Empire, Race and the Politics
of *Anti-Caste*

Empire, Race and the Politics of *Anti-Caste*

Caroline Bressey

BLOOMSBURY
LONDON · NEW DELHI · NEW YORK · SYDNEY

Bloomsbury Academic
An imprint of Bloomsbury Publishing Plc

50 Bedford Square	1385 Broadway
London	New York
WC1B 3DP	NY 10018
UK	USA

www.bloomsbury.com

Bloomsbury is a registered trade mark of Bloomsbury Publishing PLC

First published 2013

© Caroline Bressey, 2013

Caroline Bressey has asserted her right under the Copyright, Designs and Patents Act, 1988, to be identified as Author of this work.

All rights reserved. No part of this publication may be reproduced or transmitted in any form or by any means, electronic or mechanical, including photocopying, recording, or any information storage or retrieval system, without prior permission in writing from the publishers.

No responsibility for loss caused to any individual or organization acting on or refraining from action as a result of the material in this publication can be accepted by Bloomsbury or the author.

British Library Cataloguing-in-Publication Data
A catalogue record for this book is available from the British Library.

ISBN: HB: 978-1-7809-3663-5
PB: 978-1-4742-3339-2
ePDF: 978-1-7809-3579-9
ePub: 978-1-7809-3757-1

Library of Congress Cataloging-in-Publication Data
A catalog record for this book is available from the Library of Congress.

Typeset by Integra Software Services Pvt. Ltd.

Contents

List of Figures		vi
Acknowledgements		viii
1	Loving Ghosts	1
Part 1	Questioning Caste	17
2	Awakening in America	27
3	Building a New Community	51
4	Magazine to Movement	73
Part 2	Geographies of Oppression	95
5	The American Question	107
6	Firing at Long Range	129
7	Criticizing Empire	151
Part 3	The Personal is Political	173
8	A Broken Fraternity	183
9	A New Bond of Brotherhood	203
10	Triumph of the Colour Line	227
11	Hauntings	253
Bibliography		261
Index		275

List of Figures

Figure 1.1	Portrait of Catherine Impey from her scrapbook	2
Figure 1.2	Catherine with classmates and teachers from Southside	3
Figure 1.3	Mistletoe and the view from Catherine's window in 1867	4
Figure 1.4	Ida B Wells' entry in Visitors at Askew	8
Figure 1.5	Pages from Catherine Impey's scrapbook	11
Figure 1.6	Pages from Catherine Impey's scrapbook including a view of Askew House	12
Figure 1.7	A portrait of Catherine Impey	14
Figure 2.1	Portrait of Catherine Impey from *Watchword*, 1879	28
Figure 2.2	A volume of the Street *Village Album*	30
Figure 2.3	The opening page of Catherine's essay, 'Lines Left Out of My American Journal'	35
Figure 2.4	Catherine with temperance workers	38
Figure 2.5	The opening page of Catherine's essay 'Diverse Views'	40
Figure 2.6	*Anti-Caste* subscription forms	45
Figure 3.1	Pages from the Tuskegee Institute's *Southern Letter*	60
Figure 3.2	Advertisement for John Whitby & Son	61
Figure 3.3	Cabinet card with Mary, Ellen and Catherine Impey	69
Figure 4.1	A portrait of Ida B Wells, c.1893–1894	75
Figure 4.2	A portrait of Celestine Edwards	82
Figure 4.3	Location of agents for *Lux*	86
Figure 4.4	Portrait of Celestine Edwards	87
Figure 5.1	'A Lynching Scene in Alabama'	114
Figure 5.2	Scene of Lynching at Clanton	115
Figure 5.3	'You Shudder at the Picture! Of Course You Do'	116
Figure 6.1	Portrait of T Thomas Fortune	130

List of Figures

Figure 6.2	Locations of the free distribution of *Anti-Caste*, 1889	135
Figure 6.3	Portrait of Orishatukeh Faduma	136
Figure 6.4	Firing at Long Range	147
Figure 7.1	The South African Native and Coloured People's Delegates in London, 1909	156
Figure 7.2	The Rhodes Colossus	158
Figure 8.1	The Annual Report for the Society for the Recognition of the Brotherhood of Man, 1894	187
Figure 8.2	Locations visited by Ida B Wells during her tours in 1893 and 1894	188
Figure 8.3	A portrait of Isabella Mayo	191
Figure 9.1	A letter from Joseph Malins printed in the *Bond of Brotherhood*	208
Figure 9.2	An issue of the *Bond of Brotherhood*, November 1894	210
Figure 9.3	Portrait of Frederick Douglass	212
Figure 9.4	A sketch of Ida B Wells	213
Figure 10.1	A portrait of Sylvester Williams	230
Figure 10.2	An edition of *African Romances*	234
Figure 10.3	A page from Visitors at Askew 1922	237
Figure 10.4	A page from Visitors at Askew 1919	238
Figure 10.5	A portrait of Georgiana Simpson	240
Figure 10.6	Party of Conscientious Objectors	241
Figure 10.7	*The Keys*, journal of the League of Coloured Peoples	246
Figure 10.8	The Chalet	248
Figure 11.1	Catherine and Ellen Impey	259

Acknowledgements

Like the networks that were foundational to *Anti-Caste*, this book has been built upon networks of friendships, archives and archivists, libraries and librarians, seminars and the scholarly work of colleagues in the academy and in the community. I am pleased to be able to acknowledge my great thanks for the teaching and guidance of Linda McDowell, Philip Howell and Gerry Kearns, who first inspired my commitment to feminist, historical geographies and critical geographies. Philip Crang was instrumental in encouraging me to think about continuing my research at a postgraduate level and this book has its roots in my PhD thesis undertaken at the Department of Geography, UCL. My former supervisors Richard Dennis and Claire Dwyer remain an important source of encouragement and inspiration for my research. As a member of our department's cultural and historical research group and the broader geography community at UCL, I have benefitted greatly from the lively discussions with lecturers and students, including Tamsin Cooper, Jason Lim, Russell Hitchings, Peter Wood, Hugh Clout, Hugh Prince (an almost uninterrupted and active member of UCL Geography from 1946 until his death in 2013), Leandro Minuchin, Ben Lampert, Kezia Barker, Jo Norcup, Jennifer Robinson, Ben Page and Matthew Gandy. James Kneale is always generous with his advice, ideas and support and has provided me with valuable references and comments on earlier drafts and chapters. I have also been fortunate to work with Gemma Romain at the UCL Equiano Centre; her encouragement and enthusiasm for the breadth of our research projects has provided me with personal support and intellectual challenges. I also owe a great deal of thanks to Miles Irving in the Drawing Office at UCL, who spent many hours producing the maps and working on the illustrations, and to Nick Mann, who has always been on hand to help with numerous issues from computer failures to map searches.

Being based in London has enabled me to access the many thought-provoking seminars held at the Institute of Historical Research. I have particularly benefitted from the material presented and discussions held at the Reconfiguring the British seminars convened by Catherine Hall, Michael Collins, Keith McClelland, Clare Midgley, Zoe Laidlaw and Sonya Rose and those of the London Group of Historical Geographers, now convened by Miles Ogborn and Felix Driver. I have had valuable opportunities to present my work at seminars, and from participating in international and national conferences, in particular sessions organized by David Lambert, Steve Legg and David Featherstone and others supported by the RGS with IBG's Historical Geography Research Group and the Women's History Network. An early invitation from my old geography friend Alpa Shah to speak to her anthropology students encouraged me, with the help of her references, to think of Catherine's activism and theorization of caste/race in a broader interdisciplinary context.

These and other events provided an opportunity to present ideas and in some instances formed the basis of papers published in the *Journal of Historical Geography*

(Reporting Oppression: Mapping Racial Prejudice in *Anti-Caste* and *Fraternity* 1888–1895, 38, 2012: 401–411, http://dx.doi.org/10.1016/j.jhg.2012.04.001 and *Women: a Cultural Review* (Victorian Anti-racism and Feminism, 21/3, 2010: 279–291, www.tandfonline.com/doi/full/10.1080/09574042.2010.513491), from which material in this book has been drawn. My thanks are extended to the editors of these journals and the anonymous reviewers whose comments helped sharpen my thinking, as did the questions and notes of fellow students on two valuable courses on non-fiction writing organized by City Lit adult education college, London. In developing the proposal and manuscript, I am greatly obliged to Clare Midgley, Vron Ware and Antoinette Burton for their careful readings and thoughtful suggestions. At Bloomsbury I would like to thank Frances Arnold, for seeing the potential of the project and commissioning my proposal, and Emily Drewe, who has seen it through to its completion.

Direct funding from the ESRC (RES-22-0522) supported a number of visits to the Schomburg Center for Research of Black Culture at the New York Public Library that proved invaluable. The Schomburg Center's commitment to collecting and caring for material of interest to the African diaspora means that archival papers no longer available in Britain can still be accessed by researchers, even when, such as in the case of *United States Atrocities*, they were published in London. In 2009 the award of a Leverhulme Prize enabled me to visit archives that I would not have otherwise been able to access, including Yale University Library and the National Library of Australia, Canberra. During my stay in Melbourne and association with the Monash Indigenous Centre, Jane Carey introduced me to a network of researchers that are examining complex issues of 'black history', antiracism, feminism and the fragility of archives, as did Fiona Paisley during my too-brief visit to Brisbane. Listening to their discussions, absorbing the richness of their empirical work and reflecting on their questions was important to my own rethinking of the gaze of my own writing. During my stay in Australia I also found the time to rewrite a large part of the manuscript. My old friend Toby Ansell, his wife Louise and their son Angus were on hand to help me with whatever I needed, including last-minute repacking of overweight bags filled with books and manuscript notes.

For over a decade I have benefitted enormously from the energetic and pioneering network of community scholars, activists and teachers I have been introduced to through BASA, including Hakim Adi, Jonah Albert, Kathy Chater, Sean Creighton, Jeff Green, Daniel Grey, David Killingray, Dan Lyndon, Fabian Thompsett, Martin Spafford and Marika Sherwood, who early on in this project generously passed on material she had gathered on Catherine. The many BASA conferences, the *Newsletter* and seminars have provided spaces for me to discuss my work with a variety of specialist audiences in addition to placing this project in the context of my broader research activities on the black presence in London, and I extend my thanks to Sandy Nairne, Jan Marsh, Bernardine Evaristo, Makeda Coaston and Tom Wareham for their enthusiasm and support for my endeavours.

At a time when archives and libraries in Britain are under great financial pressure, I have still been able to benefit from the enormous commitment, specialized knowledge, professionalism and enthusiasm for collections that numerous archivists and librarians have shared with me. I am particularly grateful to Lucy McCann at the Bodleian Library at the University of Oxford, who answered many queries, and Tim Crumplin and Charlotte Berry, who have worked diligently to enable me to access Catherine's papers held among the archives of the Alfred Gillet Trust with a generosity of time and cups of tea that made all my trips to Somerset greatly enjoyable as well as academically rewarding. Staff at the History, Philosophy and Newspaper Library, University of Illinois kindly made the missing issues of *Fraternity* available to me in a very short space of time so they could be included in this publication. Those issues would not have come to light without the diligent work of Anya Pearson, who provided invaluable research assistance during the final months of the manuscript's preparation, particularly tracking down images, and grateful acknowledgement is given to those who have kindly granted permission to reproduce copyright images in their possession: material from Catherine Impey's scrapbook and Visitors' at Askew, *Anti-Caste* subscription forms, private family archive; Catherine Impey in *Watchword* (Figure 2.1), portrait of Sylvester Williams (Figure 10.1), portrait of Orishatukeh Faduma (Figure 6.3), *African Romances* (Figure 10.2) and *The Keys* (Figure 10.7) by permission of the British Library; *Village Albums* (Figures 2.2, 2.3 and 2.5), photograph of Mary, Ellen and Catherine Impey (Figure 3.3), The Chalet (Figure 10.8) and portrait of Catherine and Ellen Impey (Figure 11.1), Alfred Gillett Trust; temperance workers (Figure 2.4), courtesy of Bristol Record Office; *Southern Letter* (Figure 3.1), General Research Division, the New York Public Library, Astor, Lenox and Tilden Foundations; advert for John Whitby & Son (Figure 3.2), courtesy of Somerset Record Office; portraits of Celestine Edwards (Figures 4.2 and 4.4), courtesy of the National Archives; A Lynching Scene in Alabama (Figure 5.1) and Frederick Douglass (Figure 9.3), courtesy of the Religious Society of Friends in Britain; Scene of Lynching at Clanton (Figure 5.2) and portrait of Ida B Wells (Figure 4.1), Special Collections Research Center, University of Chicago Library; 'You Shudder' (Figure 5.3), Virginia Broadside Collection; Firing at Long Range (Figure 6.4), courtesy of The Library of Virginia; Isabella Mayo (Figure 8.3), by permission of the University of Aberdeen; *Bond of Brotherhood* (Figures 9.1 and 9.2), Annual Report for the Society for the Recognition of the Brotherhood of Man (Figure 8.1) and *Fraternity* (Figure 9.2) The Bodleian Libraries, University of Oxford; Georgiana Simpson (Figure 10.5) by permission of the Moorland-Spingarn Research Center, Howard University; portrait of T Thomas Fortune (Figure 6.1), courtesy of Documenting the American South, the University of North Carolina at Chapel Hill; *Great Thoughts* (Figure 9.4), reproduced by kind permission of the Syndics of Cambridge University Library; The Rhodes Colossus (Figure 7.2), reproduced with the permission of Senate House Library, University of London; South African Native and Coloured People's Delegates (Figure 7.1), courtesy of the National Library of South Africa: Cape Town campus.

During the weeks I spent at the National Library at Cape Town, Inca Waddell and her parents, Kathy and Gordon, were wonderful hosts as usual. I am deeply saddened that Gordon is not here to see the completion of the book. I am also very sorry Jill Black is not here to see the manuscript to completion as she always greatly encouraged my research, as have our fellow Nenwnhamites Bethan Cobley, Fflur Jones, Charlotte Ross, Catarina Tully and Inca along with Tim Prosser, Justine Waddell and my old friends Sarah Loch, Sam Rich, Chris Watts and Martyn, Lynn and Sally Milner. Their support has come not only in the form of encouragement and a willingness to listen to woes about unfulfilling archive trips and disheartening slow progress but also in the form of their patience when visits out of London and the solitude of writing meant I was not around to hear their stories of everyday life. For always supporting me in my studies I am grateful to my family – Stephen, Jeanie and Sylvia Bressey – and my grandmother Eleanor Bressey, who is sadly not here to read this; I think she and my great aunt A L Wright would have greatly admired Catherine's tenacity and independence.

On many of my trips away I was accompanied by Andrew, who has been instrumental in the production of this manuscript in a myriad of ways from the carrying of bags to the reading and suggestion of changes on drafts of presentations, papers and chapters and instigating my introduction to Gay Edwards. Gay's generosity in opening her family archive meant I was granted an opportunity to get closer to Catherine than I had thought would be possible. I hope this book goes some way to fulfilling the *West Somerset Gazette's* trust that Catherine's activist spirit would not be forgotten.

1

Loving Ghosts

Among the objects on the table is a book. The cover still holds some colour: black, blues and faded reds. In the top right-hand corner there is a sticker with a handwritten note: 'Scrap Book of Catherine Impey of Street'. It is fragile and I handle it as delicately as my hands allow. The cream paper has faded. The edges are dirty with age and the binding is disintegrating, exposing the cotton threads that hold the pages together. These bulge out of the brown binding which strains to contain precious mementoes. Inside, on the first page, there is a sepia photograph of a young woman. This is the first time I have seen a portrait of Catherine. She is 20 years old. The print is small and many details of the image have faded, but the face of a serious young woman can still be seen. With a neat centre parting, Catherine's hair is pulled back from her face into a bun. Her blouse is buttoned to the neck. She stares determinedly into space, her gaze fixed beyond me (Figure 1.1).

Catherine Impey began to fill her commonplace book as a 15-year-old schoolgirl, in the Easter week of 1862. The scrapbook comprises reminiscences she saved for over a decade: her first cheque, trips to Essex agricultural shows, train tickets to London; photographs of weddings and school friends and teachers from Southside, Western-super-Mare (Figure 1.2). There is a list of Quaker friends who took a pony and trap or horse and cart to the woods at Kingweston in Somerset to attend nutting party picnics under a giant oak tree in the woods a few miles from Street.[1] The pages reflect the three themes that would form the most important focus of Catherine's adult life: family, faith and philanthropy. Catherine's love of botany is revealed in the collection of seeds and pressed flowers. Some of the leaves have decayed and form a fine layer of dust on the pages. Silk spun by her own worms has been carefully attached to a page, followed by a jay's feather, letters, newspaper clippings and cartoons. Watercolours, sketches and postcards capture memories of Malvern, the Bristol Channel, trips to the Crystal Palace and views from her bedroom window. A membership certificate for the Street branch of the temperance movement's Band of Hope marks Catherine's commitment to her teetotal life, made when she was 14.

The book gives a sense of Catherine's interest in nature and people, politics, both local and international, poetry and literature. The pages of text, printed, cut and pasted and handwritten, are interspersed by photographs and pictures. Catherine's 'first landscape from nature' was painted from a window at Askew House in January 1866. The bare trees and snow-laden ground are disturbed only by three

Figure 1.1 Portrait of Catherine Impey from her scrapbook

sheep picked out by their black legs and brown tinges to their wool. Catherine's initials are printed in a tiny font in the bottom right-hand corner of the 4-by 3-inch painting. On the same page are two small portraits of two men drawn by her friend Emily. The pictures are surrounded by writing overflowing from the previous page and notes on their provenance. A piece of paper clipped behind another illustration contains a piece of French poetry Catherine had to learn. There are quirky mementos like the long since decomposed scrap of bread found in a great oak chest inside a church and brought home in December 1867. The scrapbook was a place to keep things that did not go into Catherine's diary. For more information on a paper bill used as money in a charade on 25 December 1865, she makes a note to 'see page 131–145 in volume 2 of my diary', but if these diaries still exist they are yet to be recovered.

As Catherine grew up politics took the place of schoolgirls' portraits and dance cards record evenings with friends: a quadrille with Paul and a polka with Isabella. A pale lilac dance card from 18 January 1870 is tucked into a tiny envelope at the back of the book. The miniature slender blue pencil that Catherine used to mark her card is still attached to the small social record of her gallop with Harry and waltz with Charlie. Newspaper articles, programmes and sketches reflect Catherine's growing interests

Figure 1.2 Catherine with classmates and teachers from Southside 1863, taken from her scrapbook

in political affairs and literature. These appear among quotations from the Bible and poems including a neat copy of verse by Henry Wadsworth Longfellow.

Trust no future howe'er pleasant!
Let the dead Past bury its dead!
Act, -act in the living present!
Heart within and God O'er head!

Another certificate records Catherine's enrolment to the National Reform Union in 1867. Established in 1864 the Union aimed to promote the common interests between the middle and working class, campaigning for an extension of the vote to men, secret ballots, a national distribution of MPs in proportion to population and property and the reduction of the life of a British parliament to three years to give the public more frequent opportunities to express their national opinion. A number of newspaper articles on the general election of 1868 have been cut out of columns and carefully pasted onto the cream pages. The 1868 election returned a Liberal majority of 108 to

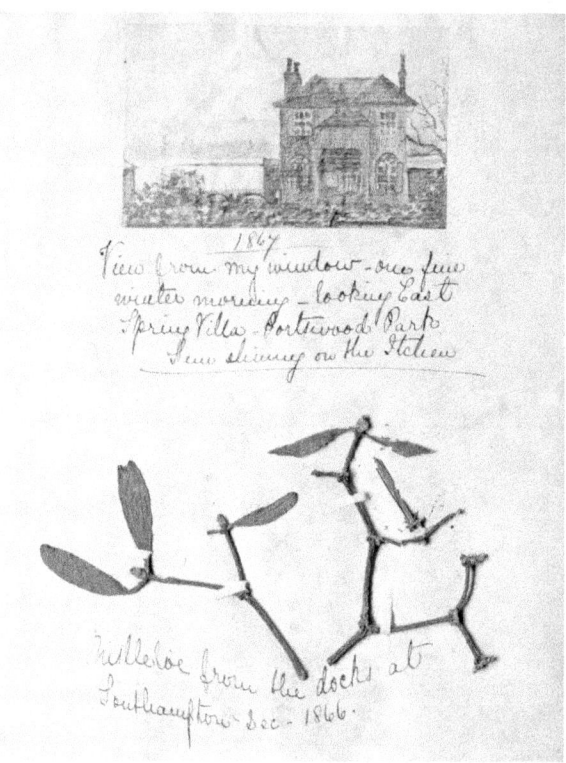

Figure 1.3 Mistletoe and the view from Catherine's window in 1867 from the pages of her scrapbook

Parliament, although in Catherine's constituency of Mid-Somerset their representatives were Conservatives. Catherine saved a postcard with the portraits of Neville Grenville and Richard Paget with her handwritten observation 'Our Successful Candidates. Tories!' Below the card, folded neatly inside a small envelope is a leaflet supporting the Liberal candidates Tagart and radical-leaning Edward Freeman. The pamphlet, written in verse, appealed to the working electors of the area who had won the right to vote in the 1867 Reform Act.

> Ye working men of every grade, who live by sweat of brow,
> Awake! Obey brave GLADSTONE'S call, for you have power now.
> Unfurl the flag of LIBERTY, to FREEDOM's cause be true,
> And give your vote to honest men, who will be true to you.
> ....
> Care not for malice or for threat, be faithful and be just;
> Your power used for Labour's rights, be mindful of your trust;
> Let Labour's voice speak freely out, and if its wants are fair,
> 'Tis honest TAGART who will make your wants his daily care.

Rise! Sons of cheerful labour, then, obey your chieftain's call;
Send Senators of fearless name, to grace the Senate Hall,
Send feeling ones for IRELAND'S cause, who would her happy see,
To DISENDOW the church she scorns, and see Religion FREE.

Who would the BALLOT try to gain, see useful knowledge spread?
The scales of wages justly held, your children better fed?
The cost of War fast dwindle down, the wrongs of nations cease?
Your COUNTY RATES get less and less, and years of smiling peace?

Do, then, your duty, Working Men, be foremost at the poll,
Be zealous for your country's cause, and vote with heart and soul.
Strike terror in the Tory breast, its power crush and bruise,
And honour bring to GLADSTONE's name, and FREEMAN proudly choose.

Catherine also cut out a poem by 'Venison' that suggests she may have shared his more cynical view of the political process, in which as a women she could not directly take part.

I stood in Mid-Somerset,
And the Rads and Tories met,
And political feuds were rising;
And I said 'O men, of tongue and pen,
Have you aught that is worth the prizing?
Promises of plenty and pledges,
Bluster of ends of wedges,
And jokes that have lost their edges;
But anything worth the prizing?'
Rads of all shades were combining,
Conservative cymbals clanging,
Greenville and Paget dining,
Freeman and Tagart haranguing.

Compared to the swollen pages of the scrapbook, the visitors' book alongside it is a slender volume. Its brown cover, embossed with small diamonds, may have once been gold. It too has lost most of its binding, two wide bands of cotton hold the covers and 300 pages together. The cream sheets are faintly lined and now mottled with brown spots. Some of the pages are loose and have to be turned gently, the pages softly teased apart to reveal signatures in pencil and ink. Clear copperplate typographies and long, scratchy scrawls have been left by friends, relatives and colleagues: *Caroline King, Isabella Metford, Richard Fry, Connie Clothier, Joseph Malins, Anna Hogg* from Dublin and *Harriet Goff* from New York. The first entry records a visit from James Cadbury in March 1876. He simply signed his name, as many guests did. Occasionally visitors left messages, poems and short essays, marking days and weeks spent within the homely sphere of the Impeys' generous hospitality. They mark the progress of political struggles and animate family memories. They tell us that Catherine was a popular member of her extended family. When James Rae visited from Reading in 1878, he wrote that he would never forget the lament of the family's young relations while Catherine was away – 'what are we to do, when will she come home?'

Tucked inside the first few pages of the visitors' book are subscription forms for early issues of *Anti-Caste*. Catherine founded *Anti-Caste* – DEVOTED TO THE INTERESTS OF COLOURED RACES in 1888 to present the British public with articles that exposed and condemned racial prejudice across the British Empire and in the United States. A close reading of *Anti-Caste* and its successor *Fraternity*, published between 1888 and 1895, reveal how some Victorians attempted to make sense of racism, imperial power and oppression at the end of the nineteenth century. The relatively short life of these radical publications is revealed by the discarded subscription forms printed for subscribers that never were. Put to use as scrap paper, they now cover over an entry to the visitors' book from Isabella Metford in January 1877.

Negro.
Question.
Spoilt.
Digestion.

The visitors' book covers 40 years of Catherine's life. It records happy family reunions as well as the lamented deaths of friends and relatives including her parents, Mary Hannah Clothier and Robert, and her older sister, Ellen. There is an entry in Swedish and messages left by visitors from Karachi and South Africa. All visited the Impeys in the small Somerset town of Street, the home of Catherine – Katie or Kate to her family and friends – from her birth in 1847 until her death in 1923. Street sits in the Somerset levels close to Glastonbury, eight miles southwest from Wells and five miles north of Somerton. It remained a stage post on the Turnpike Road from Exeter to Bristol and London until the coming of the railways, but at the beginning of the nineteenth century Street remained a small village with only 500 residents. In the early 1800s, for most people who lived in Street the highlights of their year were the midsummer Revel and the annual fair held on St Thomas' Day (21 December). The fair centred on animals with large numbers of sheep and cattle exhibited for sale. Both events declined during the nineteenth century with the increasing dominance of the temperance movement in the area, but a small fair continued in the Street Inn yard until the latter part of the century.[2] By 1851, four years after Catherine's birth, Street had tripled in size. In 1901 it contained over 4000 residents, though it still marked only a small point on the map when compared to the heaving metropolis London had become with a cosmopolitan population of 4.5 million, a total that grew to 6.5 million when the inhabitants of Greater London were included.

Kelly's 1894 directory noted that the register for Street's Church of the Holy Trinity dated back to 1639. Built of stone in a perpendicular style, the church consisted of a chancel, a nave of three bays, a north aisle, a south porch and a western tower containing a clock and six bells. In addition there stood a Congregational Chapel founded in 1814, a Wesleyan chapel erected in 1893, a Primitive Methodist chapel and a Meeting House for the Society of Friends.³ The simple grey stone Meeting House of the Friends still stands on Street's High Street opposite the Mullions Hotel. Set back from the road, the Meeting House looks over a small burial ground for Quaker members of the district. Catherine is buried here next to her sister and close to her parents and her Clothier cousins. As a committed Quaker, Catherine's life was profoundly influenced by the principles of the Society of Friends. As the author of an obituary for Catherine in *The Friend* reflected in 1924, 'she *lived* her religion – it was not part of her life but the *whole* of it – it dominated all of her actions.'⁴

Industry in Street came from numerous blue lias stone quarries and two shoe factories. Street became a company town and its built heritage remains closely linked to the Clarks shoe business. The Clark family funded a number of buildings for Street's workers including cottages and Greenbank Swimming Pool. Listed by English Heritage as a fine example of a 1930s lido, originally its waters were heated by cooling water from the Clark factory.⁵ The Impeys made their living from agriculture. Robert Impey, born in Essex in 1820, travelled down to Somerset to learn the arts of grazing and grass farming, but ended up specializing in the production of seeds, fertilizers and farming tools. At the time of the 1881 census the Impey farm covered 57 acres, employed ten men and two boys, with both Catherine and Ellen working as their father's assistants. The family lived in Askew House, built for them in grey stone and set in an old-fashioned garden filled with flowers.⁶ From here, beginning in March 1888 Catherine edited, published and distributed monthly editions of *Anti-Caste* to build the foundations of an international antiracist movement to unite 'blacks and whites and Indians, Africans, Americans and Europeans' and work 'for the emancipation of all men everywhere from disabilities imposed on the ground of colour or race'.⁷

A small town in Somerset far from spaces of cosmopolitan exchange in London may seem an unlikely place to have hosted the publication of a radical paper that challenged racial prejudice in the British Empire and the United States, but the Impeys' home welcomed men and women from across the world. Among the names in Askew's visitors' book are some I recognize from black American history: Bishop Tanner, the feminist teacher Fanny Jackson Coppin, the linguist Georgiana Simpson, the poet Paul Laurence Dunbar and William H Hillery. Elected and consecrated as the nineteenth bishop of the African Methodist Episcopal Zion Church (AMEZ) in 1876, Hillery visited the Impeys in September 1879.⁸ Tracing its roots to eighteenth-century New York, the AMEZ served black congregations who found themselves excluded from Methodist churches. Organized as its own denomination from 1821, the AMEZs' activism served as an important focus for black community solidarity in the United States throughout the 1800s.⁹ As a memory of his stay with the Impeys, Hillery left a pen and ink drawing of a dove beneath his farewell poem.

To Father, mother, and sisters dear,
Farewell! For we must part,
And if should be we no more meet here
Be Sure you've, won my heart.

And, when over distant lands I roam
Away from <u>sweet</u> Askew,
I'll think so fondly, of this bright Home:
And the Friends in Street I knew.

Farewell! Farewell! and again, Farewell!
Our parting gives me pain,
But hope is bright, for the Bible tells:
The just shall meet again.[10]

I stop at page 84. Here there is an entry from Ida B Wells, dated 17 April 1893. Her flowing handwriting preserves in black ink her memories of the first Sunday she spent in England (Figure 1.4).

'*For whatever men say in blindness*
And in spite of the fancies of youth
There's nothing so kingly as kindness,
There's nothing so royal as truth.'
Sincerely yours, Ida B Wells, New York Age

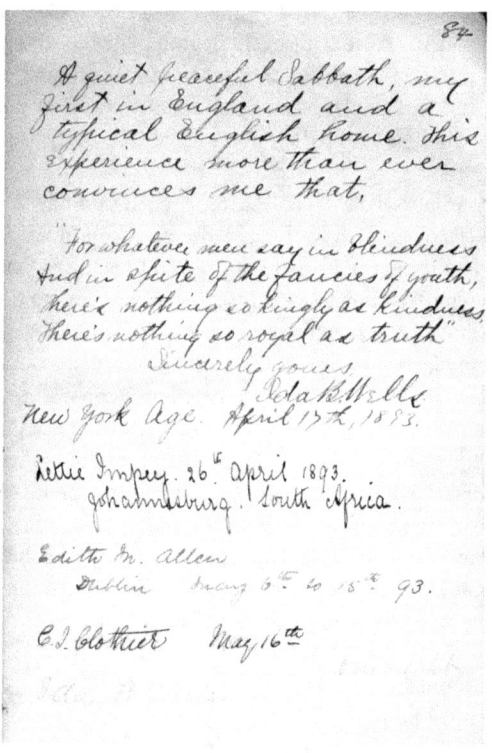

Figure 1.4 Ida B Wells' entry in Visitors at Askew. The verse Wells quotes is from 'Nobility' by the American poet Alice Carey (1820-1871)

I first read about Catherine Impey in the autobiography of Ida B Wells, a journalist, civil rights and feminist activist who worked with Catherine in the 1890s. As the historian Vron Ware observed in 1992, Wells seems to be the only one of Catherine's contemporaries to write about her political work and personal networks.[11] Since Ware highlighted Catherine's presence, a few scholars have sought to piece together different aspects of her philanthropic work, particularly her place and role in international humanitarian networks that developed at the end of the nineteenth century.[12] Of particular interest has been Catherine's high-profile collaboration with Wells on her antilynching campaigns. It was this work that brought Ida B Wells to Britain in 1893, marked by her first entry in Askew's visitors' book.[13]

The eldest of eight children, Wells was born in Holly Springs, a northern Mississippi town, in July 1862. Her parents James Wells and Elizabeth Warrenton were both born enslaved and remarried after freedom came. Elizabeth, born in Virginia, had two sisters, with whom she had been sold to slave traders as young girls. Sold on again in Mississippi, where her sisters were sold on again, she lost track of them and her remaining seven siblings. Wells remembered her mother often wrote to Virginians trying to find some trace of her family, always without success.[14] Wells' birth came on the cusp of the end of slavery and the start of Reconstruction, the years between 1865 and 1877 when black and white Americans tried to reconstitute their family and political lives within the post–Civil War paradigm.[15] The Thirteenth, Fourteenth and Fifteenth Amendments outlawed enslavement and guaranteed all Americans due process and equal protection before the law, regardless of their 'race, color, or previous condition of servitude'.[16] The period of transition was marked by political struggle and change during which, W E B Du Bois argued, the establishment of 'Negro Governments' in the South brought forward benefits of new social legislation and free public schools.[17] These years were also marked by continuing racial conflict and a resurgence in the politics of white supremacy as states in the South introduced poll taxes, literacy tests and other restrictions on the black vote.[18] Following the election of Rutherford B. Hayes as the nineteenth president of the United States in 1876, southern states rewrote their constitutions and approved legislation that removed the social, civil and political rights of their black citizens.[19] When federal troops were withdrawn from the South in 1877, the US government's abandonment of its black citizens was seen to be complete.[20]

The failure of Reconstruction represented for some the 'great moral failure' of the American nation.[21] The decades following Reconstruction were 'decisive in the development of American modernity, both anxious and triumphal' and a key component in the making of that modernity was the violent maintenance of racial segregation and the systematic removal of social and civil rights from black Americans.[22] As *Anti-Caste* observed in 1892, the infringements on their civil liberties included not only the inability to live or shop where they chose but the denial of the right to vote and everyday racist violence, including the shooting, burning and hanging of people 'euphemistically called "lynchings"'.[23] Wells' refusal to ignore the injustice of white supremacy caused her to be fired from her job as a teacher and consequently shaped her decision to work full time as a journalist. She wrote about the inequality of black and white education and schools, and became a key voice in the debates that sought to shape American modernity through the treatment of black Americans in public spaces and the violent disciplining of black bodies through the practices of lynching.

Evidence of this violence appeared on the January 1893 cover of *Anti-Caste*. A young black man hangs silently from the unseen bough of a tree; his top is dirty from the troubled ascent. His trousers, wide and crumpled at the hem, cover the heels of his bare feet. His eyes are closed. His head slumps awkwardly away from his chest towards his right shoulder. His arms are pulled back, forcing his chest to barrel forward. His hands are out of sight. The rope that suspends his body forms a taut line between him and his killers. A young white child looks up at the body, his wide brimmed hat protecting his face from the August sun. He is one of the few boys who stand among the crowd of men. It is hard to tell how many there are, for those standing at the back get lost in the dappled light. Hats on heads, hands rest nonchalantly on hips and thighs or are neatly held together. Shirts buttoned up to the neck are kept in place with braces. The crowd of men and boys face the camera, posing boldly and proudly for their portrait. Catherine's outrage at 'A Lynching Scene in Alabama' is printed beneath the image in thick black type, in which she clearly linked the violent expression of racial violence, captured by the modernist technological tool of photography, to the failure of Reconstruction to end ideas of racial supremacy that underpinned the slave system.

> Many hundreds of similar lawless scenes (AND WORSE) are enacted every year in the Southern States of American – and NO ONE IS PUNISHED. These laws are administered solely by white men – who are *corrupted* – not by bribes, but by a fierce and terrible prejudice – the outcome of slavery.[24]

While in Philadelphia during the fall of 1892, Wells spoke to a gathering of white liberals as the guest of William Still, author of *The Underground Railroad*. It was in the 'City of Brotherly Love' that Catherine and Wells talked together for the first time. Their meeting led to an invitation from *Anti-Caste* for Wells to tour Britain in the spring of 1893. A photograph of Wells dated to around the time she travelled to Britain lies in the University of Chicago archives. Although torn, it remains strong in colour and clear in tone. Her hair is pulled into a soft bun; her soft dark skin reflects her youth, though her eyes hold a sadness and weariness of the violence to which she bore witness. Her gaze, gentle but determined, is focused away from the centre of the lens.

Details of Wells' tours to Britain in 1893 and 1894 come from newspaper reports, her memoirs and letters she wrote during her second tour for the Chicago newspaper *Inter-Ocean* (a white liberal daily), reproduced in her autobiography *Crusade for Justice*. This text, which Wells had not completed when she died in March 1931, was edited by her daughter and first published in 1970. It may not be as polished as she intended, but it does narrate her friendship with Catherine. Although Catherine must have written vast numbers of letters to colleagues in Britain, the United States and across the Empire, even just in connection to the writing, editing, publishing and distribution of *Anti-Caste*, very little of her correspondence survives. Two house fires damaged a large proportion of Wells' personal and business papers in 1915 and 1923, and it is likely that correspondence between Catherine and Wells was destroyed in one or both of these.[25] As a result Ida B Wells' memoir remains one of the most detailed sources on Catherine's political activism. Aside from her presence in Wells' memoirs some of Catherine's letters to civil rights activists based in the United States, including Frederick Douglass, Booker T Washington and Albion Tourgée, survive in North American libraries and archives.

The most comprehensive compilation of Catherine's personal papers in England is held at Rhodes House, within the collections of the University of Oxford's Bodleian Library of Commonwealth and African Studies. A small brass plate for the 'Rhodes-Mandela Foundation' at the entrance to Rhodes House acknowledges the changes in African politics that have occurred since its completion in 1928.[26] The house built in part as a memorial to Cecil Rhodes reflects influences from styles of Cape Dutch farmhouses, the English country house and the arts and crafts movements and is set in gardens with green lawns and herbaceous borders which can be viewed through the windows of the first-floor library.[27] The library is a quiet and calming place, the small number of seats occupied by scholars researching Commonwealth histories and the extensive antislavery collections. It is here that a few personal letters and Catherine's record of the establishment of the Society for the Recognition of the Brotherhood of Man founded during Ida B Wells' first tour to Britain have been preserved. It is an ironic home for the collection as both *Anti-Caste* and, especially, *Fraternity* despised the greed and manipulative actions of Cecil Rhodes in Africa. Rhodes' exploitation of Africa under the British flag earned him a fortune and a prestigious legacy at the University of Oxford. Catherine was not on the side of the victors and this is perhaps why not even the British library holds a complete run of *Anti-Caste* or *Fraternity*. Only one near-complete copy of *Anti-Caste* appears to have survived in Britain. It is held at the Quaker archives in the Library of the Society of Friends in London.

Figure 1.5 Pages from Catherine Impey's scrapbook

Figure 1.6 Pages from Catherine Impey's scrapbook including a view of Askew House

Catherine lived in Street with her sister Ellen until she died in 1921, two years before Catherine. In a photograph pasted onto card, protected by a piece of patterned paper and then enclosed in a Christmas envelope the siblings stand close together. Beyond middle age they still resemble each other although the black-and-white print does not reveal if their hair still held its reddish tone. Born on 7 June 1845 Ellen was the eldest by two years. Following Catherine's birth in 1847 the pair lived together for their entire lives. Their younger sister Marion, born in 1854, died in 1860. Throughout all of Catherine's political endeavours, Ellen endured as her staunchest supporter. Neither of the sisters married and they had no children. Some of Catherine's papers can still be found closer to their home in Street. The collections of the Somerset county record office contain legal documents relating to deeds of property and trusts operated by Catherine and Ellen. More personal papers have survived as part of the Alfred Gillet Trust, housed within Clarks' former shoe-manufacturing estate in Street.[28] Among the collection are family photographs, some marked with the sisters' pet names of Nelly and Katie, others from the nutting parties Catherine memorialized in her scrapbook. One picture is framed with a note of the 'Nutting Tea party Copley Woods, Street, Somerset 1894'. In it a large group of men and women sit and lean on the grass in a clearing in the wood, the tree boughs around them dense with foliage. One older man appears to be sitting on a stool, as his bearded face sits above the rest. At the front of the group another bearded man sits on the grass, a teacup and saucer on the ground next to him. The women wear light-coloured blouses and long skirts. Most, but not all, wear straw boaters with broad ribbons, bows and flowers, or all three in some combination. Most of the men and women face the camera. I search the faces looking for Catherine, but I do not recognize her among the crowd.

Perhaps the most informative objects in the Somerset archives are the essays Catherine wrote for the Street *Village Album*. This handwritten journal is filled with entries on the thoughts and reflections of Quakers in Street. Here Catherine explained her reasons for becoming a vegetarian and reflected on some of her visits to the United States, her political activism and memories of her youth – a 'time when dancing was delightful' when 'the rhythm and throbbing of the music was all but resistless'.[29] In addition to the *Village Albums*, there is a blue sketchbook which is worn down the deep-blue binding and battered around its edges. Attributed to Catherine on the inside cover, the book contains larger watercolours than those in her scrapbook. The pictures are mostly of rural landscapes painted between 1872 and 1873, houses and hills bathed in sunlight. On one page a windmill sits on the bend of a quiet river washed in gloaming shades of blue. Resting our gaze over the artist's shoulder, we sit in a boat or perhaps lean against the side of a bridge looking down the river into the fading light. Sailing boats and small paddle steamers are painted from a bank. Blue skies with white clouds sit above a Welsh valley. One picture records the working side of rural life. Five men 'Threshing on a wet day in October' are shown moving through their tasks in brown work trousers, white shirts and dark hats, the light catching on their tools. Unusually for images of workers they are named: J Gover, H House, T Difford, John Fisher and J Green.

The pages following Ida B Wells' 1893 entry in the visitors' book are filled with inked and pencilled memories: Sophie Fox, who especially enjoyed her visit to a flower show and who, as given two pages later, was glad to be back in Street after 13 weeks of school; Harold Sessions, who came for lectures on animals; and Ida Delvade, who stayed in May 1894 in 'an atmosphere of peace, kindness & love'. The ink stops just before the book is filled. Turning through the last empty pages I feel a sense of sadness for the loss of comradeship and family represented by the bare sheets. But then, at the back of the book, and upside down, I find a short series of entries. Rotating the book it falls open to a page on which a black and white photograph is pasted in among Catherine's dense handwriting. The photograph shows Catherine and Ellen sitting with seven men who have recently been released from prison. Framed against dense foliage, the young men stand proudly for their portrait in the spring sunshine. With their jackets buttoned, ties tucked beneath waistcoats and hands neatly folded together, some smile.

On the following page is a photograph of a group of children from the East End of London who visited Street for a holiday in 1919. Next to it a subscription form for Anti-Caste Work on Behalf of Coloured Races has been written over. No longer needed, the lines reserved for the names and addresses of subscribers are covered with details of the children's visit that summer. The discarded subscription papers are among the few original remains of Catherine's vision of an international society that would challenge racism. Did *Anti-Caste* fail because it wanted to engage people in debates that too few were willing to face? A number of the themes that Catherine Impey and her colleagues raised remain familiar: the need for a greater understanding of Islam, our role as consumers in networks of consumption and exploitation, the opaque links between British military foreign interventions and capitalism, the importance of giving voice to the oppressed and how to do it effectively and how to create a language of antiracism that encapsulates the theoretical folly and real violence of race thinking.

The notes reveal that the seven men in the photograph are conscientious objectors who stayed with the Impeys following two years of imprisonment, a punishment for their refusal to fight during the First World War. Catherine and Ellen sit to the

Figure 1.7 A portrait of Catherine Impey

side of the portrait. They are far older now, both in their seventies. Like her sister, Catherine's white hair is drawn back into a bun, softer than the style she wore when she was 20. Wisps of hair fall around her still determined but tired face. I look into her eyes, which this time stare straight back at me. I lean into her gaze and struggle to capture something of that day, trying to find answers to the many questions I have. What happened to the archive of their lives? To their friends and colleagues? To the mass of administration associated with the production of a monthly paper distributed to subscribers across Britain, in the United States and Africa? To the hundreds of subscription and membership forms, the addresses for readers, letters to the editor, personal letters to Catherine and her instructions for the production of *Anti-Caste* to her printers John Whitby & Son in Bridgwater? Why did she stop? But the sisters remain silent. Our eyes remain locked until I close the page and sever the trace.[30] I sit back in the chair and once again open the book at the first page. I have read through it many more times since then. I remain apprehensive of what I'll never know, of what I might be missing and the dangers of loving a ghost.

Notes

1 On Nutting Parties see Dawe, *Clarks Courier*, 2 October 1970, 6.
2 McGarvie, *The Book of Street*.
3 *Kelly's Directory*, 1901.

4 *British Friend*, 4 January 1924, 19, original emphasis.
5 English Heritage List Entry for Greenbank Swimming Pool, Wilfred Road, http://list.english-heritage.org.uk/resultsingle.aspx?uid=1390874, accessed 20 March 2013.
6 Fahey, *Collected Writings*; McGarvie, *Guide to Historic Street*.
7 Impey to Tourgée, 21 March 1893, The Albion W. Tourgée Papers 6772.
8 Hillery's drinking led to him being disrobed in 1884 on charges of 'intemperance and immorality'. See Martin, *For God and Race*, 98.
9 Martin, *For God and Race*; Lincoln and Mamiya, *Church in the African American Experience*.
10 *Visitors at Askew*.
11 Ware, *Beyond the Pale*.
12 For example, Lorimer, 'Reconstructing Victorian racial discourse'; Holton, 'Segregation, racism and white women reformers'; Bressey, 'Anti-racism and feminism'.
13 For example, Kercher, 'Ida B Wells'; Silkey, 'Redirecting the tide'.
14 Duster, *Crusade for Justice*.
15 1865–1877 are more conventional dates given to Reconstruction. See the preface to Foner, *Reconstruction*.
16 Quoted in Smethurst, *African American Roots of Modernism*, 5.
17 Du Bois presented a paper on 'Reconstruction and its benefits' 25 years before publishing *Black Reconstruction*, see Lewis, *W E B Du Bois*, 384.
18 McDaniel and Julye, *Fit for Freedom*.
19 Alexander, *Army of Lions*.
20 McDaniel and Julye, *Fit for Freedom*.
21 Forrest Wood, quoted in McDaniel and Julye, *Fit for Freedom*, 167.
22 Smethurst, *African American Roots*, 7.
23 *Anti-Caste*, September 1892, 3. In the issue available through the British Library microfilm the original printed date for this issue is given as September (vol v, no 9), but this has been crossed out and October inked in by hand. However, this issue does come after August (vol v, no 8) and before a 'Double number' for November 1892 (vol v, nos 10 & 11), which in turn is followed by the December issue (vol v, no 12), which would suggest that the original printed month of September is correct and so it is referred to as the September issue throughout.
24 *Anti-Caste*, January 1893, 1, original emphasis.
25 Personal correspondence with Ben Stone, University of Chicago Library, Department of Special Collections, 8 November 2000.
26 Rhodes House, www.rhodeshouseoxford.com, accessed 14 June 2013.
27 Rhodes House, South Parks Road, Oxford, The English Heritage Protection List, http://list.english-heritage.org.uk/resultsingle.aspx?uid=1076964, accessed 14 June 2013; www.rhodeshouseoxford.com/the-venue, accessed 14 June 2013.
28 My thanks to Tim Crumplin and Charlotte Berry for locating this material within the Alfred Gillet Trust archive.
29 'A Jumble', *Village Album*, 36, March, original emphasis.
30 The sense of the 'photographic trace' here comes from Susan Sontag's essay in which a photograph is not only an image, an interpretation of the real, but 'it is also a trace, something directly stencilled off the real, like a footprint or a death mask.' *On Photography*, 154.

Part 1

Questioning Caste

'A Lynching Scene in Alabama' published on the cover of *Anti-Caste* in January 1893 contains many of the horrors of racism that Catherine Impey sought to challenge through the publication of her monthly periodical. At the centre of the scene is the body of a lone black man, without his shoes, without friends, without justice. In *Anti-Caste*, Catherine identified the mistreatment of black bodies in the United States in the 1880s and 1890s as a legacy of the slavery system abolished barely a generation earlier in 1865. Although lynchings of black men in the United States appeared to illustrate an exceptional response to political change, the consequences of racial hierarchies embedded in the slavery system equally infected the British Empire. Britain had been actively engaged in the development and expansion of this global system of exploitation, resulting in normative assumptions of white superiority and institutionalized animosity and disgust towards others based upon the colour of their skin. A sense of the injustice that so many of God's children could be systematically mistreated because of an accident of birth drove Catherine's political criticisms. In *Anti-Caste* the abuse of Chinese workers in Australia and the United States and the violent displacement of cultures under capitalist expansion in southern Africa were reported alongside the racial violence of lynchings in the United States.

The lone black man in 'A Lynching Scene in Alabama' is not alone. Beneath him a crowd of white men and boys arrange themselves for a viewing of his body and of themselves by the camera. Their pride and ownership of their 'white supremacy', a phrase Catherine used in her writing, is clear. For Catherine, white people's insistence of their superiority lay at the heart of racial prejudice and its unjust consequences for people of colour. Altering the politics of racial difference could not rely upon issues of 'racial uplift' for so-called 'backward races'. If such circumstances of vast inequality between populations existed, Catherine argued, they did not represent innate differences between people. Racist systems, particularly slavery but also other forms of exploitation, ensured that people of colour were unable to access the resources required for their development on an equal basis with white people. Racial prejudice did not reflect a natural response to difference or the failure of 'barbaric' peoples to 'civilize' themselves. White people produced and maintained their racial prejudice and it remained their responsibility to reverse both its ideology and its consequences. Accountability for the practices of racial prejudice lay not only with those who took part in murderous acts and photographed them but also with those apathetically watching from beyond the frame.

Although women and girls attended lynchings in the United States and on occasions had their photographs taken with the bodies, there are no women in 'A Lynching Scene in Alabama'. Though they are not pictured on this occasion, white women were intimately connected to the politics of lynching. Ida B Wells maintained that the accusation of the rape of white women by black men was a tool mobilized by white communities, especially those in the Deep South, to control sexual and platonic relationships between black men and white women during Reconstruction. Catherine supported Wells' argument that often the accusation of the rape of white women, usually not proven and sometimes entirely fabricated, was used as a justification to kill black men. The complicated gender and racial politics revealed by antilynching campaigners coincided with an emergence of a new wave of women's political movements. Catherine understood gender discrimination to be one of many forms of prejudice that faced men and women on a daily basis. As outlined in *Anti-Caste*'s first editorial, the paper intended to address mainly issues of 'colour caste' – the politics of racial segregation and the racial prejudice it supported and encouraged. But Catherine also believed that '*all* arbitrary distinctions or disabilities based on differences of social rank' were unjust. Of such divisions, she argued, the 'most cruelly irritating to the victims are those which are based purely on *physical* characteristics – sex, race, complexion, nationality – in fact form or deformity of any kind'.[1]

In her examination of activists who strove to challenge gender inequality at the end of the nineteenth century, Sheila Rowbotham identifies women reformers and radicals as possessing 'optimistic imagining'.[2] Catherine certainly shared this characteristic. *Anti-Caste* came out of her belief that an international movement to fight racism could be formed and could succeed. Attempting to shape an anticaste movement through print networks, Catherine incorporated institutions associated with women's publishing in Britain that, since the establishment of the *Englishwoman's Journal* in 1858, had encouraged politically engaged women to harness the power of print to affect change.[3] *Anti-Caste* did not maintain a direct link to the women's press; although edited by a woman and inclusive of women contributors, Catherine did not imagine or aim to create a specifically female community of readers. Though Catherine may not have undertaken work explicitly labelled feminist, some of the campaigns highlighted in *Anti-Caste* were 'gender-conscious, justice work'.[4] She supported women's suffrage, but understood gender inequality within the context of broader claims for equality for all. A number of women known to be pioneers of 'first wave' feminism in Britain, including Isabella Ormston Ford and Annie Besant, overlapped with Catherine's anticaste network, but Catherine never became an outspoken contributor to their campaigns. The failure of the women's movement to address broader issues of inequality, especially racial prejudice, may have estranged Catherine from their struggle. In turn, although the term 'Brotherhood' took on an increasingly secularist meaning throughout the final decades of the nineteenth century, Catherine's religious language, particularly her consistent use of 'Brotherhood', may have also alienated women who sought a more radical language for their political concerns.[5] Catherine did not deconstruct the gendered implications of language as she did with racialized words and their meanings.

The presence of 'A Lynching Scene in Alabama' on the front page of *Anti-Caste*'s January 1893 issue reflects Catherine's international links, her grasp of and support for challenging ideological debates made by black activists and her intention to push the boundaries of publishing to support the antiracist cause. Catherine instructed her publishers in Somerset to make a copy of the lynching portrait in 1892. The photograph had been sent to her friend and colleague the white American activist Albion W Tourgée. Becoming a popular author with the publication of *A Fool's Errand by One of the Fools*, a largely autobiographical account of Reconstruction published anonymously in 1879, his second Reconstruction novel, *Bricks Without Straw*, depicted black Americans struggling in the face of white Southern 'aristocratic tradition and economic selfishness' to redefine their place in postslavery society.[6] Perhaps best known for his role in the case which forced the US Supreme Court to make a decision in 1896 on the legality of segregation in *Plessy vs Ferguson* Tourgée challenged racial injustice in the United States throughout his life.[7] He received the lynching photograph from a representative of an Alabama 'Lynching Committee' who wanted to provide him with confident and menacing evidence of a 'black Christian hung by white heathens'.[8] Through its publication in *Anti-Caste*, Catherine inverted the Committee's intended meanings of white supremacy and the intimidation of black men and women and their supporters. Her publication of the image in January 1893 places Catherine among the earliest editors to publish a lynching photograph in an antilynching form.

Part of Catherine's ability to invert the intended meanings of 'A Lynching Scene in Alabama' came from her naming of the picture and her placement of the image below the heading of her periodical: *Anti-Caste: Advocates the Brotherhood of Mankind Irrespective of Colour or Descent*. It would be easier to directly link Catherine to twentieth-century forms of antiracism if she had called her paper *Anti-Race*, but she wanted to shun the word 'races' wherever she could. For Catherine using the term immediately implied 'in itself a distinction that is <u>unreal</u>'. We are, she argued, 'really <u>one</u> "race" – the "human race" the world over though of different <u>varieties</u>'.[9] The use of grammatical markings including underlining, italics and inverted commas all contributed to Catherine's attempt to create a language of antiracism that exposed racial prejudice while trying to avoid reinforcing the rhetoric of race. By employing 'caste' Catherine drew on analysis of racial segregation in the United States, which had utilized the term for several decades.[10] By invoking caste as a social construction rather than a religious one, Catherine found a way to avoid formulating her analysis of racial prejudice around the absurdity of 'races', but she continued to struggle with the paradox of finding a language with which to discuss racism without reinforcing its divisions. Her attempts to be more specific about what it meant to be against race prejudice, and how to distinguish the politics and principles of *Anti-Caste*, were reflected in the changing straplines that appeared on the periodical's masthead. The first issue of *Anti-Caste* declared itself DEVOTED TO THE INTERESTS OF COLOURED RACES. The final series published in 1895 appeared with the greatly extended: Assumes the Brotherhood of the entire Human Family, and claims for them their equal right to Protection, Personal Liberty, Equality and Human Fellowship.

Geographies of *Anti-Caste*

In addition to exploring the overlapping and intertwining debates of race/caste, gender and language adopted and pursued in *Anti-Caste*, this book also investigates the varied and multiple networks activated in the paper's production, distribution and consumption. *Anti-Caste* can be seen as a 'discourse network', Friedrich Kittler's term for the linkages of power, technologies, signifying marks and bodies involved in the production of media.[11] In her deployment of Kittler's methodology, Laurel Brake examines networks – Kittler's 'technic whereby cultural exchange takes place' – as part of the structure of nineteenth-century journalism.[12] Kittler's emphasis on networks focuses attention upon the processes of journalism, such as wood-cut illustration, of ink, of paper, distribution and centres of production such as London. Brake argues that by studying the material networks of media as discourses in themselves helps us to understand how production and function shaped newspapers. It can also allow us to consider how technologies, along with editorial, graphic and advertising content, as well as authorial and editorial interventions, supplement their meaning, adding the agency of science and the material to the primacy of human and individual agency.[13] As possible examples, Brake suggests exploring networks of publishers or printers and families of periodicals emerging from the same 'publication stable'. Although not framed through Kittler's structure, Jonathan Senchyne's examination of 'bottles of ink' and the printing of black ink onto white paper and the challenges this presented for illustrators attempting to depict racial ambiguity in nineteenth-century American print cultures provides another.[14] Examining networks as structures of production is a valuable tool in the biographical assembly of *Anti-Caste*.

Approaching *Anti-Caste* as a discourse network requires an examination of the multiple microgeographies of production, distribution and consumption operating at personal, local, national and international scales from which the periodical was made. *Anti-Caste* took form because of existing transnational networks of publications, people and ideas. Networks of campaigners, printers, writers, newspapers established by social groups and global postal networks were operating parallel to new ones created by Catherine to provide for *Anti-Caste*'s production. These networks overlaid, intersected with and influenced each other, building nodes of connectivity that fused personal friendships with political cultures and forged political solidarities between strangers. The culture of transatlantic reprinting of material from the American press in British newspapers and magazines and the tools of reportage utilized by the temperance movement provided a model for the 'scissors and paste' reporting technique used in *Anti-Caste*.[15] Networks of newsprint established by the black American press provided essential content to be cut and pasted together, as did newspapers published in Africa and India. The global postal service and a reduction in foreign postage allowed hundreds if not thousands of copies of *Anti-Caste* to be distributed within Britain, the United States and Africa, and spaces associated with the women's movement in

Britain provided places for topics of concern to be discussed by *Anti-Caste's* reading community.

At the heart of Catherine's personal networks lay her Quaker kinship associations. As Sandra Stanley Holton has identified for Catherine's Street neighbour Helen Priestman Bright Clark, a Quaker 'network family' could variously serve business interests, humanitarian campaigns and middle-class radical politics.[16] For Catherine, her immediate and extended family gave foundational support for *Anti-Caste*. Although from a middle-class family, Vron Ware observes that Catherine did not move in quite the same social circles as Helen Priestman Bright Clark.[17] Catherine was not independently wealthy and after her father's death she relied upon her sister Ellen to support her and by extension her editorship of *Anti-Caste*. The viability of the paper also came from technological developments in newspaper production and the subsequent fall in costs for both proprietors and readers. The sisters' extended family in Street initially provided spaces for Catherine to outline and discuss her ideas on inequality. These arose in private meetings, the pages of the *Village Album* and debates during dinners – which on at least one occasion spoilt Isabella Metford's digestion. A number of these Quaker friends and relatives later gave direct support to *Anti-Caste* as readers and regular subscribers.

Catherine's kinship networks intersected with long-established humanitarian associations, particularly those forged by the Aborigines Protection Society (APS), founded in response to a House of Commons Select Committee on the treatment of Aboriginal Peoples in 1836, and the Anti-Slavery Society. In his examination of Victorian humanitarianism Roderick Mitcham presents the APS and the Anti-Slavery Society as two nodes within a larger network of organizations that formed to 'protect' or speak for particular social groups. Organizations within what he identifies as a 'humanitarian complex' were linked through overlapping memberships, flows of people and correspondence.[18] Catherine took a keen interest in the work of the APS, and her family were committed subscribers to an organization whose members placed themselves at odds with mainstream opinion.[19] Over time Catherine did not find the kind of political reflection she thought was needed within the pages of the *Aborigines' Friend*, the association's organ usually published three times a year between 1847 and 1909.[20] She established *Anti-Caste* because 'no one else was saying what I wanted said – or not saying it to the people I felt I might reach'.[21] Moreover, although influenced by the political cultures of both the Anti-Slavery Society and the APS, *Anti-Caste* did not seek to 'protect' or 'speak for' anyone. Aware that in order to challenge racial prejudice there was a need to talk '*with* instead of *talking about* the negro', Catherine intended *Anti-Caste* to serve as a space for the publication of material by authors from a diversity of ethnic backgrounds, though she found sourcing material beyond her US contacts difficult.[22]

The abolition movement had debated ideas of 'brotherhood' from its inception in the eighteenth century but though Catherine acknowledged her political inheritance from the antislavery movement as Clare Midgley has emphasized, the antislavery movement was not an anti-imperial movement.[23] Catherine intended to include regular notices and brief summaries of the proceedings of the Anti-Slavery Society in *Anti-Caste* but she saw her periodical as having a different focus on the structuring of racial inequality and sought to promote a new narrative on issues of equality. *Anti-Caste*'s primary concern was not with slavery, nor necessarily with legalized forms of oppression, but with 'social oppression', a form of prejudice that could 'sanction cruelties and disabilities' beyond the reach of legal redress and was able to re-establish and maintain 'legislative encroachments on the primary rights of citizenship' in the United States and British colonies and protectorates.[24]

Building on Bernard Porter's 1968 assessment of *Critics of Empire*, scholars have sought to examine the nature of imperial critiques and their authors' relationship to 'anti-imperialist' sentiment and movements.[25] Many historians mark the Anglo-Boer conflict between 1899 and 1902 as the moment reformers began to develop more systematic critical engagements with imperialism.[26] Yet, as Antoinette Burton emphasizes, there is a 'back story about empire and progressive politics that remains to be told'.[27] By the 1880s 'native' activists in the Americas, Africa, India, New Zealand and Australia were consistently challenging the ideas of 'native rights', belonging and identity held by organizations such as the Aborigines Protection Society. Black American-owned-and-run newspapers such as the *New York Age*, *Cleveland Gazette* and *Richmond Planet* reported and analyzed the injustices of white supremacy. Aboriginal peoples in Australia adapted technologies of writing and print to challenge the colonial government. At the Maloga Mission in New South Wales, which featured in *Anti-Caste*, Aboriginal people's letters and petitions challenged the presence of white settlers and set out their own claims for land and fair treatment.[28] Although they may not meet the definitions of anti-imperialism applied to radicals of the twentieth century, a variety of Victorian liberals, socialists, positivists, activists and nationalists had engaged in critical discussions on the existence and expansion of the British Empire from within the United Kingdom.[29] These men and women wrestled with debates on race and imperial expansion, and their discussions resulted in a variety of opinions and policies on how British imperial power might be curtailed. *Anti-Caste*'s editor placed her readers among them.

Many early anti-imperial ideas came from collaborative politics, but not all sought to redefine social or political equality. Niamh Lynch argues that between 1840 and 1875 anti-imperialism became an important theme within Irish nationalism, but acknowledges that strands of anti-imperialism had a complex relationship with antiracism.[30] While the Irish nationalist Thomas Davis argued in an article in his paper *The Nation* in 1842 that justice and pity knew 'no distinctions of clime, or race' and that imperialists were driven by a lust for blood, power and plunder – arguments stressed in *Anti-Caste* and particularly *Fraternity* – his ideas were formed through ideas of nationhood.[31] Although criticized for it by other Irish nationalists, John Mitchel was able to argue for Irish nationalism and against British imperialism, yet staunchly support slavery in the United States.[32] Conversely, Albion Tourgée, a staunch supporter of civil rights for black Americans, was not an anti-imperialist. Although he held genuine concerns that if Cuba found itself brought under the control of the United States its hard forms of racial segregation would be introduced to the island, he also reasoned that the United States could no longer live within its own borders. He subsequently argued for the necessity of annexing the Philippines, proclaiming in a newspaper column that 'the American sense of justice toward all men' would help create 'a new civilization in the gloom of Oriental darkness'.[33]

Later in the century Indian nationalists were often sympathetic to Irish Home Rule and Kate O'Malley illustrates moments of collaboration between the two groups in the late-nineteenth-century and interwar Britain.[34] The work undertaken by activists Alfred Webb and Dadabhai Naoroji, who formed a close friendship and political ties of 'cosmopolitan nationalism', illustrates how effective these connections proved in the 1890s.[35] It is within this context of early progressive politics that *Anti-Caste* was established and both Webb and Naoroji supported *Anti-Caste* in its latter configuration. In the same year that *Anti-Caste* began publication, William Digby founded the Indian and Political General Agency in London in collaboration with the Indian National Congress in order to raise grievances from India in the British press and Parliament.[36] As Marilyn Lake and Henry Reynolds illustrate, the insistence of white settler colonies that the world should be imagined as white and nonwhite along with their determination to realize these divisions in policies of active racial discrimination prompted an increasing conflict within the British Empire between the self-governing white dominions and India.[37] In establishing *Anti-Caste*, Catherine aimed to challenge the increasing segregation or the 'colour line' that was being drawn throughout the world, particularly in the United States.

To challenge these hardening divisions Catherine aimed to mobilize an international counternetwork. She deliberately resisted support for nationally based organizations arguing that a broad-based, integrated international organization was needed, one 'that was as truly English as it was American as truly Indian as English'.[38] By presenting the voices from the African and Asian diasporas in the same place, *Anti-Caste* produced a space that challenged conventional interpretations of international race relations. Though critical of imperial expansion, neither *Anti-Caste* nor *Fraternity* demanded the immediate dismantling of the British Empire. In a tactic similar to that used by early Pan-Africanists, the editors argued for an end to the expansion of the Empire and an increase in the respect for and conditions of those unfortunate enough to be ruled 'Under the British Flag'.[39]

Created as a site for affecting change, Catherine relied upon the readers of *Anti-Caste* to dynamically engage with the knowledge it brought to them and generate the energy required for active change. She aspired to create a community of black and white readers who crossed national boundaries and cultural differences. Through their commitment to *Anti-Caste*, as formal subscribers or beneficiaries of free copies, these men and women formed a community of readers and, Catherine hoped, through their readership, a community of activists. The growing scholarship from reception studies suggests it can be argued that a regular engagement with a single periodical facilitated the Victorian reader's membership of a definable 'textual community' with its own ideologies, cultural assumptions and political aims.[40] Although readers may have united around broad principles such as the brotherhood of man or equality of women, it becomes clear that communities of readers did not form homogenous groups. Studies exploring how readers understood their place within such communities have revealed the tensions between the implied and real readers of periodicals.[41]

Attempts to enter the minds of such ordinary readers and understand how they ignored or engaged with textual cultures have become an engaging focus of 'book history'.[42] Memoirs, diaries, library registers and letters to editors have all provided sources for personal reflections on the importance of reading for all social classes.[43] *Anti-Caste* aimed to reach a broad working-class audience through its free distribution to reading rooms, libraries and cafes. Who these individual readers were is more difficult to recover. The publication of a number of subscriber lists in *Anti-Caste*'s annual reports allows for the periodical's community of real readers to be reconstructed only to a limited extent, for these lists are always partial. Readers can also become visible through letters to the editor. Their lines of encouragement, or on occasion attack, hint at how for some readers an engagement with *Anti-Caste* and later *Fraternity* influenced their everyday lives and their aspirations for a different political future. While an international community formed the theoretical ideal of the implied *Anti-Caste* reader, the readers were primarily British.

Kittler argues that each discourse network alters corpora of the past.[44] In drawing together and reshaping material into a new discourse on racial prejudice, *Anti-Caste* forged a discourse network that revised and reworked past debates on inequality, presenting new formulations of language and analysis for discussion and debate among its readers. Although a small and now relatively unknown periodical, a close examination of the geographies of reading and writing connected to *Anti-Caste* draws out understandings of racialized power and oppression at the end of the nineteenth century.[45] The approach here follows Burton's argument that in the history of imperial political culture it is details of historical narrative that provide the terrain upon which anti-imperial histories of the British Empire can be written.[46] These narratives require political histories of antiracism as a thread within British history to be addressed in a form that examines the transnational imaginations and international solidarities such movements sought to build. Geographers and historians of 'new imperial history' have sustained a critique of 'nation-centred historical models', arguing for the importance of examining networks, connectivity and the flows of ideas, people and objects.[47] This need applies equally to the political histories of anti-imperial solidarities, where, as David Featherstone has observed, a focus upon writing about political groups within a model of national political histories has tended to sideline or ignore the contributions made by indigenous and anticolonial intellectuals and activists to movements on the European left.[48] A multiple and layered microhistory is a means of producing a transnational historical geography of *Anti-Caste*'s production, distribution and consumption. Such microhistories of specific periodicals allow for attempts at detailed examinations of content, reception and a consideration of the extent to which seemingly small and marginal papers influenced discourses within broader, more popular, public spheres in Britain.

This book presents a genealogy of *Anti-Caste* as a periodical that emerged within the context of a critical black press forged in the racial politics of enslavement, Reconstruction and post-Reconstruction in the United States. The second part of the book focuses on the making of an antiracist narrative in *Anti-Caste* through a close reading of production techniques and geographies of reading to draw out the counternarrative to racialized power and oppression *Anti-Caste* published. Still,

Anti-Caste's biography is intimately linked to the genealogies of Catherine Impey, and her biography remains central to this reassembling of a Victorian antiracist network. Within an examination of unknowable readers and intersecting international networks is a microhistory of a woman's life, which are the focus of the first and third parts of this book.[49] The account begins by tracing Catherine's political awakening to the politics of race during her first visit to the United States in 1878 through until the inaugural issue of *Anti-Caste*, published a decade later, and the succeeding Society for the Brotherhood of Man established in 1893. The United States proved to be a place of revelation for Catherine. Her interaction with the ghosts of slavery and the black civil rights activists she met during her visits motivated her to transform her personal politics. She created this change within the context of her unwavering Christian faith in a global brotherhood. Her belief in universal equality convinced her that overcoming racism required an international community of activists, for such an entrenched and deadly form of prejudice could not be defeated by oppressed groups or their supporters if they solely focused on their own national concerns.

Notes

1. *Anti-Caste*, March 1888, 1, original emphasis.
2. Rowbotham, *Dreamers of a New Day*, 1.
3. Tusan, *Women Making News*.
4. Thompson, 'Multicultural feminism', 352.
5. Ware, *Beyond the Pale*.
6. Olsen, *Carpetbagger's Crusade*, 225.
7. Thomas, 'The Virtue of Defeat'.
8. Wells-Barnett, *On Lynchings*.
9. Impey to Tourgée, 16 June 1890, 4785 Albion W. Tourgée Papers.
10. Horton, *Race and the Making of American Liberalism*.
11. Wellbery, 'Forward'. Wellbery explains that the original German title of the book *Aufschreibesysteme 1800/1900* more closely translates into English as 'systems of writing down' or 'notation systems', xii.
12. Brake, 'Time's Turbulence', 116.
13. Brake, 'Time's Turbulence'.
14. Senchyne, 'Bottles of ink'.
15. Nicholson, 'You kick the bucket'; Kneale, 'The place of drink'.
16. Holton, *Quaker Women*.
17. Ware, *Beyond the Pale*.
18. Mitcham, 'Geographies of global humanitarianism'.
19. Heartfield, *Aborigines' Protection Society*; Impey to F. Chesson, 18 March 1885, MSS Brit Emp. s. 18 C138/167, The Bodleian Library of Commonwealth and African Studies, University of Oxford.
20. Heartfield, *Aborigines' Protection Society*.
21. Impey to Booker T. Washington, 5 March 1890. *The Booker T Washington Papers*, 3, 33, Illinois 1974.
22. 'Supplement to *Anti-Caste*', January 1891, 1, original emphasis.
23. Midgley, 'Bringing the empire home'.

24 Appeal Concerning the Treatment of Coloured Races, MSS Brit Emp. s. 20 E5/8.
25 Porter, *Critics of Empire*. An overview of some contributors to the field can be found in Howe, *New Imperial History Reader*.
26 Burton, 'New narratives', 120; Claeys, *Imperial Sceptics*.
27 Burton, 'New narratives', 120.
28 Van Toorn, 'Authors, scribes and owners'; McLisky, 'The location of faith'. On an evolving Maori print culture during this period, see Paterson, 'Print culture and the collective Māori consciousness'.
29 For an examination of this historiography and examples of actors from the Peace Society and Irish nationalists, see Claeys, *Imperial Sceptics*.
30 Lynch, 'Defining Irish nationalist anti-imperialism', 91.
31 Lynch, 'Defining Irish nationalist anti-imperialism', 91.
32 Lynch, 'Defining Irish nationalist anti-imperialism'.
33 Quoted in Olsen, *Carpetbagger's Crusade*, 345.
34 O'Mally, 'Metropolitan resistance'.
35 Regan-Lefebvre, *Cosmopolitan Nationalism*. For links between black US struggles and India, see Slate, *Colored Cosmopolitanism*.
36 Owen, *The British Left in India*.
37 Lake and Reynolds, *Drawing the Global Colour Line*.
38 Impey to Tourgée, 21 March 1893, 6772 Albion W. Tourgée Papers.
39 For example, the African Association, formed by members of the African diaspora living in London in 1897, sought to promote and protect the interests of subjects of African descent who lived 'in British colonies and other places' through 'appeals to British and the colonial governments to redress their wrongs'. Quoted in Mathurin, *Henry Sylvester Williams*, 45. This narrow focus on British imperial rule was broadened out for the Pan-African conference hosted by the association in London, 1900 see Schneer, *London 1900*.
40 Brake, Bell and Finkelstien, 'Introduction', 3.
41 Brake, Bell and Finkelstien, 'Introduction'.
42 Rose, *Intellectual Life of the British Working Class*.
43 For a review of some of this literature, see Rose, *Intellectual Life of the British Working Class* and the Reading Experience – www.open.ac.uk/Arts/reading.
44 Kittler, *Discourse Networks, 1800/1900*, 344.
45 Ogborn, *Indian Ink*.
46 Burton, 2006, 'New narratives'.
47 In addition to other publications referred to throughout, see, for example, Lester, *Imperial Networks*; Howell, *Geographies of Regulation*; Lester and Lambert, *Colonial Lives*; Hall, *Civilising Subjects*.
48 Featherstone, *Solidarity*.
49 Holton, 'Challenging masculinism'.

2

Awakening in America

It is pitiful to see how by this system of caste the careers of many of our fellow creatures are straitened, their cultivation and growth in civilization checked, their liberties in a thousand ways abridged.

Anti-Caste, 1888

In a letter she wrote to the great civil rights activist Frederick Douglass in February 1883, Catherine explained that she had been 'awakened' to the 'colour question' during her first visit to the United States in 1878.[1] She travelled to the United States as a representative of a temperance association led by Joseph Malins. Catherine's account of her first trip to the United States was written out for friends and family in Street and bound into their *Village Album*. Her extended essay reflects the observations of an English middle-class tourist featuring sounds, natural and urban landscapes, tourist sites, food and the weather. But while these unremarkable observations dominated her early experiences in the United States, she increasingly notes the conversations with black Americans that pricked her political consciousness. In the essay, based on her journal entries, Catherine travels through the United States and the geographical journey forms the foundation of a personal awakening. As Catherine retraces her journey, her commentary on black Americans changes from distant 'negroes' seen working in fields from train coach windows, or waiters bringing iced water to a hotel table, to named colleagues and temperance 'brothers'. Her talks with black men and women made her even more determined to challenge the politics of racial prejudice. Unwilling to compromise her principles on racial segregation, when the colour line became established within her temperance organization, Catherine initially resigned her elected position, before leaving the movement entirely. Instead, as she outlined in her letter to Douglass, Catherine believed that those committed to fighting racial prejudice had to come together to form a single union 'or Anti-Caste Society – to take up the work where the Anti-Slavery Society had dropped it'.[2]

A Quaker woman

The roots of Quakerism were established during the turbulent years of the English Civil War and the following years of Republican government from 1649 to 1660. Their

Figure 2.1 Portrait of Catherine Impey from the Good Templars' *Watchword*, 1879

religious practices focusing on introspection and contemplation created forms of worship undertaken in silence, the absence of creeds, clergy or consecrated buildings and they acknowledged women as ministers. By the nineteenth century Quaker families thrived among the commercial classes, and their antislavery campaigns had forged a wide network of political allies, although the community as a whole was declining. In 1680 Quakers numbered around 60,000, and by 1840 they had fallen to barely 16,300.³ A period of reform which sanctioned members marrying beyond the community and no longer required them to follow strict forms of dress or speech stimulated an intellectual revival within the movement.⁴ The community also established a network of schools committed to educating girls as well as boys to be 'good citizens'.⁵ A typical curriculum in a Quaker school during the first half of the century included reading, writing and arithmetic, along with some geography and history.⁶ The poem Catherine copied out and placed in her scrapbook suggests she learned French at Southside, the school she attended in Western-super-Mare, which catered for Quaker girls as well as those from other denominations. Elizabeth Sturge, born two years after Catherine, remembered the curriculum she studied at Southside included French (not well taught), some geography, history and 'such Arithmetic as was compatible with teaching a whole class, bright and stupid, together'.⁷ With lessons completed in the mornings, the afternoons were spent drawing or practicing needlework, with sewing lessons enlivened with reading allowed from books such as Thomas Macaulay's *Essays*.⁸ Though educationally Sturge felt the syllabus at Southside left much to be desired, she recognized it to be 'a good school for its day'.⁹

Although women ministers were part of Quakerism from its inception, in practice their roles were not defined equally to those of men, and women performed their roles within separate meetings.[10] Women did not form part of the central national structure governing the Quakers, but the arrangement of relationships between men and women within the Society of Friends allowed for more flexible gender roles than those generally prescribed in British society.[11] Catherine and Ellen both benefitted from the Quaker commitment to educate girls as well as boys, although like other Quaker family kinship networks the Impey sisters shared caring responsibilities for other members of the family. At times her domestic obligations limited the amount of political work Catherine could do. This is not to suggest Catherine resented her domestic duties. They formed part of her responsibilities as a Quaker, and like Helen Priestman Bright, who became the Impey's neighbour in Street when she married William Clark in 1866, Catherine's political activities and private duties were entirely interwoven into her everyday life through her faith.[12] For the Quakers of Catherine's kinship and political networks these beliefs included a dedication to social justice stemming from a commitment to egalitarianism and the right of all people to enjoy the same protections before the law.[13]

Unlike Helen Priestman Bright Clark, whose father John Bright served as a radical MP from 1843 to 1889, Catherine did not have personal connections to metropolitan radical activism.[14] Catherine's political geographies were formed through the opportunities afforded to her in Street. Women within Quaker families could enjoy being part of extensive networks that included the United States and Europe.[15] Helen Priestman Bright Clark's family hosted a number of high-profile international visitors to Street. During his final trip to England from 1886 to 1887 Frederick Douglass stayed with Bright Clark; that was when Catherine met him for the first time.[16] The Impeys' home proved to be a vibrant and supportive space for Catherine and Ellen's intellectual growth. The family's visitors' book illustrates that like other Quaker homes Askew was not a 'private haven', but an open and convivial space where the Impeys' religious and political values were performed through hospitality.[17] International visitors staying with the Impeys or other Friends in Street drew Catherine and Ellen into new associations that prompted debates and discussions at home, broadening their cultural knowledge and deepening their political aspirations.

Extended Clark and Clothier family connections in and around Street also created the foundation for Catherine's participation in the *Village Album* (Figure 2.2). This literary society brought Friends together to discuss original material, which they shared regularly through reading meetings. Rules governing membership of the *Album* established in 1857 included the payment of a subscription fee of 6d and the contribution of one or more original pieces of at least 50 words every two months. Two volumes of contributions were bound each year and allotted to members through a ballot. Meetings took place on the second day of the month as near the full moon as possible, eight months of the year, starting from 7pm, with readings commencing at 7:30pm.[18] In addition to the Impeys, members of the *Album* included Clarks, Clothiers, Morlands and Metfords – all names that appeared on subscriber lists for *Anti-Caste*. They contributed material to the *Village Album* on a vast range of social and political subjects, from Turkish baths in London to temperance campaigns, family histories

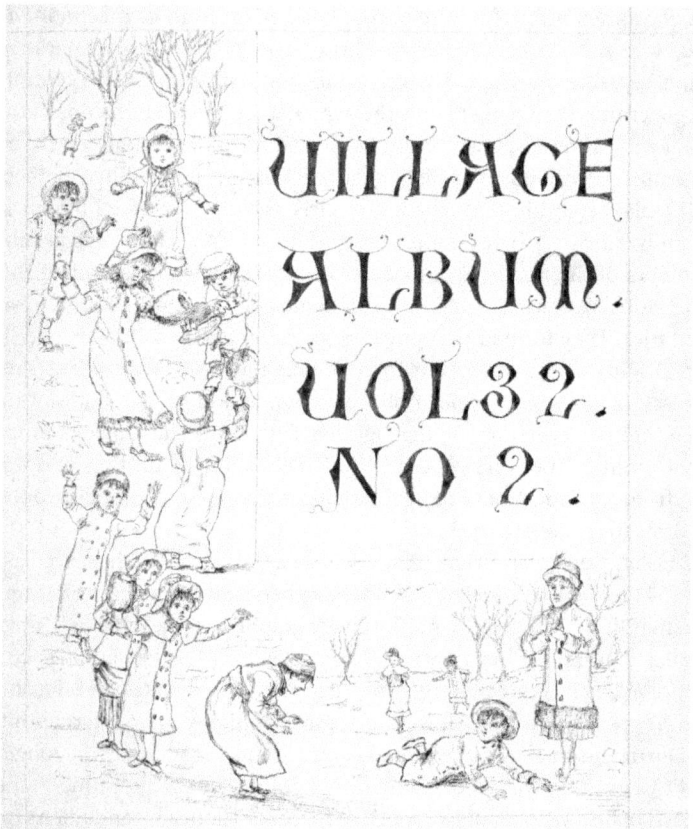

Figure 2.2 A volume of the Street *Village Album*

of Street, travel writing, poetry and illustrations. For Catherine the *Album* provided a space to develop a range of literary material. Her contributions, first appearing in the fifteenth volume bound in the 1860s, included essays titled 'Dogs', 'Week in a Welsh Country House', 'Thoughts on Two of G. MacDonald's Books' and 'A Month in Cornwall' (illustrated by Ellen), along with more probing, politically oriented essays on social equality and vegetarianism.[19]

In 1876 Catherine contributed an essay titled 'Templar Politics'.[20] Since her teenage pledge to the Band of Hope in 1861, Catherine had been involved in the campaign against drinking. British temperance associations that sought to challenge the nation's drinking habits formally began in 1829 with evangelical antispirits organizations and the radical working-class teetotal movement which emerged during the 1830s.[21] They had little effect. The Victorians continued to drink vast quantities of alcohol, reaching a peak in beer consumption of 40.5 gallons per person a year during the 1870s (in contrast beer consumption in Britain between 1919 and 1995 peaked at 27.1 gallons in 1979).[22] During the 1870s the Independent Order of Good Templars (IOGT) to which Catherine belonged, recruited widely. Originating from New York State in the 1850s, the Templars' mixture of fraternal lodge ritual with titles, passwords, insignia and companionship coupled with a strong condemnation of alcohol attracted millions of followers throughout North America, the British Empire and Europe by 1876.[23] In Britain the movement grew under the leadership of Joseph Malins, a furniture painter from Worcester. At 16 Malins had taken a total abstinence pledge, a month after the death of his alcoholic father. Between 1866 and 1868 Malins and his wife Lucy Ellen Jones lived in the United States, where he became introduced to the Templar Order. He returned to England committed to the IOGT's cause and was officially appointed to represent the IOGT in England. Within six years Malins had established a Grand Lodge with a membership of over 200,000.[24]

In addition to its uncompromising denunciation of alcohol, the Templars offered opportunities for teetotal women like Catherine to become actively engaged in political campaigning through a membership structure that espoused gender equality.[25] Establishing the IOGT in Britain Malins emphasized its universalism and commitment to welcoming men and women of all creeds and colours. In the United States, although a number of women held high office in the Templars' organizational structure their official place remained one of nominal equality.[26] They fared no better in Britain where the Executive Committee of the Grand Lodge of England contained only one woman.[27] Despite its limitations, many middle-class women including Catherine gained their first experiences of political engagement through the temperance movement. As philanthropic campaigns provided women with new avenues into public life, temperance activism supported women's participation in political campaigns and a sense of their right to address civil society.[28] For Catherine her position as the Templars' honorary secretary of the Negro Mission Committee, which she saw as an 'Equal Rights mission', provided her with opportunities to travel to the United States and Europe, to gain experience of writing essays, reports and letters and giving public lectures, while becoming part of a network of black and white activists that proved crucial for informing and establishing *Anti-Caste*.[29]

In her *Village Album* essay on 'Templar Politics', Catherine introduced her readers to internal divisions breaking the IOGT apart. Although an organizational problem, Catherine believed that the reasons for the movement's difficulties – the question of racial equality in the United States – should be of interest to a broader audience because of the centrality of racism to debates on equality.[30] She presented the structure of the IOGT as one familiar to her Quaker readers as she explained the Templars' administrative machinery ran to a similar plan to the Society of Friends, with quarterly meetings for each county (composed chiefly of representatives from particular lodges) and yearly meetings – Grand Lodges – for each country, or in the United States for each state. Beyond this the Templars held an annual international meeting – the Right Grand Lodge – composed of representatives from the yearly meetings. At this international gathering, reforms of the Templars' universal laws could be made to ensure uniformity throughout the order. In her essay Catherine emphasized a commitment to racial equality as a key motivation for the Templars, arguing that the two deepest principles laid down by their international forum from the start had been the 'Equality and

Brotherhood of all mankind, and the moral and physical evil of the use and traffic in Strong Drinks'.[31] In Britain, where segregation drawn along the colour line did not formally operate, black members joined temperance lodges in cities and port towns. A black American sailor named Henry Hammond headed a London Lodge, and a Liverpool Lodge based in Toxteth reported over 20 black members in 1881, rising to over 50 in 1884.[32] In the United States establishing lodges as spaces of racial equality created a challenge for Templar workers.[33]

Eight years before Catherine wrote 'Templar Politics' John J Hickman, a farmer-turned-insurance agent from Kentucky, had started up lodges in the South. Under his charismatic and zealous leadership Templar membership at the Grand Lodge of Kentucky flourished.[34] As soon as a sufficient number of lodges were formed in a state, they could appeal to the international Right Grand Lodge to be formed into an independent yearly meeting, with powers to make minor laws for their own government. In Catherine's version of the story, Hickman's Southern lodges had successfully attained this independent status but immediately appealed to make a bye law that the order in those states would consist of people of 'pure white blood only' shutting out old black lodges that had been in existence for years as well as preventing any new ones being formed. The request for segregated lodges was confirmed by the president of the Right Grand Lodge. In 1876 when the international meeting was held in London, British representatives carried a motion that black lodges should be recognized. The disagreement between the different arms of the movement resulted in the British Templars and their supporters seceding. These lodges insisted upon their right to be acknowledged as the only Templar Order, arguing that the original movement had forfeited its legitimacy.[35] Joseph Malins became secretary with James Yeames, editor of the weekly *Templar*, now Right Worthy Grand Templar of the Right Worthy Grand Lodge of the World (RWGL of the World).

Hickman attempted a reconciliation by travelling to London in 1876 with 'the Red Indian doctor Oronhyatekha', who, Catherine believed, hated black people worse than any Southerner.[36] Their conference with Malins and other British representatives ended without a resolution. Instead Catherine accused Hickman of setting up a new body which he alone recognized as the Good Templar Order, making the 'hot headed Dr Lees' his grand chief in England. They were now going from town to town throughout Britain trying to split up the order Catherine recognized, with all members being called on to declare which body they would owe allegiance to. Catherine could not see that her representatives had ever shown cause for distrust or acted on anything but the highest principles of justice. She argued that Hickman had to get Southerners to admit black people to their lodges before he returned with an offer of a reunion, while he could 'only promise to try to get them to be just, let us keep apart, if only as a protest against the terrible prejudice of race'.[37] In conclusion Catherine reflected on comments from Templar members who argued that the exclusion of black people from Templar lodges was a secondary concern for a movement that 'ought to be minding our temperance work and let politics alone'. 'I can't believe it!' Catherine exclaimed. Surely, she argued, it would do more good for temperance membership to be galvanized on a question of justice rather than to 'go on in apathy engrossed only in the little amusements and works of our own narrow circles'. She signed off as 'A Lover of Free Discussion'.[38]

Joseph Malins is among the first guests in Askew's visitors' book, leaving a brief entry on 5 December 1876.

Father Good,
Food nice,
House clean,
All serene!

At the time of Malin's visit to Street the split in the Templar movement was fixed, with Malins focusing on strengthening the movement converging around the RWGL of the World. When Malins visited again in August 1877 his visit came seven days after William Wells Brown, who had travelled from Boston. Born enslaved William moved with his master to Missouri Territory in 1816 and he lived in the St Louis region until he escaped from slavery on New Year's Day in 1834. He made his way to Canada, taking his surname from an Ohio Quaker named Wells Brown, who helped him on his way. He worked initially as a steamboat man and as a conductor on the Underground Railway and then, from 1843, as a lecturer for the Western New York Anti-Slavery Society. In 1847 the *Narrative of William W. Brown, a Fugitive Slave: Written by Himself* was published in Boston and went through four American editions in two years. An Irish edition was published in 1849 and a Dutch translation in 1850, and between 1849 and 1853 five British printings of a thousand copies each were published.[39] Brown first travelled to Europe to attend an international peace congress and his memories of that trip were published in 1852 as *Three Years in Europe; or, Places I Have Seen and People I Have Met*, considered the first travel book written by a black American.[40] After his return to the United States he became heavily involved with Templar politics siding with Malins' branch of the order during the split.[41]

When Catherine attended the RWGL of the World's international conference held in Boston during May 1878, she accepted an invitation to stay with Wells Brown and his second wife Anna in order to get 'a truer insight into the real position of affairs' in America.[42] She travelled to the conference with seven other British representatives.[43] Held at the Pythian Hall at the New Era Buildings in Boston, the conference welcomed delegates from England, Scotland, Wales, across the United States, Canada and beyond. Joseph Malins reported a steady growth in the movement, and William Wells Brown reported that over £200 had been collected by young British supporters of the Templars' missions for black Americans.[44] The Wells Brown home provided a rendezvous for many black Americans. Bishops, ministers, salesmen, lawyers, medical students and other visitors from all parts of the United States were among Catherine's fellow guests or callers. Through the spaces of hospitality and debate in the Wells Brown home during her stay, Catherine made quite a large circle of 'friends among coloured Americans' almost before she gained any extended knowledge of 'white Americans'.[45]

Encountering the colour line

Catherine's *Village Album* entries on her first two trips to the United States in 1878 and 1886 run to tens of pages. They are filled with observations of the American landscape, its weather and its food. Catherine found English meals differed considerably from American ones, rich with new vegetables and new ways of cooking. She particularly enjoyed courses of eggplant; she used the American name as there were no aubergines in her culinary vocabulary. She described an eggplant as a large tomato-like fruit which was exceedingly nice when fried in slices with a thick milk gravy and served with hot home-made rolls and an abundance of butter.[46] Knowing that a dislike of new food comes usually from its unfamiliarity, Catherine tried hard to enjoy the ubiquitous servings of sweet potatoes at dinner but she never succeeded. They tasted to her like a curious mixture of a very overcooked baked apple and a frozen potato, but she gulped them down to avoid insulting her hosts.[47] An American supper dished up between 6 and 7pm she likened to an English high tea. Raw sliced tomatoes, raw and stewed fruit, ice cream, cheese and butter cakes were served with coffee and ever-present jugs of iced water. The emphasis placed on cooking all meals from fresh ingredients created a focus on cookery that Catherine found almost shocking. However, wholesome bread was never seen. Instead Catherine found only thin dry slices made from miserably fine white flour.[48]

After the conclusion of the 1878 conference in Boston, Catherine and the British representatives took the long journey by boat and train to Philadelphia, arriving on 5 June.[49] Two days later a telegram from Joseph Malins summoned Catherine and the others to join him in Baltimore. With half a breakfast and lots of parcels they hurried to the station, arriving just in time to catch the train. They spent a hot day travelling, passing through woods with rare ferns and luxuriant creepers and green fields 'where a few negroes' in wide straw hats planted and hoed corn. Just south of the Susquehanna River at Aberdeen, her friends bought Catherine a bunch of the wild magnolias being sold for a few cents a handful by little 'negro boys' at the station. Catherine sat back in her seat gazing into their rich dark leaves and delicate pointed buds, while her friends laughed at her romanticism and teasingly called her a bride. The party carried on south, each station 'crowded with idling merry or sometimes listless looking negroes'. Finally they reached Baltimore, the train moving through the crowded city streets as if they were passengers in a bus or tram, its bell tolling to warn walkers off the tracks before it reached the station.[50]

Catherine shared her hotel room, more like a parlour than a room, with Jane Metford. The hotel's drawing room with a grand piano, French windows and chintz chairs overlooked a street with shop signs that amused Catherine in the differences they revealed between the English and Americans: Dry Goods (Drapery) and Gentleman's Notions (Fancy Things). Despite the building's large shutters and open windows there was little respite from the heat. Catherine found that Americans enjoyed oven-like temperatures and stifling rooms; she now understood why they shivered through trips in England.[51] In the dining room Catherine enjoyed a small feast with butter stood on ice to keep it from steaming off as oil, ice water, iced coffee and iced milk. Plates of meat surrounded by endless plates of delicious beans, asparagus, spinach, peas, greens and several styles of potatoes were brought by polite 'negro men' who catered to the party's every want.[52]

At dusk Catherine and Jane put on their bonnets and the party headed out to a temperance meeting. Housed in a boarded shed, Colonel Hoy's Tabernacle lay out on the outskirts of the city. Hoy, his wife and their supporters held meetings every night. That evening, in spite of the heat, the room was soon full. All the English visitors were invited to join Hoy on the platform. Cooling themselves with palm leaf fans (one of which Catherine brought back for her parlour mantelpiece), they tried to stop themselves melting in the intense heat. The fans did not hide the composition of the audience before them and the British group were 'vexed at seeing no coloured people there'. Baltimore was the first 'slave city' Catherine visited and she felt the burden of its history in the sultry atmosphere. The legacies of slavery maintained an active place in the city's energies, pushing against Catherine's consciousness and provoking new readings of the urban landscapes. The meeting at Hoy's Tabernacle closed around 11pm and the journey back to the hotel took them past places where men, women and children had been put up to auction and sold on slave blocks. Driving along the dark thoroughfares, Catherine 'vividly realized where we were and what an awful past, frowned at us from its streets + walls – and markets and churches even'.[53]

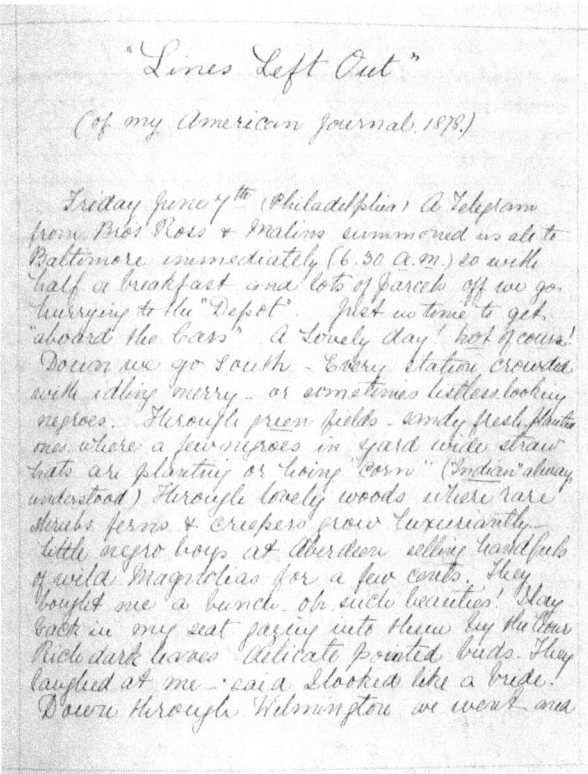

Figure 2.3 The opening page of Catherine's essay, 'Lines Left Out of My American Journal', recounting aspects of her first trip to the United States in 1878 for the Street Village Album, volume 31 (1878-1879)

The following morning the group made their way through the drizzle to the train station, this time for a gloomy journey through Maryland to Washington DC. The group cheered themselves up by laughing at caricatures of Good Templary they had bought before the journey. They were met in Washington by torrential rain so they hired a hotel bus to take them to Howard University, which Catherine noted was for 'for coloured & white students', although the majority of its students were black.[54] The university was closed for the vacation and instead the group visited the kind and hospitable family of Bishop Brown. Catherine 'enjoyed hearing his account of their difficulties in education and especially in all social relations with the whites'.[55] Through these personal conversations with Bishop Brown, Wells Brown and his guests, Catherine began to connect institutionalized forms of racism with the difficulties it caused for the everyday lives of black people throughout the United States.

That afternoon the friends enjoyed a fashionable lunch at the Arlington (although Catherine would have preferred less fashion and more food) before visiting the Capitol. Catherine compared the imposing building to the dazzling white marble of St Paul's Cathedral in London – only the Capitol was larger and set on a hill surrounded by open space. The group rose up the broad flights of marble-terraced steps, passed through the doors, admiring the frescos on the side of the dome before entering the Senate House and then the House of Representatives. They sat in the raised gallery over the speaker's head with a fine view of the semicircular array of representatives below. Leaving the representatives to their disorderly debate Catherine and her friends climbed the Capitol's white dome. They were rewarded with a glorious panorama. To one side across the grey flat waters lay Old Virginia. From the other Catherine looked down on the White House and the city. A soaked and bedraggled group made their way back down and across to the train station. Here Catherine left Jane Metford and Joseph Malins, who stayed on for a few more days, while she headed north, back to Philadelphia and then New York. Catherine spent her last night in the United States speaking at a temperance meeting in New York on another sweltering evening. Catherine found the heat stifling; the thermometer reached 105° inside the church even with all the windows open but she felt pleased enough with the talk she gave, which was perhaps her first attempt at public speaking.[56] The following day Catherine and Jane joined the *SS City of Chester* for the ten-day voyage home. Leaning over the ship's side Catherine spotted one of her 'new made negro "brothers"' on the dock and tossed him her new copy of the Templar periodical *Watchword* as a parting gift. In return he waved his handkerchief as the ship steamed out.

On 2 July the *Chester* passed through the banks of Newfoundland and the scalding heat of the northeastern skies turned to cold winds, fog and rain. Catherine sought out a warm nook near the engines to read her copy of *Thomas Wingfold* about the testing of a curate's faith written by the pastor and writer George MacDonald.[57] Later in the day she discussed John Bright's speeches with a Scottish traveller who held very decided views on Bright's work. Catherine held the opposing view (though how these fell she does not say). To avoid further confrontation with the Scotsman she crept off to bed early. The weather for the Fourth of July celebrations was cold but gloriously wild. Catherine and Jane were among the very few passengers who braved the deck. Jane wrapped herself into a shapeless mass of goat hair rug and shawls, while

Catherine watched the sailors work, enjoying the icy wind against her face. She felt invigorated and alive. On Monday 8 July the ship reached the south coast of Ireland, and a chilly wind lifted an exquisite and familiar fragrance of fresh grass and heather up from the land. At the end of July she and Joseph Malins attended the annual RWGL of the World in Belfast. Half of the *Belfast News-Letter's* article on the meeting covers Catherine's report on the mission in the southern states to bring black men and women into Templar lodges. She outlined the work of permanent and temporary agents in the South, and the funds collected and spent on the mission. Her report persuaded members to ask each Grand Lodge to promote the collection of additional funds for the mission and to print the report presented by Catherine for circulation.[58]

After her trip to the United States Catherine returned to her domestic duties at Askew, but seeing racial segregation in operation for herself caused Catherine to think about how she could work more constructively against racial prejudice. In August 1881 the orator and editor Benjamin Tucker Tanner came to Street for two weeks. Born into a poor working-class family in Pittsburgh on Christmas Day 1835, Tanner started his working life as a barber but became a Methodist preacher in 1856 and a bishop in the African Methodist Episcopal (AME) church nine years after he visited England.[59] Secretary of the General Conference of 1868, he also began editing the *Christian Recorder* that year seeking to establish it as a paper that would not only rival the most successful white religious papers but also help forge a reading community among black Americans.[60] In 1884 he helped found the *AME Church Review*, a quarterly regularly received by *Anti-Caste*, and served as its first editor. The fond memories he left of Askew reflect that visits to the Impeys were not only philanthropic meetings but also exchanges of mutual respect and the beginnings of new friendships and working relationships within trans-Atlantic networks.

Tanner travelled to England to take part in a large Methodist Conference being held in London that summer. Catherine saw the arrival of a number of black clergymen in Britain as an opportunity to discuss the racial prejudice they faced in the United States. At the start of August Catherine wrote to Charles Allen as secretary of the Anti-Slavery Society to see if the organization would help the Good Templar Mission to the Coloured people in America pay for a complimentary breakfast for 'the coloured delegates' at the Methodist Conference. She and Frederick Chesson (of the Aborigines Protection Society) had discussed the idea over the summer and before writing to Allen she had sounded out his secretary, who gave her several practical suggestions. She had initially feared that in September all influential English men would be 'away shooting and otherwise exercising their organs of destructiveness' but she now believed the event could be pulled off with the society's help.[61] The aim for the meeting was to express sympathy with 'the coloured race in their present difficult social problem' and to provide a space for those who were suffering in America 'to speak for themselves'.[62] The two societies co-hosted a breakfast meeting at the Devonshire House Hotel, Bishopsgate, in September with Edward Sturge of the Anti-Slavery Society presiding, not Catherine's preferred candidate Lord Shaftesbury.

Joseph Malins and Colonel R Osborne from the APS spoke alongside Bishop Daniel A Payne, Rev J Townshead and Bishop Brown – all black ministers. In her address to the 100 assembled clergymen and their supporters Catherine spoke out against the decision of parts of the Templar Order to exclude black people from their lodges.[63] Tanner told the audience that 'from morning till night' the hearts of his fellow black Americans 'were made to bleed at the hundred and one prejudices and the continual recital of their wrongs'.[64] No class of people was so downtrodden. They were treated as social lepers in the United States, so Tanner vowed to return home and tell his people to take hold of the hand that stretched out towards them from across the Atlantic and take up the principles of Good Templary, among whom they were recognized as men.[65] When Bishop Holsey, born enslaved and emancipated in 1865, argued that if black men and women could receive a 'Christian education' all else would follow, Catherine challenged him from the floor. 'If Christian education is to open the door', she asked, why was it that 'Christian educated men' refused to receive black people? 'How long are we to wait?' she continued. 'Are we to wait till every colored man is educated to the standard of Dr Tanner?' Her questions prompted an exchange about 'the caste question as it is now' that was eventually brought to a close by the Chair.[66]

In July Tanner and Catherine had travelled with Isabella Metford and other Templar brothers to Belfast, meeting members of the Irish Temperance League, who

Figure 2.4 Catherine Impey (in the first row, sitting on the floor) with temperance workers in Street, October 1887. The group includes future *Anti-Caste* subscribers J G Thornton (seated in the second row, third from left), Pardoe Yates (standing on the far right of the third row), F J Thompson (also standing in the third row, fifth from the right) and Frederic Sessions (standing in the back row, third from right)

showed them warmth and hospitality. Tanner, introduced as the 'African Publication House in Philadelphia', spoke at a RWGL of the World's meeting held in Clarence Hall, describing how in America caste was in operation in all aspects of social and cultural life.[67] In September Tanner and Catherine visited Llanelly for another Templar meeting, where over 150 people gathered at the Tabernacle Chapel School for a public breakfast. They listened to a number of preachers followed by Catherine and Tanner, who also spoke to a children's meeting held in the evening.[68] Her time had been crammed with engagements since the summer and Catherine did not find time to sit down and write to thank Allen for his support for the London breakfast meeting until the gloom of a December evening. Catherine had been sent a number of newspaper clippings on the breakfast from the United States, and their reports convinced her that the meeting had had some impact, or at least 'called the attention of the white people' to the fact that their actions towards black people were criticized and disapproved of in England.[69] While reports of the breakfast suggested the Templars could be an avenue for Catherine to continue her commitment to temperance and its commitment to a 'universal brotherhood', Catherine began developing a broader analysis of ideas of social and political equality.

In 1885 Catherine wrote 'Some Diverse Views on Social Equality' for the *Village Album*, examining the 'right relations' between 'rich and poor, or the cultured and the un-cultured' in America, England and around the world.[70] In the essay Catherine presented her audience with an exploratory discussion of 'social rights' as opposed to 'civil rights' within the concept of 'human rights'. These ideas were informing her writing and her theories of anticaste, although they were never directly addressed within the periodical. In 'Diverse Views' Catherine made more explicit connections between the oppression of the poor and racialized oppression than appeared in *Anti-Caste*. The essay began with the argument that just as the French Revolution had not settled issues of inequality for Europe, so the abolition of slavery had not settled matters of inequality for America. Catherine identified issues of racial prejudice to be more difficult to overcome than class alone, as she understood race as complicating issues of class rather than one form of prejudice replacing another. She argued that in America 'the question is complicated by side issues about differences of race', but in Britain she saw issues of social equality arising around the somewhat simpler question of undertaking the right relations towards people of other classes or rank in society to ones' own, and examining what just and proper claims upon the more privileged might be.[71] Although her use of language belies the need for the revolutions and campaigning she referenced, the piece reveals that what Catherine termed as caste in the title of *Anti-Caste* she meant to stand for the politics of 'race'.

Her discussion of 'civil rights' referenced the work of writer and critic George Washington Cable. Born in New Orleans in 1844, Cable served in the Confederate Army during the civil war but his literary works often portrayed New Orleans' Creole community in an unflattering light, though his collection of stories *Creole Days* (1879) earned him critical acclaim.[72] In 1885 he published a call for reform in the *Silent South*. Although Catherine does not name the book, her essay is a response to the *Silent South*, particularly Cable's argument that a distinction had to be drawn between social and civil rights made in a chapter entitled 'Civil Right not Social Choice'. As

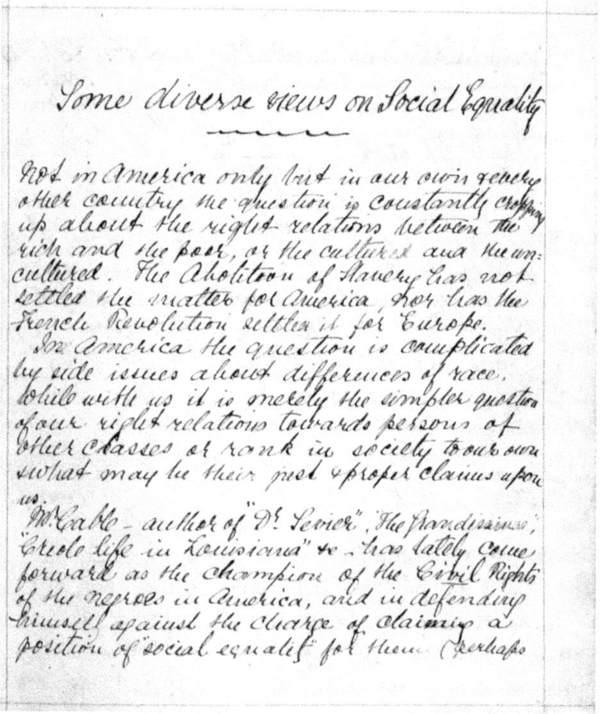

Figure 2.5 The opening page of Catherine's essay 'Diverse Views' from the Street *Village Album*, volume 38

Catherine explained, Cable saw social rights as existing within a family circle and based upon social relations and privilege that could never be claimed as a right. On the other hand, 'civil rights' covered all those impersonal interactions that created 'civil relations'. Catherine was unsure how far she accepted Cable's definitions. She remained sympathetic to his efforts, recognizing that he spoke out in a community where people's 'civil rights' were regularly flagrantly violated and his comments had made her reconsider how she viewed her responsibilities to her neighbours. Still, she did not accept his views on the limits to social relations.

Catherine took particular issue with Cable's opinion that it was a 'mischievous error' for members of the church to confuse the concept of a 'Christian Fraternity with Social Equality'. Cable based this observation on class, claiming no Protestant church in America had managed to get 'high & low life' to worship together. Although Catherine agreed that there might not be a thing called a 'social right', the idea that there might not be a way 'the stable-boy could claim as a right any social recognition from the occupant of the drawing-room' disturbed her. She argued that within each of us lies the power to genuinely interest ourselves in the welfare of others. If we choose to exercise this power we may overleap all barriers of 'class and caste'.[73] This requires combating 'the power of self', the selfishness that drives individuals to climb to the most comfortable position they can for themselves. She contrasted this focus on individual success to the 'power of human brotherliness', which before striving for personal comfort turns back and tries to assist the weaker in society, helping to lift them up to a position that without the help of others they can never attain.

Catherine further argued that an individual could not be truly free, could not benefit from the ideals of the French Revolution, unless all people benefitted from them. By slow degrees she believed the English were realizing that 'Liberty, Equality and Fraternity' could not be promoted by individuals seizing it for themselves but that it could be realized only by making 'a free gift of it to others'. Looking around her in the 1880s Catherine saw a nation slowly rising to this challenge, but she admitted individuals striving to this end were not necessarily supported or encouraged by the church. Although unfailingly committed to her faith, as she demonstrated to the audience at the London breakfast meeting, Catherine did not support Christian institutions without question. She agreed with Cable that the church was not always a complete embodiment of Christian ideals of equality. Moreover it was the church's failure to embrace fully important issues of everyday concern – peace, temperance, purity, personal freedom, liberty, fraternity – that meant they were picked up, nourished and cherished by non-Christian organizations. If the church's teachings of Christianity were too loose or too vague, it was no surprise that groups advocating for social reform sprang up to promulgate the neglected doctrines. Not hearing liberty, equality and fraternity celebrated from the pulpits of Europe the poor listened instead to voices of thunder speaking out from the revolutionary press. Catherine witheringly noted that once campaigns had been successfully developed the churches were then happy enough to claim and embrace these ideas as their own. Catherine's unease with this hypocrisy and the difficultly of living a Christian life in a world of stark inequality deeply concerned her.

> So almost impossible is it for the wretched overcrowded poor to be virtuous that this writer questions whether that society can call itself Christian which can stand by one side of the gulf, busy with the salvation of its own soul, while it leaves to the law of supply and demand the miserable thousands on the other side of the gulf.[74]

In her essay Catherine references a revolutionary press, secular ideas of fraternity and the politics of supply and demand. It is possible that Marx and other socialist writings were among the books in the Impey's library, but the conclusions of her own analysis remained rooted in Christianity. For Catherine, drawing on her Quaker practices of introspection and contemplation, the change society required was simple, a suppression of selfishness, an implementation of the 'power of the self' in order to create a society brought together through closer and kinder relationships. But the emphasis on change is placed upon men and women who were more privileged. In Catherine's theoretical model the responsibility for society's change lies with those who have rather than those who are without.

A self-imposed desire for 'kinder relations' levied by the 'self-control' of the privileged upon themselves sits somewhat awkwardly with Catherine's discussion of rights. Earlier in the essay Catherine outlines the doctrine she understood to be developing as 'human rights'. It seemed to Catherine that civilized societies (she does not list the countries she counted among these) had 'agreed upon a definition of human rights' that allowed particular conducts to be 'lawfully claimed by each man from his fellows irrespective of any particularities of person or circumstance they are his "rights".[75] Although grappling with the ideas of social, civil and human rights Catherine rarely used the phrase 'human rights' in her writing, perhaps because the term was so difficult to define and deeply contested. As one reader of the *Village Album* asked by means of an asterisk and a corresponding comment at the bottom of the page: 'But what is "a right"? Are "rights" whatever a set of men can take by force if not accorded them by law? or what?'[76] If we all have rights how are they to be brought into being if they are not in law? In Catherine's analysis personal responsibility and action are the only way these 'rights' can be realized and so it is the responsibility of individuals to ensure that the lives they lead and the institutions to which they belong uphold these principles.

Establishing a new society

Towards the end of 1885, Robert Impey's health seriously weakened and the Impey women could do little but watch as he suffered through a cold, bitter winter. He died on 30 January 1886, aged 66. In the visitors' book, five obituaries are tucked behind a remembrance card stuck in beneath Robert's fading portrait. Robert sits facing the camera, his head with a long full beard resting in his hand, a watch hanging down over his waistcoat. Obituaries note his commitment to the Society of Friends, the development of agricultural practices and local politics. Management of the farm passed to Ellen. She decided to continue to run the farm under her own name and also branched out into the wholesale selling of apples and at one stage opened a jam factory (partly to prevent them being used for cider). Although Catherine helped Ellen with some of the farm's administration, Ellen's willingness to shoulder the responsibility of running the business meant Catherine could now concentrate her energies on philanthropic work. Catherine was extremely grateful to her sister, aware that for both of them the decision to carve out their own path, rather than follow a beaten track, was not an easy option. Ellen worried about this rather more than her younger sister, and Catherine felt Ellen had chosen a business path because it seemed to be the easiest alternative available to her, but her decision did not reflect a simple choice. It was, Catherine reflected, 'a more serious matter than it seems to some – to deliberately choose a life of independence'. As women living out autonomous lives, Catherine believed that she and Ellen were 'each in our way "social reformers" or would be'.[77]

In April 1886 Catherine was elected grand vice-templar at her Templar's Grand Lodge meeting in Newport.[78] Re-elected the following April in London, this time she held the post for barely a day. Following the election of officers the meeting's attention turned to the ongoing issue of confirming unification with the Hickman lodges, a process formally underway since Malins and Oronhyatekha agreed terms at a unification meeting in Boston the previous year.[79] The committees in London submitted a proposal that every effort should be made to establish unification at an upcoming meeting in Saratoga Springs, New York State. Although sympathetic, Reverend James MacKenzie and Catherine moved to include an amendment that would insist on the total removal of the colour line from the Southern lodges before a union took place. The motion's failure left Catherine feeling she had no choice but to resign her position.[80] In May she travelled to Saratoga Springs to lead a final campaign against unification with lodges in the southern states before they agreed to erase the colour line. Catherine quoted from a letter illustrating that in Florida black people were subjected to 'unmerited indignities', which underscored her belief that race prejudice was increasing and not diminishing, but Catherine's was a lone voice.[81] Her former ally William Wells Brown had died, and no other black leaders commanded the same status to allow them to challenge the consensus of the meeting.[82] She urged the meeting to respect the voices of the journalist and editors Thomas Fortune and Benjamin Tanner who travelled to Saratoga to join the debate. As he was not a member Fortune was not given permission to speak. Delegates resented the critical comments he had made about the movement in his paper and Tanner faced hostility from colleagues who questioned his loyalty to the RWGL of the World.[83]

Although Catherine brought a number of testimonials with her to the meeting, one by one her colleagues turned against her. W W Turnbull, a representative from Scotland, argued that Catherine had only managed to collect the names of supporters she had because she misrepresented the conditions of the reunion and he read out a letter from one of Catherine's colleagues on the Negro Mission Fund, who stated that he did not see any issue of compromise of principle in the reunion. Rev J Yeames took issue with a circular Catherine had distributed in which she declared American churches were a disgrace to Christianity. He protested that those churches had 'spent millions in elevating the coloured people; that he had himself preached in nearly every coloured church in Boston', but he claimed it was 'the coloured people' who could not be induced to join in any numbers with white congregations. Joseph Malins admitted that Catherine had managed to unsettle a few of the delegates in Britain and Saratoga with her allegations of worsening racial prejudice, but he claimed that those who lived in the South, unlike Catherine, would all claim that the reverse of her accusations was reality.[84] Sorrowfully Catherine read out her final resolution to stand against 'all distinctions of race whether in societies or churches or anywhere else'. Before taking her seat she gave a final response to Yeames' claim that it was black people who segregated themselves in Boston. She told the audience that her colleague Miss Gardner had told her that during her long experiences she had known 'coloured people' like herself try to join white churches, but the feeling of isolation was so terrible and the treatment such they could not, without loss of proper self-respect, remain.[85] When the vote for reunification was taken by the delegates 47 voted for the motion, only Catherine's single vote stood against them.[86] She left the following day.

In November 1887, 18 months after her lone vote at the Saratoga session, Catherine distributed a circular to supporters informing them that she would no longer act as a collector for the Templar Mission among the Freedmen of America.[87] Her campaign had been one of determined persistence and she believed that she had managed not only to bring the issues of 'the colour question' to the attention of a new audience but also to persuade them that they had some role to play in the conditions of black people in the United States.[88] No longer able to pursue her political aims through the

RWGL of the World, Catherine considered the possibility of resurrecting an old idea for a new society and asked her supporters to allow their subscriptions to be applied somewhat differently in future. She had imagined the possibility of an 'Anti-Caste Society' as early as 1883 when she outlined her ideas for a trans-Atlantic association in a letter to Frederick Douglass. Writing through her thoughts on over a dozen pages, some printed with the Mission to the Freedmen logo of a black hand and a white hand clasped in a handshake, Catherine made the case to Douglass for a new organization to take up issues of racial equality. The Anti-Slavery Society had dropped them after their perceived success of wining arguments against inequality in the abolition of slavery. By the 1880s and the collapse of Reconstruction it was clear that although black Americans had won their freedom from enslavement, their civil and social rights were not secure. Now, Catherine believed 'some church or society – some one association at least must take the front in the cause of human equality'.[89]

Catherine did not expect to be able to spend extended amounts of time in the United States and so needed to focus on action she could undertake from England. Catherine envisaged bringing leading black Americans together with Quakers to discuss what could be done to remove racial prejudice from American society. Out of the resulting discussions, a single association could then be formed that would lead the cause of human equality and 'protest against all separation on the ground of colour'.[90] The aim of the society would be to inform the English public of the issues and restrictions and exclusions placed upon black people in churches, societies and their social life in general, all forms of social oppression Catherine had witnessed or had been told about by black men and women during her visits to the United States. Catherine's keenness to invite black Americans to speak to English audiences reflected her belief that, even if truthful and sincere, white people speaking for black people could have their arguments gravely undermined by challengers, whereas black Americans could claim an embodied authenticity. Catherine had given by her own admission a short and hurried speech about segregation at a Quaker meeting in 1882 but afterwards a woman in the audience from New York questioned the truthfulness of her allegations and Catherine felt she could not effectively refute the accusations. Catherine was convinced that black Americans would bring an authority to the debates that she and other white activists could not provide.

Catherine believed in knowledge as a transformative tool of political power and was convinced that if the English public were told a fraction of what she had learnt from the black press, her correspondence and personal conversations they would give voice to a chorus of indignation that would sting the United States into action. Although Catherine clearly envisaged a mainly white, English-speaking audience, in her mind the association's scope demanded an international geographical base. The society Catherine envisaged would include Americans, English, French and other nationals who would publicize the condition of 'coloured races in America, India or elsewhere'.[91] Catherine may have reviewed the ideas she first laid out in 1883 with Douglass when they met in Street during his visit to England in 1886 and 1887. Still many of the ideas she outlined to Douglass in 1883 are present in the updated circular she distributed to her Templar contacts in January 1888 as 'An Appeal Concerning the Treatment of Coloured Races'. In this Catherine proposed that as soon as sufficient funds were in hand the collective should arrange for the visit 'of one or two negroes or persons of negro descent (possibly ladies) competent to address our friends, and others, on the present difficulties and struggles of their people, consequent of the system of caste separations which have gradually become established in America'.[92] Aware that this shift away from a focus on alcohol consumption to issues of 'colour caste' and a rights-based activism might not be considered relevant to her old audience Catherine argued in the circular that the 'whole question of the right relations between white and coloured races is rapidly becoming one of world-wide importance in these days of frequent travelling and wide-spread immigration'.[93] These forms of international movement were directly affecting peoples' struggles for 'social emancipation', though not because of a need for an understanding of those arriving in Britain, but because those who emigrated from Britain too easily adopted the racist attitudes in their new surroundings, thus becoming 'the bitterest of negrophobists, and negro persecutors'.[94]

Catherine proposed the community initially form itself through a readership of the *Anti-Caste* periodical. As she outlined in the circular, for many years Catherine had wanted to create a way for 'large-hearted and justice-loving English readers' to learn more about the '*bitter* struggle with caste and oppression' that black people in the United States were facing. Given only 'occasional access to the ordinary press of the country' their hardships were little known 'except by readers of negro journals'. 'And who reads these journals?' Catherine asked, 'Alas! negroes only, or with very few

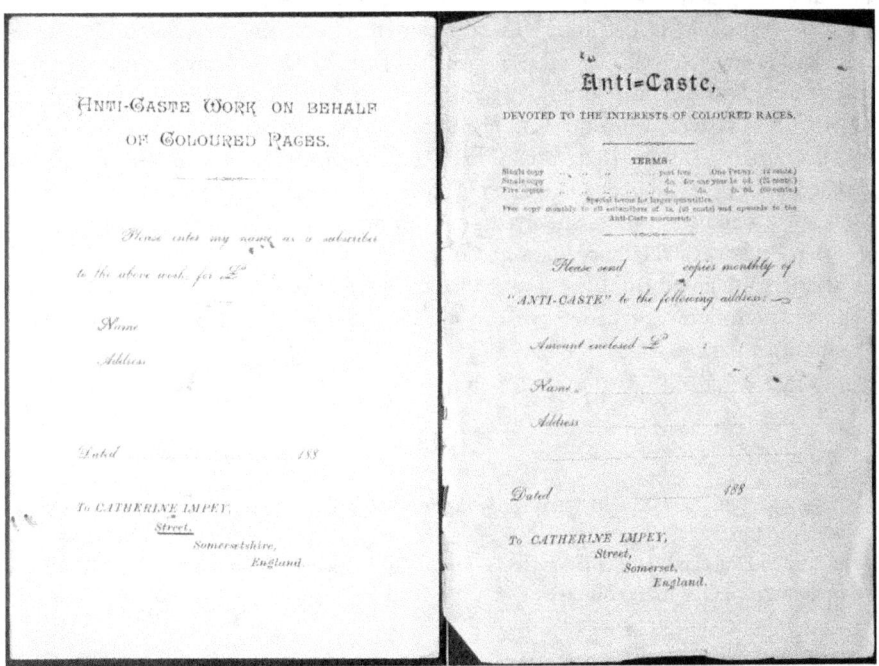

Figure 2.6 *Anti-Caste* subscription forms, the form on the left for funds, the form on the right for *Anti-Caste* in its periodical form

exceptions."[95] *Anti-Caste* would publish a 'representative selection from the current writings of intelligent negroes bearing on the position and prospects of the race' as well as notices and brief summaries from the proceedings of the British and Foreign Anti-Slavery Society and all other home organizations whose aim was the 'elevation of the coloured races'.[96] When the first issue of *Anti-Caste* appeared two months later in March 1888 the geography of its political concerns had broadened beyond the United States. *Anti-Caste* aimed to map reports of racial oppression across the globe. The principles laid out by Catherine to Douglass remained intact, including the importance of 'authentic voices' and the need for privileged people to find or provide spaces in which oppressed people could speak for themselves. A focus on the everyday violence of racial prejudice which oppressed people faced would set the readers of *Anti-Caste* aside from members of the older antislavery societies, for *Anti-Caste* would not concern itself directly with issues of slavery:

> Nor even so much with legalised oppression, as with social oppression, which – where the sentiment of a community is wrong on this point – can sanction cruelties and disabilities beyond the reach of law, and constantly tends to maintain or re-establish even legislative encroachments on the primary rights of citizenship.[97]

The January 1888 circular formally presented Catherine's proposal for *Anti-Caste*. Catherine took the opportunity to publicize Douglass' endorsement and ended with a request for practical support, however small. Although the archive remains largely silent on the extent of the initial financial support Catherine received, a letter from Priscilla Peckover of Bank House, Wisbech, in January 1888 survives. Part of a large and wealthy East Anglican family, Peckover was as a Quaker minister and temperance activist.[98] Peckover's letter to Catherine contained her strong endorsement and encouragement. She enclosed a donation of £5 for the incipient 'anti-caste Association', for she was keen to support a new kind of society, one that would act differently to the Anti-Slavery Society, which, she felt, spent too much time judging and condemning others.[99] Peckover's reference to *Anti-Caste* as a society suggests that at least some subscribers imagined from the outset that their readership formed part of an active alliance, a community of readers creating a political association through their purchase of a monthly periodical.

Notes

1 Impey to Douglass, 15 February 1883, Frederick Douglass Papers, Library of Congress, Washington.
2 Impey to Douglass, 15 February 1883, Frederick Douglass Papers, Library of Congress, Washington. Original emphasis.
3 Punshon, *Portrait in Grey*.
4 Punshon, *Portrait in Grey*.
5 Allen and Mackinnon, 'Education of Quaker girls'.
6 Allen and Mackinnon, 'Education of Quaker girls'.
7 Sturge, *Reminiscences of My Life*, 4.

8 For a discussion of Macaulay's writing see Hall, *Macaulay and Son*.
9 Sturge, *Reminiscences of My Life*, 4.
10 Punshon, *Portrait in Grey*.
11 Holton, *Quaker Women*.
12 On the political and family kinship networks of Helen Bright Preistman Clark, see Holton, *Quaker Women*.
13 Regan-Lefebvre, *Cosmopolitan Nationalism*.
14 Holton, *Quaker Women*.
15 Holton, 'Kinship and friendship'.
16 Holton, *Quaker Women*; Ware, *Beyond the Pale*.
17 Holton, *Quaker Women*.
18 *Village Album Catalogue*, Alfred Gillett Trust, Street, Somerset.
19 *Village Album Catalogue*, Alfred Gillett Trust, Street, Somerset.
20 Impey, Templar Politics, *Village Album*, 29, Alfred Gillett Trust.
21 Kneale, 'The place of drink'.
22 Kneale, 'The place of drink'.
23 Fahey, *Temperance and Racism*.
24 Fahey, *Temperance and Racism*.
25 Fahey, *Temperance and Racism*.
26 Fahey, 'Why some black lodges prospered and others failed'.
27 Fahey, *Temperance and Racism*.
28 Kneale, 'The place of drink'.
29 For Catherine's comment of the 'Equal Rights Mission' see Impey to Douglass, 15 February 1883, Frederick Douglass Papers at the Library of Congress, Washington.
30 Ware, *Beyond the Pale*.
31 Impey, Templar Politics, *Village Album*, 29, Alfred Gillett Trust.
32 Fahey, *Temperance and Racism*, 110.
33 Fahey, 'Why some black lodges prospered and others failed'.
34 Fahey, *Temperance and Racism*.
35 Fahey, *Temperance and Racism*.
36 From Fahey's research this would also seem to be an opinion held by William Wells Brown, who stated that Oronhyatekha didn't want to have a photograph taken with him because he was black, *Temperance and Racism*, 84.
37 Impey, Templar Politics, *Village Album*, 29, original emphasis, Alfred Gillett Trust, Street, Somerset.
38 Impey, Templar Politics, *Village Album*, 29, Alfred Gillett Trust, Street, Somerset.
39 Brown in Taylor, *I Was Born a Slave*; Fryer, *Staying Power*; For an examination of Brown's book, see Schoolman, 'Violent places'.
40 Taylor, *I Was Born a Slave*.
41 Fahey, *Temperance and Racism*.
42 Impey to Tourgée, 16 June 1890, 4785 The *Albion W. Tourgée* Papers.
43 'Report of the Representatives to the RWG Lodge of the World IOGT', *The Good Templars' Watchword*, 16 April 1879, 244.
44 *Leeds Mercury*, 31 May 1878.
45 Impey to Tourgée, 16 June 1890, 4785 The *Albion W. Tourgée* Papers, original emphasis.
46 Impey, On Sundry Domestic Matters in America, *Village Album*, 39, c.1886.
47 Impey, On Sundry Domestic Matters in America, *Village Album*, 39, c.1886.
48 Impey, On Sundry Domestic Matters in America, *Village Album*, 39, c.1886.

49 *The Good Templars' Watchword*, 3 July 1878, 442.
50 Impey, 'Lines left out', *Village Album*, 31, 1878–1879.
51 Reference to oven-like temperatures in Impey, 'On Sundry Domestic Matters America', *Village Album*, 39, c.1886
52 Impey, 'Lines left out', *Village Album*, 31, 1878–1879.
53 Impey, 'Lines left out', *Village Album*, 31, 1878–1879. An account of the trip also appeared in *The Good Templars' Watchword*, 3 July 1878, 442–443.
54 Impey, 'Lines left out', *Village Album*, 31, 1878–1879.
55 Impey, 'Lines left out', *Village Album*, 31, 1878–1879.
56 Impey, 'Lines left out', *Village Album*, 31, 1878–1879; *Christian Recorder*, 12 December 1878. In a letter to W.E. Axon written in 1889 Catherine explained that she made her first attempt at public speaking on the platform of a church in New York ten years earlier, Impey to Axon, 25 February 1889, Axon Papers, 2939, John Reynolds Library, University of Manchester.
57 Dearborn, *Baptized Imagination*.
58 *Belfast News-Letter*, 30 July 1881.
59 Tanner, in Gates and Higginbotham, *African American Lives*.
60 Bailey, *Race Patriotism*.
61 Impey to Allen, 4 August 1881, Brit. Emp. s.18 C61/2; Impey to Chesson, 4 August 1881, MSS. Brit. Emp. s.18 C138/163 both The Bodleian Library of Commonwealth and African Studies, University of Oxford.
62 Impey to Allen, 4 August 1881, C61/2 MSS. Brit. Emp. s.18 C61 2–8; *Christian Recorder*, 27 October 1881.
63 An extensive although not exhaustive list of attendees was published in 'Congratulatory breakfast', *Christian Recorder*, 27 October 1881.
64 *Times*, 17 September 1881, 7.
65 *Leeds Mercury*, 16 September 1881; *The Times*, 17 September 1881, 7.
66 'Congratulatory breakfast', *Christian Recorder*, 3 November 1881.
67 'The Editor Abroad. Belfast: Good Templary', *Christian Recorder*, 22 September 1881.
68 *Western Mail*, 15 September 1881.
69 Impey to Allen, 12 December 1881, MSS. Brit. Emp. s.18 C61/3.
70 Impey, 'Some Diverse Views of Social Equality', *Village Album*, 38, c.1885. Alfred Gillett Trust, Street, Somerset.
71 Impey, 'Some Diverse Views of Social Equality', *Village Album*, 38, c.1885. Alfred Gillett Trust, Street, Somerset.
72 Turner, *George W Cable*.
73 Impey, 'Some Diverse Views of Social Equality', *Village Album*, 38, c.1885, original emphasis.
74 Impey, 'Some Diverse Views of Social Equality', *Village Album*, 38, c.1885. Alfred Gillett Trust, Street, Somerset.
75 Impey, 'Some Diverse Views of Social Equality', *Village Album*, 38, c.1885. Alfred Gillett Trust, Street, Somerset, original emphasis.
76 Impey, 'Some Diverse Views of Social Equality', *Village Album*, 38, c.1885. Alfred Gillett Trust, Street, Somerset.
77 Impey to Chesson, 3 March 1886, MSS. Brit. Emp. s.18 C138/168.
78 *Liverpool Mercury*, 29 April 1886, 5.
79 Fahey, *Temperance and Racism*.
80 *Aberdeen Weekly Journal*, 14 April 1887; *Birmingham Daily Post*, 15 April 1887.

81 'Debate on Reunion in RWG Lodge of the World, Saratoga', *Good Templars' Watchword*, 27 June 1887, 402.
82 Fahey, *Temperance and Racism*.
83 Fahey, *Temperance and Racism*; 'Debate on Reunion in RWG Lodge of the World, Saratoga', *Good Templars' Watchword*, 27 June 1887, 403.
84 'Debate on Reunion in RWG Lodge of the World, Saratoga', *Good Templars' Watchword*, 27 June 1887, 402.
85 'Reunion Debate in the RWG Lodge of the World, Another Account', *Good Templars' Watchword*, 4 July 1887, 420.
86 'Debate on Reunion in RWG Lodge of the World, Saratoga', 27 June 1887, 404; Fahey, *Temperance and Racism*.
87 A reference to this circular sent on 30 November 1887 appears in 'An Appeal Concerning the Treatment of Coloured Races', MSS. Brit. Emp. s.20 E/8.
88 Impey to Douglass, 15 February 1883, Frederick Douglass Papers, Library of Congress, Washington.
89 Impey to Douglass, 15 February 1883, Frederick Douglass Papers, Library of Congress, Washington.
90 Impey to Douglass, 15 February 1883, Frederick Douglass Papers, Library of Congress, Washington, original emphasis.
91 Impey to Douglass, 15 February 1883, Frederick Douglass Papers, Library of Congress, Washington.
92 'An appeal concerning the treatment of Coloured Races', MSS. Brit. Emp. s.20 E5/8.
93 'An appeal concerning the treatment of Coloured Races', MSS. Brit. Emp. s.20 E5/8.
94 'An appeal concerning the treatment of Coloured Races', MSS. Brit. Emp. s.20 E5/8.
95 'An appeal concerning the treatment of Coloured Races', MSS. Brit. Emp. s.20 E5/8.
96 'An appeal concerning the treatment of Coloured Races', MSS. Brit. Emp. s.20 E5/8.
97 'An appeal concerning the treatment of Coloured Races', MSS. Brit. Emp. s.20 E5/8.
98 Laity, 'Peckover, Priscilla Hannah (1833–1931)'.
99 Peckover to Impey, 23 January 1888, MSS. Brit. Emp. s.20 E5/7.

3

Building a New Community

The idea that colour has any place whatever in determining the relations of members of the human family towards each other must everywhere be wiped out.
Catherine Impey, 1895

As her letter to Fredrick Douglass in 1883 showed, Catherine had been pondering the possibility of creating an 'anti-caste association' for several years before the first issues of *Anti-Caste* came out in March 1888. There were not many spaces where Catherine could express her views on racial prejudice. She had contributed to the *British Friend* and the *Temperance Watchword* but they did not allow for the expansive arguments she wanted to engage with. Once an editor herself Catherine did not have to negotiate a mediation of her ideas. In the editorial spaces of *Anti-Caste* Catherine had the opportunity to deliberate, suggest and question ideas of race and racism with her readers. Her decision to draw an active community together under the banner of 'Anti-Caste' rather than 'Anti-Race' or 'Anti-Racism' lay in Catherine's determination to undermine constructions of race in her activism and in her writing. How to convey this commitment through language and typography formed the core of Catherine's intellectual work during her years as an editor. Catherine employed 'caste' as a title and as a means of elaborating and deconstructing racial prejudice. Despite her attempts to broaden *Anti-Caste*'s geographical focus over the years, coverage of the United States remained dominant. Caste and oppression occurred of course in India, but caste as an internal structure of Indian society did not draw much attention. *Anti-Caste*'s focus fell on the oppressive relationships between British colonial governors, white settlers and people of colour in colonies across the Empire.

Although holding on to her original idea of forming international solidarities around an anticaste sentiment, the form this group initially took was not an association structured as a movement such as the Templars or APS with local branches, meetings, dances, fund-raisers, lectures and discussion meetings, but a community of readers. As a periodical *Anti-Caste* took shape because of dynamic networks of activism within associations such as temperance which Catherine could utilize. Drawing on these links enabled Catherine to develop her own *Anti-Caste* network that operated because of and in parallel to many other material networks in operation. During the 1880s changes in the structure of journalism and printing technologies, the expansion of newspapers established by civil rights and humanitarian groups and a global postal and cable system all provided a framework upon which Catherine could structure a new community. The support she received from black American activists like Frederick Douglass gave her the confidence to develop the foundations for an international association. Catherine's experience of campaign work within the temperance movement and her Quaker humanitarian kinship networks provided a base for the international membership of Africans, Americans, Europeans and Indians she envisioned. The success of *Anti-Caste* depended on Catherine's ability to draw these imagined individuals together into a community of regular and loyal readers.

A question of caste

In March 1888, Catherine's first editorial outlined that *Anti-Caste* intended to deal mainly with issues of 'colour caste', focusing on the politics of racial segregation and the racial prejudice it supported and encouraged. Her thoughts on race would be laid out in editorial addresses and articles over the years of *Anti-Caste's* publication. The columns reflect Catherine's struggle to capture in words the practice of racial prejudice and to find conceptual tools that enabled her to challenge prejudice without reinforcing it. In a notice to the *British Friend* publicizing Fanny Jackson Coppin's visit to England later in the summer of 1888, Catherine encouraged Quakers to express sympathy with those suffering under the 'oppressive system of caste (or "boycotting")' by which black Americans were 'excluded from so large a share of their civil and social rights'.[1] Although Catherine may not have chosen the header 'The Civil Rights of the Coloured Americans', beneath which her notice appeared in *The Friend*, the language of her letter suggested it. In her writing and editorial duties Catherine consistently sought a way to avoid the term 'races' wherever she could. As she explained to Albion Tourgée, 'Do you know I shun that word "races" wherever I can – It implies in itself a distinction that is unreal. We are really one "race" – the "human race" the world over though of different varieties – so that the word "race" in its plural form is as it were a hinderer of the truth we would spread.'[2] Catherine understood 'races' as social constructions of difference, and the formulation of 'colour caste' allowed her to highlight the systems of racial prejudice people built into societies, but she continued to struggle with the paradox of finding a language with which to discuss the experiences of race without reinforcing the divisions inherent in its language.

In activating 'colour-caste' as a mode of analysis, Catherine drew not directly from Indian discussions of a caste system, but from debates on racial difference that had evolved in the United States. Anthropologists working in the United States continued to use caste as a sociological concept into the 1930s and 1940s, arguing, as did Catherine, that using the term 'race' immediately implied an understanding that differences between people of different skin colour were fixed and biological. For some, caste came closer to describing the reality in which black and white communities were socially defined and relationships between them controlled not by their genetic structure but by social traditions.[3] In this context caste came to be used to describe and analyze the arrangement of black and white people in the Deep South, where the privileges, duties, obligations and opportunities within society were unequally distributed between the two 'colour-castes'. As W Lloyd Warner, professor of anthropology and sociology at the University of Chicago, noted in 1936, such a definition can also describe class. This idea had been played upon within a British context nearly 70 years earlier in Thomas William Robertson's sentimental play *Caste*. The Nottinghamshire-born playwright became known for domestic-based comedies which endorsed the decency of ordinary people.[4] *Caste*, a comedy in three acts, was first performed at the Prince of Wales Theatre, London, in April 1867, followed by the Old Broadway Theatre, New York, in August; it became one of Robertson's most popular dramas and illustrates how caste was applied to observations of England's class structure.[5] Part of the new forms of naturalist theatre, Robertson's 'cup and saucer drama' aimed for a realism in dialogue, sets and costumes, and closely focused on Victorian social habits.[6] Like his earlier play, *Society* (1865), *Caste* closely examined the English class system.

> Captain Hawtree: Of course, Dal, you're not such a soft as to think of marriage. You know what your mother is. Either you are going to behave properly, with a proper regard to the world, and all that, you know, or you're going to do the other thing. Now the question is, what do you mean to do? The girl is a nice girl no doubt, but as to your making her Mrs. D'Alroy the thing is out of the question.
>
> George D'Alroy: Why, what should prevent me?
>
> (*Returns to place on table.*)
>
> Haw: Caste! The inexorable law of caste. The social law, so becoming and so good, that commands like to mate with like, and forbids a giraffe to fall in love with a squirrel; that holds sentiment to be a dissipation, and demands the exercise of common sense from all.
>
> Geo: But, my dear Bark –
>
> Haw: My dear Dal, all those marriages of people with common people are all very well in novels and in plays on the stage, because the real people don't exist, and have no relatives who exist, and no connections, and so no harm's done, and it's rather interesting to look at; but in real life, with real relations, and real mothers, and so forth, it's absolute bosh – it's worse; it's utter social and personal annihilation and individual damnation.
>
> Geo: As to my mother, I haven't thought about her.
>
> Haw: Of course not. Lovers are so damned selfish they never think of anybody but themselves.
>
> Geo: My father died when I was three years old, and she married again before I was six, and married a Frenchman.
>
> Haw: A nobleman of the most ancient families in France, of equal blood to her own; she obeyed the duties imposed upon her by her station, and by caste.[7]

A caste system can be further defined as a system where, as George D'Alroy is asked to realize, marriage between groups is not sanctioned, but in English society, on the stage at least, 'caste' boundaries can be overcome by love and opened up to those who prove to be worthy to pass through them.

Geo: My dear fellow, nobody's a mistake. He don't exist. Nobody's nobody, Everybody's somebody.

Haw: Yes. But still, Caste –

Geo: Oh, Caste's all right. Caste is a good thing if it's not carried too far. It shuts the door on the pretentious and the vulgar, but it should open the door very wide for exceptional merit. Let brains break through its barriers, and what brains can break through love may leap over.

Haw: Why, George, you're quite inspired; quite an orator. What makes you so brilliant? your captivity, the voyage? what then?

Geo: I'm in love with my wife![8]

Social norms of caste in the United States were reinforced through legislation. In W Lloyd Warner's conception of caste, there is neither an opportunity for members of the lower groups to rise into the upper groups nor the chance that members of the upper group might fall into the lower ones. He observed that all Southern social institutions, including the family, schools, associations, temperance lodges and churches, were formed to fit the dominant white social caste.[9] The caste system in both India and in the United States secured prestige, economic and sexual gains for the groups established at the top of the hierarchy. Their desire to retain their position for themselves and their children accounted for their great efforts to perpetuate the system. The unequal distribution of school funds provided an exemplar of how the system maintained itself across generations in the Deep South.[10]

An understanding of race as caste enabled Catherine to focus on the privileges adopted and maintained by white people in employment, education and general opportunities to live. The use of the term 'caste' to express the division between black and white people in the United States appeared in the writings of both pro and antiracist writers, intellectuals and activists during the American Civil War and Reconstruction. Goldwin Smith was one of a group of English liberals who travelled to the United States during the Civil War.[11] A keen supporter of democracy in the United States, Smith simultaneously insisted on the exclusion of black people from political space. Writing to Charles Eliot Norton in 1865, Smith expressed his concern over the place of black people in the new forms of democracy that would follow the emancipation of the enslaved: 'The Negro question will, I fear, be a great difficulty. You cannot have a pariah caste without fatally derogating from the splendid principles of your Republic. On the other hand from the differences of color and the physical repugnance, amalgamation seems unlikely.'[12] In opposition, 'anti-caste liberalism' from the mid-1860s into the mid-1880s represented an important strand of radical thought and activism for those challenging racial segregation and discrimination in the United States.[13] During this time of radical antiracist thought, a small but prominent political coalition succeeded in developing a clear theory of 'anti-caste constitutionalism' that found expression in legal arguments, speeches, essays, books and political meetings.[14]

In 1869 Charles Sumner delivered a lecture on *The Question of Caste*. A leading antislavery senator from among the small number of Radical Republicans who promoted land reform for the benefit of black people following the Civil War, he later first proposed a series of bills to the Senate that would prohibit racial discrimination in public spaces such as restaurants, theatres, public transport and jury selection.[15] In 1867 Sumner had argued before the Senate that every formerly enslaved male or head of household should be given 40 acres and $100, with which to build a dwelling on their new homestead. The enslaved, he argued, 'had earned from their masters this very land and much more'.[16] In his essay on caste, Sumner outlined his hopes for a future where men would subdue their pride of birth, prejudice of class and pretension of caste. Following an outline of caste in India, Sumner compared the system to racial hierarchies in the United States, arguing that in America white people claimed the place of the Brahmin while the Africans and Chinese were treated as if Pariahs.

> The caste claiming hereditary rank and privilege is white; the caste doomed to hereditary degradation and disability is black or yellow, and it is gravely asserted that this difference of color marks difference of race which itself justifies the discrimination.[17]

Although in the mid-1860s anticaste liberals briefly argued for economic redistribution as a means of support for black communities, by the mid-1870s the need for economic redistribution largely left their rhetoric, and instead, anticaste liberalism came to focus upon the need for black men and women to be protected against discrimination in order for them to have an equal opportunity within a free market.[18] The resulting debates used the framework of caste to discuss institutionalized forms of racial discrimination such as increasing racial segregation on trains. An essay on 'Caste in America' by Michael E Strieby in *American Missionary* in 1883 discussed the reasons for racial segregation in spaces of worship, also directly contrasting the Indian caste system with a two-tiered American caste system. Strieby, an abolitionist minister and executive secretary of the American Missionary Association from 1876 to 1895, argued that in the United States the 'two castes are simply the white and the colored races' and like Sumner he understood the 'colored caste' to include Chinese and also American indigenous communities.[19]

There is no evidence Catherine saw Robertson's play or directly engaged with these particular American essays by Sumner and Strieby, but it was from debates appropriating the Indian caste system as developed in the United States that Catherine took her meaning. Reflecting on her decision to use 'caste' in a letter to Albion Tourgée in February 1890 Catherine admitted, 'I had only known of the American question when I began to publish *Anti-Caste*. The Indian religious caste I had heard of, but not the caste feeling of her rulers, towards Indian people'.[20] Though Catherine identified her understanding of 'colour caste' to have come through an American tradition, the borrowing of transnational models to enable critiques of race/caste had been adopted by both American and Indian activists. Identified as 'a vital inaugurator' of anticaste thinking in India, Jotirao Phule (1827–1890) developed an early critique of caste structures by establishing a counterhistory for the lower castes in India.[21] Though his book *Slavery* (*Gulamgiri*) published in 1873 did not closely consider the politics of Reconstruction, Phule drew on the history of American slavery and emancipation to enable him to reframe discussions on caste in India.²² His use of 'slavery as concept-metaphor' enabled him to open up complex caste structures for analysis and critique.²³ Phule's deployment of histories of American slavery to challenge caste hierarchy and Catherine's use of caste to destabilize racial hierarchies are illustrative of the importance of the circulation of ideas emerging in countercultural discourse networks. Anticaste radicals drew material from a variety of transnational print and oral cultures created by missionary and temperance reports, autobiography, plays, personal testimony and cultures of print emerging from anticolonial and antiracist networks.

Though Catherine's use of 'caste' released her from the bounded language of 'race', her utilization of American forms of caste analysis kept her within a conservative view of economic change maintained by anticaste liberalism campaigners who took on the laissez-faire ideology of the Republican Party.²⁴ Given Catherine's feeling that no Christian society could leave to the 'law of supply and demand the miserable thousands' on the other side of the economic gulf, and the interconnected relationship between race and class that she outlined in 'Diverse Views', utilizing caste as a language of discrimination had limits. Explaining exactly what she meant by or what could be encapsulated within the concept of caste also proved difficult. Catherine did not assume *Anti-Caste's* readers fully understood the political and socially constructed materiality she intended to evoke with ideas of colour caste. She found it difficult to express them herself and she recurrently tussled with the concept of caste as a replacement for race. Initially 'race' still appeared in *Anti-Caste's* masthead. When Catherine produced forms to recognize early donations for the cause, they were printed with the header *Anti-Caste: Work on Behalf of Coloured Races*. The first issue of *Anti-Caste* appeared with the slightly altered explanation that it was 'devoted to the interests of coloured races'. A few months into publication Catherine became uneasy with that description, and in August 1889 she changed it to *Anti-Caste: Advocates the Brotherhood of Mankind Irrespective of Colour or Descent*. She did not intend the change to suggest to readers that *Anti-Caste* no longer stood *devoted to the interests of coloured races*, but that title did not, for her, adequately indicate the standpoint from which the interests of people of colour needed to be considered. To illustrate her case she provided an example from the aristocracy of Europe. Among this privileged class there were thousands who were devoted to the interest of the working classes of Europe, but few who then advocated the brotherhood of rich and poor as the basis of their commitment. *Anti-Caste* advocated a genuine brotherhood, a love and respect between brothers and sisters of the human family.

While attacking segregation in public realms, *Anti-Caste* emphasized the importance of individual action, of hospitality and of not using or supporting segregated spaces in any form. In January 1890 readers were reminded that while victims of institutionalized caste systems had the strongest claims upon their sympathies, they should not forget those who lived in countries where black people found themselves in a subordinate position to white power and where it took on different forms to the clear geographies of segregation drawn by the colour line. To withstand the subtle influences of caste, these peoples needed every possible encouragement and the support of one family – of one individual – could be of unspeakable value.²⁵ Though critical of the wealthy of Europe's attitude to their poorer brethren, the limits around ideas of economic justice within anticaste liberalism maintained a presence in Catherine's thinking. Though poor, Catherine maintained, people of colour did not require money, nor did they require patronage or cheap condescension. The cure for their present ills would come from 'the warm outpouring of love' and a spirit of neighbourliness which judged people only according to merit. 'It is this which has ever been denied to them by their white Brethren.'[26]

Catherine returned to a discussion of caste in April 1891. She still struggled to find a clear, searching definition of caste which would expose for her readers where the power of its evil really lay. She first described caste as an 'arbitrary and systematic restriction of persons to particular ranks of life on grounds other than those of individual merit and fitness'.[27] But this failed to capture her meaning. As a description it remained vague and did not explain why the caste system of racial prejudice had to be dismantled. She tried again. Complexion, she argued, was not important: 'it is not the colour of his skin which fits a man or *un*fits him for this or that place in life – *nor is it his supposed race characteristics*, whatever they may be, but his ACTUAL PERSONAL CHARACTER.'[28] By what right, she asked, did those who held the keys to the upper walks of life stand in judgement of someone 'in whom they can detect "colour" (aye, though they be almost as purely Anglo-Saxon as themselves)' and thus label them weak and repulsive and therefore condemn them at sight to everlasting exclusion from their higher privileges? 'What could be more outrageously mean and unfair?'[29] These harmful processes came not only from 'absolute *prejudice* – the prejudging of an untried prisoner' – but also from thrusting people forthwith into the narrow prison house of caste – 'the *arbitrary restriction of persons to particular ranks of life, on grounds other than those of individual merit and fitness*.'[30] Her words seem to echo through into Martin Luther King's 1963 speech in Washington DC, when he spoke of his dream that his four children would one day live in a nation where they would be judged not by the colour of their skin, but by the content of their character.[31]

Perhaps crafted in response to Catherine's deliberations on caste, 'I.M.'s proposed definition was published the following month, emphasizing the social constructions of segregation which maintained the orders of caste:

> Caste restricts persons of certain colour or birth to the inferior ranks of life, and 'tends to close to them by tacit social consent, the avenues, whether of property, culture, official position, marriage, or social intercourse, by which in every free community the worthier or better endowed of the lower classes rise to take place with the higher.'[32]

The hardening colour lines of racial prejudice in the United States and southern Africa were regularly exposed in *Anti-Caste* and later *Fraternity*. These spatialized practices of segregation made racial prejudice easy to see. Throughout the 1880s and 1890s these practices presented themselves in a myriad of social and legal geographies. They ranged from legislation that denied people the right to walk along the pavement, or vote, or sit where they chose in a train or in a theatre to social norms that kept spaces such as residential settlements, churches, temperance lodges and restaurants racially segregated. As Catherine later acknowledged, focusing on these physical manifestations of the colour line made it very difficult to pull out the more subtle forms of racism such as those in operation within British life. *Anti-Caste* did try and draw attention to an uneven geography of caste formations. Caste prejudice lurked in places where black people found themselves subordinated to white communities and where racist laws, in constitution or custom, had not yet come into legal force. Segregation formed a key focus for antiracist action, and places where it did not yet have clear legal status formed key battle grounds.

On 7 June 1892 a 30-year-old shoemaker Homer Adolphe Plessy boarded a train in New Orleans. He had bought a first-class ticket to Covington, Louisiana, and took a seat in the 'whites only' car.[33] Recruited by local activists to test the Louisiana Separate Car Act passed in 1890, Plessy was chosen because of his pale skin and his subsequent ability to access a segregated train carriage. Not long into his journey the conductor inspected his ticket and questioned his right to sit in the 'whites only' car. Plessy refused to move and at the next stop he was arrested and then charged and convicted with violating the Separate Car Act. Albion Tourgée hoped that during the process of appeals, Plessy's ambiguous racial appearance would break open arguments about the category of race itself.[34] Over the next four years the case passed through the Louisiana State Supreme Court before arriving at the US Supreme Court in April 1896. The Court ruled that the Separate Car Act did not violate the Fourteenth Amendment's guarantee of equal protection and due process before the law, declaring that

> We consider the underlying fallacy of the plaintiff's argument to consist in the assumption that the enforced separation of the two races stamps the colored race with a badge of inferiority. If this be so, it is not by reason of anything found in the act, but solely because the colored race chooses to put that construction upon it.[35]

Their endorsement of Louisiana's segregated system facilitated separate railroad coaches, separate waiting rooms in train and bus stations, dual systems of public education, the back seats of the bus for black passengers 'and all the other trappings and signs of a caste system'.[36] In a lone dissent, Justice John Marshall Harlan argued that 'in view of the Constitution, in the eye of the law, there is in this country no superior, dominant, ruling class of citizens. There is no caste here.' Segregation legitimated by the decision could only further poison race relations:

> What can more certainly arouse race hate, what more certainly create and perpetuate a feeling of distrust between these races, than state enactments, which, in fact, proceed on the ground that colored citizens are so inferior and degraded that they cannot be allowed to sit in public coaches occupied by white citizens? That, as all will admit, is the real meaning of such legislation as was enacted in Louisiana.[37]

Segregation was not the result of racial difference; segregation maintained, encouraged and perpetuated racism.[38] It was, as Catherine argued, a 'superficial system of selection' and while it remained institutionalized in civic and social life, racial prejudice could not be overcome.[39] It was not until 1954, when the National Association for the Advancement of Colored People (NAACP) took on *Brown vs. the Board of Education*, that the US Supreme Court agreed that segregating schools by race was 'inherently unequal' with Chief Justice Earl Warren asserting that 'any language in *Plessy v. Fergusson* contrary to this finding is rejected'.[40]

Producing *Anti-Caste*

It is somewhat ironic that *Anti-Caste*'s physical form took inspiration from *The Southern Letter* edited by Booker T Washington, a campaigner known for his accommodationist approach to segregated education. Published monthly by the Tuskegee Institute, *The Southern Letter: Devoted to the Education of Hand, Head and Heart* was produced for supporters of the institute established as 'a Normal School for colored teachers'.[41] Now Tuskegee University, the 2000-acre campus lying 40 miles east from Montgomery, Alabama, is a National Historic Landmark. It began in 1881 as a one-room shanty near Butler Chapel AME Zion Church in Alabama. Thirty adults were taught in the first class, and Dr Booker T Washington was appointed their first teacher. By the 1883–1884 school year, over 160 students were enrolled and the school moved to a nearby abandoned plantation.[42] As the institute grew, it became synonymous with Washington's accommodationist response to racial segregation. Critics of his methods included Frederick Douglass, who argued that those who accepted segregationist policies failed to anticipate the importance of the long-term principle at stake, and W E B Du Bois, who attacked Washington's highly regarded reputation and his education programmes in his chapter on 'Booker T Washington and Others' in *The Souls of Black Folk* (1903).[43]

Catherine had been mulling over the possibility of publishing a paper for her planned association for some years when she received a parcel of Washington's *Letters* from a friend.[44] Given her principled stance against any form of segregation, that Washington's *Letter* proved such an incentive to her could appear contradictory, but Catherine took substantive not theoretical inspiration from Tuskegee's organ. *Southern Letter* did not contain explicitly political material. At a cost of 50 cents a year, the four-page monthly provided a means for former students and Tuskegee's supporters to stay in touch. Letters from graduates provided updates of their success in business and relayed their attempts to build schools for black children out of single-room buildings or old houses. Before reading *Southern Letter* Catherine assumed that the financial risk of the expense and the burden of production on her time made it impossible for her to attempt the publication of a journal. The establishment of a periodical was a major undertaking. The print entrepreneur George Newness argued in 1882 that 'to edit a newspaper, one needs to be a statesman, an essayist, a geographer, a statistician, and, so far as all acquisition is concerned, encyclopaedic. To man and propel a newspaper requires more qualities than any other business on earth.'[45] The style, structure and small size of *Southern Letter* convinced Catherine that the costs of producing a similar publication could be affordable for her.

She chose John Whitby & Son to carry out her printing instructions for *Anti-Caste*. Located in Bridgwater only 13 miles west of Street, Whitby & Sons represented a convenient choice. They also boasted gas power, modern machinery and new type

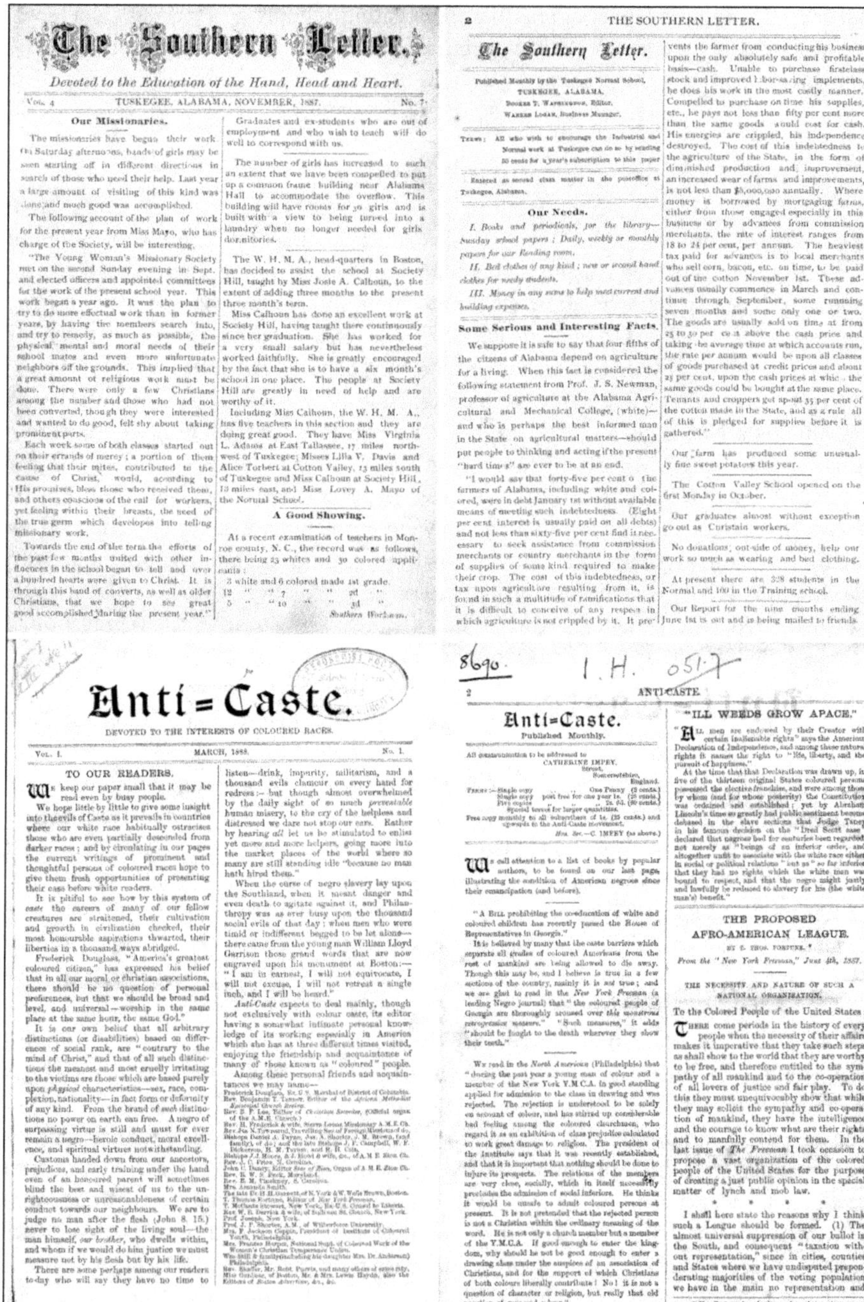

The Southern Letter.

Devoted to the Education of the Hand, Head and Heart.

Vol. 4 TUSKEGEE, ALABAMA, NOVEMBER, 1887. No. 7.

Our Missionaries.

The missionaries have begun their work. On Saturday afternoons, bands of girls may be seen starting off in different directions in search of those who need their help. Last year a large amount of visiting of this kind was done, and much good was accomplished.

The following account of the plan of work for the present year from Miss Mayo, who has charge of the Society, will be interesting.

"The Young Woman's Missionary Society met on the second Sunday evening in Sept. and elected officers and appointed committees for the work of the present school year. This work began a year ago. It was the plan to try to do more effectual work than in former years, by having the members search into, and try to remedy, as much as possible, the physical, mental and moral needs of their school mates and even more unfortunate neighbors off the grounds. This implied that a great amount of religious work must be done. There were only a few Christians among the number and those who had not been converted, though they were interested and wanted to do good, felt shy about taking prominent parts.

Each week some of both classes started out on their errands of mercy; a portion of them feeling that their mites, contributed to the cause of Christ, would, according to His promises, bless those who received them, and others conscious of the call for workers, yet feeling within their breasts, the need of the true germ which developes into telling missionary work.

Towards the end of the term the efforts of the past few months united with other influences in the school began to tell and over a hundred hearts were given to Christ. It is through this band of converts, as well as older Christians, that we hope to see great good accomplished during the present year."

Graduates and ex-students who are out of employment and who wish to teach will do well to correspond with us.

The number of girls has increased to such an extent that we have been compelled to put up a common frame building near Alabama Hall to accommodate the overflow. This building will have rooms for 30 girls and is built with a view to being turned into a laundry when no longer needed for girls dormitories.

The W. H. M. A., head-quarters in Boston, has decided to assist the school at Society Hill, taught by Miss Josie A. Calhoun, to the extent of adding three months to the present three month's term.

Miss Calhoun has done an excellent work at Society Hill, having taught there continuously since her graduation. She has worked for a very small salary but has nevertheless worked faithfully. She is greatly encouraged by the fact that she is to have a six month's school in one place. The people at Society Hill are greatly in need of help and are worthy of it.

Including Miss Calhoun, the W. H. M. A., has five teachers in this section and they are doing great good. They have Miss Virginia L. Adams at East Tallassee, 17 miles northwest of Tuskegee; Misses Lilla V. Davis and Alice Torbert at Cotton Valley, 13 miles south of Tuskegee and Miss Calhoun at Society Hill, 13 miles east, and Miss Lovey A. Mayo of the Normal School.

A Good Showing.

At a recent examination of teachers in Monroe county, N. C., the record was as follows, there being 23 whites and 30 colored applicants:

3 white and 6 colored made 1st grade.
12 " " 7 " " 2d "
5 " " 10 " " 3d "

Southern Workman.

2 THE SOUTHERN LETTER.

The Southern Letter.

Published Monthly by the Tuskegee Normal School, TUSKEGEE, ALABAMA.
Booker T. Washington, Editor.
Warren Logan, Business Manager.

Terms: All who wish to encourage the Industrial and Normal work at Tuskegee can do so by sending 50 cents for a year's subscription to this paper.

Entered as second class matter in the postoffice at Tuskegee, Alabama.

Our Needs.

I. Books and periodicals, for the library—Sunday school papers; Daily, weekly or monthly papers for our Reading room.

II. Bed clothes of any kind; new or second hand clothes for needy students.

III. Money in any sums to help meet current and building expenses.

Some Serious and Interesting Facts.

We suppose it is safe to say that four fifths of the citizens of Alabama depend on agriculture for a living. When this fact is considered the following statement from Prof. J. S. Newman, professor of agriculture at the Alabama Agricultural and Mechanical College, (white)—and who is perhaps the best informed man in the State on agricultural matters—should put people to thinking and acting if the present "hard times" are ever to be at an end.

"I would say that forty-five per cent of the farmers of Alabama, including white and colored, were in debt January 1st without available means of meeting such indebtedness. (Eight per cent interest is usually paid on all debts) and not less than sixty-five per cent find it necessary to seek assistance from commission merchants or country merchants in the form of supplies of some kind required to make their crop. The cost of this indebtedness, or tax upon agriculture resulting from it, is found in such a multitude of ramifications that it is difficult to conceive of any respect in which agriculture is not crippled by it. It prevents the farmer from conducting his business upon the only absolutely safe and profitable basis—cash. Unable to purchase firstclass stock and improved labor-saving implements, he does his work in the most costly manner. Compelled to purchase on time his supplies, etc., he pays not less than fifty per cent more than the same goods would cost for cash. His energies are crippled, his independence destroyed. The cost of this indebtedness to the agriculture of the State, in the form of diminished production and improvement, an increased wear of farms and improvements, is not less than $5,000,000 annually. Where money is borrowed by mortgaging farms, either from those engaged especially in this business or by advances from commission merchants, the rate of interest ranges from 18 to 24 per cent, per annum. The heaviest tax paid for advances is to local merchants who sell corn, bacon, etc. on time, to be paid out of the cotton November 1st. These advances usually commence in March and continue through September, some running seven months and some only one or two. The goods are usually sold on time at from 25 to 30 per cent above the cash price and taking the average time at which accounts run, the rate per annum would be upon all classes of goods purchased at credit prices and about 25 per cent, upon the cash prices at which the same goods could be bought at the same place. Tenants and croppers get about 35 per cent of the cotton made in the State, and as a rule all of this is pledged for supplies before it is gathered."

Our farm has produced some unusually fine sweet potatoes this year.

The Cotton Valley School opened on the first Monday in October.

Our graduates almost without exception go out as Christain workers.

No donations, out-side of money, help our work so much as wearing and bed clothing.

At present there are 328 students in the Normal and 100 in the Training school.

Our Report for the nine months ending June 1st is out and is being mailed to friends.

Anti=Caste.

DEVOTED TO THE INTERESTS OF COLOURED RACES.

Vol. 1. MARCH, 1888. No. 1.

TO OUR READERS.

We keep our paper small that it may be read even by busy people.

We hope little by little to give some insight into the evils of Caste as it prevails in countries where our white race habitually ostracises those who are even partially descended from darker races; and by circulating in our pages the current writings of prominent and thoughtful persons of coloured races hope to give them fresh opportunities of presenting their case before white readers.

It is pitiful to see how by this system of *caste* the careers of many of our fellow creatures are straitened, their cultivation and growth in civilization checked, their most honourable aspirations thwarted, their liberties in a thousand ways abridged.

Frederick Douglass, "America's greatest coloured citizen," has expressed his belief that in all our moral or christian associations, there should be no question of personal preferences, but that we should be broad and level, and universal—worship in the same place at the same hour, the same God."

It is our own belief that all arbitrary distinctions (or disabilities) based on differences of social rank, are "contrary to the mind of Christ," and that of all such distinctions the meanest and most cruelly irritating to the victims are those which are based purely upon *physical* characteristics—sex, race, complexion, nationality—in fact form or deformity of any kind. From the brand of *such* distinctions no power on earth can free. A negro of surpassing virtue is still and must for ever remain a negro—heroic conduct, moral excellence, and spiritual virtues notwithstanding.

Customs handed down from our ancestors, prejudices, and early training under the hand even of an honoured parent will sometimes blind the best and wisest of us to the unrighteousness or unreasonableness of certain conduct towards our neighbours. We are to judge no man after the flesh (John 8. 15.) never to lose sight of the living soul—the man himself, *our brother*, who dwells within, and whom if we would do him justice we must measure not by his flesh but by his life.

There are some perhaps among our readers to-day who will say they have no time to listen—drink, impurity, militarism, and a thousand evils clamour on every hand for redress:—but though almost overwhelmed by the daily sight of so much *preventable* human misery, to the cry of the helpless and distressed we dare not stop our ears. Rather by hearing *all* let us be stimulated to enlist yet more and more helpers, going more into the market places of the world where so many are still standing idle "because no man hath hired them."

When the curse of negro slavery lay upon the Southland, when it meant danger and even death to agitate against it, and Philanthropy was as ever busy upon the thousand social evils of that day; when men who were timid or indifferent begged to be let alone—there came from the young man William Lloyd Garrison those grand words that are now engraved upon his monument at Boston:—"I am in earnest, I will not equivocate, I will not excuse, I will not retreat a single inch, and I will be heard."

Anti-Caste expects to deal mainly, though not exclusively with colour caste, its editor having a somewhat intimate personal knowledge of its working especially in America which she has at three different times visited, enjoying the friendship and acquaintance of many of those known as "coloured" people.

Among these personal friends and acquaintances we may name—

Frederick Douglass, Ex U.S. Marshal of District of Columbia.
Rev. Benjamin T. Tanner, Editor of the *African Methodist Episcopal Church Review.*
Rev. B. F. Lee, Editor of *Christian Recorder*, (Official organ of the A.M.E. Church.)
Rev. H. Frederick & wife, Sierra Leone Missionary A.M.E. Ch.
Rev. Jas. N. Townsend, Travelling Sec. of Foreign Missions of do.
Bishops Daniel A. Payne, Jas. A. Shorter, J. M. Brown, (and family) of do; and the late Bishops J. P. Campbell, W. F. Dickerson, H. M. Turner, and R. H. Cain.
Bishops J. J. Moore, & J. Hood & wife, &c., of A.M.E. Zion Ch.
Rev. J. C. Price, N. Carolina.
John C. Dancy, Editor *Star of Zion*, Organ of A.M.E. Zion Ch.
Rev. R. W. S. Peck, Maryland.
Rev. E. M. Pinckney, S. Carolina.
Mrs. Amanda Smith.
The late Dr H. H. Garnett, of N. York & W. Wells Brown, Boston.
T. Thomas Fortune, Editor of *New York Freeman.*
T. McCants Stewart, New York, Ex-U.S. Consul to Liberia.
Rev. W. B. Derrick & wife, of Sullivan St. Church, New York.
Prof. Joseph, New York.
Prof. J. P. Shorter, A.M., of Wilberforce University.
Mrs. F. Jackson Coppin, President of Institute of Coloured Youth, Philadelphia.
Mrs. Frances Harper, National Supt. of Coloured Work of the Women's Christian Temperance Union.
Wm. Still & family (including his daughter Mrs. Dr. Anderson) Philadelphia.
Rev. Shaffer, Mr. Robt. Purvis, and many others of same city. Miss Gardiner, of Boston, Mr. & Mrs. Lewis Hayden, also the Editors of *Boston Advertiser*, &c., &c.

8690. I.H. 051.7

2 ANTI-CASTE.

Anti=Caste.

Published Monthly.

All communication to be addressed to
CATHERINE IMPEY,
Street,
Somersetshire,
England.

Terms:—Single copy One Penny (2 cents.)
Single copy post free for one year 1s. (25 cents.)
Five copies " " " 2s. 6d. (60 cents.)
Special terms for larger quantities.
Free copy monthly to all subscribers of 1s. (25 cents.) and upwards to the Anti-Caste movement.

Hon. Sec.—C. IMPEY (as above.)

We call attention to a list of books by popular authors, to be found on our last page, illustrating the condition of American negroes since their emancipation (and before).

"A Bill prohibiting the co-education of white and coloured children has recently passed the House of Representatives in Georgia."

It is believed by many that the caste barriers which separate all grades of coloured Americans from the rest of mankind are being allowed to die away. Though this may be, and I believe is true in a few sections of the country, mainly it is *not* true; and we are glad to read in the *New York Freeman* (a leading Negro journal) that "the coloured people of Georgia are thoroughly aroused over *this monstrous retrogression measure.*" "Such measures," it adds "should be fought to the death wherever they show their teeth."

We read in the *North American* (Philadelphia) that "during the past year a young man of colour and a member of the New York Y.M.C.A. in good standing applied for admission to the class in drawing and was rejected. The rejection is understood to be solely on account of colour, and has stirred up considerable bad feeling among the coloured churchmen, who regard it as an exhibition of class prejudice calculated to work great damage to *religion.* The president of the Institute says that it was recently established, and that it is important that nothing should be done to injure its prospects. The relations of the members are very close, socially, which in itself necessarily precludes the admission of social inferiors. He thinks it would be unsafe to admit coloured persons at present. It is not pretended that the rejected person is not a Christian within the ordinary meaning of the word. He is not only a church member but a member of the Y.M.C.A. If good enough to enter the kingdom, why should he not be good enough to enter a drawing class under the auspices of an association of Christians, and for the support of which Christians of both colours liberally contribute! No! it is not a question of character or religion, but really that old question of race and colour."

"ILL WEEDS GROW APACE."

"All men are endowed by their Creator with certain inalienable rights" says the American Declaration of Independence, and among these natural rights it names the right to "life, liberty, and the pursuit of happiness."

At the time that that Declaration was drawn up, in five of the thirteen original States coloured persons possessed the elective franchise, and were among those by whom (and for whose posterity) the Constitution was ordained and established; yet by Abraham Lincoln's time so greatly had public sentiment become debased in the slave sections that Judge Taney in his famous decision on the "Dred Scott case" declared that negroes had for centuries been regarded, not merely as "beings of an inferior order, and altogether unfit to associate with the white race either in social or political relations" but as "*so far inferior* that they had no rights which the white man was bound to respect, and that the negro might justly and lawfully be reduced to slavery for his (the white man's) benefit."

THE PROPOSED AFRO-AMERICAN LEAGUE.

BY T. THOS. FORTUNE.*

From the "New York Freeman," June 4th, 1887.

THE NECESSITY AND NATURE OF SUCH A NATIONAL ORGANIZATION.

To the Colored People of the United States:

There come periods in the history of every people when the necessity of their affairs makes it imperative that they take such steps as shall show to the world that they are worthy to be free, and therefore entitled to the sympathy of all mankind and to the co-operation of all lovers of justice and fair play. To do this they must unequivocably show that while they may solicit the sympathy and co-operation of mankind, they have the intelligence and the courage to know what are their rights and to manfully contend for them. In the last issue of *The Freeman* I took occasion to propose a vast organization of the colored people of the United States for the purpose of creating a just public opinion in the special matter of lynch and mob law.

* * * *

I shall here state the reasons why I think such a League should be formed. (1) The almost universal suppression of our ballot in the South, and consequent "taxation without representation," since in cities, counties and States where we have undisputed preponderating majorities of the voting population we have in the main no representation and

* Mr. Fortune is a leading coloured American.

Figure 3.1 Pages from the Tuskegee Institute's *Southern Letter*, which inspired *Anti-Caste's* format and ably fulfilled Catherine's request for *Anti-Caste* to reflect *Southern Letter* as closely as possible in both shape and style (Figure 3.1 and Figure 3.2). Like *Southern Letter*, *Anti-Caste* composed of a printed sheet folded to make a four-page periodical, with two columns per page. The front page carried news items or editorial pieces and inside in the top-left corner of page two details of subscriptions and how to contact the editor in Street were given. A single copy of *Anti-Caste* cost one penny or two cents in the United States; a single copy post free for one year was 1s or 25 cents, five copies post free for one year were 2s 1d or 60 cents. Special discounts could be arranged for those

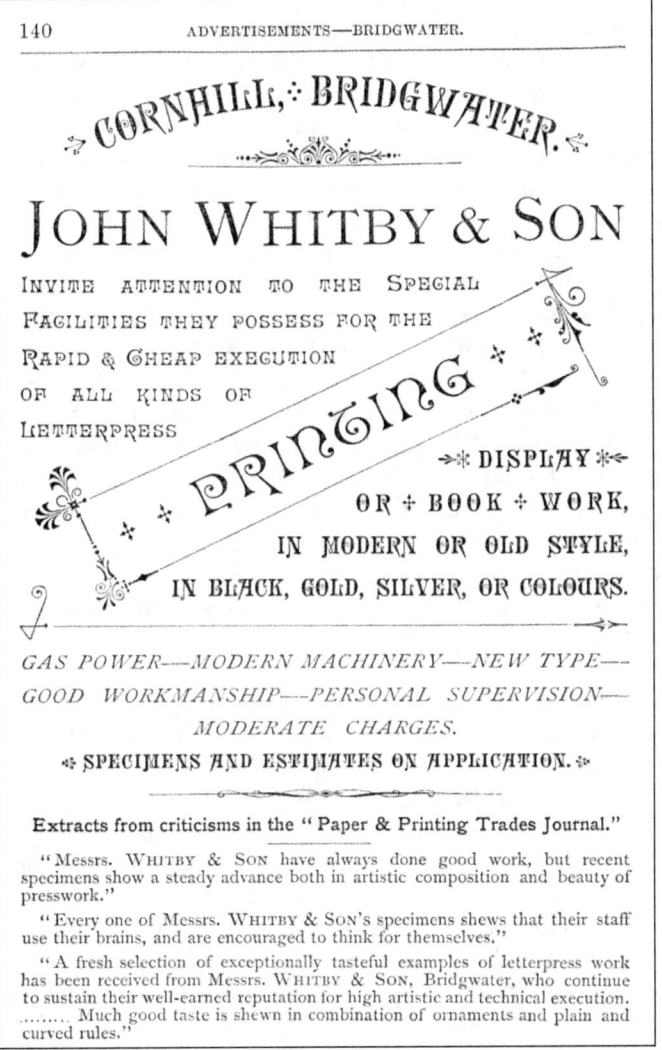

Figure 3.2 Advertisement for John Whitby & Son, who printed *Anti-Caste*, taken from the *Directory of Bridgwater*, 1883

who needed larger quantities for distribution. Such a small paper had more advantages than simply cheaper production costs. In 1887 Henry Fox Bourne reflected that few people now bothered to read the leaders in newspapers, and in an effort to cater to readers who were increasingly busy or hurrying through the modern city, newspapers and periodicals altered their formats to include attention-grabbing headlines and shorter paragraphs replaced longer columns.[46] When Gandhi started publishing *Indian Opinion* from Durban in 1903 he strove for a layout that would pause 'industrial speed' and direct readers towards a more careful 'slow reading' of the paper.[47] Catherine sort to ensure readers could fit *Anti-Caste* into the increasing speed of life and, in her first editorial, argued that *Anti-Caste's* small size would ensure that even busy people had the time or had no excuse not to read its content.

The first issue of *Anti-Caste* introduced readers to the primary aim of the paper: to distribute information on the evils of caste and to give voice to those who suffered under it. The United States, where Catherine had seen caste lines in operation for herself, entirely dominated the first issue. Her personal experiences and 'friendship and acquaintance of many of those known as "coloured" people' provided her with an inside knowledge of racial experience.[48] Among the names of personal friends and acquaintances she published were Benjamin Tanner, Rev B F Lee (then editor of the *Christian Recorder*), Rev Frederick and his wife at the Sierra Leone Missionary for the AME Church, Rev Jas N Townsend (travelling secretary of Foreign Missions), Bishop Daniel A Payne, the late Bishops J P Campbell, H M Turner and R H Cain, Bishops J J Moore and J Hook and his wife of the AME Zion Church, Rev J Price of North Carolina, John C Daney (editor of the *Star of Zion*, organ of the AME Zion Church), Amanda Smith, journalist T Thomas Fortune, Professor Joseph of New York, Fanny Jackson Coppin and Mrs Frances Harper, national superintendent of the Coloured Work of the Women's Christian Temperance Union. The extensive list gave legitimacy to Catherine's editorship and the authority of *Anti-Caste*.

Reflected in the number of clergymen cited, it was clear from the outset that religion would play an important role in the framework of *Anti-Caste's* discussions. As Catherine outlined on the first page:

> Customs handed down from our ancestors, prejudices, and early training under the hand even of an honoured parent will sometimes blind the best and the wisest of us to the unrighteousness or unreasonableness of certain conduct towards our neighbours. We are to judge no man after the flesh (John 8.15) never to lose sight of the living soul – the man himself, *our brother*, who dwells within, and whom if we would do him justice we must measure not by his flesh but by his life.

This spiritual framework allowed for a broad definition of inequality and injustice. Although gender and disability were rarely discussed independently in future issues of *Anti-Caste*, they were included in the wide-ranging understanding of inequality that *Anti-Caste* sought to challenge.

> It is our own belief that all arbitrary distinctions (or disabilities) based on differences of social rank, are 'contrary to the mind of Christ' and that of all such

distinctions the meanest and most cruelly irritating to the victims are those which are based purely on *physical* characteristics – sex, race, complexion, nationality – in fact form or deformity of any kind.[49]

As Catherine had acknowledged in her essay 'Diverse Views', however, religious institutions could not be set aside from criticism. The refusal to allow a 'young man of colour' who was a member of the New York YMCA to participate in a drawing class because he was black came under fire in the first issue.

> It is not pretended that the rejected person is not a Christian within the ordinary meaning of the word. He is not only a church member but a member of the YMCA. If good enough to enter the kingdom why should he not be good enough to enter a drawing class under the auspices of an association of Christians, and for the support of which Christians of both colours liberally contribute? No! It is not a question of character or religion, but really that old question of race and colour.[50]

Along with *Anti-Caste's* aims, the first issue highlighted a bill recently passed by the House of Representatives in Georgia which prevented black and white children being educated at the same schools. Repeating arguments she made in a letter to the *Manchester Guardian* the previous year, Catherine reminded readers that although many believed the caste barriers 'which separated all grades of coloured Americans from the rest of mankind' were dying away, in most parts of the United States this was not true.[51] Black Americans were leading challenges to the erosion of their civil rights and the remainder of the inside pages was given over to a lengthy extract from the *New York Freeman* (first published in June 1887), on the emerging 'Afro-American League'. The league was first proposed by the radical editor of the *New York Freeman* Thomas Fortune in 1887 and he had used an editorial to ask how black Americans could come together and force themselves to be heard along similar lines to the Irish Land League. Enthusiastically received by his black activist peers the league became the first national civil rights organization in the United States and the black-owned *New York Age* appreciated the attention *Anti-Caste's* article brought to the association.[52] The back page of *Anti-Caste's* first issue carried notices for the British & Foreign Anti-Slavery Society, the APS and the National Indian Association. Catherine also listed books she believed would or should be of interest to *Anti-Caste* readers. These included Albion Tourgée's *Bricks without Straw*, *The Silent South* by George W Cable, Beecher Stowe's *Uncle Tom's Cabin* and the *Life of Frederick Douglass*. Requests for further information on publication details and prices could be sent to Catherine in Street.

Prejudice 'at home'

The collective gaze of *Anti-Caste's* readership tended to avoid the politics of racial prejudice in Britain and Ireland. An exception occurred in January 1889 when Catherine commented upon a speech made by Prime Minister Lord Salisbury 'in which he sneered at our fellow subjects in India as "Black Men"'. Speaking in November 1888

Salisbury was referring to the election campaign of the Indian nationalist Dadabhai Naoroji, who had unsuccessfully stood for Parliament in Holborn in 1886.[53] Salisbury's 'scandalous', 'insulting' 'slip of the tongue' caused uproar and became part of 'highly politicized spectacles', which probably substantially contributed to Naoroji's successful election for Finsbury Central in London in 1892.[54] The *Pall Mall Gazette* suspected that Salisbury must have often wished that he had a bad cold or broken his leg or had some other impediment that had prevented him from making the speech in Edinburgh, during which he had reminded his audience, amid encouraging cries of laughter and 'hear, hear', that 'however great the progress of mankind has been, and however far we have advanced in overcoming prejudices, I doubt if we have yet got to that point of view where a British constituency would elect a black man'.[55]

Naoroji received thousands of letters and telegrams of support, and the National Liberal Club held a banquet on 21 January 1889 where he was guest of honour. He utilized the momentum to his advantage up to a Finsbury by-election in 1892, which he won by a very narrow majority.[56] The headline 'Our Indian MP' announced Naoroji's election victory in *Anti-Caste*.[57] As the first Indian MP in the House of Commons, his election marked a momentous and joyous occasion for *Anti-Caste* readers, promising brighter days for India and the oppressed of humanity the world over. In choosing Naoroji to represent them, the men of Finsbury had given 'to the millions of their fellow-subjects in India one living voice in the Councils by which they are despotically governed'.[58] Under the headline 'Colour No Bar' the Xhosa paper *Imvo Zabantsandu*, published in the Cape Colony, expressed hope that Naoroji's success marked an epoch-making moment in the political advancement of all colonial subjects.[59]

In 1888, before the excitement of Naoroji's eventual election, Salisbury's 'Black Man' comments were widely reported in the British Press. The *Dundee Courier* expressed regret that the prime minister's 'snobbery' resulted in a blunder that insulted the entire Indian empire as expressed by outraged Indian newspaper reports reprinted in the *Sheffield and Rotherham Independent*, the *Pall Mall Gazette* and London's *Daily News*.[60] Letters to the editors of newspapers around the country placed the prime minister's comments in a variety of political contexts.[61] The *Pall Mall Gazette* couched one of its editorial leaders in the context of class and caste, arguing that

> It is like cancer. Cut it out here and it will reappear there. So Caste, exorcised by Reform Acts from English politics, reappears in the shape of colour arrogance in India, and we are afforded an example in the speech of Lord Salisbury of the way in which it darkens the mind and blunts the finer sensibilities of the soul.[62]

For T Davies, who wrote to the *Bristol Mercury*, Salisbury reflected comments that were better suited to the age of the Tudors and Stuarts. Whether England had advanced in her treatment of India beyond the barbarous policy that ruled her home policies 200 or 300 years ago Davies did not know, but clearly Lord Salisbury had not and in his racism lay a real threat to freedom:

> if the spirit underlying his reference to Mr Naoroji as 'a black man' has its way, occasion is sure to arise to carry them into effect; and we believe, Sir, that it is the

imperative duty of all lovers of freedom and peace to spare no effort to remove from the councils of the Queen and from the Government of England and her dependencies a statesman who in all his sympathies is two or three hundred years behind the age.[63]

Society gossip reported that the Queen had been 'made very angry' by Salisbury's 'indiscretion'.[64] More harmful than royal displeasure the phrase made its way into political satire with *Punch* predicting that Lord Salisbury's 'Black Man' was likely to become his 'bête noirs'.[65] The *Pall Mall Gazette's* column on 'tittle tattle for the tea table' reported that Salisbury even found himself made fun of in one of the novelties of the Christmas season for sale on Regent Street. Accompanied by a striking picture (of what the author unfortunately did not say anything) a 'Salisbury's Black Man' card carried a comic verse on the affair. Despite its poor wit and polish, 'tittle tattle' expected the card to have a 'certain vogue' over Christmas.

> Oh! Lord Salisbury, how will you do?
> When this old Black Man comes for you?
> In vain you may shout with good intent –
> 'oh sir! it was not you I meant.'
> He will swing you aloft, but not in glory,
> And you shan't return to tell the story.[66]

The affair had entered the public's consciousness and made Naoroji the 'Radical hero of the hour'.[67] For Naoroji the incident came in the context of his years of campaigning to harness British public opinion and the supposedly democratic machinery of Westminster to acknowledge an Indian subject as part of its imperial parliament.[68] For *Anti-Caste* Salisbury's declaration provided a rare opportunity to discuss prejudice at home. This was not a claim that racial prejudice was usually absent in Britain but an observation that in Britain, where the colour line was not legally drawn out, the operation of racial prejudice was opaque. The 'black man incident' was an example of how language could be made to matter in discourses on racial prejudice and democracy in ways 'which affected politics at the very heart of the empire'.[69] As Catherine recognized Salisbury's speech provided a rare opportunity for racial prejudice in Britain 'the prompter of so many a cowardly and bloody act on the part of our rulers' – for once 'to be openly seen'.[70]

The first readers

From 1890 Catherine began to publish annual lists of subscribers. Enough detail can be gleaned to see that her philanthropic and 'kinship networks' of Quakers formed foundational support. In the earliest days Catherine saw subscribers to the APS as potential readers for *Anti-Caste*. One of her cousins wrote to Frederick Chesson and Charles Allen asking if they would be willing to share the details of their subscription lists or send out a circular to their members informing them of *Anti-Caste*'s arrival.[71]

Catherine's letter following up her cousin's enquiry in March 1888 indicates that they had not yet heard from the APS on how their subscribers might be directly informed of the new publication.[72] A comparison with the APS' subscribers suggests the cross-over between financially committed supporters of *Anti-Caste* and the *Aborigines' Friend* did not find much in common. The APS' publication of subscriptions and donations received between April 1890 and March 1891 allows for a comparison with subscribers to *Anti-Caste* in 1890. Of the APS' named supporters 6 per cent also appear on the *Anti-Caste* list including the Quakers Joseph Rowntree, William Rowntree, Hannah Joseph Sturge and Walter Sturge. There was probably more overlap between the two readerships than the subscriptions list suggest. Catherine does not appear on the APS list because Ellen maintained the Impey's APS subscription, while Catherine is the registered subscriber for the Anti-Slavery Society.[73] Their system suggests a greater interchange between *Anti-Caste* and the APS through joint subscriptions though it is still probably far lower than Catherine anticipated or hoped.[74]

Anti-Caste proved more successful in attracting overseas readers. In 1890/1891 the APS list identifies only 3 out of 215 supporters as based overseas compared to 35 of *Anti-Caste's* 315 subscribers, among them Frederick Douglass, then US minister to Haiti, and Harriet Colenso, a white activist from Natal, who, despite the success of her collaboration with the APS on the Zulu Defence Committee, was often at odds with the society.[75] Although not listed as a subscriber in 1890/1891, Orishatukeh Faduma subscribed to *Anti-Caste* in 1889. Previously known as William Stevens Powell, Powell had changed his name Orishatukeh Faduma by the time he began subscribing to *Anti-Caste*. Born in British Guiana in 1869, his parents returned to Sierra Leone when Faduma was nine. He travelled to England to complete his studies at Queen's College, Taunton, and matriculated at the University of London.[76] After graduating in 1885, Faduma returned to Sierra Leone to teach at the Methodist Boys High School. During this time he rejected his Western name and co-founded the Dress Reform Society, which encouraged the wearing of traditional African robes rather than the fashion for Western Victorian coats.[77] The presence of Douglass, Colenso and Faduma within *Anti-Caste's* community of readers suggests that although members of the APS saw themselves as actively engaged in challenging mainstream attitudes to racial prejudice and colonial expansion, those with more radical intent looked for associations with more uncompromising content and far-reaching political aims. On the other hand, although *Anti-Caste* had the support of prominent newspaper editors, such as Edward Russell, editor of the *Liverpool Daily Post*, its supporters did not connect it into power-making structures in the same way as the APS. The APS included a network of MPs that linked them to official power.[78] The Liberal MP Henry Joseph Wilson did subscribe to *Anti-Caste*, and although he raised questions on excessive deaths in Bengal prisons and departmental appointments in India in the House of Commons, there is no record of him asking questions on lynching or other issues directly linked to the content of *Anti-Caste*.[79]

Although well-known personalities or individuals with unusual names can be identified in the lists of *Anti-Caste* subscribers, Catherine's format did not provide comprehensive information on readers, recording their surnames and initials, and only occasionally adding a full first name or other details. This means the gender and geography of many of the readers is difficult to establish. The first full list of subscribers from 1889, published in an annual supplement in January 1890, contained 91 names, including at least 27 women. The temperance and women's rights activism of Eliza Wigham (1820–1899), brought up as a Quaker, illustrates the overlapping concerns for numerous forms of progressive politics shared by the *Anti-Caste* reading community. A loyal personal supporter of Catherine, she subscribed to *Anti-Caste* in its various forms from the outset until its final run in 1895. In 1859 she had started a 'penny bank' near her home in Causeway Side, Edinburgh, and a Women's Working Society or mothers' meeting in 1860, running both for 37 years. She was also a consistent advocate for the peace movement, arguing for systems of international arbitration instead of war and actively supporting the victims of the Franco-Prussian War of 1870 and victims of oppression in Bosnia and Armenia. Wigham acted as secretary to the Edinburgh Society for Women's Suffrage from its establishment in 1867. In 1869 she added her name to a petition against the Contagious Diseases Acts and acted as secretary for the Edinburgh Committee that worked to repeal the Acts.[80]

Aside from Wigham, at least one other woman active in the campaign to abolish the Contagious Diseases Acts was an early supporter. Bristol-born Mary Anne Estlin (1820–1902) first subscribed in 1889. In 1832–1833 she spent six months on the island of St Vincent with her father where she witnessed the cruelties of the slavery system first hand. Both she and her father corresponded with radical American abolitionists and in 1851 she became a member of the Bristol and Clifton Ladies' Anti-Slavery Society committee. She also became a leading feminist campaigner acting as a member of the executive committee of the Ladies' National Association and a founding member of the Bristol Women's Suffrage Society established in 1867, as well as co-ordinating the campaign for the repeal of the Contagious Diseases Acts.[81] Although Catherine emphasized that *Anti-Caste* would not focus on slavery, the endorsements from leading abolitionists Wigham and Estlin along with that of Frederick Douglass illustrated that respected figures acknowledged and intended to participate in the new direction *Anti-Caste* was attempting to forge.

Professor Francis William Newman sent financial support on at least two occasions and remained a constant and loyal reader. A classical professor at Manchester New College for six years before becoming Latin professor at University College London in July 1846, Newman's opposition to vivisection, alcohol and smoking and his commitment to vegetarianism meant he shared many aspects of personal politics with Catherine.[82] Following her donation of £5 in January 1888, Priscilla Peckover became a subscriber. G M Elliot of Selma and secretary of the Industrial Missionary Association in Alabama wrote to Catherine to congratulate her on her 'excellent little paper' and enclosed a subscription for himself and the president of his association.[83] Zoologist Beatrice Lindsay wrote from Port St Mary on the Isle of Man to offer her support. In her letter, published in January 1890, Lindsay argued that any real hope for the lasting influence for the movement would be through the education of young people. A graduate of Girton College, Cambridge, Lindsay put great value on educating young people, more easily persuaded than their elders and more importantly the voters of a future day. Lindsay's optimism that women would soon be granted the right to vote proved misplaced, but she would have been pleased to see the inclusion of the Second Class at Saffron Walden Girls' School among the committed readers of 1889.[84]

Expanding the *Anti-Caste* network

The combination of domestic hospitality and political exchange at Askew remained important for informing and refreshing *Anti-Caste*. Between 29 June and 2 July and then from 2 to 7 August 1888, Fanny Jackson Coppin stayed at Askew. A teacher in Philadelphia, Jackson Coppin had been invited to England as part of the Centenary Missions Conference held in London that year. Born enslaved in 1837, Jackson had been bought out of slavery as a young girl by her aunt Sarah Orr, who, earning six dollars a month, saved $125 to buy her freedom. After graduating from Oberlin College as a mature student in 1865, she began teaching Latin, Greek and maths at the Institute for Colored Youth, a Quaker academy in Philadelphia. In 1869 she became the principal of the institute, thus being the first black woman in the country to hold such a position. In 1881 she married Levi Coppin, editor of AME *Review* and later elected a bishop of the AME Church assigned to a district in Cape Town.[85] Jackson Coppin also served as president of the Women's Home and Foreign Missionary Society of the AME Church. In her role as president she was elected to represent the society at the international missionary conference in London, prompting her first trip away from the United States and she did not relish the journey.[86]

Once in Britain she spent most of her time in London, but she found her way to Street and to Askew, where she enjoyed a 'Chamber of peace' away from the busy capital. Mary H. Garnet-Barbza, also a delegate at the Missions Conference, stayed at Askew for a few days in June and July before heading to Liberia.[87] Supporting Jackson Coppin during her visit represented an important strand of *Anti-Caste's* work during the summer. In the notice published under the header 'the civil rights of the coloured race' in the *British Friend*, Catherine described Jackson Coppin as an eloquent and powerful speaker and encouraged Quakers to arrange for her to visit their neighbourhoods.[88] Over the few weeks she was in England Jackson Coppin spoke to audiences in London and other cities in the South, West and Midlands of England detailing and explaining the racial prejudice faced by thousands of young people in Philadelphia. She told audiences how hard black men and women found it to get jobs because they were barred from factory work of all kinds, from serving in shops, from smithing, carpentry, ship and carriage building and nearly all occupations that were ordinarily open to young white people of a similar age and class.

Although freed from a substantial role in running the farm by Ellen, like other Quaker women Catherine had to fit her public work around her duties as a daughter, sister, cousin and neighbour.[89] Equally her editorial commitments had to be continually balanced with her continuing domestic duties at Askew and her continuing temperance work until her complete withdrawal from the Grand Lodge of England in 1889.[90] In October 1888 Sivra Sastri, a missionary from Calcutta, spent a memorable three days at Askew, and in December Catherine filled the house with pretty hand-made

Figure 3.3 Cabinet card of Mary, Ellen and Catherine Impey (standing)

decorations for the Christmas season. Jane Metford was among those who turned up at the party thrown by the Impeys on Christmas Day extolling the warmth created at Askew for the Christmas festivities. Among the preparations for a family Christmas, Catherine had found time to edit *Anti-Caste* and prepare a New Year supplement, but in the production of *Anti-Caste* Catherine remained reliant upon herself. At times her domestic duties or illness meant her production timetable slipped, as in 1890 when 'influenza' was the only excuse Catherine had to offer for the lateness of the February number, and sometimes the publication of the periodical had to be rescheduled resulting in combined double month issues.[91]

After years of pondering the possibility of its production, the first issue of *Anti-Caste* in March 1888 activated a new reading community. It promoted a theoretical analysis that sought to undermine constructions of race while alerting its readers to the injustices of racial prejudice and asking its white readers to consider their place and their complicity in the international system of racial hierarchy. The numbers of readers who chose to join this reading community did not amount to a large group. The subscriber list for *Anti-Caste* probably never reached more than 350 households at its peak, but over the lifetime of the periodical its readers produced a textual community of progressive radicals: vegetarians, early feminists, early socialists, pacifists and international students based in Britain as well as antislavery campaigners. International readers were present from the outset, some as subscribers; others like Thomas Fortune were part of the editorial exchange network that provided *Anti-Caste* with its thought-provoking content. They were mostly located in the United States, but the paper also attracted a readership in Africa and the Caribbean. These men and women supported a larger readership through the distribution of free copies in Britain and abroad, which boosted circulation towards 3500 each month. They formed the foundation of the international movement Catherine envisaged could overcome national concerns to defeat the transnational outrages and injustices of racial prejudice.

Notes

1. *British Friend*, July 1888, 197.
2. Impey to Tourgée, 16 June 1890, 4785, original emphasis.
3. Fuller, 'Caste, race, and hierarchy'.
4. Booth, 'Robertson, Thomas William (1829–1871)'.
5. Robertson, 'Preface', in *Caste*; Durbach, 'Remembering Tom Robertson'.
6. Innes, *Sourcebook on Naturalist Theatre*; Zeleny, 'Self-appointed executioner'.
7. Robertson, *Caste*, 9.
8. Robertson, *Caste*, 61.
9. Warner, 'American caste and class'.
10. Berreman, 'Caste in India'; Warner, 'American caste and class'.
11. Lake and Reynolds, *Drawing the Global Colour Line*.
12. Goldwin Smith to Charles Elliot Norton, 22 July 1864, quoted in Lake and Reynolds, *Drawing the Global Colour Line*, 54.
13. Horton, *American Liberalism*.
14. Horton, *American Liberalism*, 17.
15. These bills eventually became the Civil Rights Act, 1875. See Horton, *American Liberalism*, 17.
16. Horton, *American Liberalism*, 18.
17. Sumner, *The Question of Caste*, 10.
18. From Horton, *American Liberalism*. See especially chapter one on 'Anti-Caste Liberalism'.
19. Strieby, 'Caste in America'.
20. Impey to Tourgée, 16 June 1890, 4785, Albion W. Tourgée Papers.
21. Rao, *The Caste Question*, 12.
22. Nico, *Colored Cosmopolitanism*.
23. Rao, *The Caste Question*, 13.
24. Horton, *American Liberalism*.
25. Supplement to *Anti-Caste*, January 1890. For an additional example of asking readers to examine their practices of hospitality, see *Anti-Caste*, April 1891, 2.
26. *Anti-Caste*, August 1889, 2.

27 *Anti-Caste*, April 1891, 2.
28 *Anti-Caste*, April 1891, 2, original emphasis.
29 *Anti-Caste*, April 1891, 2, original emphasis.
30 *Anti-Caste*, April 1891, 2, original emphasis.
31 Hansen, *The Dream*.
32 *Anti-Caste*, May 1891, 2. The source for the quotation given is not referenced. I.M. is probably Isabella Metford.
33 Davis, *Plessy Vs Ferguson*.
34 Elliott, *Justice Deferred*.
35 Quoted in Groves, 'Separate but equal', 66.
36 Groves, 'Separate but equal', 66.
37 Quoted in Groves, 'Separate but equal', 67.
38 Lake and Reynolds, *Drawing the Global Colour Line*.
39 Supplement to *Anti-Caste*, January 1890.
40 Quoted in Elliott, *Justice Deferred*, 4.
41 National Park Service, http://www.cr.nps.gov/museum/exhibits/tuskegee/btwtusk.htm, accessed 18 March 2013.
42 The Tuskegee University site references the original space as a 'Negro normal school'. 'History and mission', Tuskeege University, http://www.tuskegee.edu/about_us/history_and_mission.aspx, accessed 18 March 2013.
43 For a discussion of responses to Washington's 'Atlanta compromise speech' within the circles of the AME's print cultures see Bailey, *Race Patriotism*.
44 Impey to Washington, 5 March 1890, *The Booker T Washington Papers*, vol 3: 33–34, University of Illinois Press, 1974.
45 George Newness writing in *Tit-Bits*, March 1882, quoted in Jackson, *George Newness*, 267.
46 Hampton, *Visions of the Press*.
47 Hofneyr, *Gandhi's Printing Press*, 4.
48 *Anti-Caste*, March 1888, 1, original emphasis.
49 *Anti-Caste*, March 1888, 1, original emphasis.
50 *Anti-Caste*, March 1888, 2.
51 *Anti-Caste*, March 1888, 2.
52 For a history of the Afro-American League and its importance in the history of the civil rights movement in the United States, see Alexander, *Army of Lions*, 2.
53 *Pall Mall Gazette*, 1 December 1888, 4.
54 Burton, 'Tongues untied', 633 and 645; Visram, *Asians in Britain*. For examples of the ensuing debate, see the *Pall Mall Gazette*, 4 December 1888, 11.
55 Quoted In Fryer, *Staying Power*, 263; *Pall Mall Gazette*, 6 December 1888, 1.
56 Naoroji served in Parliament from 1892 to 1895. During the 1895 General Election Naoroji was unable to protect his slim majority of only five votes; see Burton, 'Tongues untied' and for a detailed account of the election see Visram, *Asians in Britain*.
57 *Anti-Caste*, August 1892, 3.
58 *Anti-Caste*, August 1892, 3.
59 *Imvo*, 14 July 1892.
60 *Dundee Courier and Argus*, 7 December 1888; *Sheffield & Rotherham Independent*, 7 December 1888, 6; *Pall Mall Gazette*, 10 December 1888, 7; *Daily News*, 10 December, 5.
61 *Pall Mall Gazette* published four on Tuesday, 4 December 1888, 11.

62 *Pall Mall Gazette*, 6 December 1888, 1.
63 *Bristol Mercury and Daily Post*, 12 December 1888, 3.
64 For example in *Bury and Norwich Post and Suffolk Standard*, 1 January 1889, 3.
65 Reprinted in *Wrexham Advertiser and North Wales News*, 21 December 1888.
66 *Pall Mall Gazette*, 21 December 1888, 7.
67 *Belfast News-Letter*, 27 December 1888, 5.
68 Burton, 'Tongues untied'.
69 Burton, 'Tongues untied', 636.
70 *Anti-Caste*, January 1889, 1.
71 Impey to Allen, 1 March 1888, MSS. Brit. Emp. s.18 C61/8.
72 Impey to Chesson, 1 March 1888, MSS. Brit. Emp. s.18 C138/173.
73 For example 'Anti-Slavery Society Subscriptions, 1884', *Anti-Slavery Reporter*, 1885, 274.
74 'Subscriptions and Donations Received', *Aborigines' Friend*, April 1891, 178–180.
75 Heartfield, *Aborigines' Protection Society*.
76 'Rev. Orishatukeh Faduman, Pastor at Troy, NC and Principal of Peabody Academy', *American Missionary* 63, 1909, 2.
77 Powell, *Dictionary of North Carolina Biography*.
78 Heartfield, *Aborigines' Protection Society*.
79 Wilson did raise related issues, e.g. questions on excessive deaths in Bengal prisons (Hansard HC Deb 2 March 1896 vol 37 cc.1481–1482); Departmental appointments in India (Hansard HC Deb 25 June 1897 vol 50 c.559).
80 Richmond, 'Wigham, Eliza (1820–1899)'.
81 Taken from Midgley, 'Estlin, Mary Anne (1820–1902)'.
82 Quoted by Stunt, 'Newman, Francis William (1805–1897)'.
83 Supplement to *Anti-Caste*, January 1890, npn.
84 Lindsay, *Introduction*.
85 Neverdon-Morton, 'Coppin, Fanny Jackson', in *Encyclopaedia of African-American Education*, 122–123.
86 Coppin, *Reminiscences*.
87 *Visitors at Askew*.
88 *British Friend*, July 1888, 197.
89 Holton, *Quaker Women*.
90 Letter to the G L of England, MSS. Brit. Emp. s.20 E5/7.
91 *Anti-Caste*, February 1890, 2.

4

Magazine to Movement

> [N]either creed, colour, nor nationality ought to be a barrier to any man or woman in the great battle of life; that when we go into their countries we should recognise that they were designed by the all-knowing Father of our common humanity to inhabit that particular country, and that their lives are as precious to them as ours are to us.
>
> *Fraternity* 1893

In 1886 a black woman living in Jackson, Tennessee, and working as a cook was accused of poisoning her mistress. While in custody a mob broke into the prison, dragged her to the courthouse square and stripped her naked; the crowd watched as she was hung up to die. Information transpired that her employer's husband was the murderer, but this finding did nothing to inspire the authorities to arrest her murderers or make any attempt to punish the members of the mob who attacked her. Such lynchings were the most violent example of the failure to protect the rights of black men and women as American citizens. Charged with crimes without evidence, black Americans lacked access to protection from the law. Men, women and children could be taken from their homes or jail cells and then murdered – shot, burned, hanged, sometimes a combination of all three – with the perpetrators seemingly running no risk of punishment. All of these infringements reflected a blatant disregard of black Americans' rights as full citizens. The story of the woman's death in Tennessee, one of over 1000 lynchings in the United States between 1883 and 1894, appeared in the June 1894 addition of the *Contemporary Review*, coinciding with Ida B Wells' second British tour.[1] Wells, who was a journalist, feminist and civil rights activist, had become well known to the British public during her first tour arranged by *Anti-Caste* supporters the previous year. Travelling throughout England and Scotland, she had drawn crowds of hundreds who listened to her stories of injustice and demands for equality. On occasion she shared the stage with Celestine Edwards, a Caribbean medical student and *Anti-Caste* reader. Both made a deep impression on their British audiences. In 1908 Reverend F B Cowling, then placed with the Woollahra Congregational Church in Sydney, remembered them to be the greatest public speakers he had ever heard.[2] Their inspirational speeches helped transform *Anti-Caste* from a community of readers into a national movement.

A meeting of minds

Ida B Wells' parents worked hard to establish their family during Reconstruction. Her mother Elizabeth became a cook and her father Jim was trained as a carpenter by his slave master and continued in the trade after emancipation. Both parents placed a strong emphasis upon education. Wells soaked up all she could reading Shakespeare, Dickens, Brontë and Alcott and listening intently to political discussions within the home, learning to fear the Klu Klux Klan long before she truly understood the meaning of the words.[3] In 1878 Jim and Elizabeth Wells died during a yellow fever epidemic, leaving 16-year-old Ida as the head of the family. Determined to keep her siblings together, Wells trained as a teacher so she could care for her five surviving brothers and sisters. After passing her teaching certificate she was assigned to a one-room school in a rural district about six miles from the family's home in Holly Springs, Mississippi. During the week a friend of her mother stayed at home with her younger siblings and Wells returned home every Friday afternoon on the back of a mule. Her weekends were spent washing, ironing and cooking for the family. On Sunday afternoons she returned to school. Eventually Wells secured a better-paid job in Shelby County, at Woodstock, about 12 miles north of Memphis. Now Wells travelled to school by train on the Chesapeake, Ohio and Southwestern Railroad, but her experience of racism on one of these journeys would shape her political career.

In 1884 a train conductor instructed Wells to move to another train carriage. Wells refused. She had purchased a ticket that allowed her to sit in the ladies car where she was seated, and the 'coloured' accommodation provided was a smokers' car. The carriages provided by the Chesapeake and Ohio Railroad were separate, but they were not equal. The conductor attempted to drag Wells from her seat, but the moment he caught hold of her she sunk her teeth into the back of his hand. With the help of a baggage attendant, another man and the supportive applause of white passengers, the conductor managed to drag Wells from her seat. She told the conductor that she would rather get off the train than go in the segregated smoking compartment, and so she was forced to get off. She returned to Memphis, hired a lawyer, sued the railway company and won. In December 1884 the *Memphis Daily Appeal* reported her victory: 'A Darky Damsel Obtains a Verdict for Damages against the Chesapeake and Ohio Railroad – What It Cost to Put a Colored Teacher in a Smoking Car – Verdict for $500.'[4] But Chesapeake and Ohio Railroad immediately appealed the case and Wells had to wait three years before the case came before the Tennessee State Supreme Court.

As a young woman money was always a concern for Wells. In her diary she recorded debts she owed and berated herself for buying clothes she later felt she could not really afford. On 14 March 1887 she wondered if the approaching case in the Tennessee Supreme Court would bring an additional settlement, as any money would be a great help. In the same month her grandmother died; the women had fallen out of touch and Wells was shocked to realize that her grandmother had been living without her knowledge.[5] Wells felt lost: 'I am not happy and nothing seems to make me so. I wonder what kind of creature I will eventually become?'[6] The following month the State Supreme Court overturned the decision against Chesapeake and Ohio

Railroad.⁷ Although Wells did not realize it at the time, the company fought her case so tenaciously because it represented the first time a black plaintiff in the South had appealed to a state court since the repeal of the Civil Rights Act by the US Supreme Court in 1883.⁸ A victory for Wells would have set an unacceptable precedent for racists in the South. Instead the Supreme Court of Tennessee concluded that Wells' determination to see justice done had been undertaken to 'harass' the Chesapeake and Ohio Railroad Company and forced her to pay them over $200 in costs.⁹ She was deeply disappointed and wrote despairingly in her diary: 'I have firmly believed all along that the law was on our side and would, when we appealed to it, give us justice. I feel shorn of that belief and utterly discouraged… O God is there no redress, no peace, no justice in this land for us?'¹⁰ The path for the political activist she would become had been set.

The injustice of the case formed the basis of her first published article written at the invitation of the editor of *The Living Way*, a Baptist weekly for the black community.¹¹ Under the pen name 'Iola' Wells began a regular column of letters. Other papers reproduced these and gradually Wells began to earn a reputation as a journalist. In 1886 she met Reverend William Simmons of the American Baptist Home Missionary Society, who read her work in various newspapers and arranged for her first paid assignments on his paper, the *American Baptist*, where she remained for three years. She aimed to reach a wide black American audience writing on 'Race Pride', the

Figure 4.1 A portrait of Ida B Wells, c.1893–1894

experiences of women, 'Afro-Americans and Africa' and racial discrimination.[12] On behalf of the *American Baptist* she attended her first press convention, where she met Thomas Fortune, and through her journalism Wells made a number of friends and colleagues in common with Catherine. Between 1884 and 1887 Wells developed her skills as a journalist, joining a literary society and editing its newsletter, gathering material for potential articles, writing letters to local and national newspapers and, in October 1886, becoming the editor of the *Evening Star*, a 'spicy' Memphis paper that focused on news items, literature and poetry.[13] In 1889 she was elected secretary to the National Colored Press Association, formed to bring together black editors and journalists to strengthen the influence of the black press.[14] This success all came with Wells still working as a teacher, but the issues she wrote about soon brought her into conflict with her school board employers.

In 1889 she became editor of another Memphis paper *Free Speech and Headlight*. Her purchase of a-third-interest in the paper made her an equal to her two male partners J L Fleming, who acted as the business manager, and Reverend F Nightingale, a Baptist pastor.[15] The paper had a circulation of at least 500 copies a week and Wells managed it happily for two years, but in 1891 Wells decided to write an article about the conditions of 'coloured' schools in Memphis. The article was a protest against the few and utterly inadequate buildings provided for black children. She also wrote about the poor quality of teachers appointed in black schools. Wells had heard that some of these teachers had little to recommend them aside from an illicit friendship with members of the school board and she felt sure that such a condition deserved criticism. Wells' discussions of the school board's alleged conduct in the pages of *Free Speech* resulted in their failure to reappoint her after seven years of service.[16] From then on Wells relied on journalism and *Free Speech* to support her. She put huge effort into increasing the paper's circulation, travelling around the South as an agent to raise awareness and support, but personal tragedy soon collided with her campaigning journalism.

Tommie Moss and his wife Betty were Wells' best friends and she had proudly become godmother to their daughter Maurine. Tommie Moss and his two friends, Calvin McDowell and Henry Stewart, owned and ran the People's Grocery Company at the Curve in a suburb of Memphis. The Curve was created by a sharp bend in the railroad and a white businessman had already set up a shop in the dense black community around it. He let it be known that he resented the new competition, but surrounded by supporters and protected by his popularity Tommie Moss was unconcerned by his rival's threats. Nonetheless everyday forms of racial tensions surrounding a group of black and white boys quarrelling over a game of marbles drew the men at the People's Grocery store into a dangerous tit-for-tat argument with local white men. One weekend, rumours reached the three friends that a white mob planned to destroy their shop. They arranged to stay behind after closing to guard their store. At about 10pm on the Saturday night shots were heard in the back of the shop. The men fired back on the intruders and three of them were wounded.

Agitated headlines appeared in the white press on Sunday morning, claiming law officers had been injured while chasing criminals harboured at the People's Grocery Company. Tommie Moss, Calvin McDowell and Henry Stewart, were taken to jail and a guard was placed at the jail on Sunday morning and Monday night to ensure the men were not lynched. On Tuesday news came that the wounded white men were out of danger. With the crisis averted, the guards left, but that night a group of white men were let into the jail. They took Moss, McDowell and Stewart from the cells, loaded them onto a railroad car, which took them a mile north of the city limits, and shot them. When their bodies were found the fingers of Calvin McDowell's right hand had been shot to pieces and his eyes gouged out. As news of their murder spread, the white mob was joined by those who came to ransack the dead men's store, stealing stock they could not eat or drink. The remainder of the goods were sold by creditors at an auction a few days later.[17]

Following their murders the black community turned out by the thousand to attend the largest funeral procession to have taken place in Memphis, with resolutions condemning the lynchings and recommending emigration recorded at one town meeting.[18] *Free Speech* ferociously attacked the injustices of lynch law. The city of Memphis had shown that neither character nor social standing availed black men if they dared to protect themselves against the menace of attacks. What could the black community do in the face of such injustice?

> There is nothing we can do about the lynching now as we are out-numbered and without arms. The white mob could help itself to ammunition without pay, but the order was rigidly enforced against the selling of guns to Negroes. There is therefore only one thing left that we can do; save our money and leave a town which will neither protect our lives and property, nor give us a fair trial in the courts, but takes us out and murders us in cold blood when accused by white persons.[19]

In the following months Wells and *Free Speech* continued to attack the injustice of lynch law and support the spontaneous boycott of streetcars black people in Memphis initiated. In May 1892 Wells wrote an editorial in which she questioned the persistent accusation that black men raped white women as a justification for murder. In reply the *Memphis Commercial* gave voice to the outrage the editorial sparked among the local white community. Declaring it their duty to perform a lynching on the author, the editor – assumed to be a man – was to be tied to a stake at the intersection of Main and Madison Streets, where he would be branded 'on the forehead with a hot iron' and have 'a surgical operation' performed on him with 'a pair of tailor's shears'.[20] Wells had fortunately left Memphis on a trip to visit friends in New York and Chicago.[21] In her absence the mob's anger focused on the paper's co-owner J L Flemming, and fearing for his life, he abandoned his newspaper, as he had been forced to do once before in Marion, Arkansas.[22] Wells heard that the mob descended on the *Free Speech*'s offices, destroying its furnishings and distributing death threats to any one they thought might be tempted to restart it. Wells did not return to Memphis. She accepted a position as a reporter working for Thomas Fortune at the *New York Age* and continued her campaigns to improve the civil rights of women and black Americans from the North. Increasingly in demand as a speaker, Wells gave lectures in Wilmington, Delaware, Pennsylvania and Washington DC. In Philadelphia during the fall of 1892 she was the guest of William Still, author of *The Underground Railroad*. At the same time Catherine was visiting the United States again, staying with Albion Tourgée on the picturesque shores of Lake Chautauqua in New York State, with Douglass and his wife at their home Cedar Hill in Washington DC and with the Tanners in Philadelphia. She also stayed with Fanny Jackson Coppin and attended a drawing room meeting in her home in Philadelphia. Around 50 of Jackson Coppin's friends and acquaintances including teachers, students, clergymen and professional businessmen and women attended. Sitting in Coppin's drawing room Catherine had been deeply shocked by the tales of almost daily acts of racial violence she heard described.[23]

Catherine called on Wells at Still's home and the pair talked together, agreeing in the end that 'there seemed nothing to do but keep plugging away at the evils both of us were fighting'.[24] In her autobiography Wells records that it was through their meeting that Catherine learned of the horrors of lynching. Clearly Catherine knew about the process of lynchings before she met Wells. Perhaps Wells meant that in talking with her, Catherine heard for the first time directly from someone who had personally suffered from the horror and unending injustice of lynch law. Their meeting rekindled an old idea. Catherine had always intended to try and organize a movement through correspondence with other activists, but by 1890 she had reluctantly put the idea aside realizing that it was too much for her to attempt, considering how little time she could dedicate to it.[25] Wells presented an opportunity to realize the anticaste society Catherine had long imagined. She had the skills to address audiences on the difficulties and struggles of her people, perfectly fitting the mould of speaker Catherine had suggested inviting to England in her January 1888 circular to her former temperance colleagues. In Wells Catherine saw the possibility of transforming the British public's attitude to racial inequality.

A network of activists

Back at home in Somerset Catherine resolved that once the worst of the winter had passed she would start on a tour of northern England to galvanize support for *Anti-Caste's* transformation. In March Catherine cleared enough of her domestic duties in Street to take off on a mission to meet *Anti-Caste's* most zealous and reliable friends, hoping to enlist their support for a new society. She started out for Aberdeen, where she stayed with Isabella Mayo for over a week. Better known to the public as writer Edward Garrett, Isabella Fyvie Mayo was born in London in 1843. Her Scottish parents ran a bakery in the West End and their daughter always identified as a Scottish woman. When Mayo's father died in 1851 the family business soon failed and she sought work among the new women's employment agencies. She worked as a secretary and law writer helping to clear the family's debts. Developing her interest in writing she became an established author, publishing novels, poems, reviews, biographies, essays and short stories and she was among the first to translate Tolstoy.[26] She spent most of her adult life in Aberdeen and in July 1870 married John Mayo, a solicitor, who died seven years later. After his death she took in a number of lodgers and her home became known as 'an asylum for East Indians'.[27]

Catherine and Mayo had not met, although they had corresponded since Catherine's return from the United States in October. Catherine added Mayo to her 'free list' for *Anti-Caste* soon after her return from the States, and the women frequently exchanged letters on the subjects raised in the periodical. Mayo expressed such a strong a desire to help in the movement that after about two months Catherine agreed to meet Mayo and discuss their interests. At first the pair considered holding their meeting at a hotel in Manchester or Edinburgh, but Mayo proposed Catherine visit her at home in Aberdeen. Keen to secure Mayo's support Catherine agreed to undertake the 500-mile journey to meet her. As 'a literary lady of something above mediocre fame' Mayo's celebrity could draw much needed publicity to *Anti-Caste*.[28] Catherine borrowed £5 from Ellen to cover the cost of the journey and on 13 March 1893 headed for Scotland, stopping for a night in Birmingham on the way.[29] Suffering from a severe cold Catherine ended up staying with Mayo for over a week although she kept busy, jointly editing with Mayo the double March and April number of *Anti-Caste*, which focused entirely on the United States, and drafting with Mayo a letter of invitation to Ida B Wells for her visit to Britain.

Catherine wrote out a pencil draft of the invitation, which was then copied out by 'a gentle and good young doctor half Indian by race', George Ferdinands, one of Mayo's boarders.[30] Part of the original letter to Wells was published in the American press, but Catherine also created a copy that moves between two authorial voices.[31] The letter's interchanging use of 'we' and 'I' reflects Catherine's claiming of her long-standing investment of thought and hope that a society might be created to challenge racial prejudice.[32] Mayo and Catherine asked Wells to cross the Atlantic for a tour of Britain that would draw support for Wells' antilynching campaign while generating the energy to establish a new society. The outline of the society presented to Wells in the letter closely resembles the ideas Catherine outlined to Douglass in 1883. Catherine still saw the society as an inheritor of the antislavery movement rather than emerging out of the new progressive political movements of the 1880s. She remained committed to the ideal of an international membership, publicizing the condition of people of colour across the world, but the letter suggested their union would now be called the 'Emancipation League'.

Catherine's commitment to the former Anti-Slavery Society was partly practical. There were still active campaigners from the old antislavery movement who could be pulled into supporting the new Emancipation League. The hope that Frederick Douglass would become president of the union's council in part came from Catherine and Mayo's knowledge that his name would prove advantageous on the British side of the Atlantic, where some of his former colleagues could be gathered from the fragments of the old-abandoned movement. The naming of the Emancipation League Catherine credited in the letter to 'we'. Beside Douglass as president, Catherine planned to invite a number of influential Englishmen and women, perhaps younger members of the Wilberforce family, as well as Indians and Africans to join the council. Membership of the league's guiding council would be international and multi-ethnic. Catherine wanted Thomas Fortune, William Still, perhaps Fanny Jackson Coppin, along with other influential and trusted persons that might be available to join them. Her disappointments in former friends and colleagues in the temperance movement meant trust in people's commitment to the cause was of primary importance.[33]

With Wells' invitation prepared, Catherine left Aberdeen for Glasgow, stopping at the Old Waverly Temperance Hotel on Buchanan Street.[34] Over five days she called on

Anti-Caste supporters, informing them of the proposals for the Emancipation League and discussing the arrangements for meetings if Wells accepted the offer to undertake a tour of Britain. On 21 March Catherine finally found time to finish her letter to the Tourgées, which she had begun while staying in Aberdeen. Albion Tourgée had written expressing his concern that the society Catherine imagined coming out of *Anti-Caste* would sit in competition to the National Citizens' Rights Association (NCRA) Tourgée had founded with colleagues in 1892. Opposed to all forms of oppression based on colour prejudice, the NCRA seemed little different in its aims to the Afro-American League, which primarily focused on seeking equality for black Americans through the premise that the Fourteenth Amendment had established a 'national citizenship'.[35] Catherine tried to assure Tourgée that she sought to cooperate and assist with their work, not challenge it. The NCRA focused on the rights of black people in the United States, and Catherine emphasized again the need for a broad collective to challenge prejudice across the British Empire, 'an organisation that was as truly English as it was American as truly Indian as English'.[36]

From Glasgow Catherine travelled onto Edinburgh staying with Eliza Wigham. Together the women visited Priscilla Medarew, Elizabeth Pease Nichol, who was tenderly sympathetic and warm hearted as ever, and Mrs Calow Martin, wife of the editor of *Scottish Leader*.[37] Catherine used her meeting with Mrs Martin to secure an interview with the *Leader's* editor. After two attempts he agreed to see her at his office publishing their meeting in the *Leader* on 29 March 1893. The interview appeared under four succinct headlines: THE WAR OF THE RACES IN AMERICA/NEGRO FREEDOM ONLY HALF ACHIEVED /A NEW EMANCIPATION MOVEMENT NEEDED/INTERVIEW WITH MISS IMPEY. Emphasizing her Quakerism and her long correspondence with Lloyd Garrison, Martin's article perhaps linked the Emancipation League more closely to the former antislavery movement than Catherine intended. Catherine explained that in her 'little paper Anti-Caste' she collected the reported cases of 'atrocities committed by organized bands of white citizens on negroes' who might be, and in many cases doubtless were, quite guiltless of the crimes charged against them. Despite Catherine's emphasis on a truly international organization being formed, the *Leader* mainly reported the intended aims of the movement in regard to the United States. The final point of the interview returned to Catherine's ideas of the self and the responsibilities of white people to recognize their racism explaining that the movement also aimed for 'the emancipation of the whites' from their racial prejudice though this task they expected to be 'the hardest of all'.[38]

Catherine intended to make similar preparatory visits to Newcastle, Darlington, Manchester, Liverpool and beyond up until Wells' arrival, but she had to spend some time at home over Easter. Her journey South resulted in only one unsatisfactory call on Joseph Sturge, the son of Hannah Joseph Sturge, during a short stop in Birmingham.[39] She arrived home on 30 March. By 5 April she had composed and distributed a circular to *Anti-Caste* subscribers informing them of the plans for the new society 'whose care it should be to protect the rights of the coloured members of our human family everywhere, teaching the universal application of the principle of human brotherhood to all alike, regardless of colour or nation'. Enclosing advance copies of the March/April special issue on lynching she had edited with Mayo, Catherine requested help with the distribution of 20,000 copies being printed. She was able to add a hurried p.s. that Wells had cabled her intention to accept the invitation to visit Britain.[40]

Wells received Catherine and Mayo's invitation while staying with Frederick Douglass. Filled with a sense of urgency the letter asked Wells to come 'soon – almost at once'.[41] Her hosts' financial plan relied on getting subscribers and donations at every place they could to organize meetings for Wells, providing funds for the next stage of the tour. Although unsure how to offer Wells anything like remuneration for her loss of time, they guaranteed all Wells' expenses would be paid. If she could not come they asked her to see if Thomas Fortune would come in her place, but they particularly wanted Wells. Catherine had heard her speak and knew the power of her delivery but also felt that as a woman Wells would find it easier to gain a sympathetic hearing from the British public. The unexpected letter meant Wells altering her plans for the summer but Douglass urged her to take the opportunity to visit Britain and tell her story. She began her first voyage across the ocean on Wednesday 5 April 1893.[42] An extract from the invitation from 'Miss Impey', who 'as editor of *Anti-Caste* is well known in America', was part of a letter by Wells published in the *Topeka Call* explaining her sudden departure and her anticipation of the work ahead. She was 'indeed glad that it has fallen to my lot' to aid Catherine 'however feebly' in her work.[43]

S J Celestine Edwards and *Lux*

Celestine Edwards, known to friends and colleagues as Jules, was full of life, energy and enthusiasm.[44] Proud 'of his colour and his people', he lived not for himself, but the political causes to which he was devoted.[45] Born on 28 December 1858 in Dominica, Edwards' parents were a poor French-speaking couple and he was the youngest of their nine children.[46] His father, born enslaved, held a small appointment under the French government for some years. As a boy Edwards had enjoyed walking down to the wharf to listen to sailors talking about the different countries they had seen. Hearing the sailors' yarns inspired him to go to sea, and following his father's death and while still a school boy, after a number of attempts, Edwards successfully ran away to sea with a friend. The sound of his mother imploring him to 'Come back!' from the shore tore into his heart like an arrow.[47] In 1873 Edwards found himself in New York and quickly relieved of his shipmen's pay by a 'land shark'.[48] By 1875 he had moved on to San Francisco, where he decided to try and make a life on land. Finding work in a large hotel Edwards remembered these times as his wildest days, when he hung out with 'a motely crew composed of gold-diggers, miners and sundry other bohemians' who observed no Sabbath. Narrowly missing being shot during a fight brought about 'a little sober thought'.[49] He went back to sea, hoping to return home to see his family, but never managed to arrange it. In the late 1870s Edwards settled in Britain, first living in Edinburgh for about two years where he developed his lecturing career on behalf of the temperance movement, speaking around the city and elsewhere in Scotland. Moving south he worked for a time as an insurance agent in Sunderland and for a builder in Newcastle.[50] At the time of the 1881 census he boarded at 57 Square Street, in Tottington Lower End, Lancashire. Aged 24 Edwards' employment

Figure 4.2 A portrait of Celestine Edwards. The copyright of the image was applied for in 1894 by the photographer Robert Banks, 126 Market Street, Manchester

is listed as lecturer, the craft for which he would become so well known. By the 1891 census he had moved to London and was living at 50 Tudor Road, Hackney. Listed as a medical student, he had probably been based in the East End for a number of years. In addition to his medical studies at the London Hospital, he was now a popular and active speaker on aspects of Christianity and particularly temperance.[51] The following year the Welsh language newspaper *Baner ac Amseau Cymru* described how Edwards' deep understanding of the Scriptures enabled him to explain complex ideas to the gratification of his audiences. As a result hundreds of people flocked to listen to him and he met with great applause wherever he spoke.[52]

Edwards' transformative speeches were credited with converting a hardened convict, Southampton-born Joseph Wailey, away from a life of crime. A smuggler, forger, blackmailer and notorious horse thief in the United States, Wailey spent 40 years of his life in prison, but his later years took an abrupt turn during an open-air meeting one Sunday in East London's Victoria Park. As Wailey stood among the crowd with (according to one version of the story) the intention of picking pockets, he was drawn to Edward's address. The speaker's words had such an effect on him that Wailey was converted on the spot and thereafter became a noted speaker in the park himself.[53] In the 1895 obituary that recalled Wailey's conversion what exactly he converted to is not made clear. Edwards spoke on a range of subjects from temperance politics at home and in Africa and India to Darwinism and racial prejudice. His popularity meant audiences flocked to hear all aspects of his 'anti-infidel' lectures. Between 1887 and

1894 advertisements appeared for public lectures he delivered in Bradford, Bristol, London, Liverpool, Manchester, Sunderland, Sheffield and Wolverhampton. In the earlier years of his national career his talks were closely connected to the temperance movement.[54] Often Edwards appeared among a group of speakers who had been gathered together for events such as the annual meeting of the Blackburn branch of the Church of England Temperance Society in December 1888. Despite rough weather an encouragingly large crowd heard Edwards condemn British influence in Africa and India.[55] Edwards also regularly addressed the Christian Evidence Society, helping to establish new local branches of the organization where he spoke. He was given credit for establishing the Bristol branch of the movement, and by the time he returned to speak on 'Science and Miracles' at St James' Hall, Sunderland Street in March 1893 the branch had 300 members and over 100 attended its weekly study classes.[56]

As his reputation grew Edwards became a headline speaker and then a public lecturer in his own right. Although committed to religious topics, the breadth of his themes developed. In September 1891 the *Sunderland Daily Echo* advertised Edwards' popular lecture on 'The Negro Race and Darwinism'.[57] The lecture was delivered at the Assembly Hall, Fawcett Street, to a full house of punters who paid six pence admission and 1s for a reserved seat. Edwards dealt at length with the theory of evolution, critical of Darwin's suggestion that it was somewhere in Africa that the human race first originated from the ape. Reportedly Edwards argued that Darwin had 'somehow got the negro race mixed up in his book', but it seems that Edwards' critique of Darwin came from a concern over the racial prejudice associated with Darwin's theories rather than the challenge evolution posed to religious doctrines. Though Edwards argued that 'A consistent advocate of the Darwinian theory of the *Origin of Species, Natural Selection, and Survival of the Fittest* will and can have no difficulty in allowing the obvious truth that, given favourable environment, the Negro race is just as likely to give as good account of itself as the European', at a meeting in the Morley Hall, Hackney, in 1886, Edwards had despaired that a whole generation now compared men and women with black skins to baboons.[58] In 'The Negro Race and Darwinism' Edwards continued to challenge these racist associations and dealt with 'various objections raised against the negro, and caused much amusement by the comparison he made between negroes and white men.'[59] In conclusion he argued that the time was soon coming when public opinion would be turned against racial prejudice and it would be seen that, given equal opportunity and time, black men and women would establish as good a record as any other race. Edwards delivered a lecture with the same title in Sheffield in December 1891 and closed a series of lectures with it in Liverpool the following April.[60]

Journalists rarely provide information on the eager audiences at Edwards' lectures, but the report of an accident in Portsmouth in 1893 suggests young working women were a noteworthy part of his audiences. In February 1893 Edwards gave a series of lectures at the Fuller's Hall in Landport. As usual the talks, in which he criticized free thinkers, agnostics, positivists and infidels, created a great deal of interest.[61] On Tuesday 14 February a crowd began to assemble outside the hall in Charlotte Street over an hour before the doors were due to open. By 7pm, half-an-hour before opening, over a thousand people were crowding in the doorway, filling the small lobby and queuing out across the street. To relieve the crush an additional entrance door was opened, but pressure on the Charlotte Street entrance continued and at about 7:20pm part of the lobby floor gave way and about 50 people crashed down into the cellar below. The list of the injured named Eliza Lashley, 19 (her father Charles Lashley was a police constable); Emily Taylor, 19 (who in the 1891 census worked as a dressmakers' apprentice); Beatrice Walker, 20; Caroline Shopland, 25; and Nellie Pilcher, 20.[62]

In addition to lecturing, Edwards wrote penny pamphlets and in 1891 published a biography of Walter Hawkins, a bishop within the British Episcopal Church in Canada. One of the *Times*' books of the week in November 1891 *From Slavery to a Bishopric* formed part of Edwards' contribution to the battle against racial prejudice.[63] He wrote the biography of Walters because he believed knowledge of Walter's life could be an inspiration to young black men (women are not mentioned) who, though physically free, had not yet fulfilled their potential – a duty they owed not only to themselves and to humanity at large but especially to the British public. Although feeling a great debt to Britain for the emancipation of the New World, Edwards' time in England had led him to believe that black people faced an uphill struggle to fulfil their potential.

> My experience in England has led me to think that many are somewhat disappointed that the Negro, from whom they expected so much fifty or sixty years ago, has not come up to their expectations, i.e., he has not improved his position quite as quickly as they feel he ought to have done. In this book I hope to set forth what Europeans well know: viz., that there is not a single nation in Europe who could have done more for itself, in the same time and under similar circumstances, than our race: they have expected too much of us, with far less opportunities. Besides, it is all very well to tell people what they ought to do, but it is quite another thing to give them the opportunity of doing.[64]

As Edwards toured through Derby, Sheffield, Manchester, Liverpool and Oldham in 1891, he assessed the strength of secularism as the most active form of atheism spreading among the masses. His observations compelled him to temporarily give up his medical studies in order to establish *Lux*. When Edwards took on the editorship of *Lux* in August 1892, he became, probably, Britain's first black newspaper editor.[65] *Lux: A Weekly Christian Evidence Journal* particularly aimed to counter the influence of atheist papers among the working classes. Printed in London for publication every Thursday, the paper cost one penny and ran to about 16 pages plus advertising space. Adverts of 30 words and under cost 2s. The first issue included 'Why I left the Secular Party' by James Marchant, a former president of the West Ham Secular Society, and 'The Atheists Creed Examined' by Robert V Allen.[66] Along with 'Rays of General News' (which in April 1893 noted with despair that there were 14,000 licensed public houses in London), regular columns included Edwards' weekly editorial 'Our Conviction' and a regular women's column, 'Written by a Woman to Women' originally by Helen Sillitoe, but also contributed to by 'A L O S' and 'Jennie'. The paper's list of agents and letters to the editor suggest that by drawing on the Christian Evidence Society's networks *Lux* quickly established a national readership.

Within the first few weeks E G Atkins sold 133 copies during a day of public debating around London at the Midland Arches, Hyde Park and Kilburn, and James Payne, chairman of the Sheffield Christian Evidence Society, recommended it to all he met.[67] By September 1892 the paper claimed a circulation of 15,000 copies a week and in October Edwards urged *Lux* readers to increase their support by asking their newsagents to show one of the paper's bills or buying an additional copy and sending it to a friend. He hoped the upcoming Christmas number could reach a circulation of 100,000 copies.[68]

Initially the majority of *Lux's* London agents were located in the East End, with only one, Mr Foster on the Camberwell Road, based south of the Thames, but the network soon expanded. In Liverpool, Conland & Son in the Abbey Buildings on Victoria Street, Williams Jones on Caryl Street and W. H. Smith & Son on Dale Street all stocked the paper. Four sellers in Manchester included two booksellers, one on Oxford Street and one at The Market. J Arthur Bain at 13 High Street acted as the sole stockist in Sheffield. To increase the security and distribution of the paper, Edwards encouraged friends and supporters to become founding members of the Lux Newspaper Company. With capital of £2500 in £1 shares, the Board of Managing Directors was to control at least 500 of the shares. If financial support did not come as quickly as he hoped, by March 1893 Edwards and other Luxites, as they came to call themselves, had secured a substantially increased network, with 90 stockists in London, 42 in Manchester, 5 in Sheffield and 14 in Liverpool as well as vendors in Newton Heath, Sunderland (5), Jarrow on Tyne (5), Bolton (3), South Shields (4), Great Driffield, Southampton, Norwich, Oldham (20), Newcastle on Tyne, Derby, Bristol (7), Stockport, Rochdale, Leicester (3), Portsmouth, Doncaster, Hull, Denbigh, Cardiff, Aberaman (2), Belfast and Melbourne (Figure 4.3).[69]

Alongside the editorial responsibilities of *Lux*, Edwards continued to lecture throughout England. The first issue of *Lux* advertised a forthcoming engagement in Manchester, where Edwards would lecture three times in one day: 11am – Miracles, 3pm – Is England Atheistic?, 7pm – Jesus of Nzara. In addition Edwards ran Bible and Christian Evidence classes at 8:30pm every Friday evening at St Andrew's Hall, Cambridge Heath Road in Bethnal Green, East London. Papers for the weekly discussion were advertised in *Lux*. They covered a broad range of topics under the headers 'Mahomet and the Koran', 'Utility Actually a Moral Guide' and 'Secularism v. Christianity'.[70] In October 1892 Edwards split the class into two, taking an advance class of men and women from 8 to 9pm and then an elementary class from 9 to 10pm, with each class studying different texts. He also began a men's Bible class at St Andrew's Hall at 11am on Sundays. At the end of October, he went to lecture in South Shields from 30 October until November 4th, before St James' Hall Manchester on November 6th and Rosamond Street the following day. He returned to London to speak at Shoreditch Town Hall on November 8th, back to Gorton-Manchester on November 9th, Miles Platting, November 10th, St James' Hall Manchester again from 18th to 20th November and then the Free Trade Hall, on 21st and St John's School, Deansgate on the 22nd.[71] In December 1892 Edwards published the schedule for another lecture tour. Four months later Ida B Wells arrived in Britain and Edwards enthusiastically embraced her campaign (Figure 4.4).

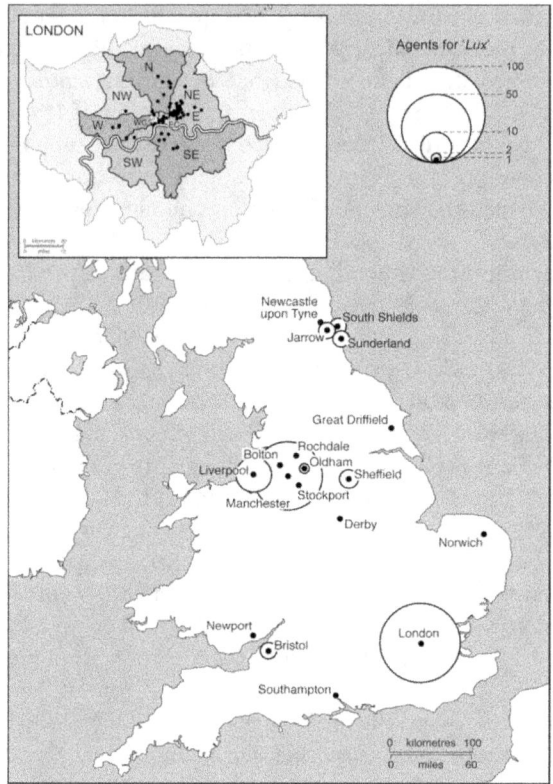

Figure 4.3 The location of agents where Edwards' weekly newspaper *Lux* could be purchased after 3 months of publication as advertised in *Lux*, 19 November 1892, iv. At this stage no international agents were listed

Geography of a new society

Wells suffered badly from seasickness during the eight-day Atlantic crossing, only managing to feel better once she had swallowed a large quantity of medication from the doctor's cabinet. She woke on the ninth day to find the ship finally standing in the Mersey opposite Liverpool. Both Catherine and Mayo had engagements that prevented Wells' tour starting immediately, so she travelled to Somerset to stay with Catherine and Ellen. She spent her time quietly and peacefully, recovering in what seemed to her to be a typical English home. Wells' schedule originally began with work in London and the south of England before heading north, but Mayo could not come down to Somerset for an additional two weeks. Mayo had become an influential supporter and so the programme was revised to accommodate her. Catherine banked on pledges and about £2 collected from supporters in addition to £5 borrowed from *Anti-Caste* to start a travel fund for the tour.[72] Catherine and Wells journeyed up to Aberdeen via Weston-super-Mare, where they called on Professor Newman and a local newspaper editor.

Figure 4.4 Portrait of Celestine Edwards. This image was one of a series for which the photographer William Harry Horlington of South Shields applied for copyright in August 1894 and may have formed part of a series advertised in *Fraternity*, which could be obtained post-free for 1s 1d each. *Fraternity*, October 1894, 8

Once in Aberdeen, Catherine, Wells and Mayo spent two weeks preparing for the tour with George Ferdinands and another two of Mayo's boarders. The group wrote letters, arranged meetings and mailed out several thousand copies of *Anti-Caste*.

A drawing-room meeting held in Mayo's home opened Wells' tour. The audience who heard Wells speak in Aberdeen formed itself into the first branch of not an Emancipation League but the Society for the Furtherance of the Brotherhood of Man (SFBM). In the discussions preceding the opening lecture those present agreed that the label of an Emancipation League was too narrow. The new collective felt the Society for the Furtherance of the Brotherhood of Man would more easily include those in India and other British colonies. With the new movement established, Catherine would soon leave Scotland so she could confirm arrangements for the English part of the tour. Wells and Mayo travelled on through Scotland visiting Huntly, Glasgow and Edinburgh, where they were the guests of Eliza Wigham. Here Wells undertook a full programme of talks. On Friday afternoon she addressed a meeting in the Bible Society Rooms, on Saturday she spoke to a drawing-room meeting convened in the Free Church and then she addressed a crowded assembly in the hall of the Carubbers' Close Mission. On Monday she spoke in the rooms of the YMCA. On Tuesday she moved on to speaking at the Friends' Meeting House in Glasgow. At each venue the audience was encouraged to commit itself to form a branch of the SFBM.

In Edinburgh a new circular was printed: 'To the Friends of Justice and Humanity everywhere, especially those who interest themselves in the future of the Coloured Race; also to the remnant of the Anti-Slavery Workers, and the Members of the Society of Friends.'[73] The signatories, Eliza Wigham, Elizabeth Pease Nichol, both from Edinburgh, William Gowan Smeal of Glasgow, Ellen Robinson in Liverpool and Catherine Impey, asked for funds to support the public meetings planned during Wells' trip. They announced the formation of the new association and its aims of 'instilling principles of *justice* and human brotherhood in our own people *at home*, in India and in the Colonies'.[74] No subscription was required to become a member of the SFRM, simply a pledge to uphold its principles. The *Edinburgh Evening Gazette* reported that the SFBM was the proposed basis for protests against violence and prejudice and had already enrolled many names, with every post bringing more. Within the first few weeks over 1200 people signed a pledge to uphold the society's declaration to 'secure to every member of the human family, Freedom, Equal Opportunity, and Brotherly Consideration'. The SFBM was, as Edwards argued in *Lux*, an opportunity to tell the American public that their bloodthirsty barbarities were an abhorrence to the British, and that 'their cruelty and inhumanity to a weak people kindle in us a feeling which will only be changed by justice and mercy towards the Negroes whom they have wronged and are wronging'.[75]

As Catherine and Mayo envisaged, the new society sought pledges, subscriptions and membership from the fired-up audiences following each of Wells' talks. She spent six weeks on the road speaking to audiences in Scottish and English towns and cities. At each of the meetings the audience established local branches of the SFBM.[76] Edwards' presence during Wells' English leg of the tour added to its popularity. In May he joined Wells in Liverpool before they travelled onto Ashton-under-Lyme. At the Vegetarian Restaurant on Fountain Street, Manchester, a branch of the society was established with 146 members. On 8 May they travelled together to Newcastle to deliver lectures before moving on to Sunderland and Sheffield. When they spoke at the Friends' Meeting House, Pilgrim Street, on 9 May, so many people arrived to hear them that the audience was divided into two halls. Edwards delivered his lecture in one, Wells in the other, and the pair then swapped places.[77] Here 438 members agreed to sign up to the aims of the Brotherhood. On 12 May 40 members were signed up in Darlington, and five days later another 77 in Birmingham. *Lux* recognized the long-term efforts Catherine had committed to the cause through *Anti-Caste* and encouraged its readers to embrace the movement.

> Miss Catherine Impey deserves every praise for her tact and courage in the Anti-caste Movement. To her belongs the credit of the enthusiasm which is being raised

in England and Scotland on behalf of the oppressed and badly treated Negroes of America, Hindoos, and Kaffirs. We trust that the members of the Christian Evidence Societies will get to know more about this movement, and demonstrate their love for Christ and sympathy for humanity by doing something to further the principles of this noble cause.[78]

At a drawing-room meeting at Mill Field, the home of Helen Priestman Bright Clark, where a print of George Richmond's 1833 water colour of William Wilberforce hung on the dining-room wall, an enthusiastic audience assembled, and encouraged by Helen Priestman Bright Clark 50 people formed a branch of the SFBM in Street.[79] The following day at a meeting chaired by Reverend James Bartlett another 59 members enrolled. Between 23 and 28 May Wells travelled to London to galvanize support in the capital.[80] Wells sailed home from Southampton at the end of May but returned to build on her success ten months later.

Edwards continued with a gruelling lecture tour combining his work for the new society with the Christian Evidence Society. On 3 July he spoke in Bristol before addressing a crowd of 1200 in London, and on 10 July he spoke to an audience at St James' Hall, Manchester, on 'American Atrocities'. On 19 July he took the stage at Victoria Hall, Southsea, to discuss 'Christianity and Freethought'.[81] Catherine's work also continued. While staying at Eccles House, at Colwyn Bay in north Wales, she wrote to Dadabhai Naoroji to see if she could enlist his support for the society, outlining that the object of the society was to cultivate a greater spirit 'of justice & brotherliness regardless of differences of colour & "race", so called'.[82] She explained that the readers and supporters of *Anti-Caste* had begun to organize 'in order as it were to provide a platform from which protest may be issued in defence of any who suffer injustice on the ground of race prejudice'.[83] A second version of the call to 'Friends of Justice and Humanity' published a more extensive list of supporters: Isabella Metford in Switzerland; Robert Spence Watson and David Richardson from Newcastle; F S Webster, the Rector of St Thomas, Birmingham; and Arthur Albright also in Birmingham; Rev Urijah R Thomas and William Somerville, J P Walter and Margaret Sturge and Anna and Mary Priestman – all based in Bristol; Josephine Butler in London; Edward Russell in Liverpool; Henry Mason Joseph from Antigua; Harriet Colenso and Anne Yardley Warner, a resident for some years in Tennessee; and three MPs, Henry Wilson in Sheffield, Alfred Webb MP of Dublin and Dadabhai Naoroji of London and Bombay. In Street Catherine was joined by James Clark, William and Helen Bright Priestman Clark. This high-profile and multi-ethnic list of collaborators appealed again for support and cooperation in completing the work of the 'Anti-Slavery movement by securing, not mere *declarations of emancipation*, but the full enjoyment of FREEDOM, EQUAL OPPORTUNITY, and BROTHERHOOD within the pale of the one great human family'.[84]

On Saturday 12 August Edwards took his campaign to working men, joining the list of speakers addressing a Trade Union march in Portsmouth. Among the 3000 demonstrators were members of the Boilermakers' Society, the General Labourers' Amalgamated Union, coppersmiths, bricklayers, joiners, plasters, dockers, railway workers, stone masons, iron founders and insurance agents. Speaking to the crowd from 'Platform No 1' Edwards proposed a motion for the meeting to push for the improved conditions of workers and the placement of labour representatives on all local governing bodies. He encouraged the unionists to better educate themselves by meeting together in club rooms so they could discuss 'the vital questions which lay at the very root of happiness and peace'. [85] Following the applause for that point he added that when they had settled their petty differences workers could then conduct a peaceful war against the capitalists. That month he also spoke to audiences at Ginnett's Circus in Newcastle, the sweltering heat reportedly causing some of the women in his audience to faint. Between 3000 and 4000 people were reported to have heard him speak on issues of segregation in America the following day.[86] He stopped at Liverpool on 28 August, where he lectured on 'Black and White in America' at Hengler's Circus to those who paid the 1d admittance charge.[87] In September he addressed a crowd in Plymouth before travelling to Aberdeen to speak before an audience at Blackfriars Hall and a crowded YMCA on 'The Racial War in America'.[88]

The last issue of *Anti-Caste* and the first issue of *Fraternity*

On 1 July 1893 Edwards announced in *Lux* that the June and final issue of *Anti-Caste* 'organ for the Society for the Recognition of the Brotherhood of Man' (SRBM) had been published and could be purchased from the numerous agents for *Lux*. Over the summer, as the new society evolved and discussed its position, its members decided the Society for the Furtherance of the Brotherhood of Man did not fit their purpose. The brotherhood of man existed; it could not be furthered. Instead the society believed that it was more accurate to describe their campaign as one that fought for the recognition of this equality, hence the small but significant change. Edwards and Wells edited the final issue of *Anti-Caste* with help from Catherine, as it had also been decided to launch a new periodical for the SRBM. The July issue appeared as the newly launched *Fraternity* using *Anti-Caste*'s columns until the new layout of Edwards' vision of the paper could be arranged.[89] Under Edwards' editorship after August 1893, *Fraternity* became a far larger paper than *Anti-Caste*, giving Edwards more scope for articles of analysis and reportage, but with far higher production costs: the circulation costs of 1200 copies of *Fraternity* equalled about 4000 of *Anti-Caste*.[90] With ambitions of selling three to four million copies in the first year, Edwards needed to utilize the new SRBM networks launched by Ida B Wells' tour, his own distribution networks for *Lux*, which he continued to edit, and the original supporters of the *Anti-Caste* movement. As promoted in *Lux*, the inaugural issue of *Fraternity* contained articles on 'The Angora Trials', 'More Brutality in America', 'Around the World' and other matters relevant to the society's propaganda. Its publishing offices were located at 18 Paternoster Row, where Edwards continued to publish *Lux*. Although the first issue of *Fraternity*'s masthead proclaimed it to be the 'official organ of the Society for the Recognition of the Universal Brotherhood of Man', the second and following issues dropped the 'universal'.[91]

Edwards sought to reassure his readers that *Fraternity* would not forget its *Anti-Caste* routes. As *Fraternity* declared on its first front page:

> For more than six years Anti-Caste has been doing a quiet work in England, slowly but surely permeating society, and winning the hearts of good men and true women to the cause of the helpless races in America, India, Africa, and Australia, and wherever tribes, races, and nations have been oppressed by the accursed enemy of mankind – Caste.... In this country if a man ill-uses a horse, tortures a cat, maltreats a cow, thousands cry shame upon him for his inhumanity. But alas! How different the same English speaking people treat the Negro in the United States! How unkind the same people have been and are to the pariahs of India and the Kanakas in Australia! All this ill-treatment we conceive to have sprung from a feeling of superiority existing in the mind of the English race over his darker Brethren and this feeling in process of time breeds caste, and caste ends in reckless cruelty.[92]

Original subscribers enthusiastically embraced the arrival of *Fraternity*, excited to see the little paper they had supported for so many years transformed into a substantial monthly periodical. Eliza Wigham wrote to the new editor expressing her hope that 'Anti-Caste, under its new title' would prove to be an opportunity for an expansion in its meaning and application.[93] Edwards' encouragement of *Lux* readers to support the SRBM provided an avenue of new readers. The Liverpool branch secretary of the SRBM reported that their local branch of the Christian Evidence Society had taken up the new paper with 'a spirit in which success is written'.[94] Unlike a stagnation of readers Catherine reflected upon in her January 1893 address to *Anti-Caste* readers, reports from SRBM branch secretaries on their region's progress over the first year reflected the establishment of an invigorated and growing community. In *Fraternity's* inaugural issue, Mayo's Aberdeen branch printed details of its local setup. Their president Reverend David Brown (principal of the Free Church College) served alongside their vice-president Miss Melville (formerly honorary secretary of the Aberdeen branch of the Anti-Slavery Society). Their committee included George Ferdinands and Mayo, with John Leith and Samuel Woodrow acting as treasurer and secretary respectively. Mayo's declaration that they had secured £4 of subscriptions in addition to the highly organized structure of the branch set a high standard for others.[95]

On 1 March 1894 the Somerset branch of the SRBM met to mark the sixth anniversary of the first publication of *Anti-Caste*. The group, gathered together by their secretary Miss Waterfall, agreed to meet at Catherine and Ellen's home, but as the anniversary fell on a particularly stormy night, only 12 out of the 40 or so members were present.[96] Reflecting on the work undertaken since she first published *Anti-Caste* in 1888, Catherine must have been hopeful. The movement no longer solely relied upon her personal energies or Ellen's finances, but rather showed the potential to grow into a national movement. There were, she argued, opportunities for developing the usefulness of the society and for increasing funds for its work. The group established a regional West of England branch of the SRBM with an appointed executive committee, in whose name fund-raising for the SRBM could take place. As a national movement the SRBM held great promise, with the potential for a truly national reach through its branch secretaries. In September 1894 these numbered over 25 in England, 3 in Wales, 6 in Scotland and 1 in the West Indies, with at least 2000 people signed up to the society at some level. Readers of *Fraternity* followed Edwards' angry editorials against the imperialist expansions undertaken by Cecil Rhodes in Africa and the shame of inequalities spread 'Under the British Flag', and read of numerous injustices in the column 'Things that Are that Should Not Be', but they could take some hope from 'Things as They Should Be'.

Notes

1. Aked, 'The race problem in America'.
2. *Adelaide Advertiser*, 30 December 1908, 7.
3. Giddings, *Ida*; Duster, *Crusade for Justice*.
4. Duster, *Crusade for Justice*, footnotes 4 and 19.
5. Decosta-Willis notes that it is surprising Wells had fallen out of touch with her paternal grandmother, who helped Wells take care of her younger siblings following her parents' death until she suffered a stroke, see Decosta-Willis, *Memphis Diary*.
6. Decosta-Willis, *Memphis Diary*, 138.
7. McMurry, *Waters Troubled*.
8. Weaver, 'The failure of civil rights 1875–1883'.
9. McMurry, *Waters Troubled*, 29.
10. Decosta-Willis, *Memphis Diary*, 141.
11. Duster, 1972; For a discussion of Wells' early writing see McMurry, *Waters Troubled* and Giddings, *Ida*.
12. Decosta-Willis, *Memphis Diary*.
13. Duster, *Crusade for Justice*, 23; Decosta-Willis, *Memphis Diary*.
14. McMurry, *Waters Troubled*.
15. Duster, *Crusade for Justice*, 35.
16. Duster, *Crusade for Justice*.
17. This account of events comes from Wells' recollections in Duster, *Crusade for Justice*.
18. Tucker, 'Miss Ida B. Wells and Memphis lynching'.
19. Duster, *Crusade for Justice*, 52.
20. McMurry, *Waters Troubled*, 148.
21. McMurry, *Waters Troubled*.
22. Nightingale had sold his share of the paper to Flemming and Wells sometime before. See Duster, *Crusade for Justice*, 39.
23. *Anti-Caste*, September 1892, 3.
24. Duster, *Crusade for Justice*, 82. In her memoirs Wells remembers that her first 'interview' with Catherine took place in November 1892, but in the archive records of the SRBM Catherine recalls (in a draft letter written in 1893) that she returned to England in October.
25. Impey to Tourgée, 16 June 1890, 4785 The *Albion W. Tourgée* Papers.
26. From Plaskitt, 'Mayo, Isabella (1843–1914)'.
27. Duster, *Crusade for Justice*, 89.
28. Impey to Tourgée, 2 March 1893, 6700 The *Albion W. Tourgée* Papers.
29. MSS. Brit. Emp. s.20 5/7.
30. Impey to Axon, 9 November 1894, Axon Papers 3329, John Rylands Library, University of Manchester. In her memoirs Wells identified Ferdinands as 'a native of Ceylon', Duster, *Crusade for Justice*, 89; also see Moore 'Reputation of Isabella Fyvie Mayo'.

31 'To whom it may concern', 17 August 1893, MSS. Brit. Emp. s.20 E5/7.
32 'To whom it may concern', 17 August 1893, MSS. Brit. Emp. s.20 E5/7.
33 Impey to Tourgée, 25 March 1893, 6772 The Albion W. Tourgée Papers.
34 Scottish Post Office Directories, *Post-Office Annual Glasgow Directory*, 1893–1894.
35 Quoted in Elliott and Smith, *Undaunted Radical*, 4; Alexander, *Army of Lions*.
36 Impey to Tourgée, 25 March 1893, 6772 The *Albion W. Tourgée* Papers.
37 'To whom it may concern', 17 August 1893, MSS. Brit. Emp. s.20 E5/7.
38 *Scottish Leader*, 29 March 1893, 4.
39 'To whom it may concern', 17 August 1893, MSS. Brit. Emp. s.20 E5/7.
40 'Untitled circular', 5 April 1893, MSS. Brit. Emp. s.20 E5/7.
41 'To whom it may concern', 17 August 1893, MSS. Brit. Emp. s.20 E5/7.
42 Duster, *Crusade for Justice*, 86.
43 *Topeka Call*, 15 April 1893, 2. My thanks to Mia Bay for sending me this reference.
44 'Outline sketch of the life of S J Celestine Edwards', *Fraternity*, March 1895, 3.
45 Quoted by Fryer, *Staying Power*, 277.
46 This material comes from a series of columns published in *Fraternity* on the life of S J Celestine Edwards, based in part on his recollections or memoirs in progress, which ran over several issues. Edwards was not sure if he was born in 1858 or 1859, 'Outline Sketch of the Life of S J Celestine Edwards', *Fraternity*, November 1894, 3–4. Although the published biographical information in *Fraternity* states Edwards was born in the small village of Burns, Dominica, the 1881 census records that 'Samuel Edwards' was born in St John, Antigua, West Indies (Class: *RG11*; Piece: *3849*; Folio: *47*; Page: *26*; GSU roll: *1341920*), with a similar record in the 1891 census which states that 'Samuel Jules Celestine Edwards' was born in 'West Indies, St Johns, Antigua' (Class: *RG12*; Piece: *205*; Folio: *9*; Page: *11*; GSU roll: *6095315*).
47 'Outline Sketch of the Life of S J Celestine Edwards', *Fraternity*, December 1894, 3–4.
48 'Outline Sketch of the Life of S J Celestine Edwards', *Fraternity*, March 1895, 3.
49 'Outline Sketch of the Life of S J Celestine Edwards', *Fraternity*, May 1895, 3.
50 'Outline Sketch of the Life of S J Celestine Edwards', *Fraternity*, May 1895, 3–4.
51 See *Hampshire Advertiser*, 3 September 1887, 2.
52 *Baner ac Amseau Cymru* (Denbigh), 17 February 1892, 4. My thanks to Fflur Jones for the translation.
53 *Pall Mall Gazette*, 25 September 1895.
54 In London, *Pall Mall Gazette*, 26 February 1887; in Wolverhampton, *Hampshire Advertiser*, 3 September 1887; in Bradford, *Morning Post*, 7 October 1887.
55 *Blackburn Standard and Weekly Express*, 8 December 1888, 7.
56 *Bristol Mercury*, 28 March 1893, 8.
57 *Sunderland Daily Echo and Shipping Gazette*, 28 September 1891.
58 *Lux*, 10 December 1892, 1; *Fraternity*, September 1894, 3.
59 *Sunderland Daily Echo and Shipping Gazette*, 30 September 1891, 3.
60 *Sheffield Daily Telegraph*, 11 December 1891; *Liverpool Mercury*, 28 April 1892.
61 *Portsmouth Evening News*, 2 February 1893.
62 *Portsmouth Evening News*, 15 February 1893; Eliza Ashley, 1891 Census Record Class: *RG12*; Piece: *857*; Folio: *58*; Page: *48*; GSU roll: *6095967*; Emily Taylor, 1891 Census for England Class: *RG12*; Piece: *857*; Folio: *83*; Page: *2*; GSU roll: *6095967*.
63 All from *The Times*, 13 July 1888, 4; *Marylebone*, 16 July 1889, 9; *Books of the Week*, Thursday 26, 1891, 4.
64 Edwards, *From Slavery*, xi.
65 Fryer, *Staying Power*, 278.

66 *Lux*, 6 August 1892, 4 and 8.
67 *Lux*, 27 August 1892, 59 and 60.
68 *Lux*, 3 September 1892, 73; 29 October 1892, 201.
69 Agents are listed 22 April 1893, iii–iv, which also gives information on the scale of charges for advertisements.
70 'Mohamet and the Koran', *Lux*, 12 August 1892; 'Moral Guide', 27 August 1892.
71 *Lux*, October 1892.
72 'To whom it may concern', 17 August 1893, MSS. Brit. Emp. s.20 E5/7; Duster, *Crusade for Justice*, 86.
73 'To the friends of justice and humanity' (marked Edinburgh 1893), MSS. Brit. Emp. s.20 E5/8; Duster, *Crusade for Justice*, 86.
74 'To the friends of justice and humanity' (marked Edinburgh 1893), MSS. Brit. Emp. s.20 E5/8; Duster, *Crusade for Justice*, 86.
75 *Edinburgh Evening Gazette*, 1 May 1893; *Lux*, 20 May 1893, 242.
76 'Early record of "brotherhood" society', MSS. Brit. Emp. s.20 5/7.
77 *Lux*, 1 May 1893, 250.
78 *Lux*, 20 May 1893, 250.
79 On Helen Bright Priestman Clark and the importance of her role in Quaker political networks, see Holton, *Quaker Women*. A picture of the dining room of Millfield (now a boys' common room at Millfield School) is held by the Alfred Gillet Trust. My thanks to Judeth Saunders for confirming this.
80 *Anti-Caste*, May and June 1893, 4; *Lux*, 20 May 1893, 242. For an analysis of the content and style of Wells' talks and lectures while in Britain, see Zackodnik, 'Ida B. Wells and "American Atrocities" in Britain'.
81 Bristol and London, *Portsmouth Evening News*, 19 and 20 July 1893; *Manchester Evening News*, 10 July 1893, 1.
82 Impey to Naoroji, 29 June 1893, original emphasis. National Archives India. My thanks to Dinyar Patel for sending me this reference. Colwyn Bay was home to Congo House, a 'practical' training institute in a Christian environment for African men and women that at one point received support from the *Anti-Caste* subscriber Joseph Jackson Fuller, see Draper and Lawson-Reay, *Scandal at Congo House*.
83 Impey to Naoroji, 29 June 1893, original emphasis. A note at the top of the letter suggests they met at the House of Commons in early July.
84 'To the friends of justice and humanity' (no date), MSS. Brit. Emp. s.20 E5/8.
85 *Portsmouth Evening News*, 14 August 1893, 2.
86 *Lux*, 5 August 1893, 10.
87 *Liverpool Echo*, 28 August 1893, 1.
88 *Aberdeen Journal*, 4, 11 and 12 September 1893; *Liverpool Echo*, 9 September 1893, 6.
89 'Early record of "Brotherhood" society', MSS. Brit. Emp. s.20 5/7.
90 'To the subscribers of "Anti-Caste"', March 1894, MSS. Brit. Emp. s.20 E5/7.
91 *Fraternity*, July and August 1894, 1.
92 *Fraternity*, July, 1893, 1.
93 *Fraternity*, July, 1893, 7.
94 *Fraternity*, August, 1893, 15.
95 *Fraternity*, July, 1893, 6.
96 MSS. Brit. Emp. s.20 E5/8.

Part 2

Geographies of Oppression

Anti-Caste intended to galvanize the support of those who lived under the British flag, in the United States and beyond, by presenting them with irrefutable facts and experiences of racial prejudice, with content created by and disseminated to an international and multi-ethnic readership. It formed part of the vast array and diversity of periodical titles that emerged in Britain at the end of the nineteenth century. Those who read *Anti-Caste* entered into the dynamic encounter that marks the process of engagement between a reader and text. It is a process structured by layers of interlocking public and personal geographies. These 'textual geographies' are situated within the spaces of the text – how and where the text is produced, the places where a text is circulated, read and discussed, and the spaces of the text – the geographical news, analysis and meanings contained within the text.[1] The networks of newsprint established by the black press in the United States provided essential news content for *Anti-Caste*, as did newspapers from Africa and India.

The ability to reach readers beyond those who committed to annual subscriptions depended upon the number of subscribers, the generosity of additional donations and the costs of distribution. Some subscribers took hundreds of copies to deliver around their networks; others took dozens to deliver to clubs and public reading rooms. Yet others took two or three to distribute among kinship circles or to enclose within a letter to friends and families abroad. During the early years of *Anti-Caste* Catherine travelled to conferences in Bristol and London. Such meetings meant that 'despite living in a West-country village, far from any of the great centres of public life', Catherine found opportunities for extending her knowledge of the workings of racial prejudice in many parts of the world.[2] The collage of print cultures in *Anti-Caste* created a 'space of exchange' between African, Caribbean, and British humanitarians and anti-imperialists, and black American, Indian and South African activist print cultures. Through letters to the editor *Anti-Caste* became a place in which readers could express and exchange views not found in other sections of the British media.

Producing news

In April 1888 the *New York Age* warmly welcomed *Anti-Caste's* new contribution to the political arena. The *Age* was founded and largely edited by the self-defined radical journalist T Thomas Fortune, considered by many of his peers to be one the most important men in black American journalism. Born to enslaved parents in Jackson County, Florida, in 1856, Fortune's mother died when he was barely a teenager. His father Emanuel, 'a conspicuous character' during Reconstruction politics in Florida, became a respected citizen of Jacksonville.[3] Growing up working in print rooms, Fortune believed a newspaper committed to a fearless tone that spoke up for its editorial convictions and held itself aloof from party politics could provide a voice that could challenge and help shape American politics.[4] He believed strongly that the United States was governed by public opinion and that newspapers could successfully mould and control this. In November 1884 Fortune became the editor and sole proprietor of the New York *Freeman*, which quickly became the most popular paper among black American newspapers.[5] The *Freeman's* independent reputation made it impossible for the publication to attract political subsidies, so Thomas handed control of the paper to his brother Emanuel and friend and business partner Jerome B Peterson.[6] They changed the paper's name to the *Age* and it was under Emanuel's editorial tenure that the *Age* introduced *Anti-Caste* as a potential beacon of 'great light set upon a hill'.[7] When Emmanuel died in 1890 Thomas returned to the helm of the *Age*. Known as the 'dean of the Afro-American journalists', he gave Ida B Wells a job when she found herself exiled from the South.[8]

Speaking to the Afro-American Press Convention on the syndication of news in 1891, Thomas Fortune hailed the growth of the press as one of the most striking phenomena of the nineteenth century. A considerable number of black newspapers contributed to this trend, among them his paper the *New York Age*. Supporting literacy within the black community was a key tool in black America's fight to consolidate their freedom and civil rights. A number of black literary societies formed between 1828 and 1860 had established libraries and institutions which supported readings, public lectures, opportunities for publication and spaces to discuss and develop literary engagement for men and women.[9] By 1891 Fortune estimated that about 100 black newspapers were publishing in the United States. Most were young and none were wealthy, but the demand from increasingly literate black American readers meant they seldom died.[10] As Ida B Wells' experience with *Free Speech* demonstrated though, the right of the press to freely express and publish opinions remained a fragile notion in the American South. Despite the vulnerability of the black press in parts of the United States, Fortune still believed deeply in the power of the press to animate social change and he celebrated the technological transformations that powered those changes.

During a political protest on 3 May 1886 Chicago police fired into a crowd of protesting workers at the McCormick Reaper Works, killing two men. The following evening during a meeting to denounce the violence at Haymarket Square a bomb thrown into the crowd killed a policeman and numerous civilians. In the chaos that ensued seven policemen and an unknown number of working people were killed. The event led to the aggressive repression of political radicals culminating in the trial of eight anarchists who were convicted of murder, four of whom were hung on 11 November 1887.[11] Looking back at the execution of these men Fortune explained how he had experienced their deaths as they happened, though he was not reporting in Chicago, but standing next to the telegraphic batteries in a newspaper office in New York.

> There was stillness of death. The sympathetic click, click, click of the keys of the sentient machines was unheard. Every word spoken, every movement made in the jail, a thousand miles away, was accurately recorded. So intense was the interest, so close did we all feel to the great tragedy progressing, that we really felt as if we stood onlookers of it and participators in it. And so we were. And when the drop fell – when the condemned enemies of law and order sprang into the darkness of the infinite, out of the light of the finite, every man's blood ran cold, every man's breath was suspended for the second, and then a long sigh broke the awful solemnity, and each mortal there turned away from the machines as from the gallows a thousand miles distant, with the horrors still upon him.[12]

Fortune's recollection of this crushing of organized labour illustrated his sympathy for the Chicago anarchists and the possibility of multi-ethnic solidarities in the United States, and in 1886 he argued in an editorial that the experiences of black Americans gave them an 'honest sympathy' for the Irish people and he encouraged those of his readers who could afford it to send money to Charles Parnell for his parliamentary campaigns.[13] But before the Afro-American Press Convention, he argued that 'race papers' were an essential part of the battle for black American's equal rights. Shawn Leigh Alexander argues that as Reconstruction disintegrated and black leaders lost their political positions the black press became more important as a voice in and for the black community, and editors of the increasing number of black newspapers and journals commanded greater respect.[14] The potential of the press to successfully change or mould public opinion accounted for their great value, and a power akin to a kind of sovereignty that clothed their editors and owners.[15] But black Americans could not get justice in the pages of the white press. Their unbalanced and racist reporting came from the editorial positions held by the white press, their editors and owners, as well as the syndicated news those papers relied upon.

By the 1850s foreign news had become a staple of national dailies in Britain, their collation of overseas news supported by rapidly developing international communication infrastructure. The geography of this coverage developed unevenly. Countries closely connected to Britain through imperial networks or with the greatest political and economic power featured most often with other nations hardly ever discussed.[16] The contents of these reports were themselves shaped by the decisions of news agencies. The trans-Atlantic telegraph cable, and cables to the Black Sea in 1868 and India in 1869, facilitated new speeds in the communication of news, but few newspapers could afford to employ their own foreign correspondents.[17] Instead they relied upon news agencies who employed 'a vast army, scattered in all parts of the world' to report on events day and night.[18] In Europe three agencies dominated the business of international news, agreeing to carve the geography of journalism between them. Havas, the oldest agency founded in Paris in 1832, covered the French empire, Italy, Spain and Portugal. Wolff, established in Berlin in 1849, reported from German, Austrian, Scandinavian and Russian territories, and Reuters of London, set up in 1851, covered the British Empire and the Far East.[19] Although running in an early form since 1846, the Associated Press Association was formally founded in New York in 1848.[20]

For Fortune, the role of agencies grew ever more important as the business of gathering the news became one of the most important industries of the age. Fortune was right to be sceptical of the reporting of American news overseas. In Britain foreign news was reported with little deconstruction or analysis. Before the creation of the *Time's* Foreign Department in 1891, foreign news was printed in the newspaper in the form in which it arrived.[21] Those who controlled agencies such as the Associated Press Association held great power. They controlled public opinion, Fortune argued, because public opinion was formed by the information put before it, from whatever source from which it was derived. Fortune accused the Southern Press Association, which gathered information for the national association, of biased journalism at every stage of reporting relating to racial politics in the United States. Instead of a presentation of facts that news agencies purported to provide, each item of news was doctored, either by the reporter who gathered the information or by the State to whom it was sent, ensuring that events would always be presented in favour of white Americans. As a result, year in, year out, public opinion was every day poisoned against black people.[22] Although in the black press black communities could read stories about their lives that were usually ignored in the white press, their black editors relied upon press agencies to bring international news to their readers.[23] They were limited in sympathetic sources. Even journals such as the *Aborigines' Friend* or Annie Besant's increasingly socialist paper *Our Corner*, which 'recognised in theory the brotherhood of the entire human race', rarely published voices belonging to those from the African and Asian diasporas.[24]

To overcome the power of the international press agencies, Fortune argued that the black American press needed to come together to create and control their own news agency. Fortune's enterprise was not realized until 1919, but an unofficial syndication of news operated among antiracist periodicals, newspapers and newssheets that produced and distributed countercultural narratives. As Mary Louise Pratt observes, those who found themselves on the receiving end of European imperialism produced their own forms of knowing and interpreting.[25] Catherine heard the echoes of the horrors they faced which reached her from:

> all quarters of the Globe, from Central Africa, to ice-bound Siberia from the United States with her slaughtered Indian babes and women and her downtrodden millions of dark-hued workers, thoughtful cultured India under the heel of British militarism, from the Australian forests, to the islands of the Southern sea.[26]

Acting as a 'relay station' within this information network, Catherine read through a mass of material, usually sent by people who themselves suffered from the oppression of caste.[27] Letters came in by every post, sometimes by the dozen.[28] Believing herself to be a 'slow laborious reader' who was 'easily distracted by talking in the room', Catherine often received more material than she could effectively process and she asked readers to clearly mark out the passages in the newspapers they sent which they felt most important for her to read.[29] While an active temperance worker, Catherine had contributed to and read a variety of temperance publications. These provided highly heterogeneous forms of evidence for their readers combining a use of tables, maps, quotations from literature and historical sources, personal eyewitness accounts, news cuttings, statistical data and, as technology allowed, photographs.[30] *Anti-Caste* followed this structure. Catherine displayed skills as an essayist and a geographer, accessing extensive sources of information on the experiences of people of colour in the United States, Australia and colonies in Africa and the Caribbean. As a 'relay station' Catherine processed a mass of diverse material, extracting news items, statistical data and eyewitness accounts, augmenting them with biblical and literary quotations, letters to the editor and later, reports on *Anti-Caste* in the national and international press.

Although viewed disparagingly by contemporary journalists this 'scissors and paste' method had become a staple feature of many late Victorian newspapers and magazines during the *fin de siècle*.[31] Editors viewed rivals who relied heavily upon 'scissors and paste' as undercutting the true costs of production and jeered at their poor business success, suggesting their inability to survive in a truly competitive market.[32] Across print cultures 'scissors and paste' represented a broad range of editorial tactics from the unacknowledged lifting of news reports to acknowledged and formal agreements, to the compilation of detailed social reports such as those produced by temperance organizations.[33] For *Anti-Caste* the use of 'scissors and paste' became its essence and its strength. *Anti-Caste* usually referenced its sources and these articles from an 'Afro-American' newspaper or a 'native' South African paper demonstrated *Anti-Caste's* ambition to speak with, not merely about oppressed men and women. The articles from these newspapers provided evidence not just content. In the United States, for black American journalists *Anti-Caste's* reproduction of their articles and reports as evidence exemplified the possibility of white-owned papers honestly reporting events in America as the black community understood them to be.

Geographies of writing

As women in control of the editorial voice, Annie Besant and Catherine remained rare examples of women working as managers in journalism. The 1841 census reported only 15 women holding positions as authors, editors or journalists; in 1881 this had risen to just 660.[34] At the 1891 census Catherine's mother Mary, now retired, formally remained the head of the Impey household. Ellen continued working as an agricultural seed grower and apple agent while Catherine is recorded as living on her own means, in addition to being an 'editor and publisher' and agent of a building society. Living at home with her sister, Catherine did not rely solely on journalism to earn a living and so her editorial aspirations were not restricted to material more usually associated with women such as domestic advice columns, scriptural reflections or fashion and frippery in magazines.[35] In the early decades of the nineteenth century British women faced stringent patrolling of their creative outputs, confining them to poetry, novels and moral tales, with frustrating limits placed on their ability to write directly about politics.³⁶ In response to increasing literacy rates and affordable printing technologies throughout the century, women found new ways to position their writing within an array of publications.³⁷ By the end of the century the literary market had dramatically expanded. The foundation of the *English Woman's Journal* in 1858 represented the beginning of a new era for women's political journalism, and Michelle Elizabeth Tusan argues that its founders, Bessie Parkes and Barbara Bodichon, believed that through the publication of a newspaper they would be able to draw greater public attention to the issues surrounding the changing economic status of women.³⁸ The women's political press, which developed over the remainder of the century, played a vital part in the construction of women as public citizens.³⁹ The periodical press provided women with an outlet for promoting causes, debating contemporary issues, passing on information and providing a forum for new ideas.⁴⁰

In *Anti-Caste*, engaging in an examination of the discourse of race became a regular issue. Miles Ogborn has illustrated how in the seventeenth and eighteenth century forms of writing played with calligraphy, using the capitalization or italicization of words to help convey forms of knowledge between scribe and reader.⁴¹ Similarly Catherine attempted to use type and print to convey, mark out and highlight the problematic language or racism she had been writing against since her earliest political essays in the *Village Album*. There can be complications with deciphering the meanings in print, resulting in fractures and uncertain outcomes when texts are read outside their intended community of readers.⁴² Kittler argued that there is no psychological bridge between the encoding author and the decoding reader; there is a technical exchange. With luck the elements and associative rules used in the author's textual medium can be reproduced through the associative rules of the reader's medium.⁴³ In *Anti-Caste*, Catherine laid out her attempts to create a medium of antiracism. She built on people's understanding of the formatting and reading of print to stress the constructed nature of the language of race. Using commas, underlines, and italics she marked out a typography of antiracism. In the making of these political typographies *Anti-Caste* generated and institutionalized particular modes of readability, placing 'white' in adverted commas, capitalizing the word 'Negro' and implementing new definitions of black America such as 'Afro-American'.⁴⁴ This attention to the technology of race and text further marked out *Anti-Caste's* critical contribution. In Annie Besant's *Our Corner*, for example, descriptions of 'natives' on the West Coast of Africa, 'Negroes' in Jamaica and 'half-breeds' in Canada were used without editorial comment or typographical reflection.⁴⁵

Spaces of reading

During the 1870s and 1880s the market for periodicals in Britain expanded dramatically.⁴⁶ They became extremely interactive and intertextual print mediums, and readers performed a key role in their production.⁴⁷ Readers endorsed an editors' line by purchasing a periodical week after week or month after month, and through their regular engagement with an individual periodical such as *Anti-Caste*, they became part of a clearly definable reading community.⁴⁸ Regular readers became part of the periodical's textual community, accepting its ideologies, social aspirations and cultural assumptions. They were also its financial supporters. Although newssheets were relatively cheap to produce, *Anti-Caste* did not have a preformed institutional base and often such publications had to rely on subsidies from their editors.[49]

Reading is both a solitary and a communal and participatory activity, serving to shape both individual and group identities.[50] *Anti-Caste* disseminated news not only to inform and rouse individuals but also to shape and animate an evolving anticaste movement. To this end Catherine saw the readers of *Anti-Caste* as active 'co-workers'.[51] It is difficult to extricate how far individual readers embraced their co-worker status in the manner their editor intended. All readers construct themselves in the process of reading, in choosing what to read in what order and what to skip altogether, whether to reread certain sections and whether to refer back to previous issues or to just follow particular interests from month to month, even within a selection of news and comment as restricted as that provided in *Anti-Caste*.[52]

Matthew Arnold coined the phrase 'New Journalism' in 1887 as a disparaging term to encapsulate the lamentable changes he saw developing with the democratization of print. Mark Hampton reflects that many of the transformations Arnold attributed to New Journalism seemed to have developed more gradually than journalists realized or wished to recognize. In particular commentators understood topics recently regarded as 'private' or 'domestic' becoming the subject of news and comment.[53] As Thomas Fortune argued, news could be anything that was of interest to people.[54] For black peoples in the United States, those oppressed by imperial rule and their friends and colleagues attentive to racial oppression, the lines between a political sphere and the 'private' or 'domestic' were complexly blurred.[55] These spaces were relatively indistinct because the colour lines drawn inside, outside and around their homes affected all aspects of their lives. The news published in the antiracist press reported on a wide range of 'human interest' stories for the personal contained the political within them. Catherine's creation of 'A Lynching Scene in Alabama' as an antilynching cover held much in common with the worst traits of New Journalism. It was eye-catching and sensationalist. It was also an editorially brave and bold decision that unflinchingly presented to readers the complexity of human interest stories shared by the living and the dead.

Readers of *Anti-Caste* purchased yearly subscriptions or single issues or accessed it through the network created by readers who distributed free copies to places where working-class readers would be expected to see them, including 500 YMCA Reading Rooms in the United States and public reading rooms in Yorkshire.[56] The system seems to have worked relatively well, for when Catherine sent five of the first issues of *Anti-Caste* to her fellow journalist W E A Axon, she apologized for being unable to send him the April and June numbers as these had effectively sold out.[57] How individuals who read these paid for or free issues responded to them is even more difficult to access, though Catherine believed that the success of the April and June 1888 issues was because 'they were rather more interesting' than others published during the year that had not been so extensively distributed.[58] Few memoirs or biographies record reading material as ephemeral as *Anti-Caste*.[59] Bob Stewart, a shipyard worker born in Dundee in 1877, recalled how important reading was to him in his political awakening. He consumed topical pamphlets, books theoretical and popular, including several by Karl

Kautsky. Though he particularly remembered several American temperance books and socialist pamphlets held a particular appeal to him, he did not name any of them in his memoirs.[60] Since the early nineteenth century, people had found ways to overcome the limits placed on their access to literary material by financial or racial restrictions. In the United States black communities came together through literary societies.[61] In some factories in Britain, if the noise of machinery still allowed, workers continued to take turns to read aloud from a collectively purchased newspaper as they had done since the end of the eighteenth century and would continue to do so until the cheap mass circulation of daily papers became established in the early twentieth century.[62] Whether or not *Anti-Caste* was shared in such a way through its free distribution list, it assumed a multiclass readership. Making efforts to reach those who she assumed might not be able to afford it, Catherine left *Anti-Caste* vulnerable to claims by other editors that a key marker of a periodicals' success and influence was its ability to get readers to commit to buying copies week and week.[63] If *Anti-Caste* was important enough, or interesting enough, readers would commit to buying a copy.

Even if all the thousands of printed copies of *Anti-Caste* or *Fraternity* were eventually distributed, their circulation does not mean they were all read. In general subscriber lists are scarce and assessing which readers participated in more active engagements with the periodicals is difficult. Where individuals can be identified, their contributions to *Anti-Caste's* literary community can remain opaque. Correspondence pages remain the most useful source of identifying real readers of periodicals and newspapers. *Fraternity's* larger format allowed for a greater interaction with readers and Edwards introduced some of the formats he used in *Lux*. Edwards directly engaged Luxites through 'our post box' and a column in which readers gave answers to fellow readers' questions. Correspondence columns revealed readers in conversation with the editor and placed them in public conversations with each other.[64] The pages of *Anti-Caste* were initially intended to provide a place where the thoughts and ideas of prominent black writers could be circulated before a new readership. In describing this ideal Catherine revealed that she envisioned *Anti-Caste's* readership would, in the beginning at least, be an audience that was mostly white.

Geographies of solidarity

An important success of *Anti-Caste* and then *Fraternity* was their ability to speak to the local, regional and international concerns of their readers. Through *Anti-Caste* and *Fraternity* readers felt they could become part of a community that supported them with interventions into their own local politics. This is illustrated in the cross-cultural analysis of experiences readers shared and also in the example of a man who wrote from the United States enquiring about the charter status of the SRBM so he could establish a branch of the organization in the South, seeing it as way for him to form a political solidarity among his peers. With the formation of the SRBM, for some readers their textual encounters in *Fraternity* became real encounters through the formal meetings, lectures and debates organized by the Society. The community of readers created through the circulations of *Anti-Caste* became an active community.

Anti-Caste did not provide the new platform for a broad range of political writing by African and Indian writers that Catherine originally aspired to, but it did help forge an international dialogue on racial prejudice, contributing to an unofficial syndication of news, and images, that helped disrupt the narratives purported by conventional white media. While doing so *Anti-Caste* and *Fraternity* challenged ideas of stable 'white' textual communities that unquestionably supported white supremacy or racial hierarchies. *Anti-Caste's* challenge to an international community of white solidarity found support among the black American press while drawing the ire of some white Americans. Concerned primarily with racial prejudice in the United States and the British Empire, *Anti-Caste* rarely directly addressed the experiences of race and racism across the British Isles. This may have been because friends and fate led Catherine to focus on events overseas. Or Catherine may have believed it was not an urgent an issue. The daily violence facing black Americans in southern states had no comparison for the black community in Victorian Britain, and it was the everyday embedded nature of prejudice and related violence that Catherine wanted to highlight. Though Britain remained largely absent from both *Anti-Caste* and *Fraternity*, to some in Britain the principle of equality advocated by the Society for the Recognition of the Brotherhood of Man appeared dangerously subversive. Edwards took pains to reassure the public that neither the SRBM nor *Fraternity* had formed common cause with revolutionary agents. Though he argued that *Fraternity's* mission was purely humane and should not have to justify its political position, in November 1893 he felt the need to clearly state in an editorial that *Fraternity* had nothing whatever to do with any revolutionary party or movement in Britain.[65]

Through their international print networks *Anti-Caste* and *Fraternity* became spaces in which readers were informed about oppression in other places, enabling them to locate their own experiences within a global context. Many readers found their 'horizon of expectations' challenged by *Anti-Caste*.[66] For black American editors and readers *Anti-Caste* represented a novel model in journalism. A white edited newspaper that presented news material from their own pages to a white audience without doctoring their words against them. For readers an encounter with *Anti-Caste* could be extremely confronting. As a result some changed their opinions of racial prejudice and engaged with *Anti-Caste's* campaign. For others, although it failed to undermine their commitment to white supremacy, *Anti-Caste's* existence challenged their assumptions of, if not a universal white community, an understanding of a universal sympathy and solidarity among white people for whiteness. For black American readers the creation of a space where black voices were published and discussed with seriousness and respect among a largely white audience seemed valuable and filled with exciting potential. As an editor Catherine encouraged the active reception of her readers. She incorporated their views, expressed through letters to the editor, as commentary, news and original contributory material for her own editorial observations. Readers' contributions published in *Anti-Caste* and more extensively in *Fraternity* allowed for an easier flow of information between disparate and distant political communities, creating spaces of exchange between schoolgirls in Britain, black American professors, radical African clerics and an English couple living on an Aboriginal mission in Australia.

Notes

1. Saunders, 'Literary geography'.
2. *Supplement to Anti-Caste*, January 1891, 3.
3. Penn, *Afro-American Press*, 133.
4. Penn, *Afro-American Press*.
5. Penn, *Afro-American Press*.
6. Alexander, *T Thomas Fortune*.
7. *The New York Age*, 7 April 1888, 2.
8. Quoted in Moses, 'Writing *the Age*', 2.
9. For example, the Colored Reading Society founded in 1828 in Philadelphia was for 'men of color' but the New York Phoenix Society, founded in 1833, welcomed both men and women. See McHenry, 'An association of kindred spirits'.
10. T Thomas Fortune, 'On syndicating news'.
11. Dabakis, 'Martyrs and monuments of Chicago'; A day before the executions one defendant committed suicide and the Illinois Governor Richard Oglesby commuted the capital sentence of two other defendants to life in prison. The eighth defendant was sentenced to 15 years hard labour, 'The Dramas of Haymarket', www.chicagohistory.org/dramas/, accessed 14 June 2013.
12. T Thomas Fortune, 'On syndicating news', 233–234.
13. Alexander, *An Army of Lions*, 10.
14. Alexander, *An Army of Lions*.
15. T Thomas Fortune, 'On syndicating news'.
16. AG, Global Journalism, *Dictionary of Nineteenth Century Journalism*.
17. Gray, 'Introduction'.
18. T Thomas Fortune, 'On syndicating news', 236.
19. JEM/MaT, News Agencies, *Dictionary of Nineteenth Century Biography*.
20. LL, Associated Press, *Dictionary of Nineteenth Century Biography*.
21. Brown, *Victorian News and Newspapers*.
22. T Thomas Fortune, 'On syndicating news'.
23. Alexander, *Race Man*.
24. McKay, 'A journal of her own', 332.
25. Pratt, *Imperial Eyes*.
26. *Supplement to Anti-Caste*, January 1891, 3.
27. *Anti-Caste*, December 1890, 2; Kittler, *Discourse Networks*.
28. Impey to Axon, 16 June 1890, Axon Papers, 3036, John Rylands Library, University of Manchester.
29. Impey to Axon, 16 June 1890, Axon Papers, 3036; Supplement to *Anti-Caste*, January 1891, 3.
30. Kneale, 'The place of drink'.
31. CCF, 'Scissors and paste' journalism, *DNCJ*, 561; Nicholson, 'You kick the bucket'.
32. Nicholson, 'You kick the bucket'.
33. CCF, 'Scissors and paste' journalism, *DNCJ*, 561; Kneale, 'The place of drink'.
34. Tusan, *Women Making News*.
35. Gray, 'Introduction'.
36. Rendall, 'Condition of women's writing'.
37. Gray, 'Introduction'.
38. Tusan, *Women Making News*.

39 Tusan, *Women Making News*.
40 Fraser, Green and Johnston, *Gender and the Victorian Periodical*, 16.
41 Ogborn, '*Geographia*'s pen'.
42 Korhoen, 'Textual communities'.
43 Kittler, *Discourse Networks*.
44 Brosseau, 'Geography's literature'.
45 *Our Corner*, March, September, December 1883, September 1885, 178.
46 Tusan, *Women Making News*.
47 Jackson, *George Newness and the New Journalism in Britain*.
48 Brake, Bell and Finkelstein, 'Introduction'.
49 Tusan, *Women Making News*.
50 Towheed, Crone and Halsey, 'Reading communities'.
51 Impey to *Tourgée*, 16 June 1890, *Albion W. Tourgée* Papers 4785, original emphasis.
52 Brown, *Victorian News and Newspapers*. On an attempt to direct and slow down reader's engagement with a periodical, see Hofmeyr, *Gandhi's Printing Press*.
53 Hampton, *Visions of the Press in Britain*.
54 T Thomas Fortune, 'On syndicating news', *AME Church Review* 8, 1891: 231–242.
55 For a discussion of these issues in the context of 'second wave' feminism in Britain, see Carby, 'White woman listen!'.
56 For the last half of 1890, 500 copies were posted for free, *Supplement to Anti-Caste*, January 1891, 1.
57 Impey to Axon, 25 February 1889, Axon Papers, 2939.
58 Impey to Axon, 25 February 1889, Axon Papers, 2939.
59 Warren, 'Women in conference'.
60 Stewart, *Breaking the Fetters*.
61 See McHenry, 'An association of kindred spirits'.
62 Vincent, 'Reading and writing'.
63 Fraser, Green and Johnston, *Gender and the Victorian Periodical*.
64 Tusan, *Women Making News*.
65 *Fraternity*, November 1893, 1.
66 Jauss, 'Literary history as a challenge to literary theory'.

5

The American Question

In America we shall oppose lynching because it is inhuman, and the spirit which prompts it is diabolical.

Fraternity, 1893

Reports on the brutality of black life in the United States regularly came to the attention of *Anti-Caste* and *Fraternity* readers. Finding a way to challenge the injustice of racial segregation inspired Catherine to establish *Anti-Caste*, and debates on the 'American question' appeared in most of its issues. Although not the only form of racial prejudice in North America to be featured, the experiences of black individuals and their communities dominated reporting from the United States. In July 1900 delegates of the first Pan-African Conference held in London declared that the problem of the twentieth century would be the problem of the colour line.[1] Their prediction was formulated with ideas from a text prepared by W E B Du Bois for a photographic exhibition illustrating the history and conditions of black Americans, part of the 'American Negro Exhibit' at the 1900 Paris Exposition.[2] The 'Lines of Caste' or the 'Colour Line' was regularly discussed in the pages of *Anti-Caste* and *Fraternity*.[3] Reports on 'color/colour lines' identified material markers of social and economic segregation in American life as well as 'a nexus of competing gazes' in which the process of constructing colour caste was 'understood as the effect of both intense scrutiny and obfuscation under a white supremacist gaze'.[4] Reporting from the colour line in *Anti-Caste* and *Fraternity* thus touched upon a wide range of everyday experiences of racism from spaces of education and public transport to the development of the women's movement, conceptions of justice and lynching photography.

Reporting from the colour line

In October 1891 *Anti-Caste* recounted the case of a black clergyman who was ejected from a Pullman sleeping car and the legal action taken by the Afro-American League on his behalf.[5] In May 1892 an extract from *National Pilot*, a Virginian magazine, highlighted debates around separate train cars for white and black people on the railway system. The cars, if separate, were supposed to provide 'equal accommodation', but according to a report by Reverend G B Gordon, this was not the case. In October 1891 Gordon had undertaken a 5000-mile tour of the South including states where segregated train car laws were in force. He did not find a single state where first-class accommodation for black passengers equalled that of white customers.[6] This was no surprise, but how to tackle the caste privilege the white community engineered through unequal schools' budgets, unequal transport systems and access to job security remained a subject of debate among black Americans.

Discussions revolved around two major positions: 'Radical Reconstructionism' promoted by Frederick Douglass and 'Accommodationism' propagated by Booker T Washington. As a 'radical reconstructionist' Douglass sought to remove racial barriers in American life through the establishment of legal rights.[7] Others embraced the accommodationist view closely associated with Booker T Washington. While Douglass argued for a new social order and a remaking of the American nation, Washington sought a way through the existing structures. Given the racist conditions they were forced to live under, particularly in the South, Washington argued that black Americans should try to create an independent economic base for their communities. Educational establishments like the Tuskegee Institute provided black men and women with an opportunity to establish themselves in professions from which they could slowly ascend to claim broader economic and political rights.

Catherine's personal politics were deeply influenced by the ideas of 'radical reconstruction', but material in *Anti-Caste* illustrated that steering a clear path between the two ideologies was difficult. In January 1889 *Anti-Caste* reported the actions of a Philadelphia-based millionaire who had endowed a mechanical school that would educate white students only. The donor's explicit exclusion of young black students was resolutely condemned.[8] But *Anti-Caste* had gladly supported Fanny Jackson Coppin's visit the previous summer, which included raising money to build a boarding house for black students to attend an educational institute for 'colored youth'. Frederick Douglass saw enhancing segregation as deeply problematic. In a letter to Catherine, published in *Anti-Caste* in 1889, Douglass argued that black people should not separate themselves any more than they were forced to by white Americans. As an example Douglass discussed mixed schools which he supported. He realized that many black people opposed them because they feared that mixed schools controlled by white people would mean that black teachers would not be employed, but he thought this view shortsighted. He argued that with mixed schools would eventually come a staff of mixed teachers. He also criticized the tendency for Americans to place the burden of finding a solution for these problems upon the South. 'The American people', he wrote, 'are talking of a "Southern problem", a "negro problem"', forgetting that the real problem was 'whether American civilisation and the American people and government are capable of protecting the negro in the rights of human nature'.[9]

As hinted in Douglass' letter, in addition to the inequalities embedded by racial prejudice in all aspects of social and cultural life, black Americans, particularly those living in the South, faced the sadistic and orchestrated violence of lynchings. Defined as murder committed by three or more people, during the tumultuous times of Reconstruction and its aftermath, lynchings predominately became acts undertaken by white men who killed black men.[10] The Virginia-based *Richmond Planet* registered the number of black Americans lynched every week, and in her first annual editor's address Catherine used the *Planet's* statistics to tell the grim story of lynching. Between 26 July 1887 and 26 July 1888, 109 lynchings had taken place; since then a further 56 bodies had been added to the count. Among the crimes punished was 'marriage to a white woman'.[11] Three months later *Anti-Caste* carried a report of the death of an unknown man who had been shot and killed because he had refused to give up his seat to a white captain on an Atlantic and West Point train.[12] Debates about American lynching appeared in the British press throughout the nineteenth century, contributing variously to discussions of the corruption of slavery in American society to the exploitation of fears of 'mob rule' by conservative politicians seeking to fuel opposition to constitutional reform at home.[13] Between 1889 and 1918 a lynching occurred in the United States roughly once every three days.[14] Between 1888 and 1895, the years of *Anti-Caste's* publication, hundreds if not thousands of articles on lynchings appeared in the British press. These included a broad range of stories from sensational telegrams reporting the impending burning of a black man, the lynching of 11 Italians in New Orleans in 1891 and longer editorials reflecting the spike in reports of lynchings of black men in 1890 and 1891, which left the *Bristol Mercury* thinking that in some states 'negro lynching appears to be as fashionable a pastime as bear-baiting used to be' in Britain.[15]

In February 1890 *Anti-Caste* called attention to the Barnwell Outrage, a case written up by the *Virginia Planet* from a report in the *Charleston News and Courier*.[16] In this instance eight black men were tied to a tree and shot outside the Barnwell Court House. Two days later another man was 'tied to a tree and put to death like a dog; and his body was left to feed the carrion birds for two days'.[17] Six months later Catherine printed a letter from 'A Negro professor of a Southern University', who wrote to update *Anti-Caste* readers 'fearing that you may not get it elsewhere' on the aftermath of the murders. He regretfully informed them that not one of the lynchers had been brought to trial. The solo murderer had been tried the week before, but despite the clear evidence of his guilt, with the jury standing six to six, the judge declared a mistrial. 'People may read of the south and think they know all about it', the professor lamented, 'but they know nothing of the grievances we have to suffer.'[18]

Two years later Catherine reflected on the gruesome lynching of Edward Coy, which had caught attention across the mainstream British press. In February 1892 a mob at Texarkana, Arkansas, had burned Edward Coy to death. Reports later ran that Coy had been involved with a married white woman for over a year before she accused him, perhaps under the threat of violence, of assault. Knowing the outcome of an accusation of rape by a white woman the young man fled. A mob trapped him and delivered him to the public square. Reports differed to the exact manner of his death. Some versions described him tied with wire to a post, others that he was bound to a tree and tortured by men and boys cutting flesh from his body. Reports agreed that while Coy still lived piles of wood were heaped around him and his clothes soaked in oil. The woman who accused him of assaulting her was brought out from the crowd to apply a light to the pyre. Coy died after the most excruciating agony before a crowd of 5000, although Ida B Wells later claimed as many as 15,000 watched the macabre spectacle.[19] The *New York Times*, which gained a reputation for being broadly critical of lynching, reported that although the 'good people of Texarkana' deplored the necessity of mob law, that night popular opinion espoused that 'Coy had been rightly served'.[20]

Articles about Coy's death in the British press came from a mixture of sources. The *Manchester Courier*, the *Sheffield and Rotherham Independent* and *Belfast News-Letter* all carried a story sent from their own correspondent in New York. Either they had the same correspondent or their correspondents used the same press source as the papers' versions of events are almost identical. They gave a succinct account of events: Coy had been charged with the rape of a white woman, so he was hunted and captured by a 'crowd of citizens' and was taken into the town where thousands of people had gathered. Knowing there was 'no hope of mercy' Coy apparently 'met his fate without flinching'. As the light was applied to the pyre he 'asked the foremost of his tormentors to keep back and stand aside, so that the ladies might see how a negro could die'.[21] The *Glasgow Herald* reported the same details, perhaps more honestly, attributing the material to telegrams from Reuters and special agents.[22] The *Manchester Evening News* reprinted a story similar to the *Manchester Courier's* report, reprinting the same account as their opening paragraph and supplementing it with another more lengthy account that detailed the alleged attack, the search for Coy, the debate as to whether he should be burned in town or beyond the city limits and the role of Mrs Jewell, the white woman at the centre of the allegations, who, 'pale and determined' and with the 'support' of two male relatives on either side, struck a match and lit Coy's kerosene-soaked clothes in two places.[23] Although the *Manchester Evening News* gave a far more detailed account of the events, like the other dailies it offered no analysis or contextual detail for the case.

Anti-Caste condemned the mob and its self-proclaimed laws outright. In her analysis Catherine supported arguments pioneered by Ida B Wells that lynchings were sentences of death given not to those guilty of crimes but to black men who challenged the caste laws of the South, particularly those regulating sexual encounters. Wells' analysis of lynchings appeared in *Red Record* published in 1895, an elaboration of material outlined in *Southern Horrors* (1892) and earlier talks and newspaper columns, particularly 'Exiled', a series of articles in the *New York Age*. In *Red Record* and *Southern Horrors* Wells criticized Southern white leaders, ministers, governors, judges and editors, who perpetuated the belief that black men embodied a constant threat of physical assault upon white women and that lynchings represented a reasonable response. Wells argued that during slavery, when white men retained an economic interest in the black body, arguments that black men were a constant threat to white women were not present. In the wake of Emancipation and Reconstruction, however, the white man's interest in the black male body had turned to fear and anxiety over the battles for identity and citizenship.[24] The production of the stereotype of the black male rapist was 'the new cry', the most recent technology of control developed by white communities to maintain their economic, social and cultural dominance.[25]

Wells' analysis of lynchings produced material that was severely confronting for white commentators, particularly two arguments she made in *Southern Horrors* and *Red Record*.[26] Her first was that white women engaged in consensual sexual relationships with black men. Though the spectacle of lynching in the United States focused on the body of the black male, the regulation of women's sexuality was key to maintaining caste structures in India and the United States. In both countries, gender and genealogical knowledge were essential to marking distinctions between castes that were 'played out on the field of intimate life and familial relations'.[27] In his anticaste criticism Jotirao Phule's focus on gender and sexuality 'enabled a powerful critique of the reproduction of caste through the regulation of gender'.[28] Wells also developed a powerful critique of the regulation of racial/caste hierarchy through gender relations. Wells reminded her readers that not all victims of lynchings were men. A 15-year-old girl had been hung in Louisiana, a woman hung in Jackson, Tennessee, and another in Hollendale, Mississippi. Both Wells and Catherine also wrote about the differential application of womanhood upon the bodies of women from different parts of the caste/race structure. For though merely the suspicion of an assault on a white woman's position, not necessarily her person, could bring out the full force of lynch law, similar attacks as well as acts of physical violence on black women were routinely left unpunished.

In both India and the United States violence was a key tool in maintaining caste order.[29] Wells also argued that in the United States lynchings were administered as the punishment of a myriad of crimes and sometimes for no crime at all, as and when particular white communities felt the need to control black advancement and regulate caste boundaries. To support her theories, Wells presented her evaluation of 1115 lynching cases which occurred between 1 January 1882 and 1 January 1894. Of these only 348 were connected to charges of rape; the remaining 'were lynched for any other reason which could be manufactured by a mob wishing to indulge in a lynching bee'.[30] In *Red Record* Wells outlined a number of cases where men had been accused of rape after consensual affairs with married women turned sour or were revealed through town gossip or after their girlfriends gave birth to 'mixed-race' children. To illustrate the importance of the narrative of rape as a justification of lynching among the white press and pulpit, Wells presented the case of Daniel Edwards. Edwards who lived near Selma, Alabama, worked for a farmer and embarked on a relationship with one of his daughters for over a year and she fell pregnant. Following the birth of her child, it became known that Edwards was the father. He was first thrown in jail and then was taken by a mob, hung from a tree and his body riddled with bullets. The following morning a notice was found pinned to his back: 'Warning to all Negroes that are too intimate with white girls. This the work of one hundred best citizens of the South Side.' The notice contained local acknowledgement that a consensual relationship between Edwards and the girl had taken place, but when press dispatches went out describing the event they reported Edwards was lynched for rape.[31]

Wells did not argue that violent and sexual assaults by black men upon white women did not occur, but she insisted that black and white criminals should be punished equally before the law. Black men should receive the same opportunity to defend themselves against accusations and if found guilty their sentences should be the same as those given to white men convicted of similar crimes.[32] Wells presented a number of cases in which white men who had raped or murdered black women or girls were never arrested, acquitted or, if convicted, received only prison sentences for their crimes. This inequality she labelled 'Color Line Justice': that some black men were guilty of rape could not account for the manner of their deaths, nor of the many innocent men who were murdered by mobs.

Anti-Caste's analysis of Edward Coy's murder was published before Well's 'Exiled' articles appeared in the *New York Age* and before Catherine had met Wells in the fall of 1892, but Catherine would have read Wells' accounts in the *New York Age* and perhaps discussed the issues with black activists during her previous trips to the United States. *Anti-Caste*'s report on Coy's murder aligned with Wells' published theorizations on rape and lynchings. *Anti-Caste* told its readers that it was the charge of a black man with rape – rather than Coy's conviction, for he never was convicted of injuring a woman – that had enraged the mob. If it had been the case of a white man assaulting a black woman the public would not have been appalled.[33] It was because 'the *man* being of the despised colour and the *woman white*, he had defied the white man's law, and broken through the lines of Caste'.[34] Catherine linked Coy's death directly to the legacy of slavery and the gendered nature of the new forms of white supremacy evolving in the Deep South. In their violent treatment of black men, the white men of the South 'passionate, revengeful, intoxicated by centuries of uncurbed license and mastery' proved that they recognized 'no "human rights" except those of their own white community'.[35]

Picturing Southern horrors

In January 1893 Catherine published the first of only two issues of *Anti-Caste* with an illustrated cover (Figure 5.1). The second reproduced a gentle portrait of an aging Frederick Douglass following his death in 1895. The first presented 'A Lynching Scene in Alabama' taken in August 1891. The image constructs a familiar frame in the surviving albums of lynching portraits. Partakers from the mob pose patiently below the lifeless body as travelling photographer W R Martin memorializes the evidence of their racial superiority. Producing portraits of lynch mobs proved to be a lucrative trade for travelling and local photographers, who turned the images into souvenir *carte-de-visite* and later postcards that sold by the thousand.[36] The postcards served multiple purposes for members of the mob. They documented the consolidation of white power while compounding the pain and fear of the victims' families and the black communities from which they came and they turned a lynching event into a memory that could be possessed, recalled, celebrated and shared among members of the mob and those who were never present.[37]

Following the lynching of Will Stanley, who was hung and burned in Temple, Texas, in the early hours of 30 July 1915, a young man called Joe posed with the crowd for his lynching portrait.[38] The focus of the picture is not so much on the crowd in this instance. The viewer's eye is drawn to the broken, charred and twisted remains of Will Stanley's body hanging in the centre of the frame. On the far left of the picture wearing a hat low on his forehead, Joe stands tall facing the camera. He bought at least one copy of the group photo in the form of a postcard, allowing him to explain that the picture commemorates the sociable 'barbecue' he attended the night before. The rapid reproduction of the image suggests the photographer sensed or well knew people wanted to quickly share their excitement of being part of the spectacle. In the same year as Will Stanley's death, Thomas Brooks was lynched in Fayette County, Tennessee. Following the lynching Du Bois' *Crisis* carried a report that hundreds of personal Kodak cameras had clicked at the scene of Brooks' murder all morning. To maximize their profits from the people who had come in carriages and cars to view Brooks' body hanging beneath the Nashville, Chattanooga and St Louis Railway bridge, picture card photographers set up a portable printing plant.[39] Joe sent his picture postcard of Will Stanley's murder to his parents. He also inked a cross on the photograph in the space above his hat so that they could easily identify him among the crowd.

The meanings of lynching photographs changed depending on the context of the circulation and political interests of each viewer and how they read its content.[40] While for the majority of white viewers lynching postcards disseminated narratives of solidarity and power, among black viewers they contained ominous warnings and illustrated the ugly powers of whiteness. Although lynching was always illegal, individual perpetrators were confident that they would never be prosecuted.[41] Even within communities where lynchings never occurred the circulation of lynching images intimidated black people, instructed them on the power of whiteness to manipulate and control the law and strengthened oppressive racial codes of conduct operating in social and cultural life.[42] These racist codes received tacit support from the government, whose postal workers delivered cards to the families and friends of murderers through the federal postal system. Although the mailing of lynching postcards became illegal in 1908 as they fell within statutes which forbade the sending and circulation of lewd and obscene material through the post, Joe's postcard to his parents illustrates lynching images continued to be circulated.[43]

Catherine received a copy of the lynching scene in Alabama because a member of the self-appointed 'lynching committee' sent a copy of the photograph to Albion Tourgée. These men, and perhaps women, sent the image 'With the Compliments of the Committee' to the president of the Citizens' Rights Association so he might have a good example of a 'black Christian hung by white heathens'.[44] In September 1892 Catherine had confessed to readers that she had failed to find the words to describe the violence of lynchings.[45] She asked her printers to make a copy of the photograph sent to Tourgée to enable her to make reproductions. The resulting copy from this block appeared on the cover of *Anti-Caste* in January 1893. By displaying 'A Lynching Scene in Alabama' on the cover of her periodical, Catherine aimed to convey the shocking violence of the South in a way that she thought 'perhaps only a photograph can do'.[46]

Catherine inverted the intended meanings of the photograph by the text she constructed around the image. By placing the picture beneath the bold *Anti-Caste* title on the cover, rather than on an inside page, she challenged the caste and gender solidarities demonstrated by the crowd. Between the title and the image is the periodical's declaration that it 'advocates the brotherhood of mankind irrespective of colour or descent', further emphasizing that editorial sympathy lies with the lone black figure, not the white men and boys below him. This is confirmed by the explanatory text placed beneath the image. Although the image may be unfamiliar to readers, the text underlines that the picture represents violence that is common, rather than an event that can be dismissed as exceptional. By describing the scene as 'lawless'

Figure 5.1 'A Lynching Scene in Alabama', *Anti-Caste*, January 1893

while explaining that the perpetrators always go unpunished, Catherine emphasizes the injustice and inequality of power the image contains. Finally, she is clear that the actions of the mob are racialized. Although in the late nineteenth century white, Jewish, Mexican and indigenous American men, and women, were lynched, following the end of Reconstruction in the South lynching came to be understood as a ritual for killing black men.[47] Catherine acknowledges that white men have been lynched, but by comparing their four murders in 26 years to the 'many' carried out against black men, she again underscores the injustice faced by the black community because of 'a fierce and terrible prejudice', a legacy of slavery that had 'corrupted' white people.[48]

'A Lynching Scene in Alabama' inverted the meanings of whiteness the 'lynching committee' meant to represent. On *Anti-Caste*'s cover the black body is not evidence of an effective public execution but the murder of a lonely man. He is an innocent victim of racial violence, regardless of the crime he may or may not have committed.

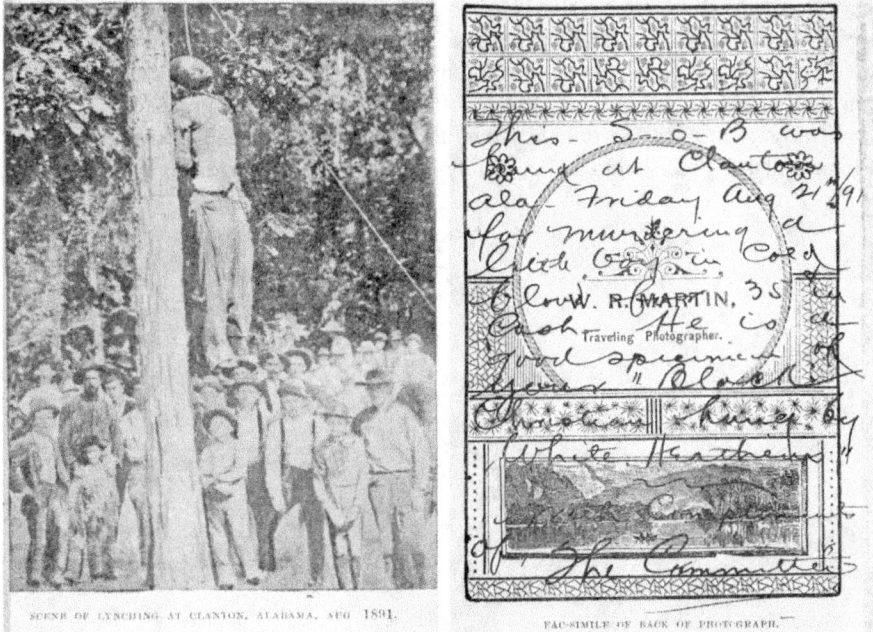

Figure 5.2 Scene of Lynching at Clanton, Alabama, August 1891, as reproduced in Ida B Wells' *A Red Record* (1895)

The white bodies around him are no longer civilized protectors of the law, but revealed as uncivilized perpetrators of, or witnesses to, a murder, as is the imagined community of white Americans beyond the crowd in Alabama who 'look on' at the scene through photographic evidence but voice no complaints. Lynching photographs asserted political identities of whiteness. The presence of skilled labourers, white-collar workers, planters and rising members of the middle classes standing side by side in these images illustrates the opportunity lynchings presented to a town's 'best men' to produce a sense of solidarity among otherwise different white Southerners.[49] Speaking out against the manner and the means used to justify lynchings, Catherine placed herself outside a 'white community' imagined by men and women of the Deep South. In doing so, before an international audience of mostly white readers, Catherine challenged their claims of white superiority and a unified white community. 'How long', Catherine asked, 'will the callous nation look on!'[50]

Catherine's decision to commission a copy of 'A Lynching Scene in Alabama' may have been encouraged by editorial illustrations in the *Richmond Planet*, which she received regularly. Each week above a list of names of those who had been lynched, the *Planet*'s editor John Mitchell Jr published a picture of a black man hanging from a tree. The caption asked, 'Shall this barbarity continue until the God of retribution marshals his strength against the barbarians?' In 1891 Mitchell replaced this with a picture made from a photograph of three lynched men hanging from a tree at Clifton Forge, Virginia.[51] The picture's form is familiar but unlike 'A Lynchng Scene in Alabama' it does not show any members of the white mob to be present. The image, part of an advertisement for the *Planet*, asked potential readers if they shuddered at the picture – 'Of Course You Do', Mitchell retorted (Figure 5.3). In turn *Anti-Caste*'s bold reproduction on a front page may have encouraged other journalists to continue pushing for ways of reproducing images of lynchings as forms of protest.

In August 1893 the *Richmond Planet* and *Fraternity* reported the murder of C J Miller – at Bardwell, Kentucky, on 7 July – who was later proven to be innocent of

Figure 5.3 'You Shudder at the Picture! Of Course You Do', an advertisement for *The Planet*, 1891, created by John Mitchell Jr, who made the drawing by tracing the image from a photograph

the charge that he murdered Ruby and May, two white girls killed near their home in Kentucky. Doubts over Miller's guilt at the time meant the crowd consented to hang rather than burn him as they had originally planned. Exhausted from the weight of the 100lb log-chain used to lead and drag him around the village, Miller's stripped body was hoisted high above the drunken crowd and dropped from a telegraph pole as a result of which his neck broke. Then bullets were fired into his limp body, which was left hanging from the telegraph pole from 3 to 5pm to allow photographers to bring out their cumbersome equipment and capture the scene.[52] Souvenir hunters took Miller's fingers and toes as mementoes. At 5pm his mutilated body was taken down and burnt and soon there was nothing left of C J Miller save a few bones and ashes and the photographs of his body.[53]

Reports about the lynching appeared in the British press the following day including columns in the *Manchester Evening News*, *Glasgow Herald*, *Pall Mall Gazette*, *Yorkshire Evening Post* and the *Sheffield Evening Telegraph*, although at this stage reports from across the Atlantic were sent in anticipation of the lynching taking place. According to the telegram the newspapers had to hand, the huge stake at which Miller would be burnt was being constructed, with the father of the two murdered girls ready to strike the match. Farmers and other spectators were arriving from the surrounding district, ready to bear witness.[54] A similar report appeared in the *Glasgow Herald*, although this included an update from a later telegram that confirmed Miller had been killed, though hung rather than burned.[55] Reports of lynchings in the white American press often assumed or accepted the guilt of the black men involved.[56] Reprinting these accounts without refinement meant these assumptions circulated within the majority of the British newspapers that covered Miller's story. On Monday the *Hull Daily Mail*, *Aberdeen Evening Express* and *Western Mail* were among the papers which circulated the same updated report on the death of the 'murderer and ravisher' of two little girls and that he was baptised by a Methodist 'coloured minister' on the scaffold before his body was hoisted up and allowed to drop.[57] The number of newspapers reporting on the case dropped off during the week until the following Saturday when the *Illustrated Police News* and a number provincial weeklies including the *Tamworth Herald*, *Wrexham Advertiser* and the *Lancaster Gazette* ran reports. These papers all used the original version of the report that circulated on Monday 10 July and despite the days that had passed, like the dailies before them, they offered no additional comment or analysis.[58]

Publishing accounts in August, the *Richmond Planet* and *Fraternity* both took the opportunity to reproduce detailed accounts of the events with an illustration of the mob with Miller's body. Their reproductions were based on line drawings taken from a photograph Wells had acquired while reporting on the event for *Inter-Ocean*.[59] The version published in the *Planet* is a crude reproduction, but clearly shows the familiar motif of the lynching portrait. Miller's hanging body fills the foreground of the frame. The chain around his neck is clearly depicted reaching up towards the unseen bough of a tree. The sketch appeared beneath the headline 'Kentucky's Crime'. Below the picture the *Planet* printed the reported last words by Miller, in which he reinforced his claim to be innocent of the crime, giving his alibi and the address of the home he shared with his wife in Springfield, Illinois. The rough sketching of the image in the *Planet* means that the faces of the crowd are no longer so easily identifiable and become a flat mass of features facing towards the camera. Umbrellas and parasols are held aloft to help keep the sun off some viewers or help them identify themselves more easily in the prints they will buy later.

The deaths of the two girls, Mary and Ruby Ray, had been violent. Mary (18) and Ruby (nine) had their throats cut, their clothing torn and their bodies mutilated.[60] Edwards drew *Fraternity's* readers into the story by comparing their murders to those carried out in London by Jack the Ripper a few years before. Edwards went on to explain that witnesses of the likely suspect all testified that the man they connected to the crime was white, or, according to a fisherman and ferryman, possibly a very light-skinned mulatto man who appeared to be white. It had been Miller's misfortune to be stealing a ride on a freight train going out of Sikeston, Missouri, at the time. Miller fought the brakeman who ordered him off and he was arrested. He wore a woollen shirt, light trousers and a coat to match; he had 12 dollars in paper, two silver dollars and some change in his pockets along with four gold rings, a knife and razor which were rusty and stained. The Skikeston authorities concluded that this must be the man the Kentuckians across the river were searching for.[61]

In *Fraternity* the drawing of Miller's lynching is placed in the centre of the page, interrupting the columns. It is more clearly defined than the *Planet's*. Faces towards the front of the crowd are recognizable individuals. Miller's face is also clearer although the pencil lines have smoothed his skin, removing the dirt and wounds that he must have endured before his hanging. The symbol of violence that does remain clear is the fabric knotted around his waist, an indication that he may have been castrated, the cloth acts as a screen to protect the sensitivities of viewers of the photographic prints.[62] Neither the *Planet* nor *Fraternity* made explicit attempts to draw their readers towards a closer interpretation of the images of C J Miller which they used. There was no further explanation of what the original photograph was meant to do or what particular aspects of the images such as the presence of children at the scene of a social occasion might represent within Southern life. It may have been that by 1893 Mitchell and Edwards felt their readers had enough contextual understanding of their own to place the image in a broader context themselves. Wells used the image as an illustration for her own report on Miller's death in *Red Record* and during a meeting with British MPs in 1894. In this version members of the crowd retain their individuality. *Red Record* also includes a copy of the lynching scene in Alabama. The version used by Wells is not the cut used for *Anti-Caste's* cover, but a copy of the photograph sent to Tourgée (see Figure 5.2). Wells also reproduced the handwritten note inked onto the backing of the photograph. By showing readers the committee's handwritten message, Wells illustrated the dual purpose of commemoration and intimidation served by lynching photographs.

Anti-Caste's commentary on 'A Lynching Scene in Alabama' highlighted the presence of children in the summer scene as illustrative of the white community's indoctrination of a new generation into the ideas and norms of a white supremacist society. 'A Lynching Scene in Alabama' shows only men and boys in the crowd, but other lynching portraits show women and girls participating in lynching events.[63] Parents brought their children so they might effectively learn the consequences of participating in a transgression of caste boundaries, and how black men were punished for challenging white racial superiority. In July 1935 after Rubin Stacey was tortured and killed at Fort Lauderdale, Florida, for 'threatening and frightening' a white woman called Marion Jones, a small number of white girls were photographed viewing his body.[64] The picture shows a young figure hanging from a tree, his feet almost brushing the ground. Stacey's dungarees are ripped and dirty, his hands cuffed in front of him and his neck angled awkwardly as the rope digs into his flesh, pulling his neck out of the collar of his shirt. Around him a group of men, women and girls stand around observing, chatting, grinning.

The NAACP used a version of this image in an antilynching leaflet published around 1936.[65] Placed beneath the photograph, the text directs readers away from Stacy's body, for his 'earthly problems have ended now'. Instead viewers are asked to consider the white children who observe the gruesome display; is the tiny four-year-old child able to comprehend 'the barbarism her elders have perpetrated'? 'Is it horror or gloating on the face of the neatly dressed seven-year-old girl on the right?' To gain the sympathetic attention of white readers the NAACP pamphlet compares the physical torture of Rubin Stacy (brutal but now ended) to the permanent and ongoing psychological damage viewing such horrors had on white children. Catherine explained the presence of children in 'A Lynching Scene in Alabama' as 'Planters teaching their children how to treat offending (defenceless) negroes'. There is no attempt to garner sympathy for the white individuals pictured in *Anti-Caste's* text: 'The look of shameless satisfaction on the faces of the men' and of 'innocent wonder on those of the children as they gaze at the form of the murdered man' were simply 'shocking'. White men, with 'astounding effrontery', were teaching their boys 'how an accused negro ought to be treated – no trial – no defence – murder for murder – or perchance murder for helpless innocence' – 'If 'tis only a nigger, what matter if sometimes you do hang the wrong man!'[66]

The first account of Miller's killing in *Fraternity* appeared in July 1893. A short paragraph, preceding the details of the lynching of William Shorter at Kernstown Station on the Baltimore and Ohio Railway, gave a thin outline of Miller's death as opposed to the graphic detail relayed in the following August issue. The July issue carried no image of C J Miller, but it did contain a poem written by 'E. B. P.'

When and Where?
. . . .
There, where the southern summer
Smiles on a fruitful land,
Where all should share the bounty
Of the great All-Father's hand,
where black and white together
One Brotherhood should be,
Son of a common country,
Equal, erect, and free.

There justice is dishonoured,
Law hangs her head in shame,
Humanity is outraged,

> And Freedom but a name;
> Not liberty, but license –
> Such is the white man's creed,
> With cord and bullet ready
> For each ferocious deed.
>
> Nor these alone – hot irons
> To pierce the quivering frame,
> Stakes where the living victims
> Meet the devouring flame,
> While savage mobs assemble
> And gloat with cruel hate
> Over the fiendish tortures
> Their hard hearts perpetrate.
>
> How long, O Great Republic,
> Wilt thou endure this shame?
> How long shall Freedom suffer
> These insults to her name?
> How long, in suffering patience,
> Will *Christ*, behold this wrong,
> Ere *He* arise in Judgment?
> How long, O Lord, how long?[67]

The creation of the poem in June 1893 suggests E.B.P. was a reader moved to write to express their response to articles they had read in *Anti-Caste*, *Fraternity* and possibly other newspapers in Britain or the United States. There is no indication of whether the author was black or white, a man or a woman, but by sending their poem to *Fraternity* they deliberately placed their prose before a multi-ethnic audience with a majority white component at least receptive to engaging with views critical of whiteness.

Like Catherine's text around 'A Lynching Scene in Alabama', the poem condemns and inverts the intending meanings of lynchings. In E.B.P.'s depiction of society controlled by traditions of colour caste, white Southerners are greedy, refusing to share the produce of a wealthy nation. Lynchings are condemned as not only unlawful and shameful acts but as acts that will incur the wrath of God upon the uncivilized and 'savage' white men who assemble to carry out these torturous crimes motivated not by a desire for justice but by hatred. By declaring the outrage of 'Humanity' at their crimes, the poem breaks down assumptions of universal white identities, for among the humanity that condemns the white Southerners are the white readers of *Fraternity* who are imagined to stand alongside the rest of the human race. E.B.P.'s poem also echoes Catherine's belief that the fates of black and white were intimately intertwined. While racial violence against black people persisted, white people could not be free.

Catherine returned 'A Lynching Scene in Alabama' to Tourgée in March 1893, apologizing that her printers had taken so long to produce the block. With her letter she enclosed a proof copy of the resulting image explaining to Tourgée that now she had the block she could reproduce as many as he needed.[68] Though Catherine did not publish another image of a lynching scene in *Anti-Caste*, like Ida B Wells she did use reproductions to give weight to her arguments. In her interview with the *Scottish Leader* in March 1893, Catherine took the image with her as proof of the atrocities she discussed. The *Leader* chose not to reproduce the image, but it printed a description of the scene in which 'an assembly of men and boys have taken up a position before the camera with the air of having accomplished a worthy deed, while the body of their victim dangles from a branch overhead.'[69] The image was reproduced in the British edition of *Southern Horrors*, produced by the 'Lux' publishing company. *United States Atrocities: Lynch Law* by Ida B Wells included an introduction by Edwards alongside 'A Lynching Scene in Alabama'.[70] Though they had access to the technology to reproduce lynching images, how to use images of lynchings in order to make evident their horror without reproducing the voyeurism inherent in their framing remained a difficult question for activists, artists and curators into the twentieth century.[71]

The Waco Horror appeared as a supplementary report to the July 1916 issue of *Crisis*, the official organ of the NAACP edited by W E B Du Bois. It gave a detailed account of perhaps the most horrific spectacle of lynching that had so far taken place in the United States. The disturbing carnival took place at Waco, about halfway between Dallas and Austin, Texas, on 15 May 1916. The *Crisis* report contains 11 photographs purchased as commemorative cards in Waco by Elisabeth Freeman, a white NAACP supporter who travelled to Waco to investigate the events surrounding the lynching.[72] The first five show important buildings in the city: Baylor University with its American gothic towers; the First Baptist Church, the Court House and City Hall with the Stars and Stripes flying high; The Riggins Hotel – an early skyscraper-like structure with ten stories of comfort and safety for 'sleep where life is safe'.[73] These images were used to illustrate the ordinariness of Waco as a typical Southern city, 'alert, pushing and rich'.[74]

On 8 May the body of 53-year-old Lucy Fryer was found by her children on the floor of the seed shed of the family farm in Robinson, a small community seven miles south of Waco.[75] Jesse Washington, an illiterate 17 year old, who worked as a hired hand on the Fryer farm, quickly became the prime suspect. Initially the entire Washington family was taken into custody although Washington's parents and his brother William were soon released. During questioning Jesse Washington, reportedly discovered in bloodied overalls, gave several conflicting statements but denied any knowledge of Lucy Fryer's death. He did eventually confess to her rape and murder describing where on the Fryer's farm he had buried the murder weapon. Unable to read or write Washington signed his confession with an 'X'. The first attempt to lynch Washington failed as law enforcement officials had taken him out of Waco for his own safety, but he returned for the trial which began on Monday 15 May before a packed courtroom. The audience did not have to wait long for the performance to reach its finale. Despite the importance of rape in the ideology of lynching, there was no mention of this allegation during the trial, and Elisabeth Freeman became doubtful that the rape ever took place.[76] And although there seemed no particular motive for Washington to have turned on Lucy Fryer on that particular day the defence called only Jesse Washington as a witness.[77] The jury took four minutes to find him guilty.

As the judge wrote the verdict into the docket book a group of men seized Washington, forcing him out of the back of the courthouse where a crowd of about 400 people waited in the alley. With a chain around his neck Washington was dragged towards city hall as individuals attacked him, tearing his clothes, stabbing him with knives and battering him with bricks and clubs.[78] The sixth photograph in the series published in the *Crisis* is of 'The Waiting Crowd' taken at the back or among the growing masses waiting for Washington to arrive. The photographer F A Gildersleeve had advance warning of the events enabling him to set his equipment up in city hall.[79] The next photograph is taken from his position above the crowd. Hundreds, perhaps thousands, of people are in the frame, packed into tight circles around the lynching tree where Jesse Washington's naked body lies twisted at its base. Hats at the back of the crowd are titled up as the heads beneath them strain up to get a better look. 'The Waiting Crowd' becomes 'The Mob'.[80] The remaining images are lynching portraits; close-up pictures of a burned and charred body with absent limbs and molten flesh. 'The Victim' and 'The Torture' all show members of the crowd, facing into the lens, once again among them on the ground. The final image in the series Du Bois published is of Jesse's head resting among white hot logs at the base of the lynching tree. The chain, later sold to souvenir collectors at 25 cents a link, still reaches up beyond the frame. The heat from the fire blurs the foreground of the photograph. This is 'Finis'. Du Bois made no apology for including such brutal pictures in the Waco report. He knew that some would question the decision. In publishing the lynching portraits, he intended to directly challenge those who 'so hate the evil of this world that they are unwilling to be disturbed by it'.[81] Lynching photographs provided an arresting form of evidence alongside the statistics, reports, stories and letters that appeared in the *Planet*, the *New York Age* and *Anti-Caste*.[82]

At least part of the reason 'A Lynching Scene in Alabama' appeared on the front page of *Anti-Caste* was to draw readers' attention to the content of the lynching report carried on the inside pages and shock them into action: to force them to see evil. By ending the cover caption with the capitalized rhetorical question 'How long will the callous nation look long!', readers were also being asked how long they could look on. The image is dreadful. The isolated, lonely body juxtaposed with the comfortable crowd below remains deeply upsetting and unsettling. The image still holds the shocking qualities images need to accuse and possibly alter the behaviour of viewers.[83] The transmutation of lynching images to antilynching images is a challenging manifestation of the idea that a photograph is truly subversive not when it frightens, repels or stigmatizes, but when it is pensive and forces viewers to think.[84] Catherine was the first and perhaps the only white editor to use a lynching portrait, of a black body among a white crowd, as an antilynching image before the Second World War.[85] In 1893 Catherine and E.B.P. asked how long white Americans would look on as lynching scenes were enacted again and again across the South, but many did not want to look at all. It remained rare for newspapers edited by white liberals across the United States to reproduce lynching images well into the 1950s.[86]

Things as they should not be

Edwards maintained a high and relentless profile of lynchings in *Fraternity*. They illustrated only too well 'Things as They Are and Should Not Be'. Introduced by Edwards, this regular column covered the social and economic disadvantages placed upon black people, especially Americans from the proposed racial segregation of tax allocations in Alabama to the pervasive attempts to keep black Americans from the ballot box. The reports varied in length from a couple of sentences to detailed paragraphs, covering stories from violent murders to the strange expressions of racism in public spaces. A single column in April 1894 reported the burning of a Catholic school for black children in Tampa, Florida, the murder of two black men in an Arkansas jail, the lynching of two others in Missouri and the ejection of C S Smith from his first-class sleeping car in Jacksonville, Florida, because he was not white. It also reported that H C Smith, editor of the *Cleveland Gazette* and member of the Ohio Legislature, was contemplating suing the restaurant in Columbus, Ohio, that had recently refused him service. *Fraternity* suggested that in all probability Smith would prosecute 'the wretch who keeps oatmeal and large spoons for coloured people'.[87]

Edwards countered these depressing stories with the columns 'Things That Are as They Should Be' and 'To Their Credit'. In these columns more heartening reports were shared, often telling stories of everyday heroism, kindness and conviviality in the United States and Britain: An 'Afro-American' who died saving his fellow workman in Atlanta, the funeral of an 'Afro-American' woman whose pall-bearers were white men from the organization where her husband worked and a Parsee law student from Bombay who received an Honorary Testimonial from the Royal Humane Society for saving a ten-year-old girl from drowning in a canal.[88] An examination of black education in the American South celebrated the development of schools and further education facilities under difficult circumstances. More than 25,000 schools had taught over 2 million black Americans to read and write with 150 schools providing advanced education for the community.[89]

The columns laid claim to and celebrated the successes of people of colour, primarily heralding stories of 'Good Business Men', 'Coloured Inventors' and scientists in North America, where newspapers collected and reported the progress of their communities. The personal achievements of individuals were closely linked to community politics. So the election of Dr N H Hudson from Alabama to the Medical Society of the County of King, Brooklyn, was noted, as he was only the second 'coloured man' to be elected.[90] The successful return of the 'Afro-Canadian' William P Hubbard to a seat on the City Council of Toronto was celebrated as was successful emergency surgery undertaken at Provident Hospital in Chicago, which was owned and staffed by 'Afro-Americans'.[91] Women did appear in these columns, usually as humanitarian benefactors, such as Harriet Hayden, who was born enslaved in Kentucky but, with her husband and child, had escaped to Canada with the help of the Underground Railway. The Hayden family returned to the United States and settled in Boston and when Harriet died she left $5000 to endow a scholarship for 'coloured students' at Harvard University at a time when there were only 15 black students studying at the university.[92]

The aim of integrating the black community into all levels of society in its current form meant that interconnecting issues of class and race were not often directly challenged. As suggested by Rev Gordon's focus on the inequality of first-class train carriages during his train sojourn of the South, issues where race and class fused were not broken open for analysis. In November 1893 *Fraternity* reported on the strike by a group of white waiters at the Avenue Hotel, St Louis, who took exception to a black waiter being placed in charge. As a result of their strike all of them found themselves replaced by black workers. Given the exclusion of black people from so many employment opportunities *Fraternity* celebrated this reversal of fortune.[93] But here were signs of the problematic outcomes of segregation present in Douglass' earlier warnings. The failure of white labour to support black labour, and the burden of inequality this placed on black workers, could still be clearly seen in civil rights struggles in the 1960s, memorably in Martin Luther King Jr's final campaign supporting the rights of black sanitation workers in Memphis.[94] At the end of the nineteenth century, the interests of white workers in the United States and across the British Empire became solidified within narratives of whiteness.[95] This was not an identity imposed upon them, but one they demanded.[96] Unable and unwilling to separate their concerns for their own exploitation from their aspiration to remain within the dominant racial structure, white working men in southern states posed side by side with their town's 'best men' among black bodies.[97] In addition to the collapse in the possibilities of uniting black and white labour in the United States, these divisive forms of solidarity expressed themselves in conflicts between white and Chinese workers in Australia and the United States and between white, black, Chinese and Indian workers in southern Africa – conflicts Catherine and Edwards highlighted in *Anti-Caste* and *Fraternity*. They were able to do so by maintaining links with editors and reporters of newspapers in the United States and across the Empire which focused on the experiences of the oppressed and so created their own place in the counternarratives of white supremacy.

Notes

1 'Address to the nations of the world by the Pan-African conference,' in Langley, *Ideologies of Liberation*, 738–739.
2 Smith, *Photography*, 1.
3 'Mr Moody and the colour line', *Fraternity*, January 1894, 13.
4 Smith, *Photography*, 1.
5 *Anti-Caste*, October 1891, 1.
6 *Anti-Caste*, May 1892, 6.
7 On Douglass as a 'radical reconstructionist' see Gooding-Williams, *Du Bois*.
8 *Anti-Caste*, January 1889, 3.
9 *Anti-Caste*, August 1889, 4.
10 Smith, 'Lynching photographs'.
11 *Anti-Caste*, January 1889, 2.
12 'A negro wantonly shot', *Anti-Caste*, April 1889, 3.
13 Silkey, 'Evolving morality'.

14 SoRelle, 'The "Waco Horror"'. SoRelle bases this on the record that 3224 occurred in the United States between 1889 and 1918.
15 'On the impending death of C J Miller', *Manchester Evening News*, 8 July 1893, 2; 'The lynching of Italians', *North Eastern Daily Gazette*, 18 March 1891, 4, among many others. The event caused a serious diplomatic incident between the United States and Italy; for an account of this, see Silkey, 'Evolving morality'. On the spike in reports of lynchings see 'The negro question', *Bristol Mercury*, January 22, 1891, 5.
16 *Anti-Caste*, February 1890, 3.
17 *Anti-Caste*, February 1890.
18 *Anti-Caste*, July and August 1890, 4.
19 Wells-Barnett, 'A Red Record', in *On Lynchings*, 112.
20 *New York Times*, 21 February 1892, 6; on the reputation of the *New York Times* and lynching, see Perloff, 'Press and lynchings'.
21 *Manchester Courier and Lancashire General Advertiser*, 22 February 1892, 5; *Sheffield Independent*, 22 February 1892, 5; *Belfast News-Letter*, 22 February 1892, 5.
22 *Glasgow Herald*, 22 February 1892, 8.
23 *Manchester Evening News*, 22 February 1892, 2.
24 Gunning, *Race, Rape and Lynching*.
25 Wells-Barnett, 'Southern Horrors', in *On Lynchings*, 39.
26 See Collins, 'Introduction'.
27 Rao, *The Caste Question*, 48.
28 Rao, *The Caste Question*, 49.
29 In the context of India see Rao, *The Caste Question* and Chandra, *The Sexual Life of English*.
30 Wells-Barnett, 'A Red Record', in *On Lynchings*, 109.
31 Wells-Barnett, 'A Red Record', in *On Lynchings*, 115.
32 Wells-Barnett, 'A Red Record', in *On Lynchings*, 2002.
33 Carrigan narrates one such example from Texas in *The Making of a Lynching Culture*, 112.
34 *Anti-Caste*, February and March 1892, 4, original emphasis.
35 *Anti-Caste*, November 1892, 4, original emphasis, also material by Tourgée reprinted on page 3.
36 Apel, *Imagery of Lynching*.
37 On the multiple roles of a photographic print, see Sontag, *Regarding the Pain of Others*.
38 Both sides of the postcard are reproduced in Allen, *Without Sanctuary*. It had originally been assumed this to be a picture of Jesse Washington, murdered in Waco, Texas, in 1916, but based on the post stamp of Temple, Texas, William Carrigan argues that it is an image of Will Stanley. See Carrigan, *The Making of a Lynching Culture*.
39 *The Crisis*, 2 June 1910, 71. The report was based on an article by Bishop Gailor of Tennessee, who urged people to speak out against the lynching in an article for an unnamed Memphis newspaper.
40 Samuel, *Theatres of Memory*; Ryan, *Picturing Empire*; Apel, *Imagery of Lynching*.
41 Smith, 'Lynching photographs'.
42 Apel, *Imagery of Lynching*.
43 On the Statutes see Smith, *Photography*.
44 *Anti-Caste*, January 1893, 5.
45 *Anti-Caste*, January 1893, 5.

46 *Anti-Caste*, January 1893, 5.
47 Apel, *Imagery of Lynching*.
48 *Anti-Caste*, January 1893, 1.
49 Wood, *Lynching and Spectacle*.
50 *Anti-Caste*, January 1893, 1.
51 Alexander, *Race Man*, 41.
52 *Fraternity*, August 1893, 8.
53 *Fraternity*, August 1893, 8; *Richmond Planet*, August 26, 1893; Wells-Barnett, 'A Red Record', in *On Lynchings*, 92.
54 *Manchester Evening News*, 8 July 1893, 2.
55 *Glasgow Herald*, 8 July 1893, 5.
56 Perloff, 'Press and lynchings'.
57 'Baptised on the scaffold', *Hull Daily Mail*, 10 July 1893, 3; 'A negro's terrible fate and the presence of a Methodist minister', *Portsmouth Evening News*, 10 July 1893, 2.
58 *Illustrated Police News, Tamworth Herald, Wrexham Advertiser*, and *Lancaster Gazette*, all 15 July 1893.
59 In its article, the *Planet* reported that Wells gave a graphic account of the lynching in the *Inter-Ocean* and in her memoir Wells references her use of the image for the article and when presenting her arguments in Britain. Duster, *Crusade for Justice*.
60 *Fraternity*, August 1893, 6. These are the ages of the sisters given by *Fraternity*, although earlier reports gave their ages as 16 and 12, for example, see *Manchester Evening News*, 8 July 1893, 2.
61 *Fraternity*, August 1893, 6–7.
62 *Fraternity*, August 1893, 8.
63 For a discussion of the presence of women in lynching images, see essays by Apel and Smith, *Lynching Photographs*; Apel, *Imagery of Lynching*..
64 As Apel observes in this picture a black woman is also present, her face turned away from Stacey's body, see Apel, 'Lynching photographs', 42–78.
65 The cover picture of the pamphlet is reproduced in Apel, 'Lynching photographs', 60.
66 *Anti-Caste*, January 1893, 5.
67 *Fraternity*, July 1893, 6, original emphasis.
68 Impey to Tourgée, 2 March 1893, 6700, The *Albion W. Tourgée* Papers.
69 *Scottish Leader*, 29 March 1893, 4.
70 Wells, *United States Atrocities, Lynch Law*, Schomburg Center for Research in Black Culture, New York Public Library.
71 The NAACP and American Communist Party developed rival antilynching exhibitions in New York in 1935. 'An art commentary of lynching' organized by the NAACP opened in February. Curated by a collective of leftist activists, 'Struggle for negro rights' opened 1 March. For a discussion of artists' responses to lynching photography, see Apel, *Imagery of Lynching*; Langa, 'Two antilynching art exhibitions'.
72 For more on Elisabeth Freeman, who was an active militant suffragette during the six years she spent in England before returning to the United States in 1911, see Bernstein, *First Waco Horror*.
73 'Waco's new hotel', The Texas Collection, Baylor University, http://www.flickr.com/photos/texascollectionbaylor/6170018804/in/set-72157624609439808/, accessed 8 March 2013.
74 'The Waco Horror', Supplement to the *Crisis*, July 1916, 2.
75 This account of the events leading up to the lynching of Jesse Washington is taken from SoRelle, 'The "Waco Horror"'.

76 Bernstein, *First Waco Horror*.
77 Bernstein, *First Waco Horror*. Bernstein recounts that on 10 June 1916 the *Chicago Defender* published an article that Lucy Fryer's husband was responsible for her murder though word of the story had not been sent out to the daily papers or the Associated Press.
78 SoRelle, 'The "Waco Horror"'.
79 Bernstein, *First Waco Horror*.
80 *Crisis*, July 1916, supplement, 5.
81 *Crisis*, July 1916, 135.
82 Raiford, *Imprisoned*, 2011.
83 Sontag, *Regarding the Pain of Others*.
84 Barthes, *Camera Lucida*.
85 On the contrast between the circulation in the press of images of white and black men who had been lynched, see Wood, *Lynching and Spectacle*.
86 For an examination of the white press preventing the circulation of images of 14-year-old Emmett Tills' body following his lynching in Mississippi in 1955, see Berger, *Seeing Through Race*.
87 *Fraternity*, April 1894, 12.
88 'Parsee student and died to save a friend', *Fraternity*, September 1893, 6; 'Funeral in Albuquerque', *Fraternity*, November 1893, 12.
89 *Fraternity*, March 1894, 7.
90 *Fraternity*, September 1863, 7.
91 'Afro-Canadian councillor', *Fraternity*, February 1894, 4; 'Afro-American surgery', *Fraternity*, September 1893, 7.
92 'To their credit', *Fraternity*, February 1894, 7.
93 *Fraternity*, November 1863, 12.
94 Honey, *Going Down Jericho Road*.
95 See Lake and Reynolds, *Drawing the Global Colour Line*.
96 Hyslop, 'Imperial working class'.
97 Wood, *Lynching and Spectacle*; Hyslop, 'Imperial working class'.

6

Firing at Long Range

They are firing the cannon at long range. Its balls may not strike the object at which it is aimed, but its noise is directing to the South the attention of the civilized world.
Richmond Planet, 1895

Although the 'American Question' dominated the inaugural issue of *Anti-Caste*, within six months it had included discussions on Australia, Brazil, Canada, India and colonies in the Caribbean and Africa. Catherine mapped out experiences of prejudice in these countries through firsthand accounts and letters to the editor, but primarily her sources came from foreign news reports. Conscious of the dominance of the United States in the first issue, Catherine wrote to the APS asking to be put in touch with potential contributors for future editions. She needed 'a larger number of African and other news' if *Anti-Caste* was not going to be dominated by the politics of the United States.[1] The diversity of contributions she hoped for did not come to fruition, but by keeping in touch with black American, Indian and African newspapers such as Fortune's *New York Freeman* and *Age*, *India* and *Imvo Zabantsandu* (*Native Opinion*), Catherine presented *Anti-Caste* readers with voices that challenged the normative narrative of white supremacy. Through their newspapers black American editors such as Thomas and Emanuel Fortune and H C Smith of *The Cleveland Gazette* expressed their support for *Anti-Caste* republishing its news items and opinions for their own readers. Receiving attention in the international Indian and black press placed *Anti-Caste* within a network of newsprint that sought to report 'the truth' of geographies of oppression. *Anti-Caste* performed a rare role, a white-edited newspaper that did not twist the words and opinions of black people against them. For those fighting racial oppression, *Anti-Caste* represented the possibility of equality in print. But geographies of empire, particularly language, determined Catherine's access to print cultures, shaping the geographies of oppression placed before *Anti-Caste*'s readers and leaving some out on the margins of the periodical's geographical imagination.

T. THOMAS FORTUNE
Editor *New York Age*: Author of " In Plain Black and White "

Figure 6.1 Portrait of T Thomas Fortune, from J W E. Bowen, ed., 'Africa and the American Negro', Gammon Theological Seminary, 1896

Networks of newsprint

In 'An English View of the Afro-American Problem', published in April 1888, the *New York Age* reported that Liverpool's *Daily Post* had recently devoted a column to race relations in the United States. For sources the *Post* used an article in *Contemporary Review* by George W Cable, a report from the British Consul in Texas and material on Fortune's call for a new Afro-American League taken from *Anti-Caste* – 'an English periodical conducted by Miss Catherine Impey, the famous friend of the Afro-American'.[2] The *Age* analyzed the *Post's* piece, appreciative of the paper's broad discussion and the fact that such an influential paper had addressed itself to the 'Afro-American question'. The credit for capturing the *Post's* attention was given to Catherine, 'the brave little woman of Somersetshire who has for years fought the demon caste not only in England but America as well'. The *Age* hoped her new periodical would prove to be a beacon of light for the English public, so that they might not veer away from facing – 'as they had shown signs of doing' – the real conditions and feelings of black Americans.[3]

By October news of *Anti-Caste's* publication reached the readers of *The Cleveland Gazette*. Founded in 1883, the Ohio-based *Gazette* was edited by one of its founders, H C Smith. One of the youngest editors in the country, Smith ran what was considered by some to be one of the best edited newspapers in the United States, and his brilliant and fearless writing made the *Gazette* essential reading for ordinary citizens as well as all black members of the Ohio legislature.[4] The *Gazette* commented on a number of articles published in *Anti-Caste* which highlighted the politics of the United States and the importance of syndicating news. Referring to *Anti-Caste* as 'our English contemporary' the *Gazette* endorsed Catherine's method of reprinting material from American journals to advance the cause for 'equal rights in America by gaining English sympathy' on behalf of black Americans.[5] The *Gazette* remained convinced that without international pressure the hopes of gaining civil rights in the United States were remote. Supporters such as the known and imagined readers of *Anti-Caste* were important allies in their local and national battles.[6] The paper approved of *Anti-Caste's* content and tone, commending its 'vigorous and unrelenting fight against American prejudice and any germs of that prejudice that may be sown in the soil of our English friends by American tourists and renegades'.[7] Reprinting a piece in which an *Anti-Caste* editorial focused on the difference between knowing about racial prejudice and doing something about it, the *Gazette* confirmed the importance of Catherine's aim to ensure her readers not only knew 'about Caste, but to make them *set their souls against it*'.[8] Like the *Age*, the *Gazette* wished Catherine a long and prosperous voyage on the political waters she had chosen to navigate.[9]

Two months later the *Age* drew its readers' attention to *Anti-Caste's* November issue. This piece, beneath the headline 'An Englishwoman's work', praised the geographical span of reporting in *Anti-Caste*, highlighting articles on the evils of caste in India, the manumission of slaves in Egypt alongside the ill-treatment of 'American Negroes' in the South. The *Age* reprinted an extensive extract from an editorial on the perfidious treatment of Chinese workers, concluding that the 'compact but powerful pleader of the cause of oppressed nationalities' continued to be full of promise.[10] For the *Age*, Catherine acted as an agent from within, awakening the conscience of white people to the politics of responsibility and duty they had towards people who carried a different skin colour to their own. With distribution in Britain, India and America through friends of the movement, the *Age* saw much promise and undoubtedly productive results ahead. The following June the *Christian Recorder*, published weekly by the African Methodist Episcopal Church *'for the Dissemination of Religion, Morality, Literature and Science'* in Philadelphia, also published an admiring review, informing its readers that Catherine stood among 'the bravest and most correct of Caucasian on the race subject.'[11] Although small, *Anti-Caste* bristled with news and notes on the mistreatment by white people of their Asian and African brethren. The *Recorder* knew of no other journal that maintained such an impressive philosophy on the subject and suggested *Anti-Caste* be read by every family of 'Negro descent', its analysis and content providing both 'an inspiration as well as an instruction.'[12]

The *Liverpool Daily Post* professed similar hopes for *Anti-Caste* in an extensive editorial review published in March 1889. Established as one of the first penny dailies in Britain, Edward Richard Russell edited the *Liverpool Daily Post* from 1869 to 1919. Under his tenure the paper maintained a consistently radical stance, giving full support to the Northern states during the American Civil War and to Irish Home Rule.[13] As the *New York Age* noted the *Post* had a broad and prominent readership in Liverpool. Growing to cover the city of Liverpool, west Cheshire, southwest Lancashire and north Wales, the paper claimed (along with the *Liverpool Echo*, its cheaper evening sister paper) daily circulation figures of 65,000 a day in 1889, rising to 165,000 in

1892.[14] Russell and Catherine had known each other since the early 1880s and Russell supported *Anti-Caste* through editorials in the *Post*.[15] His 1889 review of recent *Anti-Caste* issues began by acknowledging that 'caste rules the world, and race prejudice is its sinister and effective ally'. Attempting to fight against such a gigantic evil might seem hopeless to most readers, but he cautioned those who would dismiss a small monthly tract and 'a woman's intellect' as effective weapons with which to challenge the 'hydra-growth' of racial prejudice over centuries. Reflecting on the legacy of *Uncle Tom's Cabin*, Russell considered that when Beecher Stowe's story appeared in an American newspaper, long before any thoughts of worldwide circulation, its influence against the power of the Southern States must have seemed slight. Who could now say whether it did not prove as effective as the military legions of Grant or the policies of Lincoln? Russell agreed with *Anti-Caste's* premise that slavery represented a campaign against a tangible evil, whereas untangling the cultural and political consequences of racial prejudice would prove to be far more difficult; tackling caste prejudice required a battle against theoretical ideas of racial difference that rather than being condemned were instead at times applauded as the most admirable patriotism.[16]

Reflecting on the influence of *Anti-Caste* the following year, Catherine admitted that measuring its effect was in fact an impossible task. One encouraging gauge came from the movement's co-workers who wrote to tell Catherine that they had held little interest in the cause before reading *Anti-Caste*.[17] Their deeper engagement prompted them to supply their editor with newspaper notices, pamphlets and magazine articles on the caste question, giving examples of the injustices so often suffered by people of colour.[18] Readers who sent in journals 'from the poor and oppressed of many lands' formed the staple of the paper's existence providing 'its daily food'.[19] Material in the Alabama *Plantation Missionary*, the *Minneapolis Appeal* and the *Richmond Planet* complemented material from the Calcutta-based *Indian* and other Indian papers, and *Brotherhood* and *Lux* published in Britain. Although *Anti-Caste* obtained information weekly from English and colonial papers supplied by the London News cutting agency, it subscribed directly to *India* (the organ of the National Congress Movement introduced to *Anti-Caste* readers in 1890 as a new and important monthly journal for the discussion of Indian affairs, published in London), the *American Missionary* and the *New York Age*.[20]

Imvo Zabantsundu, 'the first African newspaper of significance published in the Cape Colony' founded by John Tengo Jabavu (1859–1921) in 1884, provided a black perspective from southern Africa.[21] Catherine highlighted *Imvo*, which she initially received from the secretary of the APS, in December 1890 when she gratefully acknowledged the receipt 'week by week from foreign lands' of numerous newspapers and magazines 'evidently often sent by those who themselves suffer by caste'.[22] She was especially indebted to the editors of the *Boston Courant*, *Philadelphia Sentinel* and the quarterly *AME Church Review*, which by 1891 had a circulation of 1500 with copies distributed in the United States, Africa, Europe and Haiti.[23] Along with the editor of the Bahamas *Freeman*, these 'Afro-American publications' regularly sent complementary copies of their papers to Street.[24] These networks of periodical exchange created a significant source of content and contextual information for journalists constructing counternarratives of imperial cultures. In November 1894 *Imvo* acknowledged receiving the *Statesman*, 'an organ of the Coloured People in Colorado'. Jabavu presumed the paper came as an 'exchange' and gratefully added it to his list.²⁵

These dynamic exchanges of print culture continued under Edwards' editorship. Not all articles in *Fraternity* referenced their source but many of them were presumably drawn from the international papers *Fraternity* received including the *Richmond Planet*, *The Monitor*, *New York Age*, *Boston Courant*, *Cleveland Gazette*, *Barbados Tax-payer*, *Demerara Daily Chronicle*, *Asia* and the *Johannesburg Star*.²⁶ Articles and comment referencing the *Colored American*, Chicago's daily *Inter-Ocean*, *San Francisco Call* and the *Nashville Citizen* appeared alongside material gathered from British newspapers such as the *Manchester Guardian*, *Daily News* (London), *Leeds Mercury*, *Sheffield Independent* and the *Liverpool Daily Post*.²⁷ A list of newspapers received in June 1894 included longstanding associations with the black American press plus *Hindostan*, *The Gold Coast Methodist Times*, *Demerara Daily* and *The Cornwall Times*.²⁸ Receiving a large number of locally published newspapers allowed *Anti-Caste* and *Fraternity* to challenge the dominance of news agencies in reporting overseas news. Edwards acknowledged the great debt the paper had to friends in all parts of the world who sent in their local papers. But there was a geographical unevenness to the material that arrived at *Fraternity*'s offices on Paternoster Row, one of the centres of the London publishing trade, a five-minute walk from St Paul's Cathedral.²⁹ The Americans sent their material in regularly and punctually, but not enough local news came in from the British colonies and Africa.³⁰ During the discussions that established *Fraternity* in the summer of 1893, Edwards proposed the paper send its own 'travelling agent or correspondent' to report from the United States.³¹ The expense of foreign correspondents undoubtedly played a part in the SRBM's decision to rely upon their own authorized and registered 'trustworthy' correspondents and local agents who, they believed, would be more able to get reliable information.³² Articles from 'our own correspondent' on the Chinese Restriction Act and from Johannesburg did appear though. Thomas Fortune wrote extended letters especially for *Fraternity* readers on at least three occasions and John Stuart, editor of the *Isle of Wight Express*, wrote a column on his time 'Among the American Negroes' for *Anti-Caste*.³³

For material that did not find its way into the main body of the periodical, Edwards introduced a new regular column 'Concerning Ourselves in the Magazines', which directed readers to items presumed to be of interest to them recently published in periodicals and newspapers.³⁴ In March 1894 the columnist's author decided there was not much around of interest to readers, but in May he or she found more to review in articles from *Nineteenth Century*, the *Forum*, *Contemporary Review*, *Review of Reviews*, *Fireside Magazine*, *Home Words*, *Leisure Hour*, *World Travel* and *Indian Magazine*, a monthly published in London by the National Indian Association which provided a unique space within British print culture for debates on colonial political and social reform in which both Indians and Britons took part.³⁵ *World Travel* was complimented for being a 'useful little periodical' which concerned itself with 'the ways and means of "getting about"' and provided useful information on the manners and customs of those living overseas. *World Travel* also knew something of *Fraternity*, referring to it in an article on the history of 'Applying the Lash to the Kafir'.³⁶ *Fraternity* also gave a positive review of the new book by Mary Marks, which had just made its appearance in the circulating libraries. Although a novel, the columnist argued that *Thorough* gave great insight into the 'subjugation of Ireland' and provided general revelations of what 'conquest' really signified, with British male characters glorying in their own shame.[37]

Geographies of distribution

Beyond the homes of individual subscribers, the geography of *Anti-Caste's* readership depended upon the localities of men and women who offered to distribute additional copies of the paper around their towns, places of work or other activist networks they belonged to. In 1889 Frederic Sessions pledged to circulate the paper among working folk offering to place it among the temperance literature which his well-networked staff of men distributed monthly to several villages around Gloucester. He acknowledged this hardly met the need, but in this way Sessions thought he could distribute a hundred copies a month.[38] The proposal made Sessions one of *Anti-Caste's* most important distributors. This illustrates how Catherine made use of pre-existing networks to circulate *Anti-Caste* both at home and abroad. Of the distributors named in *Anti-Caste's* 1890 annual report, Thomas King took the largest numbers offering to direct and post a few hundred copies each month from his home in Newcastle. Peter Mackenzie handed out 50 copies a month in Edinburgh. In Bristol Elizabeth Nash and Reverend Broughton Knight (a member of the Congregational Theological Institute) distributed over 40 copies a month between them. Pardoe Yates took 18 copies for Wiltshire, Lydia Bunting 18 for Charlbury, Oxon, and the same number went to Herbert Nicholson in Sunderland (Figure 6.2).

By the end of 1888, irrespective of those who received *Anti-Caste* for free distribution, the list of subscribers had reached 189. A year later 137 had renewed their subscription (with a few more late payers to come) and 123 new subscribers had joined including Fanny Jackson Coppin, Mary Estlin, Orishatukeh Faduma (Figure 6.3), W F Mackenzie from Demerara and G E Symonette in the Bahamas. From these subscribers an international network of 50 individuals, at least 13 of whom were women, distributed 1700–1900 copies a month. Some like Eliza Clarke in Milverton, Miss Brown in Eversham and Mrs C A J Mann in New Haven, Connecticut, took just a few copies each.[39] Rev T R Couch distributed 100 copies in London, alongside Celestine Edwards, who, although not a subscriber, took 8 copies for distribution in the capital. Closer to home Catherine continued to enrol the help of a number of her neighbours. Reverends Bartlett and Boulter, J A Seymor and John Tapleton, all from Street, distributed 62 copies between them. Although the majority of *Anti-Caste* subscribers continued to be based in Britain, copies were sent to individual subscribers in the United States, the Caribbean, Australia and West Africa. The January 1890 annual address reported 150 copies of *Anti-Caste* were sent monthly to an elder of the AME Church in South Carolina for distribution among leading workers in his district.[40] A year on in Philadelphia Fanny Jackson Coppin and Dr Nathan T Mossell took 18 copies each, and Dr E C Young took 9 copies for distribution in Ohio. In the Caribbean half a dozen copies were sent to the Bahamas, 15 to two men in Barbados. Nine copies were sent care of R H Habgood to West Australia.[41]

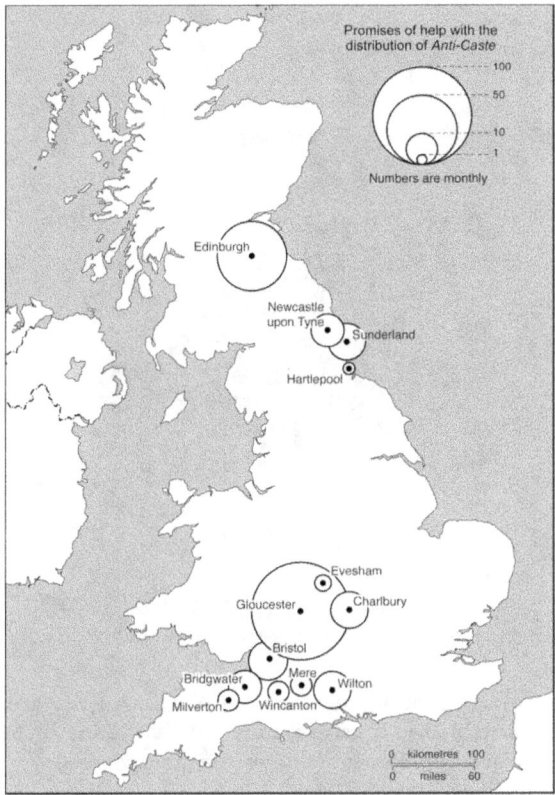

Figure 6.2 Locations given for the free distribution of *Anti-Caste*. The circulation of issues beyond the core subscribers of *Anti-Caste* relied on a network of men and women who distributed issues to cafes, libraries, reading rooms and among their own activist and kinship networks. This map shows the locations of those who made 'Promises of Help in Distribution' during the first year of *Anti-Caste*'s publication, highlighting the importance of Catherine's kinship networks in the west of England to the foundation of *Anti-Caste*'s reading community, *Anti-Caste*, March, 1889, 4. This list also included Mrs C A J Mann of New Haven, Connecticut

Access to working-class readers came mostly through connections with charitable or public institutional organizations. Some, such as a Seaman's Mission in London, requested copies (in this case 100 copies monthly) directly from Catherine. Others came from successful lobbying by supporters like Peter Mackenzie, who, in addition to the 50 he distributed personally, persuaded the principal public libraries in Glasgow, Leith, Dundee and Inverness to take regular issues in 1889. A large provincial Sunday School took 100 copies, as did the headmaster of a school in South Wales. These institutes, which received free copies thus not financially supporting the anticaste movement, were never listed as subscribers, though the distribution of *Anti-Caste* to clubs, libraries, sailors' homes and teachers was extended as fast as funds allowed. Catherine

ORISHETUKEH FADUMA, B. D.
Native of the Yoruba Tribe, West Africa ; Educated in Sierra Leone, London, and in Yale University

Figure 6.3 Portrait of Orishatukeh Faduma, from J W E Bowen, ed., 'Africa and the American Negro', Gammon Theological Seminary, 1896 (the spelling of Faduma's name here is incorrect though it does appear in this form in other sources).

wished she could get a thousand young or old friends to volunteer in its distribution, with each taking 10–50 or more copies to give out monthly. Once printed it would require little extra work for Catherine and her assistant to send out 20,000 in place of the 2000 they sent out in 1890, but it involved a considerable outlay in postage and additional printing costs.[42] As Thomas Fortune noted in 1891, running a newspaper ate up money fast.[43] Further expansion had to wait until subscribers' funds could support it. In 1892 Catherine published a plea for help for more funds, although in her 1893 annual address she reflected on another year of continuous, if moderate, growth.

By 1893 the subscribers were now mostly well known to each other. Although a number of readers had fallen off the subscription list, others, such as Celestine Edwards, had returned but only a dozen new readers had signed up. A total of £77 raised during the year supported the costs of printing 3500 copies of *Anti-Caste* every month, but the cost of posting these issues and the need to purchase foreign and British journals that were not part of free-exchange agreements meant that a deficit of £8 lay on the books. Still, Catherine remained optimistic and there were new opportunities to be seized. A reduction in the cost of foreign postage meant that a record number of free copies had been dispatched abroad in 1892, and Catherine hoped that for every free copy distributed in 1892, 99 more would be posted out in 1893.[44] Any possibilities for expansion in the distribution of copies continued to rely upon the distribution network and all those who worked to sustain it. These unpaid agents performed a variety of roles. An unnamed man in Yorkshire delivered *Anti-Caste* to 16 public reading rooms; others distributed copies among their own circle of friends or enclosed a copy in a letter to friends and family abroad; yet others encouraged readers of free copies to become committed subscribers.

With the enthusiasm levered by Ida B Wells' tour, *Fraternity* launched itself onto an enthusiastic network of volunteers. During October 1893, the Portsmouth branch of the SRBM sold or gave out over 400 copies. Their black agent for *Lux*, Mr Solomon Masse, also worked hard to support *Fraternity* and at an SRBM talk he gave a short sketch of his own experience of black life in the United States.[45] Over the coming months details of new branches were published and the influence of women on the movement became increasingly apparent with the majority of the branch secretaries being women. The publication of the SRBM's *Annual Report* for 1894 provided a national picture of the Society through its regional branches. In Portsmouth the SRBM had secured 250 signatures for membership and ensured that the issues of concern to the SRBM were raised at local discussions and literary meetings. They sent out copies of *Fraternity* to clergymen, institutions, associations and hotels in town as well as in the suburbs, in addition to securing regular places for the magazine on the public reading tables at the Free Library. Ella Fox recorded 248 members enrolled on her books in Bristol, 74 of whom subscribed to *Fraternity*.[46]

Newcastle boasted 591 members with a committee of 12 that met on a monthly basis. To spread the message of the SRBM effectively they divided the city into three districts, ensuring that copies of *Fraternity* appeared on the tables of the Free Library, cafes and the conservative club, and they sold about 250 copies each month. The Gateshead branch had sold 91 copies, but delivered almost 400 free copies onto the tables of public libraries and cocoa-rooms. The signatures of 140 members pledging to uphold the Society's aims had been secured during the year. From Birmingham, Miss Scott MacLlwaine reported a membership of 225 and the distribution of around 900 copies of *Fraternity*. Miss M Shilliton reported that when she had become secretary in Sheffield six months earlier there were only two people on her membership list, but the number had now grown to 32 and she distributed two dozen copies of the magazine each month. In London Edwards acted as the main contact for the Society while additional secretaries set up locally focused branches. Mrs Brooks, based in Victoria Park in east London, had obtained 107 signatures for membership and reported that her sales of *Fraternity* were steadily increasing. Catherine's West of England branch reported that their principal work during the first few months had been to fund the free distribution of *Fraternity*. Their efforts had resulted in mailing about 18,000 copies to India, China, South and West Africa and Europe in addition to several hundred individuals in the United States and the West Indies.[47]

Reading *Anti-Caste*

As Catherine reported, a number of British radical and humanitarian publications voiced their support for *Anti-Caste* including the *British Friend*, which encouraged its readers to become subscribers and in 1889 placed sample copies of *Anti-Caste* in the flyleaf of the journal. The *Vegetarian Messenger* gave forthright support accepting that in reporting on some of the 'burning injustices done to coloured people of various races by the scandalous insolence of the white races' and more particularly the British, *Anti-Caste* filled a political gap.[48] The *Vegetarian Messenger* also endorsed Catherine's argument that racial prejudice had to be owned by white people. Racial prejudice was not a natural event which was 'hopeless to fight against' like a rising tide, but a construction of society with a history, not within a context of centuries, but in the relatively recent history of trans-Atlantic slavery. Attempts to defeat racial prejudice could not wait for a miraculous intervention but should be addressed by those that perpetrated it and not just by those who suffered from it. The *Vegetarian Messenger* recommended *Anti-Caste* to its readers and encouraged all those who could afford it to become its subscribers.[49]

Those individuals who can be identified from the published subscriber lists suggest that *Anti-Caste* attracted an audience of white men and women who are still well known for their progressive politics, others who are no longer remembered for their politics and people of colour whose interest in eradicating racism came out of their experiences of everyday life in the United States and the British Empire. As editor of the *Vegetarian Magazine*, Josiah Oldfield supported *Anti-Caste* through his editorial comments and by being a named subscriber. The Wapping-born writer William Wymark Jacobs and one of his sisters became joint subscribers in 1894.[50] Born in Sunderland, where he lived for most of his life, Thomas William Backhouse came from a well-known Quaker horticultural family. Elected a fellow of the Royal Astronomical Society in 1873 he became a subscriber in 1889 and appeared on most of the subscriber lists.[51]

Joseph Jackson Fuller appears as a subscriber in 1891. Most likely born enslaved in Spanish Town, Jamaica, Fuller aimed for a career in the church and became ordained as a Baptist priest in 1859. He became deeply involved in Cameroon for over 30 years. He made his first trip to England in 1869 to visit the family of his second wife in Norfolk. His son (with his first wife, a Jamaican school teacher who died in 1859) was placed in an apprenticeship in a Norwich engineering company before Joseph returned to Cameroon. About a decade later Joseph settled in London, first in Barnes and then Stoke Newington. He became a popular lecturer at Baptist and missionary meetings, speaking to an audience of 4000 at Birmingham Town Hall in 1889.[52] James Theodore Holly, the first black American bishop of the Episcopal Church, first held a subscription in 1889 while he was bishop of Haiti. Born in 1829 in Washington DC, Holly was the descendent of freed slaves. He spent his early years in Washington DC and Brooklyn, where he met Frederick Douglass and other black abolitionists. Baptized and raised a Catholic, he left the church over a dispute about ordaining local black clergy and joined the Episcopal Church in 1852. He moved to Haiti as a missionary in 1861 and in 1874 was consecrated as a missionary bishop.[53]

It is difficult to glean how these and the many other readers engaged with and interpreted the content of *Anti-Caste*. A subscriber dropping off the list may indicate a lack of enthusiasm, but as Edwards' links to *Anti-Caste* show subscribers who dropped on and off the list could still maintain strong connections with the community. With so many free copies being distributed, they could continue to read month by month, even if they no longer paid. The engagement of some readers comes clearly through the letters they sent, which were published by Catherine and Edwards. James Theodore Holly wrote as 'one of the long proscribed African race' to assure Catherine that *Anti-Caste* held great interest to him and he enclosed a donation of five shillings to support the cause.⁵⁴ *Anti-Caste* did not have a formal column for letters to the editor, but Catherine published 'Words of Cheer', which included extracts of letters from readers who, like Holly, sent in their support, encouragement and endorsement. Like all letters to the editor, these illustrate the feelings of only a small proportion of readers and their letters were selected and pruned down by Catherine, possibly substantially altering their text in the process.⁵⁵

Individual readers like Henry Mason Joseph regretted the periodical remained so small. Although for others, as Catherine guessed, this remained part of its advantage. Emily Howland, a Quaker from Sherwood, New York, greatly admired *Anti-Caste*. Known for her work within the women's movement and on education, particularly among black Americans, Howland commented that *Anti-Caste* was much 'needed against the cruel race prejudice which is our sad inheritance from African slavery. It is calm, reasonable, forcible, and brief; traits which must secure it readers and influence.'⁵⁶ Dr A C Rembaugh, a temperance advocate and prominent physician in Philadelphia, just wished that, whatever its size, *Anti-Caste* could be placed in the hands of millions because the mass of readers needed it.⁵⁷ Professor Scarborough at Wilberforce University, Ohio, agreed with this sentiment and everything Catherine said about outrages committed against 'colored people' in the United States. Heartened by her efforts Scarborough hoped that the discussions in *Anti-Caste* would help direct the 'attention of the civilized world to this much abused race'.⁵⁸ Although in his autobiography Scarborough only briefly mentions *Anti-Caste*, he recalls the key role Catherine played in introducing him to William Edward Armytage Axon, an antiquarian, classicist, ardent vegetarian, temperance activist and journalist with the *Manchester Guardian*, resulting in trans-Atlantic correspondence on the classics and a lifelong friendship between the two men.⁵⁹

Reading *Fraternity*

Edwards' popularity brought readers to *Fraternity*. For SRBM branch secretaries, Edwards' lectures proved an excellent place for recruiting new members and selling copies of *Fraternity* and he maintained an active speaking programme to galvanize support for the SRBM and its new organ. A month after taking on the editorship of *Fraternity* he travelled to Liverpool to lecture on 'Black and White in America' at Hengler's Circus and as usual crowds turned out to welcome him. According to the report of the evening by 'Irene', many found Edwards' description of lynch law to be a disturbing revelation. Irene also reported on the same lecture given by Edwards the week before at the Exchange Rooms, New Street, Birmingham. Here, despite the intense heat, every available inch of space had been occupied half an hour before the lecture began.⁶⁰ The public lectures Edwards gave continued to reference the history of black people's suffering in emotive and affecting language. As he told one audience in Newcastle:

> My ancestors proudly trod the sands of the African continent; but from their home and friends were dragged into the slave mart and sold to the planters of the West Indies... The very thought that my race should have been so grievously wronged is almost more than I can bear. They have given lie to many a false prophet who, prior to their Emancipation, sought to convince the world that the black man was in all respects unfit for freedom.... To their future I look with confidence.[61]

Some readers took up *Fraternity* because they were drawn to Edwards as much as the causes he represented. In August 1893, T Davies wrote to explain that whether as editor of *Lux* or *Fraternity* Davies found Edwards' advocacy compelling.[62] The expansion of content in *Fraternity* facilitated an extended engagement with readers like Davies through 'Our Letter Box', a monthly column of letters to the editor. The published correspondence ranged from brief words of encouragement, cryptic anonymous notes sent to SRBM branch secretaries, readers' anecdotes on themes raised in the paper as well as longer commentaries and on occasion the reprint of letters to editors of other newspapers concerning members of the SRBM on themes that interested them.

In addition to the extensive article on C J Miller's murder in Kentucky, *Fraternity*'s August 1893 number published several commentaries on lynchings, including two letters from either side of the colour line. A. H. L.'s letter from Brazoria, Texas, urged the Society to expand in the United States. A. H. L.'s letter suggested he regularly read *Anti-Caste* and was encouraged by the recent transformation of the paper into a movement.[63] Challenging the injustice of lynchings lay at the forefront of his mind. In the United States he saw his people hung on suspicion, shot down on suspicion, tied to stakes and burned alive on the basis of suspicions. He believed that if he could organize with other black men throughout the South within a structure such as the SRBM, they could more effectively demand change from those with power. Asking if the new Society was chartered, he sought to establish an official branch of the SRBM in the United States. From Kansas, V. O. wrote to express his anger at *Anti-Caste*'s very existence. Written across the cover of the final issue of *Anti-Caste* V. O.'s letter, sent to Edwards, demanded an end to the publication, angrily arguing that the editor had 'no idea of what you are saying or trying to do'. Assuming that Catherine was a man, he blamed her inability to understand the situation on England's geographical distance. He maintained forcefully the belief that white women's honour was constantly under threat by black men: 'If you were here where this raping of white women by negro brutes went on, you would change your tune, especially if your wife or daughter was ravished by one of them.'[64]

Readers demanding a greater variety of periodicals drove the growth of titles at the end of the nineteenth century. As individuals they read across a number of publications and placed debates into different contexts as they read across different monthlies, weeklies and dailies which they might have bought regularly, on a one-off basis, or picked up at a public reading room by chance because of an eye-catching headline or photograph. George Gunthorpe wrote from St John's, Antigua, enclosing payment for five copies of *Fraternity* and one copy of *American Atrocities*. He also wished to support the sentiment of G D Garroway's letter sent from Casktries Street, St Lucia, published three months earlier. Both Garroway and Gunthorpe hoped the work of the SRBM would soon become better known in the West Indies, where they felt the Society would garner strong support. Gunthorpe acknowledged that while the people of the West Indies did not suffer the injustices of lynch law, many of the same principles existed and there were many minor things that galled more than the iron fetters that were put upon their forefathers: 'the iron', he observed, 'is entering our souls'. He also remarked on the failure of the journalist W T Stead to recognize the SRBM as a member of the 'Civic Church' within his *Review of Reviews*. Gunthorpe remained convinced that Stead would do so if the SRBM was brought to his attention, and argued that the principles of the SRBM had to be an essential and central factor for those working for the consummation of the principles of that 'Civic Church'; without them they would be, almost, wasting their time.[65]

As editor Edwards anticipated and acknowledged the overlapping of his audiences' reading practices. On occasion there are notes of assumption in his commentary that debates in other papers and periodicals can be referenced and continued within *Fraternity* without too much additional explanation or contextual material required. Such a discussion appeared in January 1894 when a column in *Fraternity* critically deconstructed a letter sent by Cicely Simpson to *The British Friend*. Simpson's letter was not reprinted; the column begins by challenging Simpson's prejudicial assumptions and correcting the factual and political errors seen in her attack on requests for funds for the Coloured College Scheme in Bermuda. The column ends with a hopeful plea that no readers of *Fraternity* had withheld support on account of Cecily Simpson's bitterly prejudiced letter.[66] Conversely some readers sought to address multiple readerships through their letters. Edgar Horwood wrote to the *Daily News* in March 1894 condemning the behaviour of the Chartered Company operating in southern Africa, drawing attention to their brutal actions in Mashonaland and Matabeleland. He had previously contributed an essay titled 'a South African's View of the Matabele War' to *Fraternity*, and though he addressed his letter to the editor of the *Daily News*, Horwood also sent a copy of the letter directly to *Fraternity*.[67]

When writing letters of support or commentating on issues of racial prejudice, readers often expressed their views within narratives of their own personal stories. Such a letter, signed from 'Asia', came from 'an ex-Coolie, now a Prospective Missionary', who had been introduced to the paper by Catherine. In only a few lines to the editor of *Fraternity*, he explained how as a boy of 15 he had been enticed away by Europeans to Trinidad. Here, against his will and understanding, the Government of Trinidad deprived him of his personal liberty for three years. He had stayed on the island for five years, before spending three years in the United States. Here he observed Indians, Chinese and 'coloured people' labour while white people lived off their work and called them lazy. The same he saw in India. He hoped to become a missionary but had been refused a place by London, Scottish, European and American Societies because they told him they had no precedent for sending out a man of his colour before.[68] The following month another far longer letter appeared, also signed off 'Asia'. This letter is far bolder in tone than that from the 'ex-Coolie', the author now identifying himself as from the tribe of Al-Quraish. In this letter Asia sought to draw attention to the history of Africans in India and inform *Fraternity's* Christian readers (so he assumed) of the attempts of Anglo-Indians to forbid the employment of Africans and Arabs by the Nizam government.[69]

A further engagement in cross-cultural dialogue came from Hajee A Browne's contributions. A British convert to Islam, Browne was active in a number of London-based Muslim societies and president of the London Anjuman Angrezi, which included a number of Indians among its membership.[70] Browne first wrote to *Fraternity* to comment on an article discussing 'Islam in Japan', cut from a *New York Tribune* piece and published in *Fraternity* in October 1893. Browne's response, published in November, challenged the *Tribune's* assertion that Islam should experience a growth in popularity because of its 'leniency on the score of morality' and corrected descriptions of the Hanapee and Shapee sects.[71] In 1907 he published *Bonaparte in Egypt and the Egyptians of To-day*. In the preface Browne explained that for over 30 years he had given all he had to give for two objectives: first, the establishment of a 'Pan-Islamism' identity, which he believed to be in the true interest of the Islamic world; and, second, the development of friendly relations between the Muslims of the East and the British Empire.[72] His contributions to *Fraternity* followed this second aim with a lengthy serialized essay on Islam and the Brotherhood of Man. Browne positioned his essay in the context of a renewed interest in Islam and orthodox Muslims sparked by the opening of new Islamic missions in London, Liverpool and New York. For centuries, Browne observed, Islam, often but erroneously called 'Mohammedanism', had been seen in Europe as a 'religion of blood'. Though slowly this unfounded idea was being replaced by more just and truthful teachings on Islam, there remained a lack of understanding about the moral framework of the Qur'an. Spread over three issues, Browne's article discussed the teachings of Islam and the practices of orthodox Muslims within the ideas of tolerance and humane treatment for all.[73]

Women writing in *Fraternity*

The SRBM provided an opportunity for individuals to form a basis of collective action and the pages of *Fraternity* provided an opportunity for individual actions to be shared. That *Fraternity* received support from working-class women is revealed in a letter from Ms J Simons, who wrote to Edwards on behalf of her little band of Christian 'workwomen', who regularly discussed the issues raised in *Fraternity* with their Sunday School teacher. The group had committed to save 1d a week and send their collection to Edwards once a month. They were not rich, but hoped Edwards would accept their contribution. Simons had specifically written to share their idea for collecting and giving, hoping that 'if we wrote and told you how we did you might tell someone else who had not thought of doing this'.[74] Though Catherine had withdrawn as editor, women continued to be an important part of the network of distributors, readers and activists for *Fraternity* and the SRBM. A lecture 'From Bondage to Liberty' by Rev

Peter Stanford, a 35-year-old black minister who lived in Birmingham, was reported in the 'Letter Box' in November 1893. On this occasion, despite the stormy weather, he delivered his lecture to a large audience from all classes of society, who sat and listened in rapture to his powerful discourse. He spoke of the conditions of black people in America and the treatment they were receiving. He then suggested that a branch of the SRBM be formed in the district, and Alice James, who wrote to Edwards, was elected its secretary. Of the 35 branch secretaries for the SRBM listed in September 1893, 21 were women, including Miss C Ella Fox at 74 Park Street, Bristol, Mrs Chowry Muthu in Ilford, Mrs Barnett at 3 Hume Street in Sunderland and Eliza Wigham at South Gray Street in Edinburgh.[75]

As branch secretaries some of these women contributed regular reports on the progress of the SRBM in their area or region for *Fraternity*, detailing events that had taken place or those they hoped to organize and reporting the numbers of new members who took the SRBM's pledge. Their branch reports are factual and compact, quite different in style, tone and content to the creative material produced by women journalists who contributed reviews, essays and opinion pieces. As editor of *Lux*, Edwards maintained the regular column 'Written by a Woman to Women' and a number of the same women writers contributed to *Fraternity*. As in *Lux*, their columns and essays in the paper were attributed in a variety of ways. Some were probably published anonymously with the gender of the author remaining unknown such as a piece titled 'Italian Women', which appeared in January 1894.[76] Other articles were published using the writer's full name or initials or as in the case of 'Irene', who reported on Edwards' lectures in Birmingham and Liverpool, a shortened name or pseudonym.

A column by Katharine Davis Tillman in 1894 focused on the work of 'Afro-American' women poets.[77] Born in 1870, Tillman published essays in the *AME Church Review*, *Voice of the Negro* and a number of poems in the *Christian Recorder*.[78] In addition to her plays she also published two books, *Beryl Weston's Ambition: The Story of an Afro American Girl's Life* (1893) and *Clancy Street* (1898). Tillman was one of the black women writers who committed themselves to 'race literature' and her work embedded radical political and social messages enriched by her depth of knowledge in contemporary politics.[79] Her essay in *Fraternity* began by highlighting the poems of 'slave girl poet' Phyllis Wheatley, the first 'Afro-American female poet', but Tillman's main focus was the work of contemporary poets including Josie Heard, Frances E W Harper and Cordelia Ray. Ray occasionally contributed to the *AME Review* and her poem on Toussaint L'Ouverture appeared in *Anti-Caste* in 1889. The poem's inclusion within a collection of Ray's work published in 1910 suggests that *Anti-Caste* and *Fraternity* provided on occasion a useful space for more creative political interventions.[80] When Tillman wrote her essay, Ray's collection of *Sonnets* had just been published and Tillman noted its favourable reception by one of the best 'Anglo-Saxon journals' in the United States. Tillman celebrated the work of her better-known literary sisters and drew attention to women who she believed deserved greater attention than they had so far received, including Virgie Whitsett, author of a number of poems published in various papers, and Mamie Eloise Fox, whose work Tillman admired for its originality and humour, and a brief example of Fox's work ended her contribution.[81]

Don't tell me that our famous men
Alone, the heights shall scale,
For in no strife with tongue or pen,
Will women ever fail.

'A. L. O. S.' contributed to the women's column in *Lux* in May 1893, where she advised women on how to make a mark. She contributed at least three articles to *Fraternity* during its first year of publication, a biography titled 'William Wilberforce and Slavery' and 'Prejudice'; her call to draw more women into an active role in 'Justice' is full of energy and there is a determined forcefulness to her writing.[82] Her column in *Lux* urged women to be proud of their gender and to stop believing that only men could have influence. She had no time for women who wasted their time reading 'light, trashy, sentimental literature'.[83] They allowed their heads to be filled with flighty notions that undermined their character and drew them away from their true womanly instincts. Although in her column she claimed that women's influence could not be bounded, her suggestions for how women could make their mark remained firmly within the domestic sphere. She praised the woman who, rather than wasting her time reading French novels, could 'scrub a floor and blacklead a grate in the morning and entertain a company in the evening with the greatest of ease'.[84] Mothers influenced the outcomes of the generation they reared and many great men acknowledged the role of their mothers or their wives in their lives. By living consistent and godly lives women could support the work of their husbands and 'do more for the cause of right than mere theory'.[85]

A. L. O. S.'s anticipation of a rather different readership among the SRBM perhaps allowed her to make a less bounded call to *Fraternity's* female readers both in terms of class and their political outlook. In 'Justice' A. L. O. S. argued that the SRBM offered women an opportunity to become actively engaged in a political movement. She realized that not all women would have the time to get involved, but those who did could canvass for signatures and distribute papers. The success of Scottish-based branches regularly appeared in *Fraternity*: 'Are the women of England to be found in the rear?' she asked, 'Why should they? Let us set to work and see what we can do.' The aims of the Society could be carried out equally 'by the cook in the kitchen, the mistress of the house, the employer of servants, the rulers and governors of the land'. She appealed to her 'sisters' to let their sympathy lead women into action. Let us do everything in our power to spread the 'Brotherhood', a gendered term that she placed in quotation marks for her 'sisters'.[86]

International networks

With its focus on drawing together an international picture of racial prejudice, *Anti-Caste* created a space where readers from bishops to writers, activists and Sunday School children in Britain, Africa, Haiti and America could learn about oppression in other places. Through clippings from the *Indian*, *New York Age*, *Richmond Planet*, *Cleveland Gazette* and others, readers of *Anti-Caste* could learn about differing manifestations of racial prejudice and successful challenges to it in different parts of the world. They used these comparative examples to situate and analyze their own nationally or regionally based problems. In March 1889 the *Indian Messenger* commented upon an article that appeared in *Anti-Caste* about the injustices faced by black Americans and their inability to protect themselves from violence as the courts and legal machinery of the state sat within the hands of their oppressors. The *Messenger* compared the situation to that of British India, reflecting that these were instances that would 'remind our Indian readers of many cases in this country, especially the Coolie cases in Assam, where a similar complaint was raised, and where "white was actually found holding with white in powerful race combination." Caste works out the same evils all over the world'.[87] The *Messenger* appreciated that analogies could be made across the experiences of the oppressed including the appropriation of 'caste' to discuss the meanings and formations of racial prejudice. The following year the *Messenger* commented on a piece in *Anti-Caste* on the racist treatment of black men in Bermuda under the heading 'Men and Negroes'. Their position was compared to the experience of travelling by the railways of India, where one thing had often struck the writer as very offensive: 'the peculiar meaning attached by railway workers to the word "gentlemen"'. A 'gentlemen' on the railways always meant a European. More offensive was its use as a counterword to 'Natives', as if an Indian, no matter how exalted his position, could never be fit for the title of gentleman.[88] There may have been other occasions when the *Messenger* debated material in *Anti-Caste*; these two examples were reprinted by Catherine in *Anti-Caste*, allowing readers to see how different members of their community were interpreting the material they shared.

In October 1888 the *Cleveland Gazette* reprinted a report from *Anti-Caste* that M Hurard, a 'mulatto representative' from Martinique, had been elected secretary of the French chamber, reportedly the first time a man of colour had been called to fill a post in the French legislature. Pleased as they were to hear of the progress of 'the Negro', the *Gazette* found Hurard's pioneering position surprising given France's reputation among black Americans as an 'anti-caste Republic'. The paper concluded that it must be because of the smaller black presence, rather than prejudice, that had delayed their brethren legislative honours.[89] Occasionally the treatment of American (and also Canadian) indigenous people reached the pages of *Anti-Caste*.[90] In January 1891 under the header 'Caste Passions Let Loose against American Indians', *Anti-Caste* reported on the attacks between 'American troops and Red Indians' as reported in the *Daily News*. *Anti-Caste* conveyed with dismay that 'from the expressions used in some of the telegrams from America' they had identified 'a sort of fierce delight' felt by many 'at such an exhibition of "race hatred" as has been displayed by the combatants in these recent bloody episodes'.[91] At the end of the year a report on the murder by US troops of Sitting Bull, one of the most famous of the Sioux warriors, was taken from the *New York Age* and reprinted in *Anti-Caste's* December issue. The *Age* article celebrated Sitting Bull's righteous hatred of the white race, who became the agents of ruin for his people. Would Sitting Bull finally find in the Indians' 'Happy Hunting Grounds' the justice denied him in the United States? Perhaps the *Age* concluded.[92] Catherine acknowledged that the recirculation of an article published in the *Age* in August might have seemed out of date to American readers, but she felt there was much to be learned from its content on the connections black American journalists made between their own and other people's oppression.[93]

Edward Russell gave another in-depth editorial review of *Anti-Caste* in a July 1893 issue of the *Liverpool Daily Post*. Referring to Catherine as 'now so well-known as to need no further words of introduction', the piece acknowledged the 'almost phenomenal progress in this country of the Society for the Recognition of the Brotherhood of Man' and picked up on Ida B Wells' lively description of the busy week she had spent in London furthering the Society's aims.[94] Wells' presence in Britain had focused *Anti-Caste's* reporting on lynching, and an article titled the 'Continued Lynchings in the United States' caught Russell's eye. In spite of what had been reported by correspondents in the columns of the *Daily Post*, *Anti-Caste's* article proved that lynching in its worst forms was still in operation. Although foreign news especially had a reputation for being uneven with contradictory reports appearing within a single title without explanation or corrections, *Anti-Caste's* access to reporting by people of colour on their experiences made it an authorial voice to the extent that Russell directed readers to accept *Anti-Caste's* evidence over the material provided by his own reporters.[95] In addition to the many local newspapers it sourced and received *Anti-Caste* was 'in a sense independent from newspapers' with Catherine's direct contact with those 'foremost workers for human freedom' – men and women who were 'laying down their lives in the cause of liberty and justice for the oppressed'.[96]

The respect Catherine commanded among some print cultures was illustrated in one of John Mitchell Jr's editorial cartoons for the *Richmond Planet*. Born in Richmond on 11 July 1863 'amid the roar of cannon and the smoke of battle', as a child Mitchell worked in the home of James Lyons, the attorney who owned his parents before the Civil War.[97] He became editor of the *Planet* in 1884 modernizing production with the installation of electricity in the newspaper office for lighting, the presses and a Campbell cylinder press which ran off an electric motor. Under his tenure the *Planet* covered local, national and international news but it focused on lynchings, segregation and the rise of the Klu Klux Klan. Along with the regular antilynching illustrations and later pictures, Mitchell created numerous political cartoons, including 'Firing at Long Range', which referenced Catherine. Published in February 1895, 'Firing at Long Range' depicts Catherine and the Antilynching Society based in London firing outraged public opinion across the Atlantic towards the United States. Although their canons cannot strike the Southern States, the noise from their fire draws the attention of Europe's elites. Kings and emperors look across the Atlantic to see the bodies of black men hanging from trees. In the North, while Ida B Wells lectures to crowds in the Northern states, President Cleveland uses the violence being perpetrated in Armenia as an excuse to avoid attacks on injustices prevalent in the United States (Figure 6.4).

Mitchell's cartoon provides further evidence that by 1895 Catherine's work could be referenced in black American newspapers with little explanation, her efforts pervasive within some public cultures. In June *Imvo Zabantsandu* reprinted a letter previously published in the *Cape Times* on the 'Coloured Question' in southern Africa. Under the header 'The Brotherhood of Man', the author explained that he or she had only recently arrived in the colony and so presumed it would not be surprising that the 'coloured

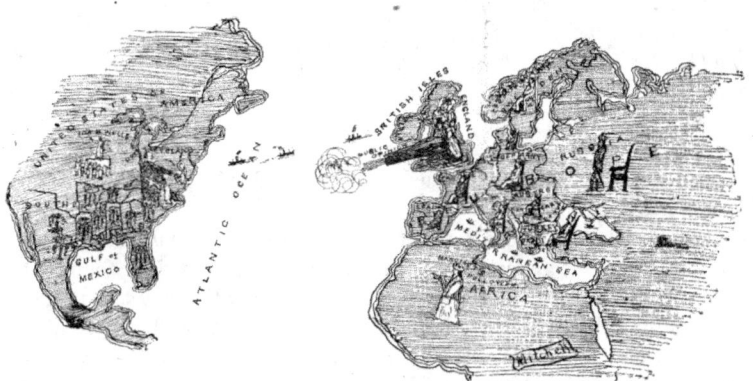

Figure 6.4 Firing at Long Range, one of John Mitchell Jr's editorial cartoons for the *Richmond Planet*, 2 February 1895

question' should be especially interesting to them. Believing 'somewhat in the brotherhood of man, irrespective of the colour Nature may have thought fit to dye his skin', the author strongly protested against views of 'Kaffirs' that had been so offensively enunciated in the Parliament recently. The writer admitted that their recent arrival meant they did know of the history of the honourable member whose language had moved them to protest, 'nor if he was a Jew, Turk, infidel, or heathen', nor 'whether his hair be *black* or *white*'.[98] They assumed from his name he could not be English and thanked God for that at least, though they quickly went on to remind the editor of the unenviable notoriety Lord Salisbury earned by his *lapsus lingua* in referring disparagingly to Dadabhai Naoroji as a 'black man'. There was no reason, the author argued, that the accidental birth right of colour, of whatever shade, should impede a man's progress or check his legitimate ambition. The reader signed off their letter Novocastrian, a reference to their origins in Newcastle upon Tyne or Newcastle, New South Wales.[99] The content of their letter is suggestive of a connection to the SRBM in some form and its continuing influence on one reader's life. If they had been a regular reader of *Anti-Caste* or *Fraternity*, they would have been alert to a highly critical analysis of politics in southern Africa particularly the military brutality and capitalist greed of Cecil Rhodes.

Notes

1. Impey to Chesson, March 1888, MSS. Brit. Emp. s.18 C138/173.
2. *New York Age*, 7 April 1888, 2.
3. *New York Age*, 7 April 1888, 2.
4. Penn, *Afro-American Press*.
5. *Cleveland Gazette*, 6 October 1888, 2.
6. *Cleveland Gazette*, 6 October 1888, 2.
7. *Cleveland Gazette*, 6 October 1888, 2.
8. *Cleveland Gazette*, 6 October 1888, 2, original emphasis.
9. *Cleveland Gazette*, 6 October 1888, 2.
10. *New York Age*, 1 December 1888, 2.
11. *Christian Recorder*, 13 June 1899.
12. 'Anti-Caste', in *Christian Recorder*, 13 June 1899 reprinted in 'Supplement to *Anti-Caste*', January 1890, npn.
13. AJH, 'Liverpool Daily Post', in *Dictionary of Nineteenth Century Journalism*.
14. AJH (who argues that the increase was probably largely due to the *Echo* founded in 1879), 'Liverpool Daily Post', in *Dictionary of Nineteenth Century Journalism*.
15. Catherine mentions that Russell had been helping her in a letter to F Chesson, 16 October 1882, MSS. Brit. Emp. s.18 C138/164.
16. 'News of the day', *Liverpool Daily Post*, 2 March 1889.
17. Supplement to *Anti-Caste*, January 1890, 1.
18. 'The editor's New Year's address', Supplement to *Anti-Caste*, January 1890, npn.
19. 'Our responsibilities', *Anti-Caste*, November 1891, 2.
20. 'Editor's address to the friends of Anti-Caste', *Anti-Caste*, January 1893, 4; 'India gentle but not weak', *Anti-Caste*, September 1890, 2.
21. Saunders, 'Ngcongco', 63. Saunders notes that earlier papers, of which the most important was *Isigidimi*, were all mission papers and not independent publications.
22. *Anti-Caste*, December 1890, 2.
23. Penn, *Afro-American Press*.
24. *Anti-Caste*, January 1891, 2.
25. *Imvo*, 28 November 1894, 3.
26. 'Papers received', *Fraternity*, May 1894, 7.
27. For example, see 'Reported massacre in a Russian church', from *Daily News*; 'Boycotting Russian Jews at Hamburg' from *Leeds Mercury* in *Fraternity*, December 1893, 8–9; 'Anti-Christian riots in Japan', from *Sheffield Independent* in *Fraternity*, December 1893, 9; 'Death of French Wilberforce' from *Liverpool Post* in *Fraternity*, January 1894, 6.
28. The list of newspapers received in *Fraternity*, June 1894, 6, included *Richmond Planet*, *Coloured American* and *New York Age*, in addition to *Monthly Review*, *Women's Tribune*, *Barbados Taxpayer*, *Nineteenth Century and St James's Chronicle*, *Hindostan*, *Gold Coast Methodist Times*, *Demerara Daily*, *Christian Mission Herald* and *Cornwall Times*. Reference to *Women's Tribune* here is curious. A British *Women's Tribune* was not published in Britain until 1906; it is possible that it is a reference to a feminist

journal published in Argentina by Carolina Muzzilli (see Rappaport, *Encyclopedia of Women Social Reformers*) but is more likely to have been an American publication such as *Women's Tribune*, published fortnightly from 1883 to 1909 by the Nebraska Women's Suffrage Association (see the Library of Congress, Washington).
29   LRB, Magazine Day, *Dictionary of Nineteenth Century Journalism*.
30   *Fraternity*, February 1894, 2.
31   'Early record of the "Brotherhood" society', MSS. Brit. Emp. s.20 E5/7.
32   The decision was announced as part of the minutes of SRBM Council Meeting printed in *Fraternity*, August 1893, 13.
33   'The Chinese Restriction Act, from our correspondent', *Fraternity*, December 1893, 14–15. Fortune's essays appeared in various issues of *Fraternity*. See 'Lynch law becomes more common', October 1893, 1; 'Black and white', November 1893, 5; 'The maddest act of the mob (since my last letter to *Fraternity*)', December 1893, 2–3. Stuart, 'Among the American Negroes', *Anti-Caste*, January 1889, 3–4.
34   Based on the scope and tone of this column, Lindy Moore argues that it is likely this section of the paper was written by Isabella Mayo. Moore, 'Reputation of Isabella Fyvie Mayo'.
35   On the *Indian Magazine and Review*, see Burton, *At the Heart of Empire*, 2–3.
36   *Fraternity*, May 1894, 2–3.
37   'Thorough', *Fraternity*, May 1894, 7.
38   Supplement to *Anti-Caste*, January 1890, npn.
39   'Promises of help in distribution', *Anti-Caste*, March 1889, 4.
40   Supplement to *Anti-Caste*, January 1890, npn.
41   Supplement to *Anti-Caste*, January 1891, 4.
42   Impey to Tourgée, 16 June 1890, 4785, *Albion W. Tourgée* Papers.
43   Fortune, 'On syndicating news', *AME Church Review* 8, 1891, 231–242.
44   'Editor's address to friends of Anti-Caste', *Anti-Caste*, January 1893, 4.
45   *Fraternity*, December 1892, 6–7.
46   SRBM, *Annual Report* 1894, MSS. Brit. Emp. s.20 5/8.
47   SRBM, *Annual Report* 1894, MSS. Brit. Emp. s.20 5/8, The Bodleian Library of Commonwealth and African Studies, University of Oxford.
48   Reprinted in Supplement to *Anti-Caste*, January 1890, npn.
49   Reprinted in Supplement to *Anti-Caste*, January 1890, npn.
50   Sadleir, 'Jacobs, William Wymark (1863–1943)'.
51   Davis, 'Backhouse family (per. c.1770–1945)'. Thomas William Backhouse (1842–1920): doi:10.1093/ref:odnb/61920; 'Obituary notices: Fellows: Backhouse, Thomas William', *Monthly Notices of the Royal Astronomical Society*, 81, 254–255.
52   Green, 'Fuller, Joseph Jackson (1825–1908)'.
53   Hein and Shattuck, *Episcopalians*.
54   Supplement to *Anti-Caste*, January 1890, npn.
55   Warren, 'Women in conference'.
56   Reprinted in Supplement to *Anti-Caste*, January 1890, npn.
57   The reference to Rembaugh's views on alcohol comes from Stowell, *A Healthy Body*.
58   Reprinted in Supplement to *Anti-Caste*, January 1890.
59   Ronnick, *Autobiography of William Sanders Scarborough*. 'Obituary', *Times*, 30 December 1913, 9; Hollingworth, 'Axon, William Edward Armytage (1846–1913)'.
60   *Fraternity*, August 1893, 14.
61   Quoted in Fryer, *Staying Power*, 277.
62   *Fraternity*, September 1893, 12–13.

63 *Fraternity*, August 1893, 14.
64 *Fraternity*, August 1893, 14.
65 Gunthorpe in *Fraternity* December 1893, 7; Garroway in *Fraternity*, September 1893, 12.
66 *Fraternity*, January 1894, 14.
67 'A South African's view', *Fraternity*, December 1893, 13; *Fraternity*, May 1894, 12.
68 *Fraternity*, January 1894, 16.
69 *Fraternity*, February 1894, 15.
70 Abd-Allah, *A Muslim in Victorian America*.
71 *Fraternity*, November 1893, 14.
72 Browne, *Bonaparte in Egypt*.
73 *Fraternity*, November 1893, 8; December 1893, 11–12; January 1894, 3.
74 *Fraternity*, October 1893, 16.
75 *Fraternity*, September 1893, 16.
76 *Fraternity*, January 1894, 10.
77 *Fraternity*, March 1894, 12.
78 Wallinger, 'Shrinking at no lofty theme'.
79 Wallinger, 'Shrinking at no lofty theme'.
80 *Anti-Caste*, October 1889, 1; Ray, *Poems*.
81 Tillman wrote a longer essay on both male and female Afro-American poets and their verse, published in the *AME Church Review* in 1898. Tillman, *Works*.
82 'A.L.O.S' wrote a column on 'Prejudice', published in January 1894, 6, and one on 'William Wilberforce and Slavery', published in October 1893, 4–5.
83 *Lux*, 6 May 1893, 212.
84 *Lux*, 6 May 1893, 213.
85 *Lux*, 6 May 1893, 213.
86 *Fraternity*, August 1893, 8.
87 Reprinted in Supplement to *Anti-Caste*, January 1890, npn.
88 'Men and Negroes', *Anti-Caste*, September 1891, 3.
89 *Cleveland Gazette*, 6 October 1888.
90 For example, see 'Canadian Indians: A Canadian Indian deputation', *Anti-Caste*, May 1891, 1; 'American Indians', *Anti-Caste*, February 1893, 1.
91 'Caste passions let loose', *Anti-Caste*, January 1891, 3.
92 'The murder of sitting bull', *Anti-Caste*, August 1891, 1.
93 *Anti-Caste*, August 1891, 3.
94 *Liverpool Daily Post*, 6 July 1893, 6.
95 *Liverpool Daily Post*, 6 July 1893, 6.
96 Supplement to *Anti-Caste*, January 1892, 2.
97 Penn, *Afro-American Press*, 183–184; Alexander, *Race Man*.
98 The letter was reprinted from the *Cape Times* as part of a long discussion in *Imvo* about the incident involving remarks made by Mr Le Roex in the House of Assembly in *Imvo Neliso Lomzi (Native Opinion and Guardian)*, 13 June 1895, original emphasis.
99 'Novocastrian, n. and adj', *OED Online*. March 2013. Oxford University Press, http://0-www.oed.com.catalogue.ulrls.lon.ac.uk/view/Entry/128816?redirected From=Novocastrian&, accessed 19 March 2013.

7

Criticizing Empire

It is as though the British Empire is not large enough; our conduct in Africa is one perpetual series of war and bloodshed. First West, then East and now South Africans fall prey to our insatiable greed.

Fraternity, 1893

As *Anti-Caste's* networks of newsprint exchanges grew so did the geographical diversity of its reporting. Edwards built on these networks in *Fraternity*, exploring not only racial prejudice in the United States but its hardening in Australian labour policies and colonial inequality in India and Africa. These were placed alongside reports of religious oppression in Russia and political oppression in other parts of Europe. Edwards emphasized this broad transnational approach in one of his early editorials:

> Thus in America we shall oppose lynching because it is inhuman, and the spirit which promotes it is diabolical; in Australia we must remind the colonists that Chinamen are their brethren; in this country, in every sphere, no one should be refused any opportunity in life on the ground of his nationality, nay, not only in this but in all countries.... Russian Stundists are suffering as badly as the Negroes, and cries come from other parts of the earth for sympathy, which they think we can give; how happy our brethren will be when they know that this Society is endeavouring to alleviate their woes, that their sorrow is ours, and that their joy will be ours.[1]

British colonial expansion in Africa particularly outraged and frustrated Edwards. In January 1896 a leader in *The Times* argued that the assailants of Cecil Rhodes were too ready to forget his important accomplishments. Rhodes and his colleagues had secured for 'the British race' an empire in southern Africa of 'immense extent and practically inexhaustible resources'.[2] The year before at the fourth AGM for shareholders of the British South African Company, the Duke of Fife (chair of the meeting and the Prince of Wales' son-in-law) reflected on the company's successful addition of two immense provinces to the British Empire. According to the Duke of Fife's analysis 'If we' – meaning the British South African Company and the British state, a political and economic fusion he so ably embodied – 'had not snapped up the territory somebody else would have done so'. The fact was 'the Scramble for Africa had set in' despite the opposition of 'a small and prejudiced section of the community'. These were 'a curious set of people, who cannot control their feelings whenever any development of the British Empire, however inevitable, takes place'.[3] Readers of both *Anti-Caste* and *Fraternity* formed a part of this critical community.

Like other political progressives in Britain, Edwards spoke against the inevitability of British colonial expansion. In the pages of *Fraternity* he argued that the British government and its military and cultural power was being manipulated by capitalist companies like the British South Africa Company for the profits of its shareholders at the expense of African lives, Africa's independent future and the reputation of the British state. Edwards' contempt for Cecil Rhodes and his anger at the success of capitalists in their schemes in southern Africa are palpable in his editorials. This was coupled with the exasperation he countenanced for the British political class, who concerned themselves with 'the woes of Armenians, Egyptians, and others' when they should have been considering how to overhaul the structures and behaviour of their own colonial constabularies, judges and governors.[4] There was much 'that should not be' operating in the British Empire.

Capital and colonialism

In her critical analysis of the age of imperialism, Hannah Arendt argued that some of the 'fundamental aspects of this time appear so close to totalitarian phenomena of the twentieth century that it may be justifiable to consider the whole period a preparatory stage for coming catastrophes'.[5] Among the agents of violence during this period of change highlighted by Arendt was Cecil Rhodes, a man who sought expansion for expansion's sake and who managed to convince the British government that the 'export of the instruments of violence was necessary to protect investments'.[6] A number of Rhodes' contemporaries who witnessed his role in the 'scramble for Africa' criticized him and protested against other British imperialist moves such as the invasion of Egypt in 1882. British Positivists considered this a shameless intervention on behalf of British bond and shareholder interests.[7] Similar arguments were to be found in *Anti-Caste* and *Fraternity*. The periodicals condemned both the process of imperial expansion and supposedly reformist organizations that failed to criticize Rhodes. In July 1892 an *Anti-Caste* editorial reflected that it was painful for those who had long trusted the instincts of the Aborigines Protection Society to find that even they had fallen for Rhodes' rhetoric. Finally though Rhodes, prime minister of the Cape Colony, had revealed his true attitude:

> Mr Rhodes has just been giving public utterance to his sentiments respecting the Natives in a pithy form which will long be remembered against him. He says that he 'PREFERS LAND TO NIGGERS' – by which he explains himself to mean that had he the choice, he would prefer territory 'bereft' of its native population, to land 'swarming' with them, regarding these as 'not to the advantage of South Africa.'[8]

Too often Catherine lamented organizations such as the APS failed to see the 'lies concealed beneath the fair clothes of Chartered African Companies, and other well sounding schemes for the advancement of the trade, colonization and exploration of poor Africa'. Their failure to detect the 'cloven hoof' of men such as Rhodes was deeply disappointing.[9]

Under the tenure of Henry Fox Bourne the APS had been encouraged to support the intervention of chartered companies in Africa.[10] *Anti-Caste's* editorial was referencing the public support given to chartered companies in the *Aborigines' Friend* in the early 1890s. Reporting on the progress of chartered companies as 'international schemes for the benefit of the natives of Africa' in 1891 the APS stated: 'Happily native interests have been to some extent, and in certain respects strictly, safeguarded' during 'the remarkable progress of the great chartered companies.'[11] Following the annual meeting of the APS in May 1891, Harriet Colenso wrote to Catherine to draw her attention to the outrageous contention made by the Duke of Fife, in the chair once again, that in the South Africa Company the APS would find one 'of their warmest and fastest allies'.[12] Colenso's letter appeared in *Anti-Caste* in the same issue as Catherine's despairing editorial on Rhodes. By January 1894 the APS had been forced to retract their support and reconsider their simplistic analysis of the relationship between capitalist expansion and 'native interests'. The *Aborigines' Friend* confessed that the 'most important and painful business in 1893, as regards English dealings with native races in Africa, has been the war with Lobengula and his Matabele followers, which has been entered upon by the British South Africa Company'.[13] As part of the APS's protests against the resulting violence in Mashonaland the colonial secretary, the Marquis of Ripon, was asked to receive a deputation at the Colonial Office. The group who visited him on 14 December 1893 comprised a number of MPs including Alfred Webb, along with the Reverend Wardlaw Thompson (foreign secretary of the London Missionary Society), the APS secretary Henry Fox Bourne and Celestine Edwards.[14]

Edwards' concerns for the people of Africa were a theme in his lectures and writing well before he began editing *Fraternity*. As editor of *Lux* he acknowledged *Anti-Caste* as one of his regular 'papers received' and their interests in Africa sometimes overlapped in print. The looming annexation of Uganda reported by *Anti-Caste* in December 1892 presented the voice of 'an indignant negro writer' who asked what guarantee the 'natives' of Uganda had that following the annexation by the British state they would find themselves any better treated than their brethren in southern Africa.[15] In *Lux* Edwards ranted against British imperial actions in Uganda over three pages. He predicated a day when the injustices pressed upon the African people would come home to the 'oppressors' children's children'.

> If the British nation stole no more, they have stolen enough and have sufficient responsibility at home and abroad to occupy her maternal attention for the next hundred years. If the British nation has not murdered enough, no nation on God's earth has. Those who are crying aloud for Uganda are not her best friends, for she cannot occupy the country without more blood and additional injustice.[16]

Lux's aim of countering the spread of atheism did not prevent Edwards from criticizing religious institutions when their practices appeared to enhance or contribute to racial oppression. In the context of Uganda he acknowledged that although in principle *Lux* wished all missionary societies well, it did not and could not join in their appeal for supporting a civil power that 'did not care a fig for the personal utility of religion'.[17] Edwards' critical commentary of missionaries and their role in the expansion of the British Empire brought him into conflict with readers. In May 1893 Edward Watts, a regularly reader of *Lux*, was pained enough by *Lux*'s editorials to write to Edwards complaining about their tone towards missionaries and their 'constant disparagement' of the CMS Mission in Uganda, as well as the editor's habit of referring to missionaries as 'Salaried Officers of the State'.[18]

With critical voices such as Edwards and Alfred Webb among its members, it is not surprising that the delegation which visited the Colonial Office in December 1893 did not speak with a cohesive voice. Although Wardlaw Thompson accepted that white settlers could not really protect the rights of Africans as they were there for their own interests, he also believed that the Matabele were 'really savages' and that it would be 'Un-English' to judge Rhodes' company without careful consideration.[19] In contrast Webb argued that the concession of equal rights to all had to be the necessary outcome of the violence. According to the published report of the meeting in the *Aborigines' Friend*, Edwards did not speak and he was probably highly frustrated by the content and outcome of the meeting. Ripon deflected any responsibility away from himself and gave full support to his 'friend Mr Rhodes', arguing that South African opinion (presumably meaning white South African opinion) could not be ignored in the region's political affairs.[20] Despite their failure to elicit a condemnation of Rhodes or a change of policy towards the South Africa Company, the report of the meeting in the *Aborigines' Friend* remained calm and measured. Edwards had published an editorial in December 1893 highly critical of the government's policy towards the company and the peoples of Africa, whose humanity seemed to be placed below political considerations.[21] The meeting with Ripon confirmed his fears and Edwards' January 1894 editorial for *Fraternity* seethed with anger:

> Cecil Rhodes and Company coveted Matabeleland, and little by little they goaded poor Lobengula into a row, called for the assistance of the British Government and got the press to poison the minds of the British public by depicting Lobengula and the Matabeles as the worst of savages, and then seized their country.... Since the war has been conducted by the British Government for the British people, we, in the name of justice and humanity, ask that the Matabeles be not handed over to the tender mercies of Cecil Rhodes and his Dutch Boer allies.... We trust that every reader of this paper will feel that, before all other considerations justice and humanity are due to the Matabeles. Whatever injustice they inflicted upon the Mashonas is no justification for the wholesale slaughter of the people with Maxim guns; the stealing of their cattle, and the free division of their land by semi-civilised savages.[22]

Edwards strongly criticized the British government's failure to act and ensure the administration of British law. In February *Fraternity* readers were informed that on 22 January Rhodes had made what some would call a stirring speech, in which he complimented his men for their courage and spirit and told them to choose the land to which they were entitled 'by right of conquest'.²³ This diametrically opposed what the solicitor-general had told the House of Commons on 9 January when he had confirmed that a British subject could not acquire proprietary rights by conquest. How then, Edwards asked, could Cecil Rhodes and the company claim Matabeleland?²⁴ The British Parliament either pathetically failed to recognize the capitalist motivations of Rhodes or were complicit with his aims.

The failure of the British government to act justly in imperial disputes had been highlighted in *Anti-Caste* while Harriet Colenso was in Britain campaigning on behalf of deposed Zulu Chiefs, who were seeking a hearing in Parliament. Colenso helped revise and correct an article for *Anti-Caste* including material from the Zulu Defence Committee.²⁵ Catherine urged readers to write to their MPs to ask them to support an enquiry when the issue came before the House of Commons, but in December that year Catherine admitted to readers that she still had not yet learnt a great deal about the complexities of South African politics, although reviewing the Xhosa paper *Imvo Zabantsandu* helped. Primarily published in Xhosa, John Tengo Jabavu's *Imvo Zabantsandu* published its editorial leader and inside paragraphs in English, allowing Catherine to access a 'Kafir' voice (Figure 7.1).²⁶ As a young man Jabavu became an apprentice in a local newspaper office and worked there in the mornings until breakfast, before returning home and getting ready for school. He later became a correspondent for the *Cape Mercury* and the *Cape Argus*, where he wrote under a pseudonym.²⁷ In November 1884 he founded *Imvo Zabantsandu*, with the translated title of *Native Opinion*, sharing the masthead. He intended this to be a voice that connected Africans to the ruling powers that hailed from Great Britain, and to provide a regular space in which Africans could see themselves as others saw them, but also for black Africans in the colony to discuss issues as they saw them.²⁸ The paper also served as the 'authorized medium for the publication of Government notices addressed to Natives' throughout the colony and gained a wide readership that extended from the Cape Colony to Natal and Lesotho.²⁹

Catherine told *Anti-Caste* readers how deeply impressed she was that *Imvo* managed to discuss the burning questions of the day without bitterness, maintaining a tone of forbearance that honoured the 'sorely harassed native population'. This was in marked contrast to the bitter contempt papers such as the *Johannesburg Star* showed 'for "natives" and all "coloured people" including at times even the Parsi colonists from India, because they are touched with the despised colour'.³⁰ Before having access to *Imvo*, Catherine had relied upon white South African papers such as the Natal *Spectator* that represented 'the colonial capitalist and employers of labour' and that, for example, valued African education

> not from the point of whether or no it tends to the enlightenment and social elevation of the masses of the people (the natives), but whether it does or does not make the native a more useful instrument for the enrichment of the colonial capitalist.³¹

Catherine compared the *Spectator*'s editorial determination to keep the 'black man' in a state of 'savagery in order to be of use' to the London *Standard*'s recent discovery of 'a supposed tendency in the negroes of the West Indies and America to "relapse" into original savagery' which they attributed to the sanguinary struggles in Haiti and contextualized with an appalling depiction of black life in the Southern United States.[32] Catherine wanted to refute the *Standard's* points individually, but already late going to press she instead referred readers to George W Cable's recently prepared series of papers on the 'negro question' in London's *Forum Magazine*.[33]

During Catherine's tenure of *Anti-Caste*, southern Africa increasingly mirrored patterns of violence and racial discrimination that had previously been associated with the Southern United States. The acquittal of two white farmers in 1892 for murder deeply shocked her and seemed to epitomize the entrenchment of racial inequality in the region. The account of events began when someone stole sheep from a farmer who determined that the thief must have been one of his workers. With the help of four brothers, around a dozen black men living nearby were taken from their beds, stripped and bound to wagon wheels or held to the ground while they were beaten with sticks. One man died from his wounds and his wife and mother were shot at when they attempted to relieve his dying agony. The evidence against the five white farmers was clear but not only did the jury acquit the men but outside the court they were met with public rejoicing, and a public dinner was given in their honour. The news left Catherine aghast. It showed the lack of any sense of justice within the colony. It was a crisis caused by racial prejudice, although not in an identical form to the United States, for in South

THE SOUTH AFRICAN NATIVE AND COLOURED PEOPLE'S DELEGATES IN LONDON, 1909.

The names of the Delegates shown in this photograph are as follows: In the front row, from left to right—Mr. Matt. J. Fredericks, General Secretary of the African Political Organisation; Dr. A. Abdurahman, President of the African Political Organisation; the Hon. W. P. Schreiner, K.C., C.M.G., M.L.A., Ex-Prime Minister of the Cape Colony; the Rev. Dr. W. B. Rubusana, Ph.D., President of the South African Native Convention; and Mr. Tengo-Jabavu, Editor of " Imvo " and President of the King William's Town Native Association. In the back row, from right to left, are Mr. D. J. Lenders (Kimberley), Vice-President of the African Political Organisation; Mr. Daniel Dwanya, Agent-at-Law and Representative of the South African Native Convention; Mr. J. Gerrans, representing Bechuanaland Protectorate; and Mr. Thos. M. Mapikela, General Secretary of the Orange River Colony Native Congress.

Figure 7.1 Tengo Jabavu, editor of *Imvo Zabantsandu* (seated, far right), as part of the South African Native and Coloured People's Delegates in London, 1909

Africa Catherine saw caste operating as 'class feeling emphasised by differences of colour'.[34] Rather than addressing how this racial prejudice could be tackled, the outraged reports in the white press betrayed their alarm for the good name of colonial farmers with no indignation at the brutal acts of injustice they had performed.

Edwards had little time for white South African opinion, noting that on Rhodes' return from Mashonaland he had not been criticized but honoured at a banquet hosted by the mayor and citizens of Cape Town. Instead of weeping over the thousands of people killed in a war 'made for the express benefit of dividend-mongers', they had gathered to laud Rhodes for the great victory he had achieved. Beneath the headline 'Murder Will Out' Edwards mused that

> By a curious coincidence in human nature, some murderers are hanged, others escape being hanged on the ground of provocation, but there are others who kill so many that, either through fear or favour, they are neither hanged nor transported, but are feasted by their compatriots as heroes.[35]

Such aggressive criticism of Rhodes did not appear in *Imvo*. An article under the heading 'Mr Rhodes and Native Progress' was published with enthusiasm in 1891 mostly because Rhodes' references to matters which could be termed 'domestic policy in the Cape' were so rare that anything he revealed was of great interest.[36] Rhodes had not made any pronouncements locally, but delivered a few comments after a talk on South Africa by Dr James Stewart at a meeting of the Royal Scottish Geographical Society in Edinburgh. Rhodes had referred with pride and pleasure to Stewart's work on the elevation of 'Native Africans' and *Imvo* gratefully noted that so illustrious a man as the Cape Premier should hold such just views about the improvement of 'native races'.[37] Compared to *Anti-Caste* and *Fraternity's* descriptions of Rhodes as a devil in disguise and a murderer, *Imvo's* evaluation appears tame. But working in the Cape Jabavu faced far more restrictive editorial freedoms. Before *Imvo* African newspapers in the region were missionary journals focusing on the promotion of literacy and Christianity.[38] Jabavu's paper served an important role in developing Xhosa as a language and was charting out an innovative newsprint culture.[39] Jabavu needed to maintain a tone of forbearance to ensure he could continue to publish the paper. During the Boer War *Imvo* was forced to close for 14 months because it advocated a policy of peaceful negotiations with the Boers rather than unconditional support for British colonial policy.[40] It never recovered from the financial insecurity this period of closure brought and remained under surveillance with Henry McCallum, Governor of Natal, arguing in 1906 that articles appearing in *Imvo* were 'calculated to promote disaffection amongst the natives throughout South Africa' and he requested action that would make the publication of such columns a serious offence.[41]

Edwards knew that white opinion in southern Africa was not homogenous and allotted space for J M Cole from Johannesburg, *Fraternity's* 'own correspondent', to write reflectively about the treatment of Africans and his place as a white man in the city. Cole reported the miserable lack of rights for 'natives': in the Transvaal no 'native' was allowed to own property and it was considered a crime for 'coloured men' to eat in the same dining room as the white population. 'Native' men and women were not allowed to walk through the streets after 9pm without permission and a pass from

Figure 7.2 Illustrating the relationship between technology and imperial power, Cecil Rhodes is depicted here 'Striding from Cape Town to Cairo' stretching out a telegraph wire to connect the African continent. 'The Rhodes Colossus', first published in *Punch* on 10 December 1892

their employers, and before being able to even get a job they had to purchase a permit which cost them 1s a month. The Johannesburg Sanitary Board had recently declared that no 'native' man or woman should walk along the pavement, and that their punishment for refusing to walk in the road would be imprisonment, or a flogging of ten lashes. Despite the establishment of these racist structures Cole was still proud to be an Englishman: 'but when I see my coloured brother walking in the road ankle deep in mud while I walk on the path, I am ashamed of my white face, and of the unfairness that robs a man of his country, and then flogs him for daring to walk on the footpath.'[42]

The politics of labour

The debates on imperial expansion and capitalism that framed discussions about Rhodes forged links between concerns for the trafficking of Pacific Islanders to work on the sugar plantations of Queensland, Chinese labour in Australia and the treatment of 'native' workers in Africa.⁴³ The proposal to annex Uganda and the debate over the proposal to allow the continuing traffic of Kanaka peoples to work for fixed-year contracts on the sugar plantations of Queensland were 'of a like nature in many respects' for *Anti-Caste*. In both cases those chiefly involved were, on the one hand, 'a mute defenceless multitude of simple black folk' and, on the other, 'the pushing mercantile and manufacturing Briton or British colonists'. The question that lay before the British public was how long white colonists would be allowed to 'encroach upon the lands, liberties, interests, and perfectly natural and justifiable wishes and aspirations' of black peoples. The white settler held the overwhelming advantage in this battle over liberty and resources.

> He, or powerful members of his class, are personally represented in the court, so to speak, his adversary is far away and unknown, almost unrepresented. He is strong acute experienced, – his adversary is weak, poor, and ignorant. He is at home, and among friends – English is his mother tongue, and he is white, his opponent is a voiceless stranger, an alien, a nobody in the world's esteem, and *black*, unmeritedly despised.⁴⁴

In examining the privilege and corruption of the colonial class, in the specific case of the Kanaka labourers, *Anti-Caste* argued that their exploitation had to be judged as American slavery had been, not under the model regulation of its 'pattern masters' but by its actual implementation in the colonies in the hands of 'averagely selfish' and 'exceptionally unscrupulous planters'. Despite assurances of '"safeguards" and "provisions"', could the Kanaka contract system being discussed by Australian politicians be something to boast of? If not, how long would England stand by and watch without voicing a protest?⁴⁵

The international persecution of Chinese workers had first been discussed in *Anti-Caste*'s first year of publication when Reverend Frederick Storrs-Turner wrote to Catherine about their treatment in the United States. A resident in China for many years Storrs-Turner was a member of the London Missionary Society. In 1867 he had helped to found the Society for the Suppression of the Opium Trade and acted as editor of *Friend of China* published sporadically from the 1880s until the early 1900s.⁴⁶ He wrote to Catherine asking if there was space in *Anti-Caste* to comment on the plight of Chinese people. In his letter he condemned British newspapers and popular platforms which insulted and calumniated the Chinese people.

> Our politicians and working men combine to exclude the Chinamen from our shores. China is weak, is slow, is cautious, but depend upon it, this outrageous injustice is felt.... Why is it that nobody seems to care about this, that everybody seems to crouch in terror before the caste prejudice and selfishness of the working classes? Being an Englishman I am reluctant to comment upon American politics; but one cannot shut one's eyes to the Exclusion Act. American statesmen have yielded to the mob. Will British statesmen imitate the humiliating example? Better that the colonies should go, and the British Empire break up, than that this breach of faith should be consummated.⁴⁷

As Storrs-Turner's letter reflects, the international movements of labour and access to work were an area where interlocking issues of race, class and national identity were becoming increasingly problematic.[48] Alongside its 'Aboriginal problem' fear of a 'Yellow Peril' had also begun to take political form in Australia. The creation of the White Australia Commonwealth in 1901 was preceded by years of anti-Chinese attitudes, which could be found in the Australian press throughout the 1880s.[49] In February 1889, Catherine published a letter written by William Jones the year before and sent to his friend John Grubb Richardson in Ireland. Jones' letter outlined his interview with the author Cheok Hong Cheong. As the pair talked at a garden party in Melbourne, Cheong argued how unfounded the 'outcry about the invasion of "Hordes" of Chinese' in Australia was, calculating the numbers of Chinese people living outside the Chinese Empire to be miniscule compared to the hordes of Europeans who were scattered over the globe. Australian grievances came from their resentment of Chinese labour and Cheong believed the agitators would 'get rid of the competition of the Chinese labourer by any means, fair or foul'.[50]

In December 1893 *Fraternity* reported the dismay of a white Australian woman who realized she was obliged to share a train carriage with a Chinese man. His treatment reflected the 'unreasoning, implacable hatred' many Chinese people faced, as reported by Arthur Sinclair. His piece on the market gardens in Melbourne revealed the everyday forms this hostility could take.[51] Trudging along Elizabeth Street one morning Sinclair was shocked to hear the crack of his driver's whip connect with the neck of a 'hapless Mongolian' walking past them. 'I hate them – thieves' was the driver's excuse. When Sinclair threatened to take his driver to the police he was scornful: 'Where's the police? And supposing you find them, they'll only laugh at you. Come alowng now, boss, when you knowe them yaller skins as well as I do, you'll hate them too.' Sinclair reported that the Chinese population were seen as amoral by the citizens of Sydney, as gamblers by the gentleman horse racers of Melbourne and were beaten to a pulp in Tasmania.[52] Alongside Sinclair's column *Fraternity's* 'own correspondent' reported on the arrest of three Chinese men of Wahgunyah, Victoria, under the Chinese Restriction Act. The men had been living and working in the Corowa and Wahgunyah region for many years but did not have naturalization papers and were caught up in the administration of different laws in the different Australian colonies. For how long, asked *Fraternity's* correspondent, were poor but industrious men who had 'done more towards the making of Australia than all the loafers sent out from English cities' to be subjected daily to the grossest cruelty?[53]

Reporting on the exploitation of workers in the Empire for the benefit of British consumers was an effective way for *Anti-Caste* to demonstrate the everyday links between the British centre and the oppressed margins of the 'big crowd of British subjects' living throughout the world.[54] The consumption of tea was one example of this relationship. The new chains of popular teashops founded in Britain during the 1880s relied upon an attractive ambience and affordable menus. The tea they served came from packets decorated with images of elegant sari-clad workers picking tea in orderly plantations, which concealed the dire labour conditions of workers.[55] The harsh realities of working life on tea plantations were an aspect of consumer culture that *Anti-Caste* sought to expose. In 1889, details from a report on the imprisonment of an assistant manager of an Assam tea plantation for 'assault on coolies' and 'outraging female modesty' were reprinted as part of 'Under the British Flag'. Placing critical articles in 'Under the British Flag' allowed Catherine to frame them in a context that directed her readers to take some personal responsibility for the injustices they read about and thus turn sympathy into action. S N Sastri wrote to signal his appreciation of the quotations taken from the *Indian Messenger* for the report on Assam, regretful that officials and 'interested motives' were so strongly united against those trying to improve conditions for the tea workers.[56]

The 'Cost of Cheap Tea', published in January 1890, developed these themes bringing the 'comfortable tea-drinking public' before the real 'cost of human lives' with which their cheap tea was procured.[57] At the centre of the article were the workers who laboured in the tea gardens of Assam and suffered the most shocking abuses 'just as under the American and West Indian slave system of old'.[58] Gathered from the poorest of the poor in villages the chief commissioner of Assam contended that such a worker was 'practically a slave for the whole period of his contract'.[59] This exploitative system was legal and supposedly under government control and supervision, but this served as little protection for the workers. Catherine compared their experiences of flogging, imprisonment and lack of control over their labour to the slave systems of the Americas. To bring the injustice of the workers home to her readers, Catherine additionally compared their plight to those of factory workers in Britain. What would readers say, she asked, if there were a factory in England where half, or even a quarter, of the workers died every year? Moreover what would they say to a government that forced employees to fulfil the full term of a contract which they had entered into while they were ignorant of the nature of the work?[60]

Four months later *Anti-Caste* returned to the 'blot on the modern administration of India' in the Assam tea gardens by reprinting material from *Despatch on Inland Emigration* published the previous year in Calcutta. The report produced by the owners of the *Sanjibani* newspaper contained a number of horrifying revelations about the tea workers' conditions and their unequal access to justice.[61] Regulations for protecting the planters were rigorously enforced while those protecting the labourers were all too inadequate. The lack of government inspections of the gardens (which might occur once a year, but frequently not at all) denied the tea pickers an opportunity to appeal against the oppressive tasks and conditions set by their employers. Planters, on the other hand, were empowered to arrest workers without a warrant and rarely faced punishment for the harsh regimes they enforced upon their employees. Physical and other abuses were rife, including the refusal to allow workers a day of rest and to leave the plantations when their contracts ended.

Although critical of inequality and exploitative trade relations that brought cheap tea to British homes and tea houses, Catherine never gave explicit suggestions as to how her readers might change their behaviour in order to bridge the gulf between the rich and poor in society or as to how consumers might use their patterns of consumption to develop their political aspirations. For Catherine change required a suppression of selfishness, the 'power of the self' to be activated in order to create a society brought together through closer and kinder relationships. But *Anti-Caste* made no call, for example, for a boycott of tea grown in the Assam gardens as had occurred around

West Indian slave-grown sugar during the abolition movement of the 1780s, 1790s and 1800s. Catherine did practice ethical consumption through her temperance work and her vegetarianism. Although for many years a meat lover, as a farmer's daughter she knew something of the horrors of the slaughterhouse. She mourned over the sufferings of animals involved in the system of meat raising and thus became a vegetarian in 1879, for she came to believe that a meat diet was a cruel and needless practice.[62] Despite her own moral codes of living and the important role of a 'tender hearted man in Newcastle' in her own conversion to vegetarianism, Catherine did not seek to evangelize others.[63] During her visit to Britain Ida B Wells encountered vegetarianism for the first time. Staying with the Axon family during a stay in Manchester, Wells found their strict vegetarian diet bewildering. While with Catherine in Somerset, though the Impeys followed a vegetarian diet they provided alternatives for visitors who 'might not be members of the cult' and Wells ate roast beef or whatever cuts the family provided for her during her stay in Street.[64] Similarly Catherine did not seek to impose nor even suggest such ethical consumption to *Anti-Caste*'s readers. It was for informed individuals to acknowledge and impose the 'suppression of self' upon themselves.

The Aboriginal people of Australia

Although Ida B Wells' tours in Britain were picked up in parts of the Australian press, her speeches were not analyzed in detail and there is no indication that Australian editors were provoked into placing the mistreatment of black Americans into the context of the devastating consequences of colonial life on the Aboriginal peoples of Australia.[65] Reports on Australia in *Anti-Caste* described the violent, arrogant and abusive treatment of the Aboriginal peoples 'by all white settlers from the day when first these took possession of their country', but the politics of Indigenous peoples in Australia stretched Catherine's imperial knowledge.[66] She does not seem to have known any Australians personally. No Australian seems to appear in Askew's visitors' book and although Catherine records sending copies of *Anti-Caste* to West Australia, Australian newspapers are not often named in the list of exchanges, suggesting that she did not regularly receive particular Australian newspapers. This pattern appears to have continued under Edwards, although in April 1894 the *South Australian Register* confirmed it had received the January and February issues of *Fraternity*.[67] The commentary accompanying the notice informed readers that *Fraternity* denounced the policy and politicians who supported race separation 'in good set' terms, but it provided no detail of the content nor any further analysis or suggestion that its readers seek the periodical out for themselves. The weaker links in the print network between Catherine, Edwards and print culture in Australia meant that in *Anti-Caste* Catherine's reports on the oppression of Australian Aboriginal peoples came primarily from missionaries working in Australia, particularly Daniel and Janet Matthews, who ran Maloga Mission in New South Wales. Although heavily reliant on Daniel Matthews' views Catherine's connection to him linked her to one of the more radically minded activist missionary networks operating in Australia.

Born in Truro, Cornwall, in February 1837, Daniel Matthews left England with his mother and brother to join his father on the Victorian goldfields as a teenager.[68] After working in the goldfields and teaching, Daniel and his brother William opened a store in Echuca, where the Campasepe River met the Murray River on the New South Wales side of the border with Victoria. The brothers later discovered that part of the land they settled had been a gathering place and Corroboree ground. They set aside 20 acres on the river front, which they called Maloga, although they probably did not realize the enormous spiritual significance the site had for the Yorta Yorta and Bangerang peoples.[69] Following Daniel's marriage to Janet in 1872 the pair established Maloga as a mission.[70] For nine years the couple ran Maloga Mission without any government, church or missionary society support and when it did begin to receive funding from the New South Wales Aborigines Protection Board in 1883 more than half of Maloga's income still came from private donations.[71] An important aspect of the Mission's work focused around the school it ran where many Aboriginal men and women learnt to write and were supported in crafting petitions to colonial governments in attempts to gain land and some recognition of their political and economic rights.[72] By around 1886, 16 white and 48 black students attended the school run by their teacher of Indian descent Thomas James.[73] Born in September 1859 at Moka, Mauritius, James moved to Australia when his mother died and his father remarried. A popular teacher he volunteered at Maloga for two years before acquiring a formal position.[74] Although a success in missionary terms with over 200 residents at its height in the 1880s, by the time *Anti-Caste* began to be published in 1888 Maloga had passed through a difficult period, with Daniel Matthews increasingly in conflict with the Aborigines Protection Board and the more activist members of the Aboriginal communities who lived at Maloga. This led to the eventual break-up of the Mission in 1888 when Maloga residents were shifted to a government reserve, Cumeroogunga.[75]

Despite the role of 'benevolent parents' that Daniel and Janet allotted to themselves, Daniel Matthews proved to be one of the few activists that worked, however partially, alongside Aboriginal activists.[76] In 1881, 42 Aboriginal men living at Maloga signed a petition appealing for a grant because their traditional lands had been taken from them. Daniel Matthews typed up their claim and presented it on their behalf to the colonial secretary. William Cooper, a founder and leader of the Australian Aborigines League, settled at Maloga in 1884 and knew Daniel Matthews well.[77] Cooper was able to accumulate only a limited formal education, but the structure of the Matthews' Christian teachings provided a vision of humanitarianism that proved to be an antidote to Australian racism and provided Cooper and other Yorta Yorta peoples with 'powerful ways of understanding and protesting their plight and so helped equip them to fight for equality'.[78] After the move to Cumeroogunga James restarted his school and supported a number of students who became well-known Aboriginal activists including his brother-in-law William Cooper, Jack Pattern and William Onus, all members of the Australian Aborigines League.[79] Born out of a meeting of Aboriginal men and women at William Cooper's Fitzroy home in Melbourne in 1933 and formally constituted in 1936, the Aborigines League was the most important of the first generation of Aboriginal political organizations formed in Australia.[80]

To inform supporters and generate financial donations for the Mission's work, Daniel produced annual reports about life at Maloga which, as it had been established on his privately owned land, continued after the break-up of the mission by the Aborigines Protection Board. The *Thirteenth Report*, published in 1888, announced plans for a visit to England to 'waken a large feeling of sympathy' among the British public.[81] In May 1889 Daniel and Janet left for England with Paddy and Jenny Swift two 'dark-coloured natives'.[82] The group spent several months in England with Daniel staying behind when Janet, Jenny and Paddy returned to Australia before Christmas. Daniel Matthews claimed he travelled over 4000 miles and spoke to over 80,000 people, but there is no report of his tour in *Anti-Caste*.[83] A letter from the Matthews' friend and fellow missionary John B Gribble published in *The Christian* did appear in *Anti-Caste* during the group's stay in Britain, drawing attention to their advocacy.[84] The group spent most of their time in London, and though there were occasions when the group might have met or spoken to an audience where Catherine might have been present, Maloga's *Fifteenth Report* that details the group's time in England makes no mention of visiting Street or Catherine.[85] Speaking at Exeter Hall in October 1889, Daniel emphasized that hundreds of thousands of Aboriginal peoples continued to live in Australia, and that they had not died out as many white Australians believed, and that their present condition was 'a disgrace to England'.[86] His claims were confirmed by Paddy and Jenny Swift, who the *Pall Mall Gazette* reported to have given well-received, humorous and interesting addresses with Paddy telling his audience that the English had not only taken their country, but they were 'shooting down our lives'.[87]

Anti-Caste's readers were directed towards Gribble's recent book *Black but Comely*, which outlined that the Aboriginal people of Australia were not as *Anti-Caste* had supposed 'a nearly extinct people' but '*a nation that is still to be numbered by hundreds of thousands*.'[88] That Catherine found Gribble's book a revelation is illustrative of how important 'local news', perspectives and testimony were in challenging prevalent views and opinions. Over three columns with quotations and a page reference supplied, extracts from Gribble's book highlighted injustice, violence, the kidnapping of Aboriginal women and the effective enslavement of the people.[89] Catherine probably first met Matthews in 1890. Having read of the Maloga Mission's work in one of Matthews' old reports, which she read on a train to London, the following evening she was surprised 'to hear one of the speakers at the Aborigines Protection Society's Annual meeting introduced as Mr Daniel Matthews' for she had not heard about his arrival in England.[90] A history of Maloga appeared in *Anti-Caste* in September 1890 and a report on 'Australian Atrocities' in May 1891 was based on two papers Matthews sent to Catherine, one 'encouraging the other extremely sad'.[91] The former came in the announcement of a mission station on Bribe Island. The other, which took up the majority of the report, focused on a controversy between Sir Samuel Griffith, Premier of Queensland, and Professor Rentoul of Melbourne University over the lack of protection being afforded to Aboriginal peoples. Their exchange of letters in the Australian press was reprinted, with one of Rentoul's letters quoted at length. This ended with the question of why a colony as wealthy as Queensland was able to take £400,000–£500,000 out of its general revenue to support the railways, yet could not do something 'wide-hearted and effective so as to bring knowledge, succour, and the pity of God, and some safety from attack, and from banishment, and from disease, to the remnant of the darkened race into whose rich territory we white men have entered with the "right" of superior forces".[92]

Anti-Caste did report on the extreme violence and brutality that produced these desperate circumstances through an interview with Carl Lumholtz, a Norwegian theologian, naturalist and anthropologist, who spent four years in Queensland from 1880, which he wrote up in his book *Among Cannibals*.[93] *Anti-Caste* repeated his description of the favourite sport of some white men to systematically hunt and kill Aboriginal Australians every Sunday. Although a punishable crime, as in the United States, only the death of a white man galvanized the full workings of the law. Lumholtz recalled that colonists repeatedly offered to shoot 'a few blacks' so he could have a few more skulls for his scientific observations. In the light of such brutality Catherine argued that Australian Aborigines needed to be given access to an education both secular and religious and vigilantly protected from the 'English settlers' who acted as 'lawless ruffians' and had 'appropriated their country and portioned it out into various colonies'.[94] The fact that the Aboriginal nations were already highly educated in both secular and spiritual forms of their own was misunderstood and ignored by many missionaries and seems to have been unknown to Catherine.[95]

Typologies of race

In a July edition of the *Liverpool Daily Post*, a leader commended Catherine on a striking article in *Anti-Caste* on the subject of the ongoing 'Angora Trial' in connection to protests against the Sultan in Angora and other cities in the Ottoman Empire.[96] In response Turkish authorities had made mass arrests among the Armenian population with hundreds taken to Angora to face trial.[97] The case Catherine focused on reportedly had seen 17 Armenian Christians sentenced to death by a court of judges, though all evidence in favour of the accused was refused, and the condemned men were not allowed to speak of the tortures to which they had allegedly been subjected prior to the trial. In his editorial leader for the *Post* Russell agreed with Catherine's analysis that the spirit of the Berlin Treaty signed between Russia and the Ottoman Empire in 1878, particularly Article 61, which included the Ottoman's commitment to undertake reforms for the Armenians, had not merely been violated through the trial, but literally treated with contempt. Russell understood Gladstone's emphatic opinion that 'the Sultan should be given plainly to understand that under no circumstances will misdeeds in Armenia be tolerated', to mean that a British military intervention might result. Russell noted that Catherine's religious scruples meant she hoped that 'the "inhuman method" of war' would not be adopted. She believed that instead England's moral persuasion ought to be focused on ensuring that the Sultan secured the fulfilment of his treaty obligations. Russell concluded that Catherine's view might be the more desirable path, but there were many who differed from her.[98] Russell's careful reading and republishing of Catherine's piece in *Anti-Caste* reflected the high esteem in which he held her work, but it also reveals that in its examination of racial oppression *Anti-Caste* on occasion included geographies of whiteness within the perimeters of its concerns.

The irregularity of discussions on oppression experienced by white people in *Anti-Caste* may have been due to its compact size and so reflected a strategic editorial decision by Catherine. She recognized early on that the paper's small size made it difficult 'to boil down good articles efficiently'.[99] Edwards' expansion of the paper from 1893 supported a broader geography of reporting including more regular references to prejudice faced by white people, with a particular focus on religious and political oppression in Europe. The restrictions upon Jewish life in Siberia and the massacre of Catholics in Russian Poland were denounced.[100] The condition of Armenia and Kurdish raids in Russian Armenia were highlighted, as was the persecution of Russian Stundists (dissenters from the Orthodox Church), and the practice of flogging them and declaring them to be insane condemned. The fact that Stundists' leaders were often imprisoned without trial was compared to the experience of black Americans.[101] The arrest of anarchists in Paris and Nice and the resulting expulsion of 15 Italians from France were reported in January 1894.[102] Ireland also made occasional appearances in articles such as 'Keynote on Modern Society', in which an unnamed author argued that the abominations of lynch law in America and the subjugating of jury trials in Ireland had the same political reasoning at their root.[103]

Although attention was not often given to the oppression of white people in the pages of *Anti-Caste*, Catherine did not ignore the complex ideas of race that relied upon normalized constructions of whiteness. Catherine's struggle to conceptualize a language of antiracism included an effort to decentre the normativity of whiteness in her writing. In addition to ideas of 'caste', a variety of terms were used to describe ethnic identities and oppression in article headlines in both *Anti-Caste* and *Fraternity*: 'The Proposed Afro-American League', The 'New York Coloured Mission', 'Mr Moody and the Colour-line', 'Women's Suffrage Movement and Caste', 'Australian Native Races', 'White Men Not Hung in Georgia', 'Race Prejudice in India', 'Is There Caste in the Bahamas?' and 'Black and White' are just a few examples.[104] The diversity of terms reflects the debates and shifting meanings of race encountered through an array of international print cultures.

How to express the politics of race in print culture was a question of debate within black American thought. Thomas Fortune and Ida B Wells supported use of the term 'Afro-American' in contrast to W E B Du Bois and Booker T Washington, who preferred 'Negro'.[105] In 1891 in response to the question 'What is an Afro-American' asked by the *Southern Christian Recorder*, Fortune replied via the *New York Age* that an Afro-American 'is a descendant of an African', and an African was a man who came from Africa and was not ashamed of the fact. An 'Afro-American' resented being called a '"Negro" or a "colored" something without a race and without a country'.[106] He made a similar statement in a letter to the American periodical *Outlook* asking why in their use of the term they had construed '"negro" to be a common noun' when the article in question plainly meant to 'designate, although erroneously, a race', in the same sense as 'Filipino and Indian' used in the same article. The whole American press followed the same rubric which was, Fortune argued, greatly resented by the ten million 'Afro-Americans' in the United States.[107] Speaking at the National Negro Business League several years later Fortune reiterated his demand to be an 'Afro-American'.

> You can take your choice of names, BUT I AM AN 'AFRO-AMERICAN.' All the white newspapers of this country regard you as 'negroes' and write Negro with a little 'n.'.... They regard you as a common noun.... Now I get around that undesirable title by adopting 'AFRO-AMERICAN,' which calls for the use of two big capital 'A's.' (Laughter and applause.) I AM A PROPER NOUN, NOT A COMMON NOUN![108]

Catherine sometimes highlighted the racial prejudice present in language by using grammatical markings. Placing the 'colours' ascribed to people in quote marks Catherine emphasized the constructed nature of the language she used, for she had no other means of communicating the real differences she observed or was reporting. In the first issue of *Anti-Caste* Catherine had told readers that *Anti-Caste* expected to deal mainly with issues of 'colour caste' because she had personal knowledge of its workings. This came predominately from her travels to the United States, where she enjoyed 'the friendship and acquaintance of many of those known as "coloured" people'.[109] Telling readers about her fourth trip to the United States in 1892, Catherine described her attendance at a drawing-room meeting in Philadelphia where an 'elderly white gentleman...and the Editor of *Anti-Caste*, were the only "white" persons present in the company though some were but little darker – if at all'.[110] When discussing prejudice faced by Chinese workers in the United States, she argued that '... legislating against particular races *as such* – each "race" composed as it is of caste numbers of individuals each different in attainments and capacity – is both unsafe and unjust'.[111]

Aware that the large majority of *Anti-Caste's* readership was based in Britain, Catherine sought to create an imaginative geography that would connect them to this international collective and the individuals whose plight they read about in the paper.

> ... we the English are, as it were, but an inner cluster of the big crowd of British subjects, the masses of whom live in lands other than ours, and have been brought under British rule sometimes voluntarily but more often, we fear, by force and fraud, and for ends not purely disinterested. Now they, like us, press round the same British Government, with its mighty and cumbrous machinery of State, looking to it, as we look to it – though almost despairingly at times – for the administration of justice, for power to carry out necessary reforms, for the redress of public grievances. To hold the power for weal or woe over tens of millions of human families is indeed an appalling responsibility. One is led to wonder how long the slender fabric of the empire shall hold together? Especially does this thought press when the bitter cry of suffering and oppression reaches us from some outer part of the great crowd.[112]

A sense of geographical diffusion is central to this imaginary, though Catherine cautioned that 'by setting people off at a distance from us' it became easy to 'imagine differences which have no existence in fact'. She was adamant that 'No matter what colour people are – yellow, brown, black, olive, white – all of them are *just men and women like ourselves*.¹¹³ Despite her emphasis on international connections, this inclusion of whiteness was a rare reference to the complex prejudices in operation against white people, particularly members of the Irish and Jewish diasporas. This absence may have been because of space or because Catherine saw these groups as being part of the migrants who took on racist views as they travelled to take advantage of new opportunities in Africa, India and the Australian 'Working Man's Paradise'.¹¹⁴ References to Russia's treatment of political prisoners and the report of the refusal to admit a 'Hebrew man', mainly owing to racial prejudices, to a social club in New York were made in *Anti-Caste*. Their atypical presence suggests that although aware of forms of oppression encountered by white people, Catherine chose not to regularly include these issues in *Anti-Caste*.¹¹⁵ She may have decided to follow Fortunes' lead, who, when arguing for the need of black Americans to establish their own news agencies in 1891, maintained that the need lay in the importance of balancing not only the 'truth' of reports circulated by white people but also the stories of oppression that circulated about white people. Fortune saw millions of dollars being spent every year to expose the poor treatment of 'the people of Ireland by the British Government, of Germany's oppressed unfortunate Jews, and of the horrors of Russia's penal colony in Siberia'. On the other hand millions were spent annually to hide from the public the 'infamies of the prison convict-camps of the South, of the massacre of defenceless blacks, of the disfranchisement of a whole race, of the uniform denial of civil rights, and of the one-sided administration of the laws'.¹¹⁶

Through *Anti-Caste* and *Fraternity* Catherine and Edwards developed a geographical imagination that sought to reveal the hidden experiences of oppression that connected racial inequalities across the uneven technologies of 'colour caste' operating in the British Empire, the United States and Europe. Underpinned by a consciousness of broader social oppression, their readers were presented with their editors' imaginative capacity for connecting critical examinations of racial segregation and the violence of racial oppression in the United States with white dominions and imperial spaces old and new in India, Africa and the Caribbean. Though early discussions in *Anti-Caste* presented racial prejudice as one of many different corporeal injustices, this did not result in the development of a geographical imagination that consistently included a politics of whiteness. This absence, particularly geographies of prejudice 'at home', meant that an opportunity to create a broader narrative of antiracism, one that included anti-Semitism and other forms of faith-based racisms, was not developed.

By drawing together experiences of racial prejudice and violence against people of colour, Catherine and Edwards drew attention and on occasion were able to give voice, although still a mediated one, to the racially oppressed. Their publications spoke to debates in operation among those who sought to criticize racial prejudice from the high-profile successes of Cecil Rhodes to the plight of unnamed workers on contracts to work under terrible conditions in the tea gardens of Assam and sugar plantations in Queensland. Among Daniel Matthews' papers in the National Library of Australia in Canberra is a box containing copies of newspaper clippings Matthews had assembled. They are mostly concerned with his campaign work with and on behalf of Aboriginal peoples, including cuttings of material attributed to him in *Anti-Caste*. The copies do not contain any notes or annotations; he does not, for example, comment on how a letter was edited before publication or if he agrees with the meanings and commentaries Catherine drew from her readings of the papers he sent. Daniel Matthews did cut out and keep his contributions, though, and these cuttings illustrate that copies of *Anti-Caste* made it to Maloga, where in 1892 there were around 50 people resident at the Mission.[117] For a few issues in 1892 at least, *Anti-Caste* may have drawn the Aboriginal men and women still living at Maloga into its community of readers.

Notes

1. *Fraternity*, August 1893, 1.
2. *Times*, 10 January 1896, 10.
3. *Fraternity*, March 1896, 7, quoting from a leader in *The Times*.
4. *Fraternity*, July 1893, 7.
5. Arendt, *Origins of Totalitarianism*, 167.
6. Arendt, *Origins of Totalitarianism*, 264.
7. For example, Frederic Harrison (1882) argued that Britain invaded Egypt 'at first in the interest of bond-holders, for whom not a penny of our taxes should have been expended.' Quoted in Claeys, *Imperial Sceptics*, 82.
8. *Anti-Caste*, July 1891, 1.
9. *Anti-Caste*, July 1891, 1.
10. Heartfield, *Aborigines' Protection Society*.
11. 'Annual report', *Aborigines' Friend*, May 1891, 187–188.
12. *Anti-Caste*, July 1891, 3–4.
13. *Aborigines' Friend*, January 1894, 378.
14. *Aborigines' Friend*, 1894, 386.
15. *Anti-Caste*, December 1892, 3.
16. *Lux*, 10 December 1892, 290–291.
17. *Lux*, 10 December 1892, 290–291.
18. *Lux*, 6 May 1893, 219.
19. *Aborigines' Friend*, 1894, 391.
20. 'Affairs in Matabeleland', *Aborigines' Friend*, January 1894, 378–394.
21. *Fraternity*, December 1893, 1.
22. *Fraternity*, January 1894, 1.
23. *Fraternity*, February 1894, 1.
24. *Fraternity*, January 1894, 1.
25. 'Under the British flag, outline of the Zulu grievances', *Anti-Caste*, April 1890, 1–2.
26. *Anti-Caste*, December 1889, 3; also see 'Testimony of a Kafir newspaper', *Anti-Caste*, October 1899, 4.
27. Jabavu, *Life of John Tengo Jabavu*; Moropa, 'African voices'.
28. *Imvo Zabantsandu*, 3 November 1884, 3.
29. *Imvo Zabantsandu*, 3 November 1884, 3; Moropa, 'African voices'.
30. *Anti-Caste*, December 1891, 2.
31. *Anti-Caste*, October 1889, 2.
32. *Anti-Caste*, October 1889, 2.
33. *Anti-Caste*, October 1889, 3.
34. *Anti-Caste*, December 1892, 2.
35. *Fraternity*, January 1894, 1.

36 Stewart was editor of *Isigidimi SamaXhosa (Kafir Express)* and principal of the Lovedale Institution; Jabavu knew him from his time serving as editor of *Isigidimi SamaXhosa*. Moropa, 'African voices'; Ross, 'Stewart, James (1831–1905)'.
37 *Imvo Zabantsandu*, 16 April 1891, 3.
38 Moropa, 'African voices'; Saunders, 'Ngcongco'.
39 Moropa, 'African voices'.
40 Newspaper clipping, c.1900, BC 749 N3 2, University of Cape Town Archives. The clipping appears to be an advert requesting British Quakers to consider investing in *Imvo*, which was floated as a company in 1900.
41 Henry McCallum to Sir Walter Hely-Hutchinson, governor of Cape Colony, 13 April 1906, PMO 218 493/06 1906, Western Cape Archives, South Africa.
42 *Fraternity*, March 1894, 15.
43 On the Pacific Islands, see Mackay, 'Muffled Slavery, the Polynesian labour traffic', *Fraternity*, December 1893, 10–11; 'The Kanaka traffic and its fruits', *Anti-Caste*, June/July 1895.
44 'Kanaka question', *Anti-Caste*, December 1892, 3; 'Traffic in South Sea Island labour', May 1892, 1–3, 6; 'Renewal of the Kanaka labour traffic', May 1892, 4–5.
45 'Kanaka question', *Anti-Caste*, December 1892, 4.
46 Lodwick, *Crusaders against Opium*.
47 *Anti-Caste*, November 1888, 1. Signed in October 1888, the Exclusion Act restricted Chinese immigration to the United States.
48 *Anti-Caste*, November 1888, 2, original emphasis. The 'expulsion' of Chinese workers by 'labour organizations' from the Puget Sounds region of the North Western USA in 1886 appeared as a report on a lecture given by Garrison, *Anti-Caste*, September 1889, 3–4.
49 Mansfield, 'Origins of "White Australia"'; Yarwood, *Attitudes to Non-European Immigration*.
50 *Anti-Caste*, February 1889, 3.
51 On the train journey *Fraternity*, December 1893, 14; at the market gardens *Fraternity*, September 1893, 5.
52 *Fraternity*, September 1893, 4, original emphasis.
53 *Fraternity*, December 1893, 14.
54 *Anti-Caste*, December 1889, 2–3.
55 de Grout, 'Metropolitan desires'.
56 *Anti-Caste*, April 1889, 1.
57 'The cost of cheap tea', *Anti-Caste*, January 1890, 2–3.
58 'The cost of cheap tea', *Anti-Caste*, January 1890, 2.
59 'A blot on the modern administration of India', *Anti-Caste*, May 1890, 1–2; 'The cost of cheap tea', *Anti-Caste*, January 1890, 2.
60 'The cost of cheap tea', *Anti-Caste*, January 1890, 2–3.
61 *Anti-Caste*, May 1890, 1.
62 Impey, 'On vegetarianism', *Street Album*, 32, 1879; 'Vegetarian dinner to delegates', *Good Templars' Watchword*, 2 May 1887, 277.
63 Impey, 'On vegetarianism', *Street Album*, 32, 1879.
64 Duster, *Crusade for Justice*, 102.
65 See *Maitland Mercury and Hunter River General Advertiser* (NSW), 24 August 1893; *Bradford Courier and Reedy Creek Times* (Victoria), 3 August 1894; *Queenslander* (Qld), 4 August 1894; *South Australian Chronicle* (Adelaide), 14 July 1894.
66 *Anti-Caste*, December 1889, 1.

67 *South Australian Register* (Adelaide), 16 April 1894, 5.
68 Cato, 'Matthews, Daniel (1837–1902)'.
69 Cato, *Mister Maloga*; McLisky, 'The location of faith'.
70 Although Daniel Matthews is most usually associated with Maloga, Claire McLisky emphasizes the important role Janet Matthews played in the establishment of the Maloga Mission. See McLisky, 'Professions of Christian love'.
71 McLisky, 'The location of faith'.
72 McLisky, 'Colouring (in) virtue?'
73 Cato, *Mister Maloga*.
74 From Nelson, 'James, Thomas Shadrach (1859–1946)'; Clements, *From Old Maloga*.
75 McLisky, 'Settlers on a mission'; Cato, *Mister Maloga*; McLisky, 'Colouring (in) virtue?'; Nelson, 'James, Thomas Shadrach (1859–1946)'.
76 McLisky, 'Settlers on a mission'; Attwood, *Rights for Aborigines*.
77 Attwood and Markus, *Thinking Black*.
78 Attwood and Markus, *Thinking Black*, 5.
79 Nelson, 'James, Thomas Shadrach (1859–1946)'.
80 Attwood and Markus, *Thinking Black*.
81 Quoted in Cato, *Mister Maloga*, 189.
82 *Pall Mall Gazette*, 4 October 1889, 6.
83 Cato, *Mister Maloga*.
84 'Gribble's letter makes no mention of Paddy and Jenny Swift', *Anti-Caste*, October 1889, 1–2.
85 *Fifteenth Annual Report*, RBJ 266.0009 MAT V1/C1, State Library Queensland.
86 *Pall Mall Gazette*, 4 October 1889, 6.
87 *Pall Mall Gazette*, 4 October 1889, 6.
88 'Under the British flag, how we treat the natives of Australia', *Anti-Caste*, December 1889, 1, original emphasis.
89 'Under the British flag, how we treat the natives of Australia', *Anti-Caste*, December 1889, 1–2.
90 *Anti-Caste*, June 1890, 3. A newspaper account on the APS' annual meeting reports that Harriet Colenso was also in attendance, London *Morning Post*, 22 May 1890, 5.
91 'Native Australians, a story of "The Truth Spoken in Love"', *Anti-Caste*, September 1890, 2–4; 'Australian Atrocities', *Anti-Caste*, May 1891, 3.
92 'Australian Atrocities', *Anti-Caste*, May 1891, 4.
93 Lumholtz, *Among Cannibals*.
94 *Anti-Caste*, June 1890, 4.
95 For discussions of Aboriginal Australia and historical transnationalism and mobility, see Ganter, *Mixed Relations*; Hunter, 'Rough riding'; Macknight, 'The view from Marege'.
96 Hansard Mr Francis S Deb, 2 May 1893, vol 11 c.1733; HC Deb, 22 June 1893, vol 13 cc.1673–1674.
97 Kirakosiân, *British Diplomacy*; Dennis, 'Debate on the Early "Armenian Question"'. The trials featured in a number of reports in the British press, for example 'The Angora Trial', London *Daily News*, 29 June 1893; 'The charge of sedition against Armenians' in the *Lincolnshire Echo*, 15 June 1893 and the following up of events in 'The Angora Trial', *Manchester Courier and Lancashire General Advertiser*, 10 July 1893.
98 *Liverpool Daily Post*, 6 July 1893, 6. Reporting continued in *Fraternity*, July 1893, 3.
99 Impey to Chesson, 23 December 1887, MSS. Brit. Emp. s.18 C138/172.

100 *Fraternity*, October 1893, 12; January 1894, 9.
101 *Fraternity*, August 1893, 9.
102 'Kurdish raids', *Fraternity*, August 1893, 10; 'Anarchists', 9 January 1894, 9.
103 *Fraternity*, July 1894, 4–5.
104 'The proposed Afro-American league', *Anti-Caste*, March 1888, 2; 'New York coloured mission', *Anti-Caste*, April 1888, 1; 'Mr Moody and the colour-line', *Fraternity*, January 1894, 13; 'Women's suffrage movement and caste' and 'Australian native races', both *Anti-Caste*, May 1888, 1; 'White men not hung in Georgia' and 'Race prejudice in India', both *Anti-Caste*, June 1888, 1; 'Is there caste in the Bahamas?', *Anti-Caste*, October 1888, 1; 'Black and white', *Anti-Caste*, July 1888, 3; 'The racial war in America', *Fraternity*, September 1893, 15; 'Black firemen', *Fraternity*, June 1894, 9; 'Official favouritism in India', *Anti-Caste*, March 1889, 2–3.
105 Alexander, *T Thomas Fortune*; Ida B Wells' discussions of this term were part of an interview with *Ladies Pictorial* while she was in London in 1893 and reprinted in Duster, *Crusade for Justice*, 108.
106 *New York Age*, 24 October 1892, 4.
107 T Thomas Fortune, 'Correspondence, Afro-American or negro?', *Outlook*, 10 June 1899, 62:6, 359.
108 'From the National Negro Business League', *Report of the Seventh Annual Convention*, 156. Emphasis and edits as quoted in Alexander, *T Thomas Fortune*, xxi.
109 *Anti-Caste*, March 1888, 1.
110 *Anti-Caste*, September 1892, 4.
111 *Anti-Caste*, November 1888, 2, original emphasis.
112 *Anti-Caste*, December 1889, 2–3.
113 *Anti-Caste*, April 1888, 2, original emphasis.
114 See Kirk, *Comrades and Cousins*.
115 'Blackballing of a Hebrew Gentleman', from *Toronto Empire*, March 1889; *Anti-Caste*, May 1889, 4.
116 T Thomas Fortune, 'On syndicating news', 238.
117 Cato, *Mister Maloga*.

Part 3

The Personal Is Political

As an activist and editor, Catherine Impey embodies Sheila Rowbotham's observation that women reformers and radicals working at the end of the nineteenth century possessed a 'capacity for optimistic imagining'.[1] Through *Anti-Caste* Catherine attempted to alter the outcome of people's everyday encounters as they were mediated through race. Although the focus of *Anti-Caste* was primarily disheartening in that it mostly emphasized realities of racial oppression rather than examples of unity or collaborative successes, *Anti-Caste* came out of Catherine's optimistic belief that an international movement to fight racism could be formed and could succeed. Catherine's attempt to shape an anticaste movement through print networks was underpinned by an optimistic imaginary of a community of readers. This, it was hoped, would be drawn together to harness the institutions associated with women's publishing in Britain which encouraged women to employ the power of print cultures to affect change.[2] Michelle Tusan argues that whether or not print journalism had the power to really facilitate social change, the women's press did radically reconfigure women's understandings of themselves as political agents.[3] *Anti-Caste* contributed to this by assuming women to be among the political actors active within its readership. Despite the utilization of institutions associated with women's press cultures, broadly speaking *Anti-Caste* did not maintain direct links with the women's press movement. Catherine herself remained largely outside their networks in London, and although edited by a woman *Anti-Caste*'s gaze did not fall solely upon women readers or their presumed concerns.

Though Catherine did not partake directly in the women's press, *Anti-Caste* sought to contribute to what Becky Thompson has identified as 'gender-conscious, justice work'.[4] Some of this work, such as raising questions around race and rape in the United States, was nuanced and challenging. Other elements such as the continual use of gendered terms like 'brotherhood' and 'fraternity' were less so. The Impey women supported women's suffrage, and Catherine argued for an understanding of gender inequality within the context of broader claims of equality for all. She vocalized this in the first issue of *Anti-Caste*, which emphasized that of all arbitrary distinctions placed upon people the most cruelly irritating were those based purely on physical characteristics including gender.[5] When the SRBM was formed, in addition to securing justice for all 'regardless of race, creed or condition', Catherine proposed the Society should 'protest against all separations in societies, based upon colour (or upon any natural and unalterable conditions)'. But the founding council members did not take up this suggestion of rights relating to gender and/or disability as well as race.[6] An article on the women's suffrage movement and caste from the *New York Age* was published in *Anti-Caste* in May 1888. However, the reason why the women's movement never drew more direct attention in *Anti-Caste* may lie with the failure of the movement in Britain and the United States to address racial prejudice as a core part of their work. For most white women working to establish the formal structures of the movement at the end of the nineteenth century, their capacity for 'optimistic imaginings' did not embrace the global elimination of racial hierarchies.

Gender and periodicals

By the end of the nineteenth century women had become more prominent in British journalism. Partaking in the dynamic encounter of reading was an important cultural function for Victorian women who sought to reconstruct themselves as active citizens. Michelle Tusan observes that the women's press movement emerged as a broad-based project which drew dedicated readers and workers into their literary communities.[7] These communities were vital to women who were reconstructing their political identities, and for many their participation in the women's movement was primarily a reading experience that incorporated a vast array of print culture.[8] Feminist publications included organizational organs, weekly or monthly reviews, news sheets and manifestos that supported a broad circulation of ideas.[9] A large number of periodicals eventually became centred around London and the city became a hub for women's journalism.[10] As Tusan illustrates the networks women established here proved crucial for creating mediums of exchange, helping to facilitate the distribution of publications and secure publicity for their content. These geographies of production created personal, social and business networks for women that expanded the scope and influence of their literary communities.[11] These informal networks of women's journalism combined with new collective spaces for women being established in the capital. Living in Somerset and without the financial means or time to travel regularly to London, Catherine could not partake in these metropolitan-focused networks. The production of *Anti-Caste* remained rooted in Somerset and reminds us that activist networks could be effectively sustained beyond the concentrations present in London, though this is not to say that an opportunity to publish in London would not have brought advantages. It is probably not a coincidence that the expansion of the paper under *Fraternity* was undertaken by the London-based Edwards.

Hilary Fraser, Stephanie Green and Judith Johnston argue that Victorian periodicals became effective 'sites of discourse', spaces where voices and dialogue performed and transformed discussions of gender.[12] Under these conditions the journalism of the periodical press was fundamentally provocative, a space where ideologies of class and gender were always connected, competing and under construction.[13] Such spaces could be, as *Anti-Caste* was, both critical and sensationalist.[14] In the main these discussions and tensions over the meanings of gender assumed a normativity of whiteness. This could be seen to be also true of *Anti-Caste*. The 'we' of the editor and her implied readers appeared to assume a normativity of Britishness and whiteness. But this is complicated by the editorship of Edwards, whose editorial addresses seem to have held a similar 'we' in mind, but clearly he embodied a disruption of whiteness and Britishness. So perhaps in her utilization of 'we' Catherine, like Edwards, meant to speak directly to those living in the more privileged and safer spaces of Britain regardless of the colour of their skin. Though the language of *Anti-Caste* and *Fraternity* remained gendered in many ways, the 'we' of its implied readers was not a gendered one. In *Anti-Caste* and *Fraternity*, geographies of gender and belonging were interlocked with dialogue that attempted to transform discourses of race. This intellectual work appeared through the rhetoric and tactics forged by Catherine and other contributors in the spaces of the periodicals. In the creations of the typologies of antiracism, Catherine constituted *Anti-Caste* as a '"geographer" in its own right', generating its own particular 'models of readability' and literary typologies that produced a particular kind of geographical forum for its readers.[15]

A battle over the form of the new woman activist who took part in the work of the SRBM also took place within the pages of *Fraternity*. The character of this debate and its consequences for Catherine and the SRBM are the focus of the following three chapters. A controversy initiated by Isabella Mayo, the leader of the Scottish branches of the SRBM, in the summer of 1894 revealed, as Vron Ware argues, Mayo's conservative attitudes to women's sexuality and discussions of race. Catherine's forward advances and proposal of marriage to a younger man active in the movement produced an outraged response from Isabella Mayo, who found Catherine's behaviour to be inexplicable and inexcusable. Mayo's ideas of a woman activist could not countenance such behaviour and she sought to impose her particular ideals of femininity and activism upon the SRBM in private and in print. Lindy Moore is right to remind us that there was much more to the political life of Isabella Mayo than the few years she spent working with the SRBM. She became an active public speaker, and in addition to her support for the SRBM she became a pacifist and 'ethical anarchist'.[16] Considering herself to be a 'Tolstoyan anarchist', she regularly corresponded with M K Gandhi and wrote to offer her support to Dadabhai Naoroji during his campaign to be elected to parliament and was a lifelong supporter of women's suffrage.[17] Moore is regretful that Mayo is now largely remembered only as a second-rate Victorian novelist, whose personal dispute with Catherine precipitated a split in the SRBM. Given Mayo's cosmopolitan networks it is fair for Moore to suggest that it is unlikely Mayo's extreme reaction to Catherine's proposal was motivated by an opposition to 'mixed race' marriages. But in declaring Catherine's behaviour as an example of lynch law in operation at home, Mayo did reveal her refusal to take on board the complex and important debates about race, sexual desire and lynching that Ida B Wells had brought before British audiences.[18] Although Wells may have toned down aspects of her rhetoric when she spoke publicly in Britain, Mayo surely had read enough of her work and discussed the themes with Wells in private adequately to know her strength of feeling on the subject.[19] Mayo's response suggests that though she may have known of Wells' theorizations of lynching, she either did not fully understand them or chose not to accept them.

Mayo's stance on racial equality and additional achievements do not mitigate her inability to accept modes of activist womanhood and femininity that differed from her own. Her intractability had adverse consequences for the SRBM, which she and Catherine had worked so hard to establish. Mayo's fictional writing suggests that despite her support for a radically inclined organization such as the SRBM, she held complexly conservative views on aspects of gender roles and, as Ware suggests, perhaps her interest in the SRBM came from a position rather different and in turn misunderstood by Catherine and Ida B Wells. In their examination of the dominance of Australia in the British periodical press during the nineteenth century, Fraser, Green and Johnston highlight the serialization of Mayo's three-part story 'The Other Side of the World' published in *Girl's Own Paper* between December 1881 and February 1882. The heroines of her story, Bell and Annie, are seemingly adventurous and aspirational young women seeking a new life in Australia. But they are not, as Fraser, Green and Johnston point out, models of 'new women' but 'modern martyrs'.[20] Mayo weaves into the narrative instructions for respectable women considering migration, and when Bell explains her reasons for leaving to her parents, she reveals that she believes her move will enable her brother to attend the art classes he covets and 'so elevate and brighten all his life'.[21]

In the summer of 1894 *Fraternity* came under Mayo's control. Although she did not become an editor she carried a strong influence over the paper. At the end of 1895 poems written for *Fraternity's* 'young folks' column appeared on the periodical's back covers. Written by St Clair Knox based in Dublin, these poems strongly reinforced gender stereotypes, introducing a new layer of gendering to the periodical's implied readers. *Boys, Be Chivalrous!*, considered suitable for boys of 12 years and over and highly recommended to be learnt by heart, informed young men that their future role was to be brave and to protect the weaker peoples they might encounter overseas.

> Boys, be chivalrous, not cowardly be,
> At home, abroad, or across the sea;
> Crush not the helpless or the weak,
> But defend those who protection seek.
> ...
> Boys, be chivalrous, and boys be brave:
> Heroes risk their lives others to save;
> Have moral courage, grow up true men:
> Scorn mean actions by word or pen.[22]

Here in *Fraternity* was the familiar narrative of imperial protection framed through the education of gender roles. Young women learned that their role was to be gentle with everyone in their homes and in all their actions.

> Be gentle, girls – gentle in all you do:
> For a rough girl is not a woman true;
> Be gentle in your movements, be gentle in your walk;
> Be gentle in your actions, be gentle in your talk.
> ...

Be gentle, girls – gentle in all you do:
Gentleness wins; anger won't get you through;
Be gentle out of doors, and gentle as a wife;
Be gentle in your homes, and be gentle all your life.[23]

For Catherine and Edwards there was much to be angry about, and through their choices of material and editorial commentaries, they sought to stir the passions of all their readers. Knox encouraged her young female readers to rue their tempers. How this could possibly equip them to contemplate the disturbing injustices of racial prejudice or begin to understand the sight of a man's body hanging from a tree was a problem wilfully ignored.

'Race' and women's advocacy

There were many women writers who took a conservative approach to the 'Woman Question', and some of the best-selling female novelists of the period were actively involved in antisuffrage. Some women journalists writing primarily on social issues also took this position, though fewer gave public voice to the cause.[24] Given her friendships and professional connections with many early feminists including Ida B Wells, Georgiana Simpson and Eliza Wigham, it is surprising Catherine did not play a more active role in the emerging women's movement, but she did support women's suffrage. Some of *Anti-Caste's* earliest and loyalist supporters closely overlapped with the women's movement. Eliza Wigham became the secretary of the Edinburgh branch of the National Society of Women's Suffrage from its inception in 1867; Mary Estlin was a supporter of women's suffrage and also a founding member of the National Union of Working Women, which aimed to protect women workers and improve their social conditions.[25] Though examples of Catherine directly participating in similar feminist activities are rare, this does not mean that she did not have strong feminist sympathies, particularly if being a feminist was centrally a reading experience in Britain.[26] Catherine was part of a radical reading community and contributed to debates through her editorship of *Anti-Caste*. She knew and relied upon the support of women who have been identified as feminists as did her family. As a businesswoman, Ellen utilized the women's movement's networks, advertising the farm's apples in a 1893 issue of the feminist paper *Shafts*.

When the franchise of the Right Worthy Grand Lodge of the World was expanded in 1885, Catherine celebrated the much larger number of voters in the Lodges and urged for an extra effort to circulate the thrill that the new power of voting should awaken in them, but she 'wished that women, too, were enfranchised' and urged the governing body give the subject its full consideration.[27] A list of names of those who supported women's suffrage in Britain was given in a *Declaration in Favour of Women's Suffrage* published in 1889. For the convenience of readers, the names of the more than 2000 women who signed the petition were divided into ten sections: a general list (which included Isabella Ormston Ford), the wives of clergymen and church dignitaries, poor-law guardians, women in education, registered medical practitioners and medical students, workers in social and philanthropic work, authors and journalists, artists and musicians, and businesswomen and landowners. Ellen and Mary Impey appear in the list 'Women Engaged in Business', Mary as a jam manufacturer and Ellen as a seed grower. Catherine could have been listed under 'Social and Philanthropic Workers' but she is placed among over 70 women associated with 'literature' presumably in recognition of *Anti-Caste* as she formally published little else.[28]

Catherine's presence on this list of journalists and authors indicates that her production of *Anti-Caste* was seen as a contribution to journalism and literary communities. This covered a vast array of genres and subjects from imperial politics, suffrage, childcare, marriage, women's work, the politics of labour, fashion and literary debates.[29] Catherine's contribution came out of a 'world of ideological printing', and as Isabel Hofmeyr reminds us, 'editor-proprietor-publishers' such as Catherine constituted important characters 'in the transnational drama of social reform'.[30] However, Catherine's ideological concerns meant her production of *Anti-Caste* did not meet the more common assumptions of a successful periodical. Although the content of its print was internationally focused, its physical production remained provincial and almost wholly reliant on Catherine. The journalistic work was not undertaken in an office and, aside from occasional help with postage and distribution, most of *Anti-Caste's* work was undertaken for free. Nor was the intended aim of *Anti-Caste* to make money. Supported by her sister, Catherine could afford not to be paid for her work; nor did she have to compromise her message to find an outlet for her writing. But nor could *Anti-Caste* afford a consistent loss. Nevertheless, this places it at odds to the contentions of scholars who have argued that printed goods had to be based on a sound financial business footing to succeed or with editors who argued that financial success reflected a periodical's influence.[31]

As Lara Langer Cohen and Jordan Alexander Stein draw out from examples of early black American print culture, circulation was not always primarily or even necessarily an economic issue.[32] Catherine's astute decision to keep *Anti-Caste* fairly cheap to produce meant a relatively small readership could support a distribution of the periodical that was far larger than its core financial base of subscribers. Whether this could have continued under Edwards' model for *Fraternity* is arguable. Though Edwards' larger *Fraternity* enabled a breadth of content impossible to meet in *Anti-Caste*, the reprinting of its columns in British national and international newspapers, particularly within early black American print cultures, suggests that though Catherine did not achieve literary fame her pithy yet provocative periodical was recognized as an important contributor to the press. Although produced and edited by a woman – Catherine always clearly indicated she was the editor and main contact for the monthly – *Anti-Caste* was held in high esteem by male editors and writers committed to journalism for social change. Fortune, Smith and Russell celebrated the political aspirations of *Anti-Caste* but also paid attention to the quality of its analysis.

Catherine, Mayo and the SRBM used a variety of feminist institutions including 'at-homes', reading rooms and clubs to promote events and debates associated with the movement particularly during Wells' tours.[33] When Wells arrived in London in May 1894 the Pioneers were celebrating the opening of their new club premises at 22 Burton Street. These consisted of beautiful rooms with a reading room supplied with the latest books – although these were not to be taken out of the Silent Room.[34]

Established in Regent Street in 1892, the Pioneer Club was considered to be one of the most democratic clubs in the city, accepting women from all classes, 'rich as well as poor – poor equally with rich'.³⁵ It had a membership of nearly 500 and exerted a strong influence on discussions around the position of women in society, one that the *Shafts*' editor felt would only increase.³⁶ The Pioneer Club's proceedings were advertised in *Shafts*, 'a magazine for women and workers', that later became a 'magazine for progressive thought'. Club dinners, lectures, debates and discussions were held on Thursday evenings and covered a wide selection of topics. The 1894 summer session, which ran from 12 April to 19 July, included debates such as 'Corporal Punishment a Mistake', 'That Women Have Nothing to gain from the Spread of Socialism' and 'Is the Needle in Its Proper Sphere?'³⁷ Wells wrote to the *Inter-Ocean* on 6 June 1894 explaining that she was due to speak to the Pioneers Club on 'Thursday next', although her talk is not listed in *Shafts* as one of the Thursday evening debates. It is possible that one of these were changed, although this is not noted or acknowledged by *Shafts*. There were alternative debates held fortnightly on Wednesday evenings at 8:30pm. These only required a week's notice for participants, and the topics of the debates were posted on the club notice board a few days before each meeting. Members and nonmembers attended these debates, providing an opportunity to meet friends and for new faces to be introduced to the club; 'at-homes' were also held every Tuesday between 4:30 and 6pm and perhaps Wells' talk was scheduled for one of these evenings instead.

Contacts from *Anti-Caste* subscribers were used to arrange Wells' visit to the Ideal Club, a space on Tottenham Court Road where vegetarians met to dance and debate.³⁸ This was a new kind of club seeking to break down class barriers through discussions, dances and fun, running classes on poetry, ethics and social evenings when members could listen to conversations, some brilliant, some profound and some silly about social and political questions of the day.³⁹ Wells also spent a pleasant afternoon at the Writers' Club, another women's organization, run by a friend of the Pioneers. Their rooms were at Hastings House, Norfolk Street on the Strand, and Wells spoke to the members and their guests about lynching. Her experience there reveals the tensions over 'truth' and 'authenticity' that existed in spaces where women debated issues of equality. During her talk to the Writers, an American woman challenged Wells from the floor, proclaiming her allegations to be lies. In the process of her reply, Wells realized that the woman had never been to the South and was a 'victim to her own imagination', but the incident reminded her of the challenges she met from American white women in her quest for equality.⁴⁰ Wells' 1894 tour gained attention in the British mainstream press but drew less attention in the women's press.⁴¹ Although an announcement for Wells appeared in the *Ladies Pictorial* in 1893 (which Wells described as one of the leading women's journals of the country), *Shafts* seems to have ignored Wells' numerous presentations in both 1893 and 1894, and although *The Woman's Signal* picked up on Wells' visit in 1894 it did not substantively reflect upon the content of her arguments.⁴²

Ida B Wells is now often included as a key actor within histories of black American feminists, but her refusal to 'compromise principle to prejudice' meant she never became a key player in well-known women's organizations such as the National American Woman Suffrage Association.⁴³ Considering Catherine's commitment to living by her principles and her refusal to endorse societies that failed to refute racial prejudice in all aspects of their politics and practice, a similar observation could be made for her absence from the women's movement in Britain.[44] The role of an imperial sensibility in feminist interventions in India illustrates that white women's ideas of 'equality' prioritized the emancipation of white women before their colonized sisters and in the United States suffragist campaigners 'never hesitated to show' that delivering the vote to 'white women would give supremacy to the entire white race'.[45] In the case of Chicago, Maureen Flanagan observes that although some white women were open to 'cross race cooperation' during the development of the movement, there were too few to produce interlocking gender and antiracist activism.[46] When black women from the Women's Era Club of Boston wrote an open letter of support for Wells during her time in Britain, they revealed the tensions between black and white women in the movement. The complex interlocking of racism and sexism meant, in most sections of American society, men and women absolutely refused to worship, live or eat alongside black women.

> We have endured much and we believe with patience; we have seen our world broken down, our men made fugitives and wandered or their youth and strength spent in bondage. We ourselves are daily hindered and oppressed in the race of life; we know that every opportunity for advancement, for peace and happiness will be denied us;... All that we ask is for justice – not mercy or palliation – simply justice.... We do not expect that white women shall feel as deeply as we.[47]

Lucy Delap argues that in general 'British feminists were both less interested in, and more critical of issues of race' than their American peers, but she reveals that anti-Semitic discussions occurred quite openly in the movement.[48] In the context of the United States, Terborg-Penn argues that only black women's campaigns for the vote reflect a true theoretical and practical understanding of equality, for their campaigns on behalf of all citizens made them universal in their outlook in a way that white women were not.[49] Catherine also worked for 'human betterment' and her outlook was far broader than many 'humanitarian journalists' operating within the women's press movement.[50] Lady Isabella Somerset, whom Wells first met briefly during her 1893 tour, was seen to combine her temperance and suffrage activism with human rights activities on behalf of 'oppressed minorities in the Near East' – notably Christian minorities living in the Ottoman Empire.[51] Michelle Tuscan identifies that these many different strands in Somerset's activism came together in her journalism, forging 'an identity as a voice for the voiceless'.[52] This is very different to what Catherine attempted in *Anti-Caste*; she did not seek to speak for people, but to provide a place where oppressed peoples could be heard. Catherine's conception of the oppressed with whom she shared common concerns had the capacity to encompass greater diversity than Somerset, whose interests remained bounded by ideologies of whiteness. She found Wells' outspoken demands for equality uncomfortably confronting.[53] The eldest daughter of the third Earl Somers, the death of her father in 1883 left Isabella Somerset with a considerable inheritance.[54] In 1892 she purchased the London-based *Women's Herald* transforming it into a campaigning penny paper renamed the *Woman's Signal*. With Somerset acting as editor from 1893 to 1895 it is not so surprising that the *Signal* failed to examine the difficult intersections of race and class raised by Ida B Wells when she was in Britain in 1894.

Catherine had a universal outlook on prejudice and, as her essay on 'Diverse Views on Social Equality' illustrated, a sensitivity to the importance of class structures. The pricing of *Anti-Caste* placed it among the 'penny papers' that aimed at a mass readership. How Catherine's broader ideals of social inclusion might have been manifest in the SRBM are hard to establish. Working-class readers of *Anti-Caste* or *Fraternity* remain largely elusive, as do working-class activists within the SRBM. Wells does not mention black working-class men or women in her memories of London, and the structures and power of the SRBM appeared to be dominated by middle-class activists. The decision to ignore issues of racism at home may have marginalized black and white working women who had been living with the politics of blackness in Britain for many years. It was their friends, lovers, husbands and children who were negotiating the opaque structures of caste in Britain and who would later be victimized in the race riots in 1917 and 1919 as were the women themselves.[55] They also seemed to be marginalized in ideals of the woman activist depicted in *Fraternity*.[56] Their absence highlights the limits in the imaginative capacity of the women's movement to champion the rights of all women as expressions of 'universal rights' and 'human rights'.

Notes

1 Rowbotham, *Dreamers of a New Day*, 1.
2 Tusan, *Women Making News*.
3 Tusan, *Women Making News*.
4 Thompson, 'Multicultural feminism', 352.
5 *Anti-Caste*, March 1888, 1. In *Beyond the Pale*, Vron Ware discusses Catherine's ideas on the women's movement in the context of an essay on suffrage produced in the 1878 *Village Album*. Since Ware undertook her research, an index for the *Album* printed in 1892 has become available, and as this attributes the essay to Isabella Metford, I have not included reference to the essay in my discussions here.
6 'Early record of the "Brotherhood" society', MSS. Brit. Emp. s.20 E5/7.
7 Tusan, *Women Making News*.
8 Delap and Di Cenzo, 2008, 'Transatlantic print culture'.
9 Delap and Di Cenzo, 2008, 'Transatlantic print culture'.
10 Tusan, *Women Making News*.
11 Tusan, *Women Making News*.
12 Fraser, Green and Johnston, *Gender and the Victorian Periodical*, 16.
13 Fraser, Green and Johnston, *Gender and the Victorian Periodical*, 16.
14 Hampton, Representing the public sphere in *Transatlantic Print Culture 1880–1940*.
15 Brosseau, 'Geography's literature', 349.
16 Moore, 'Reputation of Isabella Fyvie Mayo'.
17 Moore, 'A notable personality'; 'Reputation of Isabella Fyvie Mayo'.
18 Ware, *Beyond the Pale*.
19 On Wells tempering her arguments in Britain, see Silkey, *Evolving Morality in a Transatlantic Society*.
20 Fraser, Green and Johnston, *Gender and the Victorian Periodical*, 140.
21 Fraser, Green and Johnston, *Gender and the Victorian Periodical*, 140.
22 *Fraternity*, November 1896, npn.

23 *Fraternity*, February 1896, npn.
24 Bush, *Women against the Vote*.
25 Crawford, *The Women's Suffrage Movement*.
26 Delap, *The Feminist Avant-Garde*.
27 *The Good Templars' Watchword*, 20 April 1885, 255.
28 'Declaration in favour of women's suffrage: being the signatures received at the office of the Central Committee for Women's Suffrage', London School of Economics Selected Pamphlets (1889). Catherine did publish *What Shall We Do with Our Apples* (The Vegetarian Office, London, 1892), illustrating how cider apples could be used without turning them into alcohol.
29 Gray, 'Introduction'.
30 Hofmeyr, *Gandhi's Printing Press*, 42.
31 Lara Langer Cohen and Jordan Alexander Stein highlight Lucien Febvre and Henri-Jean Martin, Jürgen Habermas and Benedict Anderson in this context, in 'Introduction: Early African American print culture'; see Fraser, Green and Johnston, *Gender and the Victorian Periodical*.
32 Cohen and Stein, *Early African American Print Culture*.
33 Green, 'The feminist periodical press'.
34 *Shafts*, vol. 16, June 1894, 276.
35 *Shafts*, vol. 17, July 1894, 283.
36 *Shafts*, vol. 15, May 1894, 251.
37 *Shafts*, vol. 15, May 1894, 251.
38 Gregory, *Victorians and Vegetarians*.
39 Bondfield, *A Life's Work*.
40 Duster, *Crusade for Justice*, 179.
41 For example, see *Liverpool Mercury*, 6 June 1894, 4; *Aberdeen Weekly Journal*, 7 June 1894, 4 and 6; *Birmingham Daily Post*, 7 June 1894, 5.
42 On *Ladies Pictorial*, see Duster, *Crusade for Justice*, 107; *The Woman's Signal*, 19 April 1894, 265.
43 McMurry, *To Keep the Waters Troubled*, 308. For examples of Wells and her feminist activities, see Higginbotham 1992; Terborg-Penn 1998; Taylor 1998.
44 Carey, 'The racial imperatives of sex'; Bressey, 'Victorian anti-racism and feminism'.
45 Aileen Kraditor 1965 quoted in Taylor, 'The historical evolution of black feminist theory and praxis', 237. On India see Burton, 'The white woman's burden'.
46 Flanagan, *Seeing with Their Hearts*.
47 Duster, *Crusade for Justice*, 198–199; Rief, 'Thinking locally, acting globally'.
48 Delap, *The Feminist Avant-Garde*, 274.
49 Terborg-Penn, *African American Women in the Struggle for the Vote*.
50 Simpson, 'Notes: Catherine Impey', 105.
51 Tusan, 'Humanitarian journalism', 91.
52 Tusan, 'Humanitarian journalism', 91.
53 On the public disagreements between Wells, Somerset and her friend and colleague Frances Willard, see Ware, *Beyond the Pale*; August, *Rival Radical Feminists*.
54 She married Lord Henry Somerset in 1872 but separated from him in 1878, see Tusan, 'Humanitarian journalism'.
55 See, for example, letter to *The Times*, The Colour Riots. Reasons For Repatriation, 14 June 1919, 8; 'Black men and white girls', *The Times*, 1 July 1919, 4; Jenkinson, *Black 1919*.
56 See Holton, 'The suffragist and the "average woman"'.

8

A Broken Fraternity

Round the earth a whisper stealeth,
Like a thrilling undertone,
Which a subtle joy revealeth
'The new age is coming soon.'

Bond of Brotherhood, 1894

The enthusiastic reports published by SRBM branch secretaries during the first year of *Fraternity*'s run reflected an invigorated community inspired by Edwards and Wells. Despite this initial success financial difficulties for *Fraternity* and voices of discontent around the structure of the SRBM were mounting. Reverend Woodrow, Honorary Secretary of the local Aberdeen Branch, reported that Scottish branches of the SRBM felt they were restricted by the current structure and could work more effectively by forming an independent Northern Federation of Branches.[1] Woodrow cited distance and 'other causes' for his suggestion. This was a subtle reference to the personal rift that had developed between Isabella Mayo, Catherine Impey and Ida B Wells, which, behind the scenes, had broken apart the women's friendships, their activist networks and their ability to maintain the unity of the SRBM. The lively and informed debates in the page of *Fraternity* masked these internal struggles and the fact that Edwards had been ill since the winter of 1893. In addition, receipts for *Fraternity* were not meeting its costs and Edwards' ambitious plans for the paper had put a serious strain on his personal finances.

With the establishment of *Fraternity* Edwards took personal financial responsibility for the production of the paper as Catherine had done with *Anti-Caste*. He and his colleagues had no doubt envisaged that with subscribers joining up all over the country the SRBM would have soon been in a position to take financial ownership of the paper. Yet, despite the apparent success of the first year's distribution figures Edwards remained the sole owner. Expectations of Edwards' public contributions to the SRBM also grew ever more demanding. In October 1893 the Portsmouth branch reported that they had managed to double the number of copies of *Fraternity* sold in July, but felt that if only Edwards would come and lecture in the city they would be able to increase their circulation even further. Likewise in Plymouth, although work was going well, W T Lee suggested that either Edwards or Wells should visit the city as soon as possible.[2] Edwards' commitment to activism, touring and editing *Lux* and

Fraternity took a large toll on his health. In the summer of 1894 he sailed to Dominica to regain his strength at the home of his brother Albert. While Edwards controlled the voice of the SRBM through his editorship of *Fraternity*, the argument between Mayo and Catherine remained largely out of public view. But his absence prompted a crisis over the control of *Fraternity* and the SRBM.

The burden of fraternity

In April 1894 *Fraternity* shared with its readers the financial burden publication of the periodical placed upon Edwards and the need to ensure a more sustainable financial future. The following month 'an Indian reader' addressed his fellow members of the community.[3] His letter argued that the Society ought to be responsible for the expenses of the production of *Fraternity* and that a syndicate, similar in structure to the model outlined in *Lux*, should be formed selling 3000 shares at £1 each. He did not suggest this should be a charitable endeavour. Judiciously conducted, the periodical could be expected to pay a fair premium to the shareholders. His suggestions for a successful expansion of a financially committed readership relied not upon an English white audience, but an international, diasporic community. During his five years in Trinidad he had met several 'Indian and Afro-Americans' who would gladly help the organization.[4] While living in George Town for six months he had felt something like the *esprit de corps* among the people of colour there who had a flourishing reading room. Black people in the Good Templars' lodges across British Guiana, Trinidad, Barbados, Jamaica and the Bahamas would surely share in the Society's work through an annual subscription to *Fraternity*. In addition there were around 350 Indian men in Britain well able to afford the subscription for *Fraternity*. As an Indian he appealed to their generosity and patriotism, but all readers could contribute – 'No matter how little you can do singly, it is bound to be helpful'. For this reader, it would be a personal disappointment if the paper could not be made self-sustaining through the influence of the branch secretaries of the SRBM in England, Wales and Scotland: 'Fellow readers! here is an opportunity for us all to do something in this good cause.' As an added incentive he offered one free lesson in Hebrew, Greek, Latin, Sanskrit, Persian, Hindu, Arabic, Syriac, Gaelic or Hindustani to readers who purchased annual subscriptions.[5]

Edwards' arrival in the Caribbean was reported in the July issue of *Fraternity*, an issue that also revealed the shifting power relationships developing during his absence. 'Letter box' in the July issue published two readers' responses to the periodical's financial crisis at some length. A letter headed 'Life or Death' from 'A Friend' urged 'readers and friends' of *Fraternity*, particularly wealthy 'gentlemen of means', to send in donations. The 'Friend' seemed to have intimate knowledge of the production process declaring that if the readers could not guarantee the monthly expenses of printing it might be necessary to delay the next issue of *Fraternity*.[6] The other author, using the pseudonym of 'an Original Member', which lent authority and authenticity to their letter, was closely linked to the Scottish branches.[7] Their letter did not directly respond to the shareholder system suggested by 'an Indian reader' in April but focused instead on the current structure of the society. The 'original member' argued that the aim of any local branch of the SRBM should be to first pay for all the copies of *Fraternity* it received, second to pay something towards free distribution and finally to maintain a sum in hand to fund any special local events.[8] For a branch as well established as Aberdeen this may have seemed like an obvious response, but for activists slowly building up a membership from smaller bases this would have seemed a daunting task.

The 'original member' also took the opportunity to counter a claim made by Ida B Wells in a letter to the *New York Age* in June that the SRBM had broken off arrangements with her and was 'without funds'. This situation they argued had nothing to do with 'the Scottish branches'. Before Wells had left the States it had been 'made plain to her that the Scottish branches declined her services, for reasons which were fully stated'. Instead they had invited the black former senator for Cleveland, Ohio, John P Green, and did not think that 'he will complain of either the hospitality or the liberality of our cold and needy North!'[9] The letter ended with the complaint that 'the Scottish branches' had received no help of any kind from the central Society. Using language closely aligned to Woodrow's Aberdeen Branch report, they added that some branches were beginning to ask if they 'might do more and better work apart than in a union with the English branches, which is not only nominal for all helpful purposes but is also threatened by serious and indefinite risks'.[10]

The 18 August 1894 issue of *Lux* appeared with a black border confirming its readers' worst fears. With the most excruciating pain Albert Edwards had written to inform R V Allen of his brother's death in July. It was devastating news for the communities Celestine Edwards served. Both his newspapers were left without their charismatic editor. Both faced financial ruin and within a year *Lux* had folded.[11] The staff at *Fraternity* vowed that their paper would carry on along the lines that Edward had established and that its workers would remain unchanged.[12] Yet, in the same paragraph the acting editor, who is not named, had already broken one of Edwards' principles – not to bring personal disagreements between Catherine and Mayo into the pages of *Fraternity*. The paper revealed it had been authorized to announce (by whom it does not say) that following the lamented death of Edwards and the hastily convened 'General Meeting' in London in August to discuss the way forward which was 'by no means representative of the Society's most active and efficient workers', it had become necessary that 'important changes' to the SRBM be made.[13] These changes heralded a bitter and public campaign by the Scottish branches to uncouple the movement from the historical context of *Anti-Caste* as well as the personal discrediting of Catherine herself. The campaign arose from the personal animosity Isabella Mayo held for Catherine, precipitated by a personal error of judgement on Catherine's part the previous summer.

An affair of deep regret and misunderstanding

Arriving in London in May 1893 it seemed to Ida B Wells as if everyone was in town. Britain's charities were gathered for their annual meetings, Parliament was still in session and the social season was in full swing. Wells had arrived in London in time to attend the May Meetings. She hoped to meet influential humanitarians and present her case for the antilynching cause at the annual gathering of Britain's charities and societies when they held elections, dinners and lectures and celebrated the distribution of prizes. But before Wells reached the capital she found herself embroiled in a row between Mayo and Catherine. The women had fallen out over a letter Catherine wrote to Dr George Ferdinands, Mayo's boarder who had written out Wells' invitation and helped arrange the meetings which opened Wells' tour in Scotland. Wells' recollections explain that while in Aberdeen working on the foundations for the SRBM Catherine had fallen in love with Ferdinands and, believing he loved her in return, had written a letter to express her commitment to him, in essence a proposal of marriage.[14] Catherine later explained that Ferdinands had been 'so good so tender' towards her during her stay in Aberdeen that though, at not even 30, he was many years her junior she came to understand that her feelings towards him were 'more than affection' and believed that he too loved her. She referred to what she supposed was their mutual feeling in a letter that included other 'trivial matters of business'. No sooner had she posted the letter she was overwhelmed with embarrassment of what she had admitted, realizing that perhaps she was really taking a 'romantic and exaggerated view of what was really on both sides a warm and unconventional friendship'.[15] She wired Ferdinands requesting that he burn the letter without opening it, but her request arrived too late, her confession read and in turn discussed in a letter from Ferdinands to Mayo.

At the time Catherine and Mayo were in Edinburgh staying with Eliza Wigham, but Catherine obviously felt she could not turn to her long-standing colleague with such a personal matter, and without close friends around to advise her Catherine went to Mayo for help.[16] Although Mayo's initial response seemed tempered, Catherine believed that very soon afterwards Mayo's confidence in her collapsed. Everyday Mayo became fiercer and angrier and soon insisted that Catherine withdraw from all her public work.[17] She demanded that Catherine drop her editorship of *Anti-Caste* and insisted that all the issues of *Anti-Caste* that had her and Catherine's names on as joint editors be destroyed.[18] Her instruction was carried out to a limited degree. The copy of the March/April 1893 issue that survives in the National Library of Scotland retains the names of both women, whereas the copy held within the Bodleian Library has Mayo's name blacked out. These probably both represent copies of the special issue on Lynch Law that was sent to each subscriber and distributor on *Anti-Caste's* list in advance of a special edition of 20,000 copies of the issue being printed for distribution.[19] Clearly Catherine managed to intervene to change the production of some of these issues, as the copy held in the library of the Society of Friends makes no mention of either editor.

Through Mayo, news of Catherine's letter was passed on to colleagues in Aberdeen; though she did not know exactly what version of events was being circulated, Catherine heard that Mayo had wired some friends to inform them that Catherine was 'insane'.[20] Mayo told Wells of Catherine's transgression and threatened Catherine with even wider exposure if she continued on with the tour and accompanied Wells to London. Mayo also threatened to cast Wells out of her influential circle if she maintained a friendship with Catherine. Catherine knew she had made 'a mortifying blunder' but Mayo claimed that Catherine could no longer be trusted, that Catherine was 'the type of maiden lady who used such work as an opportunity to meet and make advances to men' and that if the tour went on, she was likely to write such letters to others 'who might strike her fancy' and so throw suspicion and ridicule on their cause.[21] Wells refused to accept Mayo's characterization of Catherine as 'a nymphomaniac' and she recoiled from the withering sarcasm and scorn Mayo poured upon Catherine. For Wells, being forced to choose between the two women who had offered her so much hope just a month before was a devastating blow, both to the cause she was supporting and the aspiring role of women in politics they represented. After a sleepless night Wells decided that she had no real choice but to support Catherine, her friend and a proven friend of the black community.[22] Wells left Scotland to fulfil engagements already advertised in the North of England. Mayo refused to agree to any kind of compromise, and despite writing to Mayo, Wells never saw her again. She later received a letter from Ferdinands strongly condemning her for staying with Catherine. Wells did not reply, but she did 'often wonder if he ever realized his mistake in passing on the offending letter instead of destroying it'.[23]

The war of words between Mayo and Catherine cut into Wells' tour. When Catherine and Wells said goodbye at Southampton they were both disappointed by

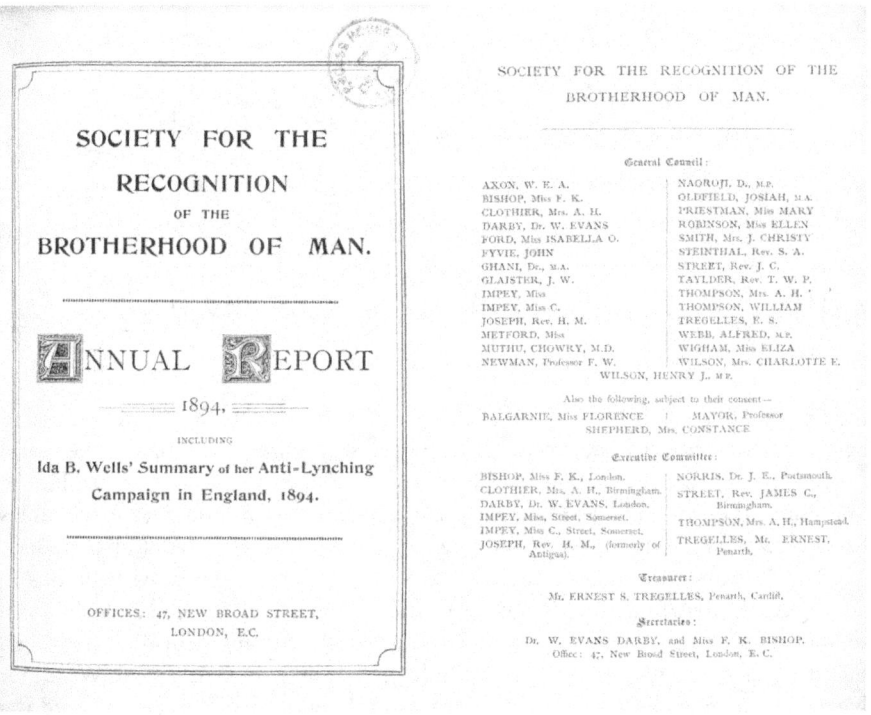

Figure 8.1 The Annual Report for the Society for the Recognition of the Brotherhood of Man, 1894, giving details of a General Council which had an international and multi-ethnic membership. Those joining Catherine and Ellen included the Manchester based journalist W E A Axon, Dr W Evans Darby (Secretary of the London Peace Society), Isabella Ormston Ford, the Antiguan Rev. Henry Joseph, Alfred Webb, Dadabhi Naoroji and Dr David Chowry Muthu, an associate of Kings College London who specialised in the treatment of tuberculosis and worked for many years in Somerset and on the Isle of Wight

Figure 8.2 Locations visited by Ida B Wells during her tours in 1893 and 1894

the unexpected end to the tour. Wells returned to the United States disappointed by the events. She was not, however, defeated. She still believed that if she could turn the 'English press and pulpit' in her favour, they would in turn influence opinion in the United States, but when she arrived she found the SRBM's troubles had followed her home. Mayo had written vindictive letters to Frederick Douglass, Thomas Fortune and Albion Tourgée, and Mayo's decision to draw friends and colleagues in the United States into the row forced an urgent response. Wells wrote to them all presenting her case and explaining why she remained loyal to Catherine, but the fallout rumbled on into the following year and nearly cost Wells her friendship with Frederick Douglass. In her autobiography Wells remembered the event as 'the most painful scene in which I ever took part'.[24] She hesitated to write about it because her colleagues in America suggested that 'the best appreciation of Miss Impey's work for humanity was to keep the story to ourselves', but Wells felt that there was still a need 30 years later to be 'just to Miss Impey' and set down 'the unvarnished truth'.[25] Mayo's memoirs published in 1910 make no mention of the women's disagreement or the debilitating effect it had on the SRBM[26].

Wells' tour of 1894

Wells arrived back in England on 1 March 1894 undertaking another busy lecture tour. Edwards announced her return in *Fraternity* and urged branch secretaries to complete arrangements for her visit to their regions as quickly as possible.[27] Wells landed in Liverpool and gave ten lectures in the two weeks she was there. She then moved on to Manchester, where she gave 12 lectures in ten days. From Manchester she went to Southport, where she spoke to 2000 people, and from there to Bristol. Here she gave ten talks during her week's stay, the first a meeting in the home of Mrs Coote, president of the Women's Liberal Association of Bristol. Under the auspices of the SRBM, the Priestman sisters invited friends to meet Wells and Catherine to discuss how and when to enlarge and strengthen the SRBM in the west of England.[28] Wells travelled across country to Newcastle, before heading south again, this time to London where she stayed for two months. She did not return to Scotland as Mayo refused to support any of her visits there and Wells wrote to Frederick Douglass expressing her surprise at the hostility she faced from Mayo because she would not consent to partake in Catherine's denunciation.[29]

As Catherine maintained a low-key role in the movement because of the events of the previous year, Wells found she had to rely on her own resources rather more than she had expected. Charles Aked, a popular preacher who hosted Wells during her stay in Liverpool, suggested Wells write to Douglass and ask him for a formal letter of introduction and support she could use while in Britain. In her request for his support Wells asked Douglass to ensure that the disagreement between herself, Catherine and Mayo remain a private matter. Thinking that to get a letter of recommendation from Douglass she only had to ask his reply shocked and hurt her deeply. To his surprise Douglass had seen in the press that Wells' lectures were already being advertised with his endorsement. He was unclear as to why she needed his public support at all, for surely those who had invited her to Britain meant to stand by her and the antilynching mission. Nor did he understand how her hosts could ask Wells to denounce anyone as a condition of fulfilling the obligations in their invitation. Mayo's attitude towards Catherine seemed no different to the one Wells had relayed to Douglass on her return from her first visit to England. Douglass asked Wells to tell him frankly and honestly who invited her on her second tour to Britain and what assurances of support they had given her. If they had made promises that they had not kept they should be exposed. If, on the other hand, Wells had made the trip on her own accord and for her own purposes she should be clear about it. Douglass wished to support Wells, but he had to do so truthfully.[30]

Wells had faced many troubles since she had been thrown off the train by a conductor to the applause of her fellow white Americans in 1884. She had spent a lot of her own money and sacrificed even more time, her home and her newspaper to the cause. But she had never felt more like giving up the struggle as when she received Douglass' letter in Manchester that April. Distressed, she wrote back to him the same day.[31] With her reply she enclosed a letter from Mayo to prove that she had not come to England uninvited. The letter sent from Mayo's home in Aberdeen on 12 September

1893 contained two requests. The first spoke to *Fraternity's* need to develop its networks of newsprint and asked Wells to arrange for the systematic posting of American newspapers to be sent to Edwards for *Fraternity*. American papers were arriving in Britain too late to be included in the most recent issue, making *Fraternity* seem dated. Thomas Fortune always promptly sent copies of the *New York Age*, but *Fraternity* did not, for example, receive regular issues of *Inter-Ocean*. In return Edwards suggested sending Wells 100 copies of *Fraternity* each month for her to sell or distribute as she saw fit.

Second, Mayo asked Wells to return to Britain for four months between February and May 1894. Edwards, who had recently held three meetings in Aberdeen, was convinced he could arrange a full tour throughout the country calling on his many contacts and local branch secretaries of the SRBM. Mayo also hoped Wells would return: 'Of Course, I wish you would come back: because I fully believe Mr Edwards' arrangement would do you justice, – and you would work *unblighted*!!' In addition to her expenses for this tour Wells would receive a fee. Mayo instructed Wells to reply directly to Edwards to avoid any misunderstandings with the arrangements, but if she wished to address anything to Mayo on any subject not meant for Edwards' eyes this should be written on a sheet clearly marked 'private'. Wells requested a payment of £2 a week, which was accepted by the SRBM's executive council in November. With their decision Wells began making preparations for the tour. She arranged a leave of absence from work and found someone to replace her at the newspaper. But in December she received a letter from Mayo which claimed that Catherine was 'still giving trouble' and that when Wells arrived in Britain there was to be no more secrecy about the situation and the 'whole truth' was to be publicly told.[32]

Wells remained loyal to Catherine and replied explaining that she could not undertake the tour if she had to speak publicly about Catherine's personal life. She sent a similar message to Edwards but received two very different replies. From Edwards and the SRBM's council, she received a letter stating that nothing was to be revealed about Catherine's indiscretion in public. Mayo's letter acknowledged that Wells' sympathies obviously lay with Catherine and so it would be better if Wells did not come to Britain after all. Mayo would have nothing to do with Wells if she had anything to do with Catherine. Wells wrote directly to Edwards again. Did Mayo's letter represent the last word of the Society? Edwards cabled his reply confirming that the SRBM still wanted her to come and that she should leave for England at once. When Wells arrived in Britain she found the SRBM in disarray. Having heard that Wells was coming to Britain regardless of her warning, Mayo resigned from the SRBM's council. Edwards was ill, suffering from influenza and rheumatic fever, but following Catherine's withdrawal and others' resignation in protest at the way Catherine had been treated, there were few who could share his workload.[33] It was into this atmosphere of confusion and hostility that Wells had found herself trying to establish her tour. She hoped that a letter from Douglass would help draw larger audiences to hear about the conditions under which Wells, Douglass and their kin had to live in the United States. Wells received Douglass' reply on 23 May while she was in London. It contained the much hoped for letter of recommendation and Douglass' words soothed relations between the two campaigners.[34]

Figure 8.3 A portrait of Isabella Mayo, taken from her published memoirs, *Recollections of what I saw, what I lived through, and what I learned, during more than fifty years of social and literary experience*, 1910

When Wells arrived in London she initially stayed at one of the city's temperance hotels, but following one of the first meetings, she was approached by Ellen Clayden and invited to stay with her and her husband. Peter William Clayden was an editor on the London *Daily News*, then the second biggest-selling morning paper in London, which claimed to have the largest circulation of any liberal paper in the world.[35] The Claydens lived at 13 Tavistock Square in the shadow of St Pancras Church, just a ten-minute walk from British Museum; when Wells sat in their breakfast room she could look out of the windows across to Charles Dickens' former home.[36] Wells' stay with the Claydens gave her access to numerous resources in London. Clayden was a passionate liberal, who was a strong advocate of the North's cause during the American civil war. He was responsible for the increased influence of the *Daily News* as an organ of liberal nonconformist opinion, although Wells claimed that he refused to take sides with any political party so he could remain without bias as an editor. He was well respected by his peers and, the year before Wells' stay, had been elected president of the Institute of Journalists.[37] To some degree Wells' presence in Tavistock Square influenced the editorial comments in the *Daily News*, and her second visit to Britain focused the subject of lynching in the minds of English liberals and seems to have attracted more attention in the British press. At the Society of Friends' annual meeting in 1894, following a debate on how to pressure countries where slavery still thrived (such as Zanzibar, Borneo and Uganda, which were under British influence or were British Protectorates), a Friend brought up the subject of lynching in the Southern United States, but was told that it had already been taken up the previous week.[38]

In her autobiography Wells recalled that the attention she received from the British press greatly outweighed her expectations. Daily newspapers such as the *Daily News*, the *Daily Chronicle*, *Westminster Gazette*, the *Sun*, the *Star* and the *London Echo*; weeklies such as *Labour Leader*, the *Methodist Times*, *The Christian World*, the *Independent*, the *Inquirer* and *Westminster Budget*; and the monthly *Review of Reviews*, *Contemporary Review* and *Review of Churches* all ran articles on lynching while Wells toured Britain. She met a number of editors personally and some, such as the editor of *Contemporary Review*, became members of the Anti-Lynching Committee founded in London at the end of Wells' 1894 tour. Throughout, the British press formed an important tool in her antilynching campaign and the international campaigns envisaged by Catherine and Edwards. Reactions in white America's press were not nearly as encouraging. *The Memphis Commercial* published a vicious article with the intention of discrediting Wells on both sides of the Atlantic, and copies of the piece were sent to newspaper editors in Britain. The *Aberdeen Weekly Journal* and the *Birmingham Daily Post* both reported on the *Commercial's* article and the strong language it used to condemn Wells' methods, reinforcing the narrative that 'a perfect epidemic of outrages by the negroes of the southern states on white women and children' had led to some unfortunate lynchings, but that Wells had been the author of an article 'justifying the outrages by negroes' in *Free Speech*.[39] The *Liverpool Daily Post's* response was the only paper Wells knew of that defended her position, strongly criticizing the *Commercial's* report. Following this trans-Atlantic debate, the Women's Era Club based in Boston wrote their open letter of support for Wells and her work.[40] She believed their public backing gave greater weight to the arguments she had been making against lynching.[41]

Wells' efforts to raise the profile of debates around lynching were not always directly acknowledged in the press. When Charles Aked wrote an article on 'The Race Problem in America' published in *Contemporary Review* in June 1894, the piece made no mention of Wells.[42] Nor did the *Spectator*, when it commented on the aspects of lynching raised by Aked in one of their June issues.[43] The *Spectator's* report illustrates that, unlike *Anti-Caste* or *Fraternity's* editorial line, British journalists, although mostly united behind Wells' cause, did not always condemn the principle of lynch law outright. The *Spectator's* columnist argued that there were periods when lynching was justified. First when society was in a state of transition (perhaps referring to America's period of Reconstruction) and then when the omission, 'inability or unwillingness' of the full rule of law made punishments inadequate, or certain crimes not punished with enough severity and so it was left for citizens to do it themselves.[44] However, in the case of southern states the *Spectator* argued against illegal action as it seemed the 'sole reason that seems to account for the determination of the white population of the south not to allow negroes to take their trial, is the race-feeling that what is good enough for the white man is too good for the black man'. It was acknowledged that 'Race-hatred, apparently, blinds the white population alike to the mischief of their actions'.[45]

In his piece for the *Review* Charles Aked was loathe to express an opinion on the way in which England's neighbours should manage their own affairs, but he felt that when 'ruffians take to skinning men alive, vivisecting them, and burning them slowly to death, no decent man can resent the expression of horror and indignation that burst from the lips of all observers'.[46] In the *Christian World* Aked visualized the geography of lynching as a contagious disease that was spreading across America, having already crossed the Mason and Dixon Line and 'invaded the Quaker State itself'.[47] He felt that if left unchecked by civil authorities, the virus of racial prejudice threatened to reach New York. But Aked also felt that the British public could play a relatively limited role in halting the spread. Moreover he claimed that Wells did not really hope to achieve anything through direct political action in Britain and that she saw 'clearly enough' that it was only possible for the British people to exert a 'strong and friendly influence' upon the American public, whose responsibility it was to see that wrongs were put right.[48] In May an interview between Wells and Keir Hardie appeared in his paper *Labour Leader*. Describing Wells as a young 'coloured lady' of medium height with a blithe face and cheery smile, he noted that as she retold the wrongs committed against 'her race' the expression of her black-brown eyes deepened and the lines on her face grew sombre.[49] The interview placed an emphasis on political activism, asking why 'negroes' did not use their political power to redress the state they found themselves in. Wells robustly responded to Hardie's questions arguing there was no truth whatever in the allegations that 'in spite of education since the emancipation, the old traits of the negro not only still exist, but are showing an increasing tendency to assert themselves'.[50] In response to a question on the success of socialism in America, Wells reflected that it had made no real impact, but felt unquestionably that the movement would do great things for black people if it could be developed.

The interview with Ida B Wells was not an isolated reflection on black Americans that appeared in *Labour Leader*. In November 1894 a piece on the 'North American Negro' was published but Wells would not have appreciated its content. The article claimed that to study the black communities of North America you could not interview men (women were not mentioned) from the cities, for their contact with the 'lower order of white folk' had robbed them of their virtues and exaggerated their vices. Instead it was in the country where they should be viewed, for here for some unexplained reason it seemed to have been assumed that the so-called lower order of white folk did not reside. Depicted as a character in a play, rather than a member of a struggling community as described by Wells, the American 'country negro' was here a figure of fun, a 'most amusing figure', 'a creature of impulse'. In the courthouse he was described as 'evasive, tricky, a witness hard to draw a plain answer from' often responding to questions with the reply, 'Don't zactly ketch yer meaning.'[51] As part of Wells' interview, Labour clubs willing to arrange meetings for her were asked to contact the *Leader* for details of how to make arrangements. But in its mixed use of racialized language and acceptance of derogatory racial stereotypes, the *Leader* reflects how entrenched understandings of racialized difference were within labour politics in Britain.[52]

On Wednesday 23 May 1894 Wells spoke at the annual meeting of the APS. She was the only woman to be mentioned in the list of attendees that appeared in *The Daily News*.[53] A fuller account of the evening written up for *The Aborigines' Friend* mentioned

Catherine, Mr Meakin from Morocco and Mr P N Browne from Barbados. In addition J E Casely Hayford (whose older brother Ernest Hayford subscribed to *Anti-Caste* in 1891) and Oguntola Sapara were in attendance.[54] Sapara, who later became a noted physician in Lagos, was one of seven black students, including two women that Wells does not name, who helped her when she first arrived in London.[55] Sapara became one of Wells' regular helpers. Each morning following one of her lectures or meetings, copies of the papers with the best review of her talks would be bought and sent across the Atlantic with letters to the president of the United Sates, state governors, leading ministers in large cities and important newspapers. During her stay in London, this campaign work took place around the Claydens' breakfast table with Sapara coming to Bloomsbury to help with the cutting and posting of clippings every morning.[56] Aside from Edwards, Sapara is the only black person Wells details in the British section of her memoirs. She recalled several amusing stories he told her of how patients were too frightened to let him minister to them. Sapara told Wells he 'didn't mind, because he knew it was an innocent fear, that there was nothing of the hatred and prejudice in it' which was expressed by white people in the United States.[57] Wells does not mention whether Sapara ever came across any black patients in Britain and, if so, how their reactions to him differed from the, presumably white, patients Wells highlighted. There is no mention of individual members of the British black working class in Wells' memoirs. She often spoke to large audiences and like Edwards she no doubt attracted a large working-class interest within them. Her writings on the geography of London are confined largely to the streets of Bloomsbury and the members of the African diaspora she comments on meeting were all students. Sapara's comments to Wells about his medical experiences also indirectly speak to this issue of class. If he did see patients who were too frightened to let him minister to them, this would imply that he worked within a particular geography of London, or among a particular class. Although it seems likely that many black families would have heard of Wells' presence in Britain through papers such as *Fraternity* and the *Labour Leader*, it is difficult to know if Wells' success in Britain impacted upon the political spheres of the black working class or helped them understand their position within British society and the Empire more broadly.

On the last night of her stay with the Claydens, friends and supporters gathered at Tavistock Place to form an Anti-Lynching Committee. With the complications of the SRBM continuing, for Wells an organization focused purely on her political campaign was a welcome outcome. Although there was some overlap in membership between the SRBM and the Anti-Lynching Committee, the new collective was comprised of far more illustrious names. In Wells' words the Claydens gathered together a most brilliant company in honour of her presence and her leaving. At the end of the social evening the Anti-Lynching Committee was formed. Florence Balgarine took the post of honorary secretary. Among those who joined her on the Committee were the Duke of Argyll, Lady Stevenson, Alderman Ben Tillet and almost 20 MPs including Dadabhai Naoroji.[58] Wells was pleased that among the first to donate funds were a dozen Africans living in London who sent nearly £14 but was disappointed that despite all the publicity there was no financial support for the committee from the United States.[59] Initially the members of the pressure group were mainly made up of activist elites with whom Wells had come into contact and lobbied during her stay with the Claydens.

John Passmore Edwards, the liberal and social reformer MP, became the treasurer.[60] A fuller list later published in the *Philadelphia* included a number of Americans as well as Lady Isabella Somerset, Sir John Gorst and James Keir Hardie.[61] The announcement of the Committee to the British public was made in *The Times* by Florence Balgarine. She wrote to the paper from 13 Tavistock Square to draw attention to the group's inception and its aims. She explained that the Committee had been formed in response to the appeal for help which had reached Britain from the 'negro population' of the United States, though Wells was not mentioned by name. Their objectives were 'to obtain reliable information on the subject of lynching and mob outrages in America, to make the facts known, and to give expression to public opinion in condemnation of such outrages in whatever way may be best seem calculated to assist in the cause of humanity and civilization'.[62]

The legacy of Wells' tours remained in the press throughout 1894 and into 1895 with the Anti-Lynching Committee and Catherine remaining the focus of reports on British activism against lynching in the English and black American press. A précis of the Anti-Lynching Committee's 1894–1895 report, which was reprinted in *The Times* in December 1895, established that the Committee had met regularly and sent letters of inquiry or protest to governors of Arkansas, Tennessee, Mississippi, Kentucky, Louisiana, Texas, Florida, Alabama, Georgia, South Carolina and Ohio. In addition, over 2000 newspapers containing antilynching material such as articles, letters and resolutions had also been sent to various governors and editors.[63] The Committee was also in contact and had kept a correspondence with between '60 and 70 coloured editors'.[64] The Committee acknowledged that some resented the interference of the British in American politics, but they had received innumerable expressions of thanks from both 'white and coloured' Americans. These assured them that if it had not been for Ida B Wells' mission and the subsequent formation of the Committee, the extent and nature of lynching horrors would never have been fully exposed.[65] They felt that public pressure had contributed to the changing attitude of the Southern press, but despite these positive changes there had been at least 138 cases of lynching between 1 January and 31 August 1895. The Committee declared its intention to hold a conference on lynching in London in May 1896, but no reports of its convening survive.

A fallen fraternity

Wells' success in Britain and the American public spheres, along with the formation of the British-based Anti-Lynching Committee, ran parallel to events evolving within the SRBM. While Edwards remained editor, *Fraternity* continued to keep the rift between Mayo and Catherine private and supported Wells' work. But following Edwards' return to the Caribbean, this balance became unstable. In August 1894 *Fraternity* published an article on the 'Female Accusation'.[66] The piece appeared next to an article by Wells that reflected on her second trip to England, in which she acknowledged the help she had gained across the country and the successful talks and press coverage she had received.[67] For the author of 'Female Accusation' too little attention was given to British women who might 'fancy' black men. In Britain, the author argued, these 'morbid egotists may only imagine that men "fall in love with them"'. Though this might seem harmless enough, it was to be remembered that such an imagination 'if indulged by a "white woman" regarding a "nigger" in some States, would mean *the death of the man*'. In women who were 'elderly, dowdy and disappointed', these imaginings and delusions were not recognized as a weakness to make such women the objects of pity and care. Instead their friends often left them 'to wander among unsuspecting strangers, heedless of the annoyance and hindrance' they caused. It was for the sake of the women's movement that the author justified her attack on such women. Those 'weak sisters' who threatened the womanhood in an era when women were entering largely into public, professional and philanthropic work should be excluded from the movement. If women refused to work with them then these 'morbid women' would soon realize 'that their only safe place is retirement'. The author ended with the observation that 'if women of the American South were all "pure in heart and sound in head," there would be fewer lynchings', and if British philanthropists, when forewarned by those in the know, set aside the dubious help of those with unhealthy imaginations 'which always gloat on temporary "horrors" rather than dwell on eternal principles, many good works, which now flagged and faltered, would go on apace'.[68]

Although no one is named in the 'Female Accusation' either as its subject or its author, it is a thinly disguised attack on Catherine by Isabella Mayo.[69] The commentary is unlike anything that appeared in the paper while Edwards held editorial control. This is not only because of the personal nature of its content but also because of the manner in which it wilfully confuses the complexities of Wells' arguments regarding the place of rape in the language of lynch law. Wells clearly emphasized that rape was used as an excuse for assault on black men. Consensual relationships between black men and white women, for Wells, should not have resulted in lynchings because they were consensual. False accusations were not based on delusional or imagined fantasies by white women; rather they were either forced upon them or were tools used by them to avoid disclosures of affairs or sexual encounters they could not countenance in public. Regardless, Wells did not argue that white women were responsible for lynchings through accusations of rape or that white women needed to be more careful with their feelings or the disclosures of their desires. The responsibility for the lynchings lay with white men who could not accept the reality of these relationships or used 'rape' as a metaphor for any assault on their superiority. The responsibility for the consequences of these accusations lay with white communities who did not accept the rights of black Americans to be tried through the justice system regardless of their alleged crime. For Mayo to compare Catherine's supposedly transgressive desires towards George Ferdinands with this confused representation of white Southern women was cruel and poorly formulated.[70]

The shift in editorial tone that allowed the publication of the essay to take place suggests Isabella Mayo had a large degree of influence over the new, still unnamed editor or that their sympathies lay with the Scottish branches. In September the essay 'The Present Position of Our Society' admitted that it was necessary to explain to readers and members that the SRBM and its work were passing through a critical period.[71] It is hard to imagine how hurt and distressed Catherine must have been reading the reformulation of the SRBM. Among the manuscript records of the SRBM in the Bodleian Library are copies of this issue of *Fraternity*, and the pencil annotations made by Catherine reflect how bewildered she felt. 'The Present Position of Our Society' reformulated the history of the SRBM around Edwards, locating its foundation with Wells' first meeting at Mayo's home in Aberdeen and Wells' first public meeting at the Music Hall Buildings, Aberdeen, in April 1893. The first organization of the SRBM followed, and the next day Wells and Mayo proceeded to Huntly establishing the branch now flourishing there. Going on southwards, however, 'they were confronted by very peculiar and trying circumstances' and the actions of 'a prominent English helper' revealed 'either mental or moral unsoundness in this person'.[72] This apparently led Mayo to conclude that she needed to involve someone with a strong knowledge of moral procedure as well as the cause itself. She chose to approach Edwards. The article did not explain that Mayo's tactics to marginalize Catherine involved appointing him as an editor to *Fraternity*, replacing *Anti-Caste*, which Mayo had demanded Catherine abandon. According to this version of events, Edwards' establishment of *Fraternity* took up all his time and so he had been unable to set up the remainder of the Society properly and so Edwards continued to be helped by 'a small clique, who had unfortunately gained some footing in the society' and attempted to force upon its council a person of '*admitted mental instability*'.[73]

As soon as Edwards' health compelled him to leave England, this 'clique' began to actively conspire to gain control of the SRBM. A so-called council meeting was convened in the summer, although Mayo claimed that she and perhaps others had not received notice of the meeting. Catherine's annotations question this. 'Who', she asks, 'was omitted?'[74] As this had all occurred in the middle of summer there was no time to request a meeting or consult all other branches. It had therefore been judged ('by whom?' Catherine asks) that a temporary council of individuals, quite prepared to resign their functions as soon as permanent arrangements were made, should take responsibility for the running of the Society. The Society for the Recognition of the Brotherhood of Man would carry on its work precisely as it had always done, but its new central organization was now led by Mayo, who was installed in this self-elected temporary council as president. Support for the coup had already been received from the Portsmouth branch, who had 'formally signified their intention to support the Scottish branches and remain loyal to Mr Celestine Edwards'. Private notices to the same effect had been received from secretaries in Manchester, Liverpool, Birmingham and Jarrow-on-Tyne.[75]

Confirmation that the Scottish branches had taken control of the Society was published on the front page of the October number of *Fraternity*. The cover also confirmed Helen Sillitoe, a writer on the women's column in *Lux*, as the new editor. Her name appeared below Edwards', who was credited as the founder of the paper in the masthead. On the cover of her first issue Sillitoe listed the new Council and structure of the SRBM. It reflected the takeover by Mayo and members of the Scottish branches.[76] The Society now had a confirmed president, a role unsurprisingly taken by Mayo, while her deputy was George Ferdinands. As well as editing *Fraternity*, Sillitoe also became honorary treasurer, and the role of honorary secretary (previously that of Edwards) was taken by Miss Fanny Kingerley. The four of them were joined on a temporary council by Dr M A Ghani, Rev S G Woodrow, William Thompson, Mrs Mary Hoppus Marks, Herr Erchkmann and Miss Mawson. Whether from Scotland or London clearly the lobbying of local branch secretaries had taken place in order to assure support for the new formation when it was announced. At the core were seven branches whose establishment was again credited to Celestine Edwards: Portsmouth, Birmingham, Sheffield, Liverpool, Manchester, Jarrow-on-Tyne and Aberdeen. Branches that did not contact the new central office would no longer be recognized as part of the movement by the SRBM or *Fraternity*.

Faced with this rewriting of the organization's history Catherine wrote an account of the SRBM as she remembered it. These form the bulk of Catherine's papers now in the archives at the Bodleian Library. Catherine never challenged the post-Edwards version of events of the SRBM in *Fraternity*; she doubtless was not given the opportunity to do so. *Fraternity*'s final break with Catherine's contribution was confirmed on the cover of the November issue of *Fraternity*. Edwards' issues of *Fraternity* were numbered as part of a 'new series' alongside the old *Anti-Caste* series; September 1893 appeared as Vol 6 of the old series, and Vol 1, No 15 of the new series. By November 1894, all traces of *Fraternity*'s relationship with *Anti-Caste* had been removed. It appeared simply as Vol II, No 4. Despite the apparent formality of Mayo's ascendancy to the presidency, the collapse in relations between key women in the movement meant that, as Wells had found earlier in the year, the SRBM remained in turmoil. Clearly Catherine was not welcome and could no longer remain within *Fraternity*'s literary community. Mayo's initial aim may have been only to remove Catherine from any position of control or influence within the movement, but whether intentionally or as an accidental consequence, she had created a major division. It was a poignant moment both for Catherine and the movement.

The West of England SRBM branch continued to meet, although their loyalty to Catherine cut them adrift from the society at large. At their meeting on 4 October, possibly having seen the October issue of *Fraternity*, in which the SRBM's *pro tempore* council and their demand for loyalty were published, they discussed the state of the Society, but no decision as to how to move forward was taken. Their activism continued; the branch agreed to call attention to South African colonists' disfranchising of Indians in Natal and to the ongoing Zulu and Kanaka questions.[77] Catherine remained active and had recently travelled to Chelmsford at the expense of the local branch to interview Florence Balgarine about the work of the Anti-Lynching Committee. In November, the white American G F Richings arrived at Askew from Baltimore to lecture in England on the 'Progress of the American Negro since Emancipation'. As the West of England branch was arranging some lectures for him, he also attended a branch meeting. Here Catherine reported on an executive meeting in London among those in the SRBM who had decided not to join the Scottish branches. Unable to influence or retain *Fraternity* they had decided to introduce a new journal, *The Bond of Brotherhood*, as the organ of the Society. The West of England branch welcomed the news ordering 100 copies of the upcoming December issue. A circular was distributed to former subscribers of *Anti-Caste* explaining that those who received requests for subscriptions from the present proprietors of *Fraternity* should remember that the paper had now passed into other hands, and as a result *Fraternity* was no longer the official organ of the Society for the Recognition of the Brotherhood of Man. The Society now published its own paper, *The Bond of Brotherhood*, with subscriptions to be paid only to the secretaries, E. S. Tregelles of Penarth, Cardiff, or Catherine Impey of Street, Somerset.[78]

The SRBM at this time had held significant promise, with a truly national reach through its branch secretaries, yet the movement would never recover from this split. Personal disagreements; differing interpretations of womanhood, of women in politics, of their sexual desires and its implications; bitter political division; and matters of principle all contributed to the fragmentation of the SRBM community at a moment it was establishing a firm foundation. The attention brought to the movement by Wells and Edwards in 1893 and 1894 had invigorated members of the public with hundreds pledging to uphold the principles of the Society every month. When Edwards left for the Caribbean in 1894, local branch secretaries were establishing local and regional networks to engage individuals with the realities of racial prejudice and injustice. By the end of 1894, divisions caused by the fallout between Catherine and Mayo had irrevocably weakened the SRBM, and any potential it had for its strongly local associations to connect and become a truly national or international lobbying organization was thwarted. For members of the SRBM and readers of their periodicals, the split created a bitter and confusing public forum in which two periodicals, *Fraternity* and the *Bond of Brotherhood*, both demanded their loyalty by claiming to be official organs of the SRBM. Both periodicals continued to focus on the politics of race but their editorial tones mediated away from the strict centrality of racial oppression followed by Catherine and Edwards.

Notes

1 *Annual Report*, 1894, MSS. Brit. Emp. s.20 E5/8.
2 *Fraternity*, October 1893, 15.
3 *Fraternity*, April 1894, 15. Although not signed off as such, the personal story he provides matches that provided in 'Asia's' first letter.
4 *Fraternity*, April 1894, 15.
5 *Fraternity*, April 1894, 15.
6 *Fraternity*, July 1894, 15.
7 *Fraternity*, July 1894, 15. The letter was probably written by Isabella Mayo, and if not, it was most likely written by someone within her circle from the Scottish branches.
8 *Fraternity*, July 1894, 15.
9 *Fraternity*, July 1894, 15.
10 *Fraternity*, July 1894, 15.
11 In February 1895, *Lux* was incorporated with *The Light of the World*. On 13 July 1895 a plea entitled 'Our Last Appeal – Is *Lux* to Live or Die' asked if that number would be the last issue published. It seems that this was indeed the last to be printed.
12 *Fraternity*, October 1894, 2.
13 *Fraternity*, October 1894, 2.
14 Duster, *Crusade for Justice*, 103.
15 Impey to Axon, 9 November 1894, Axon Papers 3329.

16 Impey to Axon, 9 November 1894, Axon Papers 3329.
17 Letter from Impey to Mrs Tourgée, 23 June 1893, 7064. Catherine wrote a letter explaining what had happened to Emma Tourgée and asked her to pass on to Albion Tourgée what aspects of the story she judged to be best.
18 Duster, *Crusade for Justice*.
19 MSS. Brit. Emp. s.20 E5/7.
20 Impey to Mrs Tourgée, 23 June 1893, *Albion W. Tourgée* Papers 7064.
21 Impey to Mrs Tourgée, 23 June 1893, *Albion W. Tourgée* Papers 7064; Duster, *Crusade for Justice*, 104.
22 Duster, *Crusade for Justice*.
23 Duster, *Crusade for Justice*, 105.
24 Duster, *Crusade for Justice*, 105.
25 Duster, *Crusade for Justice*, 110.
26 Mayo, *Recollections*.
27 *Fraternity*, March 1894, 1.
28 MSS. Brit. Emp. s.20 E5/8.
29 Duster, *Crusade for Justice*, 135, 148, 153.
30 Douglass to Wells, 27 March 1894, Frederick Douglass Papers.
31 Wells to Douglass, 6 April 1894, Frederick Douglass Papers.
32 Wells to Douglass, 6 April 1894, Frederick Douglass Papers; Letter from Unknown 1893, September 12, original emphasis (the last page of the letter, including any signature are missing, but the address and content confirm it is from Isabella Mayo), Frederick Douglass Papers.
33 Wells to Douglass, 6 April 1894, Frederick Douglass Papers.
34 Wells to Douglass, 3 June 1894, Frederick Douglass Papers.
35 *Daily News*, 26 May 1894, 4.
36 Duster, *Crusade for Justice*. Dickens lived at Tavistock House between 1851 and 1860.
37 Woods, 'Clayden, Peter William (1827–1902)'.
38 *The Christian World*, 31 May 1894, 422.
39 'Lynching outrages in the United States', *Aberdeen Weekly Journal*, 7 June 1894, 6; 'Negro lynching in America', *Birmingham Daily Post*, 7 June, 5.
40 Duster, *Crusade for Justice*, 197–200.
41 Duster, *Crusade for Justice*, 198–199.
42 Aked, 'The race problem in America'.
43 *Spectator*, 2 June 1894, 743–744.
44 *Spectator*, 2 June 1894, 744.
45 *Spectator*, 2 June 1894, 744.
46 *The Review of Reviews*, June 1894, 559.
47 *The Christian World*, 12 April 1894, 259.
48 *The Christian World*, 12 April 1894, 259.
49 *Labour Leader*, 12 May 1894, 2.
50 *Labour Leader*, 12 May 1894, 2.
51 *Labour Leader*, 3 November 1894, 3.
52 *Labour Leader*, 12 May 1894, 2.
53 *Daily News*, 25 May 1894, 8.
54 *The Aborigines' Friend*, 1894, 415. J E Casely Hayford arrived in London in 1893 to train as a barrister becoming an important writer and pan-African activist; his brother Ernest trained as a physician at St Thomas' Hospital and was admitted to the

Royal College of Surgeons in 1898, on Dr E Hayford see Sherwood, *Origins of Pan-Africanism*.
55 Though Wells spells his name as Ogontula Sapara, Duster, *Crusade for Justice*, 214; Duffield, 'Duse Mohamed Ali', vol 1.
56 Duster, *Crusade for Justice*.
57 Duster, *Crusade for Justice*, 214.
58 *The Times*, 1 August 1894, 11.
59 Duster, *Crusade for Justice*, 217.
60 Duster, *Crusade for Justice*, 217.
61 Duster, *Crusade for Justice*, 217.
62 *The Times*, 1 August 1894, 11.
63 A letter from the governor of Alabama in response to one of their letters sent to *Times* illustrates that the committee did prompt a continuing debate on the issues, *Birmingham Daily Post*, 8 October 1894, 5. For a discussion of the work of the Committee in 1894 and 1895 see Silkey, 'Evolving Morality'.
64 *The Times*, 20 December, 1895, 4.
65 *The Times*, 20 December, 1895, 4.
66 *Fraternity*, August 1894, 4–5.
67 *Fraternity*, August 1894, 4.
68 *Fraternity*, August 1894, 5.
69 Ware, *Beyond the Pale*.
70 For a discussion of this passage, see Ware, *Beyond the Pale*, and also Moore, 'Reputation of Isabella Mayo'.
71 *Fraternity*, September 1894, 5.
72 *Fraternity*, September 1894, 5.
73 *Fraternity*, September 1894, 5, Emphasis from the pencil markings made on the September copy of *Fraternity* included within the papers of MSS. Brit. Emp. s.20 E5/7.
74 Emphasis from the pencil markings made on the September copy of *Fraternity* included within the papers of MSS. Brit. Emp. s.20 E5/7.
75 *Fraternity*, September 1894, 6.
76 *Fraternity*, October 1894, 1.
77 MSS. Brit. Emp. s.20 E5/8.
78 To Former Subscribers – *Anti-Caste*, MSS. Brit. Emp. s.20 E5/7.

9

A New Bond of Brotherhood

We are banded together not so much in a crusade against lynch-law, or the more violent exhibitions of race prejudice, – terrible as these are, – as against the roots and underlying causes of these barbarities.

Bond of Brotherhood, 1894

The collective that formed around the branch of the SRBM led by Catherine and her supporters resurrected *Bond of Brotherhood*, a monthly periodical originally 'conducted' by Elihu Burritt between 1854 and 1867.[1] A temperance and antislavery activist, Burritt's original *Bond of Brotherhood* complimented his League of Universal Brotherhood, a pacifist group which he set up soon after arriving in Britain as the American Consul in Birmingham in 1846. The league became the 'first pacifist group to obtain a mass membership in England or elsewhere'.[2] When the *Bond* ceased publication, Burritt's work became absorbed into the Peace Society. The *Bond's* new editor W Evans Darby argued that as secretary of the Peace Society the paper directly transferred to his custodianship, allowing him to place it at the disposal of the SRBM. The first issue of the new series of the *Bond of Brotherhood* appeared in November 1894. Within the pages of the *Bond*, Catherine found a sense of freedom that allowed her to write thought-provoking columns on racial prejudice. The *Bond* created yet another textual format for the community of readers established around *Anti-Caste*, no doubt confusing some readers and testing the loyalty of others.

A new literary community

Priced at one penny, the *Bond of Brotherhood* moved printing and production from Paternoster Row to West, Newman & Co in Hatton Garden. Its elaborate masthead was almost identical to the one used by the *Bond* under Burritt. Re-using the motto 'God Hath made of one blood all nations of men', the paper replaced Burritt's additional motto 'Blessed are the peacemakers; for they shall be called the children of God' with the assertive claim to be the 'Official organ for the Society for the Recognition of the Brotherhood of Man'. Into the masthead design, the SRBM inserted an image of a black hand and white hand clasped in a handshake. This was the same as that which appeared on the Templar Mission notepaper that Catherine had used to write to Frederick

Douglass in 1883 (see Figure 9.2). As these changes suggested, the new formulation of the *Bond* did not 'take up in unbroken continuity' the work of Elihu Burritt, but claimed a close continuation with Catherine's original publication. The *Bond* was 'practically a new series of Anti-Caste, the change of name implying no change of identity or of purpose'.[3] Those who joined the *Bond*'s subscription list promised to help secure 'to every member of the human family, Freedom, Equal Opportunity, and Brotherly Consideration'. This formation of the SRBM declared itself fundamentally opposed to systems of racial segregation 'by which the despised members of a community are cut off from the social, civil, and religious life of their fellow-men'.[4] Lynchings and other forms of violent injustice inflicted on oppressed communities of the world had their root in racial prejudice, which in turn was fostered by a lack of understanding and estrangement between people created by racial segregation. The SRBM therefore required its members to ensure they were not personally complicit in practices of segregation, whether as individuals, or through the membership of organizations which tolerated its existence.

The new editor W Evans Darby had known Catherine for many years. He visited Askew in 1879 and became an early subscriber to *Anti-Caste*. Though Darby held his own public profile among activists in London as secretary of the London Peace Society, he had to re-establish international print networks to support the *Bond*. He wrote to H C Smith at the *Cleveland Gazette* to introduce himself, emphasizing the paper's association with the SRBM and Catherine. His letter to Smith requested help with information for the content of the new organ, primarily by being placed on the *Gazette*'s exchange list, and his letter was published in the *Gazette* by way of an announcement of the new paper.[5] Darby's letter indicated to Smith that the *Gazette*'s 'unselfish and unrequited labor in the interest of the race, extending over a period of a dozen or more years, is at least appreciated by those capable of appreciating earnest and telling effort'.[6] The *Bond*'s inaugural issue contained articles written by both Darby and Catherine.[7] A column by Catherine on 'white supremacy' relayed reports from the *New Orleans Crusader* that a 'White Supremacy League' had been organized by Democratic politicians to gain control of offices at the next election. Violent attacks upon black people were being reported alongside threats to white people considered too friendly with black families. This, Catherine observed, 'is what "white supremacy" means'.[8] She combined the report from New Orleans with encouraging updates on Ida B Wells' work in the United States and the petitions being organized by black communities to support the bill proposed by Henry W Blair in the House of Representatives to investigate lynchings.[9]

The first issue of the *Bond* also provided an opportunity to refute the version of the history of the Society presented by the Scottish branches in *Fraternity*. Darby's history of the Society covered two pages and took readers back to Catherine's original circular from January 1888. Wells' powerful advocacy was credited for paving a way for the SRBM, although Darby recalled that more than one reference had been made in *Anti-Caste* to the need for a more organized campaigning effort before her arrival in Britain. The personal acrimony between Catherine and Isabella Mayo was not mentioned. Instead, an explanation for the crisis of the Society focused on the convening of the SRBM's 1894 annual meeting. With the news of Edwards' death in the summer of 1894,

Mayo was not the only member of the SRBM to see an opportunity to strengthen her position in the movement. The 'council meeting' Mayo complained of not being invited to had been arranged by Catherine and her supporters. They contacted high-profile activists to see if they would lend their support to the SRBM. The General Council of this branch of the SRBM included original members of *Anti-Caste* and old friends of Catherine such as Miss F K Bishop, Mrs A H Clothier, Isabella Metford, Professor F W Newman, Eliza Wigham as well as Catherine and Ellen Impey (Figure 8.1). Although neither Alfred Webb nor Dadabhai Naoroji had ever subscribed to *Anti-Caste*, they both supported Catherine's branch of the SRBM along with the MP Henry J Wilson, Isabella Ormston Ford, Rev Henry Joseph, Mary Priestman and Dr Chowry Muthu.[10] The position of Dr Ghani reflects the difficulties the split in the SRBM had created. In the November 1894 issue of *Fraternity*, Ghani was still named as a member of the temporary council put in place by the Scottish branches and he also appeared on the Executive Committee of the SRBM published in the *Bond of Brotherhood*.[11] A lecture he gave at the Tyneside Geographical Institute on 'The Relations of the Moslem World to the British Empire' in February 1896, in which he discussed the fact that 'Hindoos and Mahommedans' alike were realizing more and more that they were all Indians, and must stand or fall together, was well received in *Fraternity*. Its reference to Ghani as a valued friend and constant contributor suggests that either he decided to remain loyal to the Scottish branches or some members of the network maintained connections with both branches of the SRBM.[12]

Possibly because Darby did not initially have as many international contacts as previous editors, the *Bond* carried more opinion pieces by British authors who were now usually named and their articles indexed. Catherine assured the many correspondents and readers who had sent her papers from the United States, India, Africa, Australia and elsewhere that she would continue to value and utilize their content, especially now that a committee instead of 'one over burdened individual' had taken charge of the SRBM's important and ever-widening work. Over the first four months, columns and paragraphs covered events in Swaziland, reported scandals in Cameroon, voiced support to Indian readers and gave suggestions of how representations for their concerns might be strengthened. These were placed alongside 'General News', which briefly reported on 'black labourers in Jamaica', 'the slaves of Navassa' and slavery under British Protection in Zanzibar.[13] A regular column 'American Notes', probably written by Catherine, covered issues of lynching and political developments in the United States. Alongside these recognizable forms of news, readers were confronted with a tone of language that had not appeared when the paper was under Catherine or Edwards' control, including 'News from Natives' and a lengthy serialized essay by Isabella Metford entitled 'Taking Advantage of the Weak'.

Public lectures being given by the black American educator and feminist Hallie Quinn Brown, and G F Richings who came with an endorsement from Frederick Douglass and the *New York Age*, were given prominent coverage in the *Bond* while Catherine's support for activists continued to attract the attention of the black press in the United States.[14] In January 1895 a *Cleveland Gazette* leader reported comments made by Catherine at a meeting in Glastonbury where G F Richings gave a talk on Evidence of Progress among Coloured People with illustrations from several hundred lantern slides.[15] During her address to the audience, Catherine argued that it was not only the reality of lynchings that they were fighting against but the reason they were able to happen. There was an estrangement between white and black people that meant white people could stand and see a black man tortured to death without any pity or care. To bridge this divide practically, Catherine argued that the focus of their protest had to be the religious bodies of America; while segregation existed within their own churches, they aided the path that led to other evils such as the violence of lynching.[16] Beneath their report, the *Gazette* printed a letter from Richings, who was confident that his English trip would on his return secure him a hearing with a number of white Americans with whom he had never previously been able to meet. Richings also made clear to his American readers that he was working closely with the SRBM and that it was Catherine's personal drive that was pushing forward his tour of England and Scotland.[17]

The roots of prejudice

For the *Bond of Brotherhood* Catherine produced two of her most exploratory essays on race, segregation and prejudice. In the first, 'The Obliterated Sense of Brotherhood', she formulated reflections on theoretical ideas of caste and the 'power of self', which she had discussed in the *Village Album* almost ten years earlier. Recalling her first visit to America 16 years before when she confronted caste or what was now being called the great 'Separate System', Catherine emphasized to *Bond* readers, as she would to her audience in Glastonbury, that the aims of the SRBM were not so much a crusade against lynch law or the more violent exhibitions of race prejudice such as lynchings as terrible as these were, but against the roots and underlying causes of racial prejudices. In this column Catherine argued that segregation was maintained throughout every grade of white society, in their homes, their churches, their social meetings, schools and personal relationships as they sought to avoid all relations other than those of master and servant, director and menial worker. White people adhered to these rules of separation almost without exception and those that did not obey these laws of caste forfeited the respect and even the fellowship of their white neighbours. The 'dominant race' had ruled it so, and until someone wise or braver than the rest dared to advocate and introduce another way and others dared to follow, so it would remain.[18]

The key to undermining the colour-caste line was to undermine the idea of race itself. Catherine presented racial prejudice as a disease, not something 'natural to the human mind', but something that occurred because of an interference with natural law. The unnatural barriers of racial segregation were the cause of racial prejudice, if these were removed their effects in society would cease. 'In other words, to eradicate caste prejudice, first eradicate CASTE.'

> Once abolish the colour-line, – abolish the cruel exception legislation, – unbar the doors of the schools, the workshops, and the churches, and relinquish that stony determination to exclude one gentle and forgiving race (your kinsmen) from the common life that all beside are privileged to enjoy, – and *prejudice* that offspring of misconception and *fear*, will melt in thin air.

> Caste *is an organised tyranny of human construction*, and is no less amenable to human influences and action than was the statutory slavery that it supersedes.[19]

Catherine had often acknowledged that the end of the system of slavery had not ended racial prejudice. Removing the structures of segregation would not necessarily remove the fear of the other white people harboured towards their black brethren. Nor had she managed to untangle the role of the state's interference in 'natural law' and the role of personal responsibility. Catherine maintained that as individuals it remains a personal responsibility to acknowledge the particular feelings of coldness or prejudice we hold. The remedy for this coldness, fear or prejudice also must come from personal enlightenment and change with individuals 'taking steps to place him or herself in the right attitude of sympathy towards his neighbour'.[20] Catherine understood state and institutional structures to be intertwined with personal action and responsibility, but while waiting for the governing classes to act, individuals could enforce change within the spheres of their own lives, if they could overcome their fear.

Catherine returned to the issue of fear in a column published three months later. In 'Fear: The Explanation', Catherine admitted that in thinking about the question of racial prejudice she had been led to a conclusion which, in view of the lynching horrors still being regularly reported, seemed almost paradoxical.

> We see America, or at least its governing classes (for, though the great nation is a republic, it is always the few who govern, whether by exceptional ability of person or circumstance, or by choice, or election, of their fellows), striking with deadly blows at the best elements of its coloured population. Why? From *fear*; from what by outsiders is seen to be an actually *groundless panic*.

This fear, especially in the South, meant that the idea of absorbing, amalgamating with or even granting 'civil equality' with black men and women was met with the deepest horror articulated in a fear of 'negro supremacy'. The only alternative was an insistence upon 'white supremacy', a structure of society in the minds of those in power that would ensure 'a reign of justice, morality and enlightened civilization in general'. In reality, to maintain this imaginary view of a 'Solid South', white America created a society that was 'cruel, and monstrously, *lavishly* unjust'.[21] Catherine's provocative ideas for change were limited to her focus on the situation of black and white communities in the United States. Although her first essay made a passing comment to the treatment of political prisoners in Russia, there was no other attempt to draw on other examples of racial prejudice as a means to explore further the 'American Question'. Nor did she consider how ideas of 'Aboriginality' and identities of settler communities in this context might affect the politics of fear in countries where racial prejudice could result in very violent forms of racial prejudice, although they might take materially different forms to lynching. The *Bond of Brotherhood* provided space for Catherine to present stimulating and challenging thoughts in print. The format may have encouraged a development of her thinking in conversation with other engaged readers, but this column on 'Fear' marked Catherine's last contribution to the *Bond of Brotherhood* as yet another division emerged within the SRBM.

Relaunching *Anti-Caste*

The final entry in the minute book for the West of England branch of the SRBM records a committee meeting held on 3 January 1895, when seven members including Ellen and Catherine gathered to consider their response to the publication of a letter by Joseph Malins in the January issue of the *Bond*. Malins had written at length to justify the reunification of the Templar order, which, in the first issue of the *Bond*, had been given as a major root cause for the establishment of the SRBM. The marked copy of his letter in the branch's minute book illustrates the particular points the collective disagreed with (Figure 9.1). Primarily their concerns focused on Malins' acceptance of continuing racial segregation in the IOGT lodges 'because it at least brings both

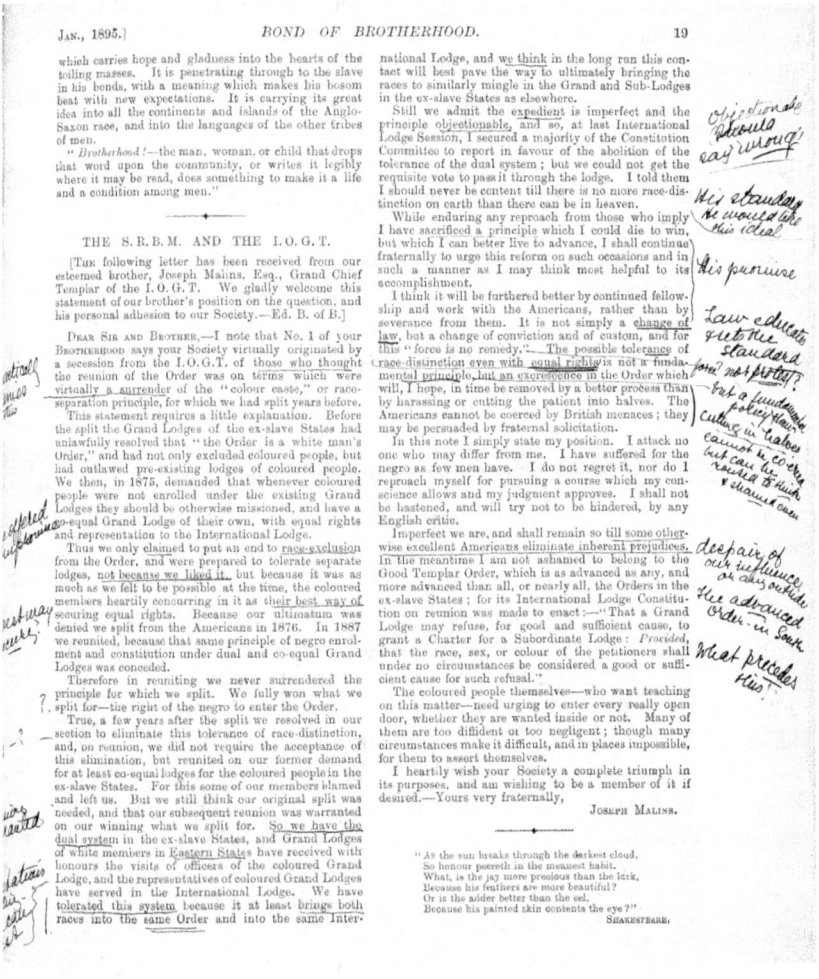

Figure 9.1 A letter from Joseph Malins printed in an issue of the *Bond of Brotherhood* from January 1895 with Catherine Impey's critical notations

races into the same Order and into the same international Lodge', which Catherine contested through her inked riposte.²² The group agreed to write a letter of protest to Darby, challenging his decision to publish and publicly welcome Malins when the actions of the Templars contravened the SRBM's fundamental principles. Their letter failed to elicit a response that satisfied them, and with regret they announced that their differences struck at such fundamental issues of principle on the personal conduct of members that they believed a working relationship with the committee could no longer function. They thus felt they had no choice but to withdraw from the movement they had helped to establish.

Catherine's personal printed letter of resignation to Darby explained that few decisions 'have cost me a more painful struggle'. She emphasized again her belief that in August 1893 the SRBM had agreed that all members would refrain 'from *all complicity*' in practices of racial segregation for this system was 'a white man's *organised repudiation* of the brotherhood of darker races, a scheme so tyrannous and *immoral*' that it was the duty of SRBM members 'to withstand it in the most practical and positive manner'. As such it did not seem to her '*brotherly* to excuse or tolerate compliance with those unjust and unbrotherly demands of the strong against the weak' and so she proposed reverting to former methods of advocating reform by 'reviving the little paper' *Anti-Caste*.²³

An explanation of yet another split amongst the SRBM was sent to readers along with their copy of a new, or for some older readers a familiar, journal. *Anti-Caste* had for a time been suspended in the hope that the cause of antiracism might be met by other publications. Now, Catherine told her readers, 'I feel, however, that its voice is again needed.'²⁴ Catherine's hope that other publications would continue to cover issues of racial prejudice, in a manner she and her close supporters felt appropriate, had come to an end. Once again personal ethics and practical politics had clashed, although as Darby emphasized to his continuing readers this division was not as acrimonious as the one that had prompted the launch of the *Bond of Brotherhood* just over a year before. In her account of the split, Catherine revealed that once again she had been deeply hurt and disappointed by her colleagues in the movement. Catherine, her close friends, family and colleagues who made up the founding core of the anticaste movement had always acted in the belief that to defeat racism they had to insure that they were in 'no way consenting to the evil' of racism, 'either actively or passively, singly or collectively'.²⁵ As Catherine saw it, racial segregation existed because of the will of two orders of people – those who openly or secretly demanded segregation, and those who, whether from apathy or policy, yielded to their unjust demands. Those at the *Bond* who supported Malins had failed to live up to their claims to equality, and their failure to do so meant Catherine could no longer work with them, for then she would be tacitly supporting racial prejudice herself.

No longer affiliated to the Scottish branches–owned version of *Fraternity* nor able to cooperate with the leaders of the SRBM attached to *Bond of Brotherhood*, Catherine felt she had no choice but to resume publication of *Anti-Caste*. She did not relish the return to publishing. Filled with 'much sorrow and a deep sense of personal unfitness for so arduous a task', she felt resuming the editorship more like a burden. The first issue of the seventh volume came out in March 1895, exactly seven years after the

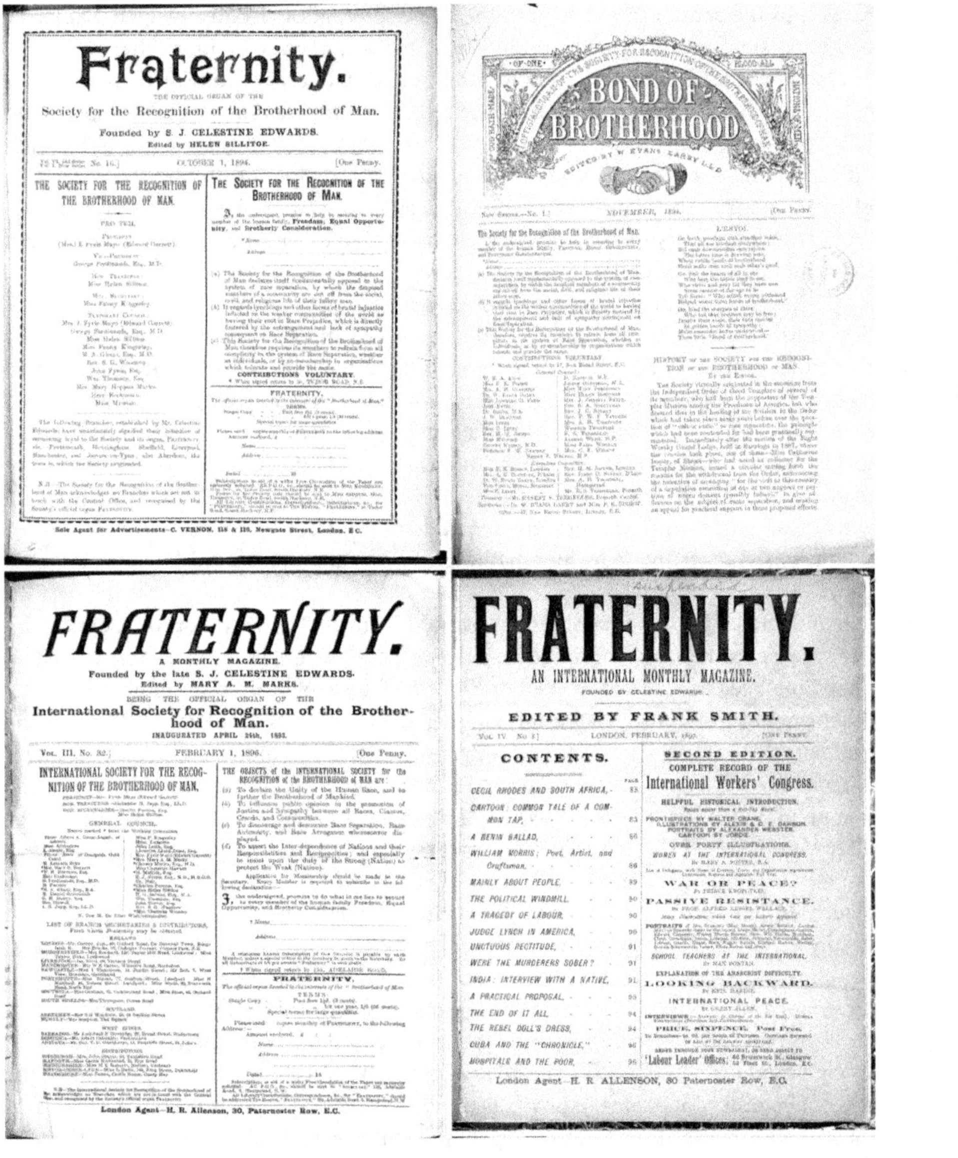

Fraternity.

THE OFFICIAL ORGAN OF THE

Society for the Recognition of the Brotherhood of Man.

Founded by S. J. CELESTINE EDWARDS.

Edited by HELEN SILLITOE.

OCTOBER 1, 1894. [One Penny.

THE SOCIETY FOR THE RECOGNITION OF THE BROTHERHOOD OF MAN.

THE SOCIETY FOR THE RECOGNITION OF THE BROTHERHOOD OF MAN.

CONTRIBUTIONS VOLUNTARY.

FRATERNITY.

Sole Agent for Advertisements—C. VERNON, 118 & 119, Newgate Street, London, E.C.

BOND OF BROTHERHOOD

EDITED BY W. EVANS DARBY, LL.D.

FRATERNITY.

A MONTHLY MAGAZINE.

Founded by the late S. J. CELESTINE EDWARDS.

Edited by MARY A. M. MARKS.

BEING THE OFFICIAL ORGAN OF THE

International Society for Recognition of the Brotherhood of Man.

INAUGURATED APRIL 24th, 1893.

VOL. III, No. 32.] FEBRUARY 1, 1896. [One Penny.

INTERNATIONAL SOCIETY FOR THE RECOGNITION OF THE BROTHERHOOD OF MAN.

THE OBJECTS of the INTERNATIONAL SOCIETY for the RECOGNITION of the BROTHERHOOD of MAN are:

FRATERNITY.

London Agent—H. R. Allenson, 30, Paternoster Row, E.C.

FRATERNITY.

AN INTERNATIONAL MONTHLY MAGAZINE.

FOUNDED BY CELESTINE EDWARDS.

EDITED BY FRANK SMITH.

CONTENTS.

CECIL RHODES AND SOUTH AFRICA,	83
CARTOON: COMMON TALE OF A COMMON TAP,	85
A BENIN BALLAD,	86
WILLIAM MORRIS: Poet, Artist, and Craftsman,	88
MAINLY ABOUT PEOPLE,	89
THE POLITICAL WINDMILL,	90
A TRAGEDY OF LABOUR,	90
JUDGE LYNCH IN AMERICA,	90
UNCTUOUS RECTITUDE,	91
WERE THE MURDERERS SOBER?	91
INDIA: INTERVIEW WITH A NATIVE,	91
A PRACTICAL PROPOSAL,	93
THE END OF IT ALL,	94
THE REBEL DOLL'S DRESS,	94
CUBA AND THE "CHRONICLE,"	96
HOSPITALS AND THE POOR,	96

SECOND EDITION.

COMPLETE RECORD OF THE

International Workers' Congress.

WAR OR PEACE?

PASSIVE RESISTANCE.

LOOKING BACKWARD.

INTERNATIONAL PEACE.

'Labour Leader' Offices.

London Agent—H. R. ALLENSON, 30 Paternoster Row, E.C.

Figure 9.2 An issue of the *Bond of Brotherhood* from November 1894, with the logo of a black hand and a white hand clasped in a handshake which was also used by Catherine on correspondence paper when she was secretary of the Templar Mission to the Freedmen of America, alongside the changing mastheads of *Fraternity* from October 1894, February 1896 and February 1897

first issue. Now printed for free distribution, the paper came with an extended new strapline on its masthead *Anti-Caste*: 'Assumes the Brotherhood of the entire Human Family, and claims for the Dark Races of Mankind their equal right to PROTECTION,

PERSONAL LIBERTY, EQUALITY OF OPPORTUNITY AND HUMAN FELLOWSHIP.' Subscribers were asked to send one shilling and upwards to support the movement, reminding readers that aside from printing and the occasional help with labelling and other administrative jobs, the work of the movement was done gratuitously.

Catherine made a number of specific requests from her readers for help in the production and distribution of *Anti-Caste*. First she reiterated the need for funds to support the publication of *Anti-Caste* literature, as well as meetings, lectures and foreign deputations, either through personal contributions or collections from the public. Funds in the form of greenbacks, postage stamps, money orders or cheques were all welcome. Second, Catherine sought to expand *Anti-Caste*'s print networks by requesting 'direct and reliable' news and information from readers. Third, she encouraged their editorial assistance by clearly marking in the newspapers paragraphs they considered relevant. In order to expand *Anti-Caste*'s reading community she asked for the names and addresses of those at home or abroad who should receive *Anti-Caste*. Finally, she asked readers to become distributors, by placing one or more copies of *Anti-Caste* into the hands of readers in public waiting rooms or on library tables, thus enlarging the circle of *Anti-Caste*'s readership and influence.[26]

Catherine's first editorial of this new series betrayed her despondent mood, one clouded by the inequality that continued to grow seemingly unabated. She emphasized the need for *Anti-Caste* to aim for the widest dissemination of its views through its own publications and the general press. It was a work that was arduous and ever growing, although Catherine trusted that the time would soon come when more widespread support would be given to the cause. Reflecting on the history of the anticaste movement at this moment of its rebirth, the racialized divisions of the United States remained at the forefront of Catherine's mind. She recalled her first, transformative trip to the United States, when she had decided that in the 'deliberate and systematic separation of those differing in colour lay the root and core of race-prejudice with all its inhumanities to the dark races and attendant moral degradation of the white, not only in America, but in India, Africa, and many countries where white and dark races come in contact'.[27] Again she reiterated to her readers that the 'idea that colour has any place whatever in determining the relations of members of the human family towards each other must everywhere be wiped out'. She emphasized the power of individual action and the important impact of Ida B Wells' visits and she drew on the scriptures to argue that no other measure of judgement than that of personal merit was sanctioned throughout the Christian and Jewish Scriptures.[28]

Anti-Caste emphasized its networks of correspondence with the British and Foreign Anti-Slavery Society, the APS, the Indian National Congress, the Anglo-Indian Temperance Association, the Afro-American League through Thomas Fortune, the National Citizens' Rights Association through Tourgée and G W Cable, the Central Anti-lynching Association and Ida B Wells and Victoria Matthews, a journalist and president and founding member of the Women's Loyal Union, one of the oldest black women's clubs founded in New York City to support Wells when she was first exiled from the South.[29] Catherine again began the task of forming an individual relay station for newspapers and reports produced by *Imvo*, John Mitchell Jr and numerous other 'Afro-Americans and West Indians', Maloga Mission and others working among 'Native

Australians'.[30] Throughout March, Catherine and Ellen again hosted G F Richings, who stayed in Street while on the road from Bristol to Leeds and then before he left for home from Southampton on 23 March. Under different circumstances Catherine would have included something of Richings' lectures in the following issue of *Anti-Caste*, but as it was the April/May 16-page issue was devoted to the late Fredrick Douglass (Figure 9.3). John Whitby and Son also printed a memorial issue of Douglass' essay 'Why Is the Negro Lynched?' A preface explained that those in the 'Anti-caste movement' felt the most fitting tribute they could pay to Douglass' memory was to support the widest possible distribution of the article published in the *AME Church Review* a few months before his death. In this, on behalf of victims of lynching, Douglass claimed 'in the name of justice, to be heard'.[31]

During the months of May and June Isabella Metford came to stay with the Impeys, and joined Ellen and Catherine on a trip to Dublin. They perhaps encroached on the time Catherine needed to produce the next issues of *Anti-Caste*, resulting in another double issue. The first two pages of this June/July number were dominated by a report

Figure 9.3 *Anti-Caste*'s memorial number dedicated to Frederick Douglass, who died in February 1895; it was only the second *Anti-Caste* cover to carry an image

A New Bond of Brotherhood 213

written by Catherine on the Tenth Annual Indian Congress held in December 1894 in Madras. Catherine reiterated the grave disappointment expressed at the way in which the Indian government disregarded the more sympathetic mandates of the Parliament and repeated assurances of Queen Victoria that Indian subjects should expect equal treatment. One of the greater complaints was of the barriers placed in the way of recruiting Indian candidates for the civil service, and the persistent rejection of demands for preliminary examinations to be available in India so the huge costs of a passage to and residence in England could be avoided. An urgent appeal was also made for the disfranchisement of Indians in South Africa to be vetoed.

In June 1895 Ida B Wells married Ferdinand L Barnett, a union announced by *Anti-Caste* and newspapers in England and Scotland.[32] *Anti-Caste* encouraged readers to study Wells' writing for themselves and to continue actively supporting her cause. The issue also reported the work that Florence Balgarnie was continuing to do in her role as secretary of the Anti-lynching Committee and an ongoing row between the leaders of the Women's Christian Temperance Union (WCTU) and staunch supporters of Wells.

Figure 9.4 A sketch of Ida B Wells which appeared on the cover of *Great Thoughts and Christian Graphic*, illustrating 'The Story of Ida B Wells' by Florence Balgarnie, Secretary of the Anti-Lynching Committee, published 16 March 1895

In June 1895 at the British Women's and World Women's Temperance Convention in London, a charge was brought against Wells once more, this time by Lady Isabella Somerset, who accused Wells of alienating some of the (white) Americans who might have helped her. Balgarnie came to Wells' defence and in an eloquent and impassioned speech, reportedly received with some disfavour by the American visitors, gave some accounts of the horrors of lynching. Balgarnie argued that American women too often apologized for, instead of denouncing, these outrages, and she called upon her American sisters to pronounce much more boldly on the subject.[33] To an extent Balgarnie's words were heeded. A resolution denouncing lynching was introduced by the executive, and was supported by 65 branches of the British Women's Temperance Association. It was carried unanimously; but it was followed by one which *Anti-Caste* viewed as

> far less satisfactory, declaring the belief of the Convention that the WCTU of America 'has maintained the attitude which all Christian bodies must adopt towards this (lynching) question, namely, that under no circumstances must human life be taken without due process of law.'[34]

The *Daily News* also picked up on the debate at the Women's Temperance Convention, agreeing that Balgarine made a powerful speech in vindication of Wells and in condemnation of the outrages which shocked the moral sense of civilized mankind. It observed that the American ladies present led by Miss Frances Willard appeared to complain that Wells had not sufficiently minced her words in her telling of these shocking outbursts of lawlessness.[35] The report concluded that in Britain more needed to be done than the shaking of heads and the repetition of words that exclaimed human life should never be taken except by due process of law. The *Daily News* supported the British use of more decisive and energetic terms to be followed up by decisive and energetic deeds.[36] It seems unlikely Celestine Edwards would have agreed with this robust view of the British response to international injustice.

In the June/July issue Catherine also advertised that Daniel Matthews was back in England and was happy to speak at meetings wherever friends might be able to arrange them. She hoped that a report on the situation of Aboriginal Australians would have been published in the June/July issue, but due to lack of space it was being held over. But this report did not appear, neither did a portrait of the son of King Cetewayo, for this was the last issue of *Anti-Caste* to be published. There is no indication within the pages of *Anti-Caste* as to why this was the case. Having rekindled *Anti-Caste* in such a dramatic fashion, it seems odd that Catherine would have given up so easily. It is possible her domestic duties could not be made to fit around the production of the paper. Her domestic duties had always torn at Catherine's ability to give all she wished to *Anti-Caste*. Finding herself 'almost buried and lost in the tangle of multitudinous claims' on her time had made it impossible for Catherine engage with the British 'general press' and attract the tens of thousands of readers she hoped for.[37] Moreover, the death of Catherine and Ellen's mother in 1895 was a great loss to the sisters and no doubt disrupted Catherine's ability to issue monthly numbers of *Anti-Caste* in the first instance. The abundant apple harvest that year nearly entirely occupied, indeed almost engulfed, Ellen, and without their mother's help other domestic and social duties now fell on Catherine's shoulders alone. Though they worked almost unceasingly the sisters still had not got everything in order by November.[38] The re-establishment of *Anti-Caste* may also have received a slow response from a readership negotiating its options or resistance from readers tested to their limits. Catherine came to recognize that though spurned by members of the Society she had founded, they continued to influence a growing circle to think on the questions *Anti-Caste* had originally raised. Viewing the work of the anti-lynching committee, Catherine believed Florence Balgarnie wrote well, and besides, she moved in more influential circles than Catherine.[39] In this context Catherine was not convinced that she could or perhaps should begin another run of the periodical.

A Scottish *Fraternity*

Backed by Isabella Mayo and a number of local branch secretaries in Scotland and England, *Fraternity* continued as a monthly periodical. The concerns discussed in *Fraternity* remained closely aligned to those in the *Bond*, reporting on lynchings, welcoming and supporting Hallie Quinn Brown's visit to Britain, reporting on the colour line in Australia and the work of the Indian National Congress.[40] Although Catherine had always seen work as a way to highlight and discuss racial discrimination across the Empire, the politics of labour *per se* did not feature in *Anti-Caste*. Although given more consideration in Edwards' *Fraternity*, the re-orientation of the paper under Mayo and her colleagues reflected a strong move to bring issues of racial prejudice together with the emerging politics of labour and the trade union movement. The presence of the *Bond of Brotherhood* forced a redefinition of *Fraternity*, and the battle for ownership of the Society of the Recognition of the Brotherhood of Man was ignored in the pages of the *Bond* but played out on the pages of *Fraternity*. Mayo's colleague Rev S G Woodrow wrote to Darby to take issue with the version of the history of the SRBM which appeared in the *Bond*. Darby refused to publish his letter and so it was printed in *Fraternity*. The accompanying editorial commentary was bitter, aggressive and once again a disproportionate response that distorted the radical narrative of its legacy.

Although he claimed he did not wish to 'underrate the services which Miss Impey has rendered to this cause through the Press', Woodrow's letter insisted that the SRBM owed its formation to the 'active brain and warm heart' of Isabella Mayo. It was true, he admitted, that 'a monthly journal called *Anti-Caste* faithfully discussed the position and prospects of the Negro race' for six years, but no organizational planning took place until Mayo invited Catherine to Aberdeen to see if something more active could be developed and was able to guarantee one-half of the costs of bringing Ida B Wells to Britain from America. Darby informed Woodrow that this was inaccurate, taking a far longer view of the movement's history. Woodrow responded that he was concerned only with the origins of the SRBM and clearly for him these arose from Aberdeen and were to be credited to Mayo and Celestine Edwards.[41] Though the publication of their exchanges brought 'gratuitous advertisement' to the *Bond*, those behind *Fraternity* deemed they had to challenge the bold and shameless claim that the *Bond* made to be the official organ for the SRBM. The editorial asked, 'Of what is the "Bond of Brotherhood" the outcome?' we unhesitatingly answer, '*it is the outcome of the spirit of Lynch Law at home!*'[42]

Challenging the *Bond's* claim to be the official organ of the Society, *Fraternity* declared itself to be 'The original and only organ of the S.R.B.M'. Ensuring that the paper remained closely associated with Edwards and his popular memory, the paper's strapline maintained Edwards' name, crediting him as the founder of the paper. Mayo, Sillitoe and their Executive Committee must have realized that their claim to the Society's name remained tenuous. Regardless, two societies bearing the same name would remain confusing for subscribers, readers and political campaigners. Couching a decision to change their name in the need to encapsulate the group's worldwide sympathies, it was announced in November 1894 that the collective would probably soon be known as the International Society for the Recognition of the Brotherhood of Man. From March 1895 the masthead changed to reflect the new emphasis (see Figure 9.2). Readers were informed that this did not reflect a changing of *Fraternity's* title, merely an addition to stress the organization's force and value.[43]

Letters from local branches confirmed their loyalty to the Scottish branches, but some such as Portsmouth and Birmingham were rather less enthusiastic than others. Their letters also reveal the confusion that surrounded the separation of the Society and the importance of a periodical to their activism. A meeting of the secretaries of the Birmingham branch unanimously decided to join with the Scottish branches because they had taken control of *Fraternity*. Without an official organ the secretaries could not see how they could undertake any work at all. As they had heard from the SRBM treasurer Tregelles that the Council (as they still recognized it) did not intend to issue a paper, they saw only two options open to them: first to remain without a paper and, consequently, drop their work entirely; or second to join the Scottish branches and carry on the work as before. They chose the latter.[44] The Liverpool branch warmly embraced the new structure. The three honorary secretaries wrote to Helen Sillitoe in October to congratulate her on her appointment to the editorship of *Fraternity* and to mark their approval of the establishment of the Provisional Council. They attributed the foundation of their branch to Celestine Edwards and had never faltered in their allegiance to him and felt fully assured that he would have approved of the steps taken by the Aberdeen branch.[45]

Helen Sillitoe remained editor throughout 1895, overseeing the continuation of a form of *Fraternity* that in structure remained familiar to readers who joined the community before the split. Columns such as 'What We Think' and 'Concerning Ourselves in Recent Magazines' and space for women writers continued to be regular features. Mary A M Marks became a prominent contributor writing articles on the National Indian Congress, political economy and 'Individualism and Collectivism.'[46] Ill health forced Helen Sillitoe to withdraw from the editorship in 1895 and she was replaced by Mary A M Marks. She inherited a periodical still in a precarious financial position; two years after its establishment *Fraternity* still did not pay for itself. A letter to the editor from J R Drummond of Edinburgh reveals some of the tensions between leaders of the movement and their supporters, and gives some reasons for their inability to develop a large enough support base to sustain *Fraternity* financially. As a supporter, regular reader and subscriber to *Fraternity*, Drummond felt bound 'to protest against the persistently carping and sarcastic tone' that dominated many of *Fraternity's* articles. For Drummond the paper had developed 'an air of ostentatious virtue' that paraded itself before the reader, as if it, the voice of *Fraternity*, were immaculate. The paper took its assumed position of superiority as a place from which it could 'pick holes in everybody else, and hold them up to the light.' Drummond named numerous examples from the February issue including 'What We Think', which managed to fall foul of the Peace Society; 'Our Circle in the World', which antagonized British Christianity and the newspapers; 'Set Thine House in Order', which challenged ministers and the Christian Church; and so on *ad nauseam*. His more serious accusation was that in every instance he named, the attacks had come with 'a grave amount of misrepresentation or untruth,' which was neither fair nor brotherly.[47] He spoke not only for himself but for all *Fraternity* readers with whom he was acquainted. It was his conclusion that if the carping and sarcastic tone could be removed the difficulty in maintaining the paper's circulation would be reduced. Marks strenuously defended *Fraternity* in her lengthy reply. *Fraternity*, she argued, could not be incompatible with plain speaking particularly when the British had gravely departed from the principles which as a nation they still professed.

Perhaps as a response to criticisms from readers such as Drummond, Caroline Martyn, who had published widely in radical journals, was introduced as the new editor of *Fraternity* by Isabella Mayo in July 1896. A leading and popular socialist teacher and lecturer, earlier in the year Martyn had been elected to the National Administrative Council of the Independent Labour Party (ILP) and was soon to become the Trade Union organiser for the North of Scotland.[48] Martyn fused her Christian faith with strong socialist leanings. Before editing *Fraternity* she had served a term as editor of *Christian Weekly*, and in February 1894 had been hired by the *Workman's Times* to raise its sales but she had little chance to make an impression before the paper closed the following month.[49] Although an important and popular speaker on the socialist lecture circuit, like other women in the movement she had found herself confined to focusing on topics within the arts, rather than economic theory or politics.[50] As such Martyn may have seen *Fraternity* as an opportunity to develop and control an editorial narrative for her labour and religious beliefs, but the opportunity for her to influence the direction of the paper was short lived. She wrote the August editorial 'What Is Patriotism', but her new editorial role came after a strenuous speaking campaign and she died suddenly in Dundee on 23 July 1896.[51]

During this time when *Fraternity* acted as the voice of the Scottish branches, a shift occurred in the style of the periodical's production and tone. Throughout 1896, visual elements were introduced into *Fraternity*, including sketches of characters active in the movement, photographs, illustrations and satirical cartoons such as the 'Transvaal Raid: Or a "Capital" Arrangement'.[52] A cartoon accompanying 'Dialogues in a Dustbin', a satirical and critical piece by Katherine St John Conway, an important lecturer for the ILP, showed a blackface 'minstrel' with gold earrings and a whitened mouth with a gleaming top hat.[53] It is a strangely stereotyping cartoon that would not have featured under the editorial control of Catherine and Edwards.[54] In a report about the second Annual Conference of Indians in Britain, *Fraternity* claimed that it was not often that

Englishmen were given the opportunity of listening 'with their own ears to what their dusky fellow subjects from India have to say of her Government'.[55] This may well have been true: Catherine acknowledged this when reporting on her attendance at one of the meetings held by the delegates from the Indian National Congress in Bristol in 1891. Among the speakers Catherine heard Naoroji, now an elderly man, with a careworn face and delicate features, who was listened to with great attention. The meeting provided Catherine with an opportunity of extending her knowledge of the workings of caste in various parts of the world.[56] An editor's access to locally produced news was an important part of this, but the diversity of newspapers received seems to have dramatically reduced during this period of *Fraternity's* production. In April 1895, only ten papers were listed, dominated by black American newspapers such as the *New York Age* and the *Richmond Planet*, as well as the *Lagos Standard* and *Free Russia*.[57]

Following Martyn's death, Frank Smith's editorship represented a clear shift towards a predominant concern with the politics of labour, both within a colonial context and within Britain. Remembered as a pioneering member of the Labour Party, Frank Smith worked as a journalist in the Press Gallery of the House of Commons when Keir Hardie had first arrived in London. The pair became close friends and colleagues.[58] Smith made immediate changes when he took the helm of *Fraternity* in September 1896, the first of which was to run monthly advertisements in the *Labour Leader*. From Smith's first issue in charge, *Fraternity's* masthead changed once again to 'Fraternity – A monthly Magazine – organ of the International Society for the Recognition of the Brotherhood of Man and edited by Frank Smith – founded by Celestine Edwards'. An advert in *Labour Leader* emphasized that *Fraternity* maintained two publication sites, at 53 Fleet Street, London, and 66 Brunswick Street, Glasgow, and was printed by Maclaten & Sons in Glasgow, on Scottish paper made by trade union labour.[59] In October Smith lectured to a large audience on America, but the *Dundee Courier's* report on the event carries no mention of racial prejudice, the violence of lynching, segregation or the opinions of black Americans. For Smith, their concerns were subsumed within the politics of labour. He argued that the diversity of America, which contained people from every country under the sun, every tongue, creed and every colour, made it especially vulnerable to capitalist exploitation. Its 'cosmopolitan nature' made it a happy hunting ground for 'the sweater, the capitalist exploiter, and that class who made their money out of the needs, sufferings, and sorrows of the human race'.[60] Smith did not address the arguments put forward by Catherine and her black American colleagues that without tackling the causes of racism, equality for all the labouring classes was impossible.

Although politics in South Africa was also picked up in the September 1896 issue, along with news from the West Indies and Ceylon and conflict in Cuba, reports from the Socialist Congress hint at Smith's primary commitment to supporting the ILP. Known as Keir Hardie's 'chief Lieutenant', Smith was himself a parliamentary candidate and developed campaigns for other ILP hopefuls.[61] Articles on how difficult it was for British workers to remain 'thrifty' on a tight wage and Britain's neglect of its aged poor were perhaps closer to his interests.[62] Smith directed the paper towards a brotherhood of man that focused on class as the primary issue of division between people. Outlining the history of the International Society for the Recognition of the Brotherhood of Man in January 1897, the group's motto was given to be 'fellow-workers'. The aims of the

Society laid down in 1893, including the declaration of the 'Unity of the Human Race and to influence public opinion in the promotion of Justice and Sympathy between all Race, Classes, Creeds, and Communities', were now all placed in the context of labour and seen to be 'parallel with the claims of Labour, since both the inclinations and the true interests of the workers make for peace and goodwill'.[63]

Like Catherine, Smith argued for the importance of living principled lives but his focus for personal enlightenment revolved around class. In January 1897, he asked readers if their daily lives were a rebuke to the selfishness and tyranny of men and women around them? Did those readers who were pastors preach at the poor as though they were inferior and not capable of their fine intellectual culture? Did readers who were employers of labour in their factories, shops or warehouses see in those who toiled from Monday to Saturday members of one family?[64] The periodicals received under Smith maintained links with the *New York Age*, the *Richmond Planet* and the *Lagos Standard* but the mention of British journals including *The Labour Chronicle*, *Labour Leader*, *Labour Copartnership*, *Forward* and the *Prison Service Review* represented a shift in focus on the local news collected and reported.[65] Still a consistent hatred of Cecil Rhodes remained. A cartoon by 'Alexis' of Rhodes sitting on top of a barrel, pumping out profits at the expense of a crushed 'native' for a respectful capitalist graced a cover in 1897.[66] News that £6000 had been raised to build a monument of Rhodes in Buluwayo elicited a dry response:

> The figure of 'Cecil the damned' should stand with his foot upon dead natives. Behind him should lie an exploded bomb. In front of him should be cases of 'liquor,' and perhaps the invoice for a billiard table. From his pockets should project budgets of 'company' documents. A letter to Jameson, torn across, should lie at his feet. His supporters should be the two whites who suppressed Logenguela's last embassy and ran away with his offerings. But we fear that this is the monument of the future, not of to-day![67]

To raise his personal and the ILP's profile, Smith spoke at Gosport's Liberal Club on the 'Housing of the Working Class' in February 1897; the same month he announced a major speaking tour on 'Our Glorious Empire, on which the sun never sets and the tax-gatherer never goes to bed'.[68] His lectures aimed to give the truth about the Empire by presenting facts and figures on all nations under the Union Jack. Boasting that nothing like it had ever been attempted, Smith planned to speak to audiences throughout March and early April at Rotherham, Keighley, Halifax, Leeds, Glasgow, Lancashire and Paisley. Reports on the talks he gave highlight Smith's use of technology: his talk at Victoria Hall, Arbroath, was illustrated by a series of animated photographs shown on a screen by means of a 'cinematograph' and at the Temperance Hall, Middlesbrough, he delivered his talk accompanied by limelight views. In one report of the talk the journalist neither makes mention of the International Society for the Recognition of the Brotherhood of Man or the perspective of the Empire from black peoples nor highlights their influence on Smith's ideas or lectures. According to the reporter in Middlesbrough, Smith was entirely associated with the Independent Labour Party and presented his reflections on the Empire through the lens of Socialism.[69]

The final issue of *Fraternity* no longer carried a masthead that associated it with the SRBM (see Figure 9.2). Rebranded as an 'international monthly magazine', the issue's contents list highlighted the breadth of its concerns. The distant inheritance of *Anti-Caste* remained with articles on Cuba and Cecil Rhodes in South Africa but an article on lynch law focused not on the injustices of lynching but on whether the murderers who took part in the violence were sober or not. More general interest articles such as 'Hospitals and the Poor', 'William Morris: Poet, Artist and Craftsman' and 'The Political Windmill' illustrated the marginalized place of racial prejudice in the editor's concerns and his understanding of international solidarity. The February advertisement for *Fraternity* in *Labour Leader* was the first to mention Celestine Edwards. It perhaps represents a final effort to reconnect with readers who recalled the original aims and history of the movement, or to draw in new readers who remembered Edwards' oratory. The appeal came too late. February 1897 is the final issue of *Fraternity* advertised in the *Labour Leader* and it appears to be the final issue of *Fraternity* to be published. Although Edwards had managed a busy touring schedule while editing two periodicals, Smith was not as committed to the cause of racial equality as Edwards had been, and it would seem that Isabella Mayo could not find anyone to take his place.

At the end of the Anti-Caste movement

When Isabella Mayo chose to make her bitter disapproval of Catherine publicly known in the pages of *Fraternity*, she initiated a fracture in the SRBM that could not be healed. For the best part of a year Catherine accepted the limited role Mayo demanded of her relinquishing her editorial and production role at *Anti-Caste*, but the consequences for Catherine's penned confession to Ferdinands and the reading of this moment by Mayo and others as the manifestation of a dangerous transgressive desire had far-reaching consequences for Catherine's reputation and activist life. Though it was deeply painful for her, like Wells, Catherine found herself having to justify her actions to family, friends and colleagues. In Street Helen Priestman Bright Clark and others arranged for a group from the Society of Friends to hear Catherine's version of events. Having listened to everything they 'dismissed *the case as in "no way"* calling for' the action that Mayo demanded, but it must have been mortifying for Catherine to have to submit to such an enquiry.[70] Though deeply grateful for their public support, even more humiliating must have been the formal record of their opinion in a letter 'Friends Dismissal of the Cause', which Catherine offered to at least one colleague as evidence of her acquittal.[71] In June 1893 Catherine wrote to the Tourgées explaining candidly why her relationship with Mayo had broken down.[72] Her letters reflect how the change of plans for the SRBM wrought by Mayo's demands brought questions and queries from activist colleagues that Catherine found difficult to answer, and at least once Ellen replied to enquiries on her sister's behalf.[73] The sympathetic letters Catherine initially received from the Tourgées were encouraging but later their silence prompted her to write to them in March 1895 asking if they were ill or too busy to write, or if perhaps they thought she really was 'rather crazed'. Writing to inform them of her split with the SRBM, caused as she put it by 'men who think they know all about it', and her decision to restart *Anti-Caste*, she asked them plaintively: '<u>Don</u>'t refuse me your reply + counsel. <u>What</u> have I done to be cast off?'[74]

Catherine had written a similar letter to W E A Axon in November 1894 to draw his attention to the new circulation of *Bond of Brotherhood*. It had been a very long time since the pair had been in touch and Catherine had often wondered if 'the malignant whisperings' of her 'moral conduct' and then her 'failing mentally' had reached him. Perhaps, she asked, the cruel and damaging reports had reached further than she and her friends feared, leading some, like Axon, 'to suppose that there was at least <u>some truth</u> in the rumours'.[75] Unsure who did and did not know, nor what they may or may not have heard led Catherine to believe that 'the veil of mystery' surrounding the events had prevented her and her friends from defending her character from attack. Catherine understood herself to be 'an unconventional woman', but the insecurity Catherine felt from the circulating 'malignant whisperings', rumours and gossip took a toll and damaged relationships with two of her most important colleagues – Ida B Wells and Celestine Edwards.[76] Catherine believed that even Wells had at one point thought it would have been easier to 'sacrifice' Catherine, and though Edwards had ensured that while he edited the paper, and was in Britain, Mayo's opinions of Catherine were not given a forum in *Fraternity*, Catherine believed that 'Edwards while thinking to pacify angry assailants really played into their hands'. Seemingly unaware of the deep dilemma Wells found herself in and the great personal distress the events had caused her, Catherine concluded that both she and Edwards had been selfish in 'believing that Mrs M was more use to their cause than I could be'. Deeply pained she had gone steadily on, organizing the work in the West of England and helping collect funds for Wells' second campaign tour.[77]

Mayo's use of *Fraternity* to present accusations of Catherine and her supporters as weak, foolish and uncommitted to the cause forced a response from Catherine. Clearly members of Catherine's kinship and activist networks remained supportive of her until, and some even beyond, the split with the *Bond*. A visit to Street by Emma Tourgée and her daughter Amiée in September 1905 suggests the difficult times of 1895 had been set aside.[78] The final letters in the run of correspondence between Catherine and W E A Axon, in which she supposed that he was 'still under the impression either that I am insane or else worse', suggest that their relationship was not so easily healed.[79] And, though Catherine acknowledged Wells wrote her 'a very pretty and gracious letter' of acknowledgement before she sailed for the United States in 1894, Catherine's feelings of disappointment might explain why the tone of Wells' memoirs seems to imply the women had lost touch.[80]

As an editor-proprietor-publisher Catherine had become used to being able to report geographies of oppression in a format she controlled without her analysis of events being mediated through editors who tempered her voice. Edwards' *Fraternity* seemed to continue along lines she broadly agreed with, but Mayo's use of *Fraternity* indicated its sociopolitical voice would change. The *Bond of Brotherhood* initially seemed to provide a positive alternative for Catherine. The establishment of a committee to oversee the production of the paper suggested that more international news could be read and analyzed, and the paper provided space for Catherine to write her own critical pieces. These advantages could not override her desire for editorial control and the need for her and her closest colleagues to work with people they felt to be absolutely committed to their principles of equality. Closer links to the politics of labour in the last run of *Anti-Caste* might have drawn a larger number of readers to the movement but that direction, as taken by Frank Smith, did not secure the future of *Fraternity*. Given their insistence on the centrality of racial equality to human equality, it is understandable that Catherine and Edwards kept a broader concern for labour politics from the pages of their papers. As the triumph of the colour line in the twentieth century showed, broadly the labour movements of the United States, Britain and the former white-settler colonies could not be trusted to hold the politics of racial prejudice equal to that of class.[81] It held true, as some readers of *Anti-Caste* felt, that ultimately 'white was actually found holding with white in powerful race combination'.[82]

With the SRBM's disintegration in England and Scotland, Catherine retreated from an active role in attempting to develop print cultures that held a critical imaginary of international politics and racial prejudice within their pages. For some US politicians and activists who took a 'radically equalitarian position' ideas formulated around 'caste' had offered a useful theoretical tool, but by the time of the *Plessy vs Ferguson* decision in 1896 'anti-caste liberalism was a relic of the past'.[83] With the final issue of *Anti-Caste* in 1895, a key instalment in radical publishing in Britain came to an end. Its conclusion overlapped with the creation of new groups such as the Increased Armaments Protest Committee, formed in 1896 to protest against increasing spending on the British Navy and the refocusing of organizations like the Fabian Society, the Ethical Movement and 'progressive imperialists' in their positions to the Empire.[84] These operated in a political forum alongside emerging movements like the Indian National Congress and the African Association founded by members of the Indian and African diasporas. Darby's branch of the SRBM morphed into the League of Universal Brotherhood and Native Races Association. In 1906 the league issued a declaration in support of President Roosevelt's policy on lynching and reported on the treatment of Japanese people in California. The Liverpool-born Charles Garnett had become honorary secretary by 1907 when the league pressed Lord Elgin on the mission of the Basuto chiefs who were visiting London in an attempt to secure recognition of their claims to land in the Orange River Colony, and Garnett actively agitated on their behalf.[85]

The readers who remained attached to the SRBM's textual community were by 1897 without a printed focus to bind together their interests and aspirations for a transformative international movement. They had been a committed readership that formed part of a community sharing critical ideas on racial prejudice and empire before the shift in political culture traditionally associated with the Boer War.[86] Drawing together a critical analysis of the Empire across a diverse collection of colonies meant that a coherent anti-imperial and antiracist international policy was not formed in *Anti-Caste*, *Fraternity* or the *Bond*, although a sense of how to constitute action against racial prejudice did emerge. These theoretical debates were presented most strongly when the periodicals were edited by Catherine or Edwards. Catherine's tussle with the language of race reflected the rhetorical struggles of antiracism, as individuals within the network sought to create the foundational principles for an international movement. The periodicals were part of the strategy of making 'black, white and brown' political actors who, through their pacifism, vegetarianism, socialism, feminism, temperance work, antiracism and readerships, imagined and contributed to alternative political landscapes.[87]

For six years *Anti-Caste* maintained a solid if small circulation among its community of readers, and Edwards' expansion of its distribution networks under *Fraternity* signalled the potential for a far larger community. Neither editor came close to realizing Catherine's ideal of an international community that brought together black and white readers who recognized their situation within an international context that was as much Indian as it was American and as much African as it was British. For some readers at least the loss of the movement's publications re-opened the political gap *Anti-Caste* once filled. In 1899, G F Richings wrote to Catherine asking for her help with his continuing antilynching campaigns, hopeful that a little newspaper agitation from England might still have an effect on US actions against mob rule.[88] What support Catherine may have given remained behind the scenes and she did not attempt to publish any more issues of *Anti-Caste*. Domestic duties may have prevented greater practical activism as they had done in 1895. Perhaps she was tired or unable to overcome the repercussions of Mayo's public vilifications. Or perhaps aware that in London a new generation of black activists were uniting and pressing the British government to implement reform across the Empire, Catherine believed it was time to let others take forward the formation of an international activist community she had previously imagined.

Notes

1 These dates are taken from the British Library catalogue.
2 Vargo, 'Outworks of the citadel of corruption', 233.
3 *Bond of Brotherhood*, November 1894, 4.
4 *Bond of Brotherhood*, November 1894, 1.
5 *Cleveland Gazette*, 5 January 1895, 1.
6 *Cleveland Gazette*, 5 January 1895, 1.
7 Articles in this first issue were mostly published anonymously, but pencil notes in the margins of the issue held in the 'Brotherhood' Society papers at the Bodleian Library indicate articles written by Darby and Catherine, *Bond of Brotherhood*, November 1894, MSS. Brit. Emp. s.20 E5/7.
8 *Bond of Brotherhood*, November 1894, 8.
9 *Bond of Brotherhood*, November 1894, 8.
10 An associate of Kings College, London, and identified as 'an Indian in England' on *Anti-Caste's* list of subscribers for 1892, Dr David Chowry Muthu specialized in treating tuberculosis and worked on the Isle of Wight and in Somerset for many years, publishing *Pulmonary Tuberculosis and Sanatorium Treatment: A Record of Ten Years' Observation and Work in Open-air Sanatoria* in 1910.
11 *Bond of Brotherhood*, November 1894, 1.
12 *Fraternity*, March 1896.
13 *Bond of Brotherhood*, 'Black labourers in Jamaica', December 1894, 14; 'The slaves of Navassa', January 1895, 28; 'Slavery under British protection in Zanzibar', February 1895, 31.
14 *Bond of Brotherhood*, November 1894, 6.

15 Miss Impey – One of Our Staunchest English Friends Talks on Lynching, *Cleveland Gazette*, 5 January 1895, 1.
16 *Cleveland Gazette*, 5 January 1895, 1.
17 *Cleveland Gazette*, 5 January 1895, 1; *The Christian Recorder*, 27 December 1894.
18 *Bond of Brotherhood*, November 1894, 5.
19 *Bond of Brotherhood*, November 1894, 6.
20 *Bond of Brotherhood*, November 1894, 6.
21 *Bond of Brotherhood*, February 1895, 29.
22 *Bond of Brotherhood*, January 1895, 19, MSS. Brit. Emp. s.20 E5/8.
23 'To the Hon. Sec. of the "Society for the Recognition of the Brotherhood of Man"', Axon Papers, 3660.
24 *Anti-Caste*, March 1895, 1.
25 *Anti-Caste*, March 1895, 1.
26 *Anti-Caste*, 'Ways of helping'; *Anti-Caste*, 'Wilson Anti-Slavery Collection (1890)'.
27 *Anti-Caste*, March 1895, 1.
28 *Anti-Caste*, March 1895, 2, original emphasis.
29 Lerner, 'Early community work'; Foreman, 'Reading/photographs'.
30 *Anti-Caste*, 'Ways of helping'; *Anti-Caste*, 'Wilson Anti-Slavery Collection (1890)'.
31 Why is the Negro lynched? 1895, London School of Economics, Pamphlet collection, HT/7.
32 *Anti-Caste*, June-July 1895, 4–5.
33 *Anti-Caste*, June-July 1895, 6.
34 *Anti-Caste*, June-July 1895, 6.
35 *Daily News*, reprinted in *Anti-Caste*, June–July 1895, 6.
36 *Daily News*, reprinted in *Anti-Caste*, June–July 1895, 6. The dispute was also reported in *Fraternity*, which published a letter from Frances Willard in October 1895, 39–40 and an extended piece by Mary A M Marks, The Lynching Question and the Women's Christian Temperance Union in November 1895, 53–58. For more on the dispute between the women, see Ware, *Beyond the Pale*; August, 'Rival radical feminists'.
37 Impey to Axon, 9 June 1890 and 16 June 1890, Axon Papers 3034 and 3036.
38 Impey to Tourgée, 13 November 1895, 8844, *Albion W. Tourgée* Papers.
39 Impey to Tourgée, 13 November 1895, 8844, *Albion W. Tourgée* Papers.
40 Hallie Quinn Brown, *Fraternity*, January 1891, March, April and May 1895; a short report on the colour line in Tasmania appeared in March 1895; Indian National Congress, February 1895.
41 *Fraternity*, January 1895, 7–8.
42 *Fraternity*, January 1895, 1.
43 *Fraternity*, November 1894, 2.
44 *Fraternity*, November 1894, 7–8.
45 *Fraternity*, November 1894, 8.
46 Indian National Congress February 1895, 12; The Gospel of political economy, December, 6 Individualism and Collectivism, February 1895, 10 and May 1895, 11.
47 *Fraternity*, March 1896, 116.
48 Our New Editor, *Fraternity*, July 1896, 7.
49 Cowman, 'With a lofty moral purpose'; DM Workman's Times (1890–1894) in the *Dictionary of Nineteenth Century Journalism*, Brake and Demor; Cowman, 'Martyn, Caroline Eliza Derecourt (1867–1896)'.
50 Cowman 'With a lofty moral purpose'.
51 Our Late Editor, *Fraternity*, August 1896, 7.

52 *Fraternity*, October 1896, npn.
53 *Fraternity*, December 1896, 71.
54 Wrigley, 'Glasier, Katharine St John Bruce (1867–1950)'.
55 *Fraternity*, March 1896, 110.
56 *Anti-Caste*, January 1891, 2.
57 The 'etc.' placed at the end of this list implies it was not exhaustive, *Fraternity*, April 1895, 7.
58 Champness, *Frank Smith*.
59 *Labour Leader*, 13 February 1897, 56.
60 *Dundee Courier*, 9 October 1896, 4.
61 On Barnsley by-election, *Morning Post* (London), 21 September 1897, 3; *Derby Daily Telegraph*, 8 January 1897, 2.
62 *Fraternity*, December 1896, 63; How Britain neglects her aged poor, 69.
63 *Fraternity*, January 1897, 84.
64 *Fraternity*, January 1897, 75.
65 Periodicals received, *Fraternity*, January 1897, 83.
66 Cecil Rhodes and South Africa, *Fraternity*, February 1897, 85.
67 *Fraternity*, December 1896, 62.
68 *Labour Leader*, 27 February, 68; *Portsmouth Evening News*, 22 February 1897, 3.
69 *Dundee Courier*, 29 March 1897, 3; *Daily Gazette for Middlesbrough*, 22 March 1897, 3.
70 Impey to Axon, 9 November 1894, Axon Papers 3329.
71 Impey to Axon, 9 November 1894, Axon Papers 3329.
72 Impey to Tourgée (the letter is addressed to Dear Friends, presumably meaning both Albion and his wife Emma), 24 June 1893, 7069, *Albion W. Tourgée* Papers.
73 Impey to Tourgée, 30 September 1893, 7366, *Albion W. Tourgée* Papers; Impey to Axon, 20 February 1895, Axon Papers 3363.
74 Impey to Tourgée, March 1895, 8391 *Albion W. Tourgée* Papers.
75 Impey to Axon, 9 November 1894, Axon Papers 3329.
76 Catherine's reflection that 'I am an unconventional woman' appears in a letter from Impey to Axon, 9 November 1894, Axon Papers 3329.
77 Impey to Axon, 9 November 1894, Axon Papers 3329.
78 Visitors at Askew. Catherine wrote about their visit in a letter to Isabella Metford, MSS. Brit. Emp. s.18 C158/79, 4 October 1905. Albion Tourgée died in France in May 1905, Olsen, *Carpetbagger's Crusade*.
79 Impey to Axon, 20 February 1895, Axon Papers 3363.
80 Impey to Axon, 9 November 1894, Axon Papers 3329.
81 For examples on the labour movement and whiteness see Lake and Reynolds, *Drawing the Global Colour Line*; Kirk, *Comrades and Cousins*; Tabili, *We ask for British Justice*.
82 *Anti-Caste*, January 1890, npn.
83 Horton, *Race and the Making of American Liberalism*, 16.
84 Thompson, 'The language of imperialism'; On the Ethical Movement and 'progressive imperialism' see Claeys, *Imperial Sceptics*.
85 *Manchester Courier and Lancashire General Advertiser*, 21 December 1906, 11; Keir Hardie's Advice to Basuto chiefs, *Dundee Courier*, 28 March 1907, 5; Killingray, 'Rights, land and labour'.
86 Clayes, *Imperial Sceptics*; Burton, *New Narratives*.
87 Burton, *Brown over Black*.
88 *The Christian Recorder*, 4 May 1899.

10

Triumph of the Colour Line

The brotherhood is a fact – a universal, incontrovertible fact. What is needed is that the fact shall be universally recognised, and so recognised that it shall have its due influence in shaping human intercourse, both individually, socially, and internationally.

Bond of Brotherhood, 1985

During the final decade of the nineteenth century, networks of anti-imperial activism began to swell inside Britain. Dadabhai Naoroji's campaigning for a political presence for India within the heart of British government signalled new approaches to challenging British rule in India. During the 1890s London also became the base for political networks forged among activist men and women of the African diaspora. In 1897 a number of them formed the African Association, which by the end of 1898 had nearly 50 members. The association's drive came from its founding secretary, the Trinidadian Henry Sylvester Williams. Williams launched the African Association to provide a focus for debate and protest against the racial discrimination and economic exploitation faced by black people living under imperial rule. With a South African colleague, Alice Kinloch as treasurer and the Rev Henry Joseph, a former member of council for Catherine's branch of the SRBM, as president, 'several representative members of the black race who lived in London' ratified the organization's constitution at its inaugural meeting in September 1897.[1] When the Association hosted the first Pan-African Conference in London in July 1900 they saw the colour line hardening around them. As they all agreed, the challenge that lay ahead of them in the coming century was the division of people along the colour line. To challenge it, black people had to join together across national, religious and cultural boundaries and form transnational solidarities.

A new Pan-African politics

Williams left the Caribbean to study law in Canada before moving to Britain and enrolling for evening classes at Kings College London in September 1896. The following year he joined three other Trinidadians at Gray's Inn and became the first black person to practice as an advocate at the Cape Bar when he lived in South Africa between 1903 and 1904.² To support his studies he developed a livelihood from public speaking, lecturing to associations including the Church of England Temperance Society and the National Thrift Society. Touring Britain at the same time was the Cape-born Alice Kinloch, who had been invited to give lectures by the APS secretary Henry Fox Bourne. She spoke to large public audiences about racial prejudice in South Africa, as well as to those gathered in the more intimate surroundings of the Writers' Club which had so inspired Wells.³

The aspirations of the African Association continued a tradition of anti-racist activism that emphasized the importance of knowledge and the power of reporting oppression. Their aims were:

> To encourage a feeling of unity to facilitate friendly intercourse among Africans in general; to promote and protect the interests of all subjects claiming African descent, wholly or in part, in British Colonies and other places, especially in Africa, by circulating accurate information on all subjects affecting their rights and privileges as subjects of the British empire, by direct appeals to the Imperial and Local Governments.⁴

Two years later, taking advantage of international travellers attending the Paris Exposition, the Association convened a Pan-African Conference, using for the first time the term 'Pan-African' to describe a new global politics.⁵ Organized by members of the African Association, white liberals had a limited hand in the conference. Writing from the Common Room at Gray's Inn to update Booker T Washington on plans for the conference in June 1900, Williams reported some opposition from the Aborigines Protection Society to the conference. Despite the APS's apprehension, many distinguished friends had signalled their intention to support the conference.⁶ Catherine may have been among them. Although only men and women of the African diaspora attended the conference as delegates, conference chair Bishop Alexander Walters recalled Catherine meeting with them.⁷ Attended by at least 32 delegates from England, Scotland, the United States, Canada, the West Indies and Africa, the conference opened for three days at Westminster Town Hall from 23 July 1900. Thomas Calloway sent a report on the conference to Booker T Washington estimating a total of 50–60 delegates, with Africa and the West Indies being particularly well represented.⁸ Though small in number, Calloway believed the conference to have been a great success and the *Colored American Magazine* agreed that the event marked a new era for black people throughout the world, bolstering the new Black Atlantic and its sense of a transnational public culture.⁹

Williams travelled to towns including Liverpool and Manchester to generate support for the conference, but conspicuously absent from the Pan-African Conference are members of the British working class.¹⁰ In the early twentieth century, political associations like the Negro Welfare Association and individuals such as Claude McKay would directly involve working dock communities in their political campaigns. There were at least hundreds, if not thousands, of black people and their families living in Britain at the turn of the century and many potential Pan-Africanists among the working communities in Britain. In 1893, Mary Buller, Honorary Secretary of Missions to Seamen, had written to inform Edwards of their progress on purchasing a house for West Indian seamen in Southampton. She reported that 'a good many coloured sailors' working on Royal Mail steamers docked in Southampton and although a sailors' home welcoming all nationalities existed, very few West Indians patronized it. Unconvinced that West Indian sailors may have been happy living among Southampton's docker communities, Buller and her colleagues sought to rescue them from manipulative harbour associates by establishing a boarding house where the sailors would always receive a warm welcome and find a safe place to leave their belongings between voyages.[11] Working-class men and women from African and Asian diasporas did not only live within docker communities; they lived in lodging houses in Bloomsbury and they worked in travelling shows, circuses and in theatres, as barmaids and singers, valets and footmen, artists' models and domestic servants in metropolitan centres and rural villages.[12]

Buller's letter is one of the rare references to black working-class communities in Britain within *Anti-Caste* or *Fraternity*, although Edwards would surely have encountered working-class individuals during his popular lectures. Some would have heard Williams speak and many might have been intrigued to learn more about the new political collective. Williams seems to have been unable to contact or persuade black workers in London to attend the conference despite the large crowds he was able to attract on lecture tours and his interest in the politics of the working class.[13] Williams was anxious for 'our folks' to attend the Pan-African conference, but perhaps he meant only members of the 'various professions' he hoped would be represented.[14]

The delegates spent the final afternoon of the three-day conference overseeing the formation of a new political organization. The resulting Pan-African Association replaced the African Association. Based in London, the committee intended to establish a global network of branches connected through their new journal, the *Pan-African*, edited by Williams. It is possible that through his temperance connections Williams may have seen a copy of *Anti-Caste* or heard of Catherine's work, but there is no record of him subscribing to *Anti-Caste* or *Fraternity*. Williams intended the *Pan-African* to be a space for writers from the African diaspora to present original material for discussion among readers from the diaspora. Like *Fraternity*, the *Pan-African* not only re-circulated information but also informed its readers of the campaign efforts undertaken by the association. The *Pan-African* focused entirely on the plight of people of African descent and did not include references to India, Ceylon or white radicals in Europe. Although narrower in its 'ethnic' focus than was *Anti-Caste* or *Fraternity*, the inaugural issue of the *Pan-African* presented the geographical breadth and richness that Williams intended, with reports on the colour line in Australia, South Africa and the West Indies. In addition he announced that the second and following issues would include photographs of leading black men and women and their families. Williams may have taken this idea from W E B Du Bois, who showed a collection of photograph albums depicting 'The Georgia Negro' as part of the American Negro Exhibit at the Paris Exposition in 1900. Displayed in a cultural context dominated by scientific racism, the large folios contained portraits that sought to challenge conventional ideas of black Americans.[15] Similarly, in the *Pan-African*, Williams intended to present photographic images of middle-class black life as reflecting 'Facts' with 'their own logic' challenging the racism that declared black men and women could not succeed or have stable happy families.[16] Such 'facts' confirmed the existence and success of a global black intellectual middle class. Williams made little reference to working-class individuals, and how their families might have been represented is unclear, but no family portraits survive from the *Pan-African*; only three issues were produced before the *Pan-African* ceased publication.

Figure 10.1 A portrait of Sylvester Williams from an interview in *Review of Reviews*, 1905

As Catherine discovered in 1888, generating a new network of readers for a publication was very hard work. Given the APS' opposition to the Pan-African Conference and their lack of direct support for *Anti-Caste* or *Fraternity*, it seems unlikely that they would have provided support for the *Pan-African*, although the paper's second number carried an item from Fox Bourne to support an appeal against pass laws introduced in the Transvaal.[17] Unlike Catherine, Williams could not subsidize running costs through family support. In 1899 G F Richings had written to Catherine for support, believing she could still mobilize supporters effectively in England. She might have been able to generate readers for the *Pan-African* through her old *Anti-Caste* networks but Williams may not have known Catherine well enough to ask.[18] Although they probably met when she visited delegates of the Pan-African conference, Williams is not recorded as a visitor to Street. Besides, Williams was convinced that 'no other but a Negro can represent the Negro' and so he may have been reluctant to ask for help beyond the Pan-African Association.[19] But Williams was not a separatist. He had a white English wife, Agnes Powell (the daughter of Major Francis Powell, a retired Royal Marine), who he married in 1898 and with whom he had three children (Henry, Gwendoline and Agnes, all born in London). Like Catherine and Edwards, Williams expected part if not the majority of his audience for the *Pan-African* to be white. He may have appealed to readers for financial and editorial contributions for the paper in later issues, but the readership's response to *Pan-African* can no longer be examined, for although reviews of the second and third issues of *Pan-African* have been found in Trinidad, only the first October issue has survived in the archives.[20]

Visitors to Street

In Somerset, Catherine maintained her philanthropic efforts, acting as a member for the Board of Guardians in Wells and supporting the Street Band of Hope, which she had joined as a teenager.[21] With few archive records documenting her activities, the extent of Catherine's political interests is difficult to gauge, but her name occasionally appears in pamphlets and press reports of political meetings. In October 1903 she attended the annual meeting of the Society for the Abolition of Capital Punishment held at the Holborn Restaurant, London. Josiah Oldfield, a former *Anti-Caste* subscriber, chaired the discussion. Aware that public opinion was not yet supportive of universal abolition, Oldfield argued that the society might persuade the public to prevent the capital punishment of women in the first instance, for few women had been executed in the previous 20 years and the murders committed by women were not considered to be ones that the fear of a death sentence would prevent. Catherine seconded a suggestion put forward by Foster Bovill to ask every parliamentary candidate at the next election to pledge support for a Bill to bring criminal law into greater harmony with justice and humaneness, and that such a Bill should contain a clause providing for the partial or gradual abolition of the death penalty.[22]

The Impeys' home remained open to family and friends and the sisters continued to support the causes of black activists and temperance colleagues. From time to time they hosted political visitors in Street, continuing their tradition of welcoming friends and strangers, and combining in their hospitality political support and activism with tourist visits and garden parties. In February 1897 Matthew Dobson arrived from Blackburn for a ten-day mission in Somerset. A month later the pioneering academic Georgiana R Simpson arrived. She stayed with the Impeys from 23 April to 2 June. A subscriber to *Anti-Caste* in 1894 and a close friend of Anna J Cooper, who spoke at the Pan-African Conference, Simpson became one of the first of three black American women to be awarded a PhD in 1921. She received her degree, aged 55, from the University of Chicago for her research on 'Herder's conception of "das Volk"'. She also undertook a critical edition and translation of a French biography of Toussaint L'Ouverture published in 1924.[23] She signed off her stay in Somerset 'With thanks that can not be expressed in words for my happy, happy stay among these dear friends.'[24] Two pages on, two sides of the visitors' book are taken up by Paul Laurence Dunbar's account of his equally memorable stay.

As one of the most successful poets of the era, he inspired the establishment of black literary societies devoted to his work.[25] Publishing *Majors and Minors* in 1895 and *Lyrics of Lowly Life* the following year, his verse pioneered the use of black American dialect in poetry. At 24, Dunbar became 'a symbol of the creative and intellectual potential of the American Negro'.[26] In an attempt to capitalize on his new-found success in the United States, Dunbar visited England, leaving New York on the *Aurania*, and arriving in Liverpool on 17 February 1897. Moving on to the capital, he met a number of Londoners who inspired him, including the self-described 'Anglo-African' composer Samuel Coleridge-Taylor, with whom he collaborated and performed.[27] It is not clear when Dunbar and Coleridge-Taylor were introduced, but their encounter, instigated by Dunbar's friend Francis Downing, sparked an industrious, if short-lived, partnership.[28] Dunbar inspired a new interest and pride in Coleridge-Taylor's own cultural origins and he increasingly engaged with narratives and themes of the African diaspora in his music.[29]

Dunbar's thoughts on 'Negro Music' had been introduced to *Fraternity* readers in 1894. In an interview with *The Chicago Record* Dunbar had discussed the African heritage present in old plantation music which deeply influenced his prose. He admitted that although the thought might have struck many others, the African origins of his musical heritage had only recently dawned upon him as he had listened to a group of Dahomeyans performing. From the group he heard the same mournful minor cadences that had been popularized through negro spirituals; 'Instantly the idea flashed into my mind: "it is a heritage"'.[30] He challenged critics who dismissed the artistic value of these spirituals, hearing in them a beauty to be celebrated and crafted into new melodies. He also argued against foreign critics who claimed that plantation songs were the only original material America had produced. This was wrong, he argued, as America had not produced even these plantation melodies – she had only taken what Africa had given her. *Fraternity*'s comment on the piece ended by observing that 'Old Mother Africa had not lost her hold on the sons who were snatched from her! They will not return to her *en masse*, for they have new ties and drawings elsewhere, but she will be *their* "Old Country".'[31]

When Dunbar first arrived in London, the literary scene of which he hoped to become a part had not yet reformed after the winter. Writing to his mother from

Northumberland Avenue, just off Trafalgar Square soon after he arrived, Dunbar relayed that that he had bumped into their friend Henry Francis Downing. The New Yorker had been appointed as a US consul in West Africa in 1887, but resigned the following year. He attended the Pan-African conference in 1900 and for several years from 1902 he worked as a manager for New Cotton Fields, a London-based company which encouraged cotton growing and helped black American farmers to migrate to West Africa.[32] As Dunbar told his mother in a letter, when he bumped into him on a London street Downing was 'looking like a prince, married to a white woman and living at ease'.[33] He spent a day with Downing and his wife, who invited Dunbar to stay with them but at this point he was distracted by his first recital at the Princes' Hall in Ealing, the 'Queen of Suburbs' in west London. Dunbar's initial excitement gave way to the reality of unpaid recitals and the miserable winter fog. Dunbar took work in clubs and smoke-filled hotel rooms, places where he despised having to perform. Put on programmes between dancing girls from Vaudeville and clowns from varieties, Dunbar at least once faced an audience that was mostly drunk. The view from his room at 16 Imperial Mansions on Oxford Street did not inspire him. From his window he looked out upon 'a row of London roofs, a street where people are passing to and fro on their way to church and above all a great patch of dark gray sky. The bells are ringing, London's numerous chimes and an inexpressible sadness creeps over me.'[34]

Life improved when he left his rooftop room for suburbia. When he wrote to his future wife, Alice Ruth Moore, on a Sunday morning in late May he had become enthused by the green, quaint, bright and beautiful world of hedges and private gardens. He wrote mostly in this green outdoor space, enjoying a freedom that, like Ida B Wells, he found truly inspiring. He hoped to return to London with Alice, to walk with her along the Thames from Kew to Twickenham and show her the leafy high-walled garden where he walked, with almost the privacy of a room, in Hampstead.[35] Now inundated by social invitations, Dunbar found constant requests for his company increasingly tedious among a society that did not pay well and which he believed to be the most corrupt he had ever come across. When he attended a dinner at the Savage Club, he was an honoured guest among artists, writers, scientists and actors and his performance was received with great enthusiasm, but he was aware and perhaps burdened by his 'unique position as the representative of a whole race'.[36] In his letters Dunbar does not mention members of London's black elite in this image of London society and he felt politically and socially isolated. Dunbar did not seem to meet with any of Sylvester Williams' politically active circle but he did meet Samuel Coleridge-Taylor.

Dunbar and Coleridge-Taylor performed their first recital together in June 1897 at the Salle Evard on Great Marlborough Street in central London. The event did not gain much advance publicity and *The Times* complained that had the recital been more widely advertised, many more people would have attended for if they had not yet heard of Dunbar, Coleridge-Taylor already commanded a reputation. It would be another year before Coleridge-Taylor would oversee the triumphant performance of *Hiawatha's Wedding Feast*. Based on a poem by Longfellow, the piece remained one of the most popular English choral works throughout his lifetime and at this recital with Dunbar three of the Hiawathan sketches were performed for the first time. Dunbar and Coleridge-Taylor's collaboration culminated in *African Romances*, published in 1897 (Figure 10.2). The collection consisted of seven songs written by Dunbar and set to music by Coleridge-Taylor. Coleridge-Taylor also put *A Corn Song*, a poem from Dunbar's *Lyrics of Lowly Life* (1896) to music published in London in 1897. Dunbar would not see the English production of their most considerable work, *Dream Lovers*, which was performed at the Public Hall in Croydon on 16 December 1898.[37]

Dunbar wrote a disheartened letter to his mother on 4 July but just over a week later he was in Somerset, and his spirits entirely revived. Catherine and Ellen had

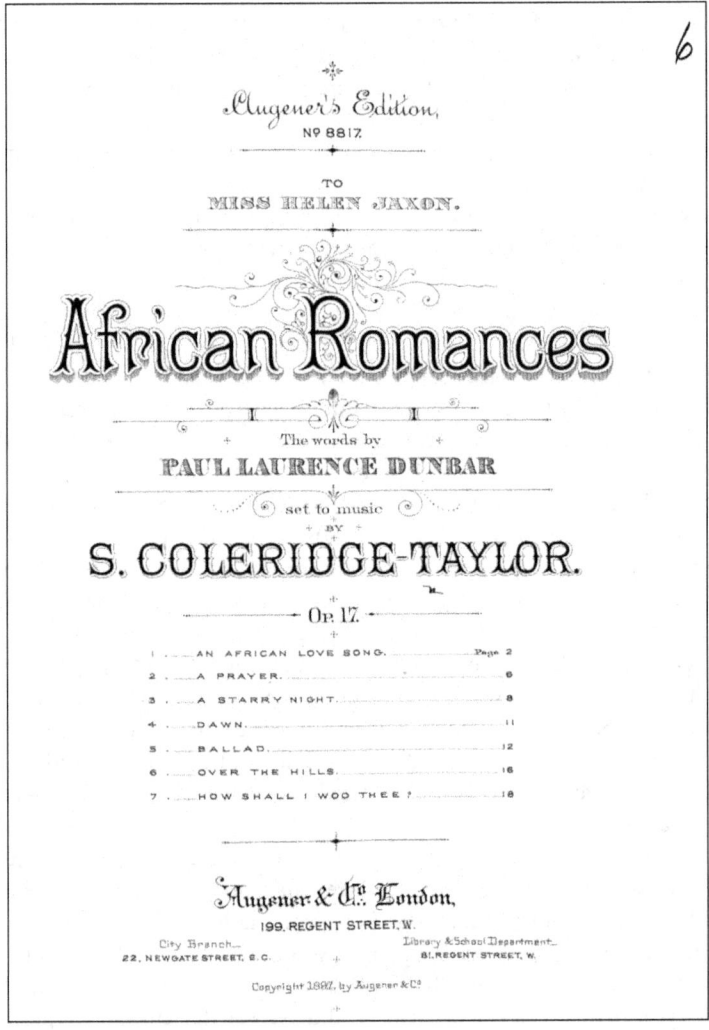

Figure 10.2 An edition of Samuel Coleridge-Taylor and Paul Laurence Dunbar's collaboration *African Romances*, first published in 1897

been in London in June and knew of Dunbar's work through *Fraternity*. Perhaps they sought an introduction to him following a performance and offered their home as a place to rest and work. However the invitation came about, Dunbar stayed with the sisters between 12 and 24 July. His time in Street proved to be fun and fruitful. On 15 July he performed a beautiful recital at the Impeys and three days later dined with Helen Priestman Bright Clark and her family, and stayed with them for a night when he left the Impeys.[38] Benefiting from Catherine and Ellen's extensive local networks, one of the recitals arranged for him attracted over 100 people and he also performed at the Congregational Church. He enjoyed being a tourist climbing up to Glastonbury Tor, walking the Cheddar cliffs and visiting the Cathedrals at Bristol and Wells.[39] While reading the books in the Impeys' library he found time to finish his own debut novel. By the time he wrote to Alice on 20 July he had finished working and was enjoying his final few days in Street lazing around among the trees and flowers.[40] When Dunbar published *Lyrics of Love and Laughter* in 1903 he dedicated it to Catherine and in the sisters' visitors' book, along with a brief account of his stay, he left a poem:

In Somerset
When days were dark & life seemed drear,
Dear friends, you kindly asked me here
I thought the year had passed its prime;
But woke to find it summer – time.
....
One thinks that days of summer pass
Like fleeting forms before a glass;
'Tis false: your house shall prove it yet,
For here, indeed, the Summer's set![41]

At the summer's end Dunbar returned to the United States and wrote his impressions of England in an essay, *England As Seen by a Black Man*.[42] Dunbar's essay picked up similar themes to Ida B Wells' articles in the *Inter-Ocean*. For Wells, the English sensibilities she encountered created spaces in which she could engage with a new sense of equality among her activist peers. Dunbar described comparable experiences in his private letters and public essay. During his first weeks in England, he had written to his mother, 'I am entirely white! My French waiter takes off his cap when I come up the steps, and my blooming rosy-cheeked English maid kisses me as if I were the handsomest man on earth.'[43] More seriously, as he wrote in his essay, it was 'a great thing to have been accepted upon the basis of work alone; to have found a people who do not assert color as a badge of degradation'. However, for Dunbar it was more important 'to have learned that an unmistakably great people look upon the black race in America with hope, interest, and admiration. It is a good thing to have been accepted upon terms of equality in excellent English families; but it is of infinitely more importance to have come away from contact with this institution.'[44]

In his essay Dunbar admitted to being 'bewildered by the magnitude of the greatest city in the world. Her temples and taverns, her homes and her hedges', but it was what he had learned in being away from the United States that was of most value to him.[45] Critics of Dunbar have decried his failure to speak out strongly against racial prejudice in the United States. Although he inspired Coleridge-Taylor with his knowledge of the discussions of civil rights in the United States, Dunbar's observations of Britain did not include an introduction to the new political movements developing among the city's African and Asian diaspora. Instead he focused upon his support for the English class structure. Dunbar believed in the right to rule by a cultured and hereditary aristocracy.[46] These structures were clearly evidenced in English society. The English, he argued, were blessed with a pure family life. He admired the 'common-sense' philosophy of the working class which sought to enjoy whatever pleasure came and make the most of the inevitable sorrows. Dunbar saw the acceptance of one's miserable lot not as a position of class oppression, but one of liberation, or at least a step along the path to this end.[47]

The degree to which Dunbar actually interacted with members of the working class, black or white, while in London is unclear. Reliant on patronage from more privileged Englanders, his opportunities may have been limited, but his poem *The Garret* suggests that when he did meet 'the common sort' he remained socially if not geographically removed from them:

> Within a London garret high,
> Above the roofs and near the sky,
> My ill-rewarding pen I ply
> To win me bread.
> This little chamber, six by four,
> Is castle, study, den, and more, –
> Altho' no carpet decks the floor,
> Nor down, the bed.
> ...
> The bore who falters at the stair
> No more shall be my curse and care,
> And duns shall fail to find my lair
> With beastly bills.
> When debts have grown and funds are short,
> I find it rather pleasant sport
> To live 'above the common sort'
> With all their ills.[48]

Perhaps if he had spent more time with ordinary Londoners Dunbar's romanticized view of the English class system would have been more open to its complexities and struggles. Reports from black American travellers depicted Britain, and Europe, as places where black people would find sympathy and regard based on merit rather than the colour of their skin, but wealth presented an equally difficult barrier to overcome.[49] When Senator John P Green, a member of Cleveland's black elite and a politician, lawyer and civil servant, visited Scotland and England in 1894, the rigidity of the class system struck him sharply and seemed as oppressive as the caste system of race operating in the United States. While Green perceived there to be a middle class in Britain, pauperism seemed much higher than in the United States and living in a society where 'the rich are very rich, while the poor are very poor' meant that Green would leave America for Britain only if he had the means of earning a comfortable livelihood, despite his feeling that 'the colour question cuts no figure here.'[50] *Fraternity* reprinted parts of Green's article as 'Africans in Europe'. While it focused on the qualities that meant black men in Europe were not always assumed to be an attendant, valet or courier and that in Britain there were always hundreds of black students to be found, especially at professional colleges, and that the colour of their skin did not, usually, exclude them from the social ranks their intellectual achievement entitled them to, Green's observation that such access came heavily yoked to the privileges of class was not repeated or analyzed.[51]

Although black and 'mixed race' families had enjoyed their lives and endured their sorrows within the cities of England for many generations, not all black

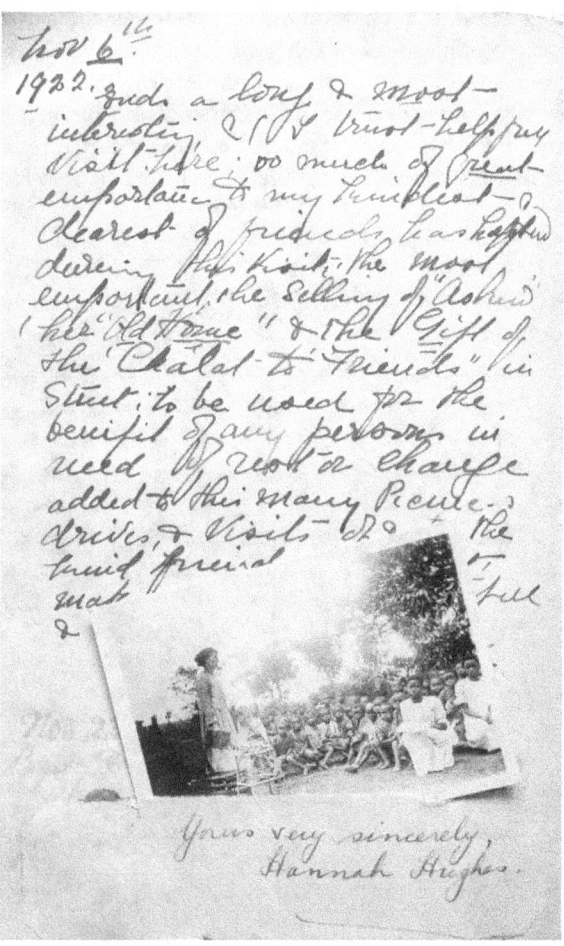

Figure 10.3 A page from Visitors at Askew from 1922

individuals were able to become part of families or integrated communities.[52] In November 1900 an American woman applied for financial assistance from a judge in Westminster to help her get home. The woman had left New York for Paris aiming to finance her trip and make more money by attending to rich American and English visitors at the Paris Exposition but they had not arrived. She had survived on her savings while trying to get work – she was willing to waitress, to cook, to take any kind of respectable work, but she had found that 'folks did not care for black people over here.'[53] Her plight stresses the diversity of the black experience and suggests the opportunity to find new political and reflective spaces in which to contemplate one's identity may well have been limited to a privileged minority. It also seems unlikely that this woman returned home to praise the virtues of the English middle class who refused to employ her.

In his essay Dunbar even displayed an air of envy that the English schoolboy believed himself to be 'a citizen of the greatest country on the earth. To him, the world is composed of England and her possessions, and a few other countries.... Everywhere he turns he sees the ramifications of this power and glory.'[54] Dunbar is not critical of these ramifications for himself or those of the African diaspora in the history of the United States, the Caribbean or Africa itself. For Coleridge-Taylor, Dunbar sparked an interest in the African diaspora that influenced him throughout his career. Coleridge-Taylor had experienced racial prejudice before he met Dunbar, enduring

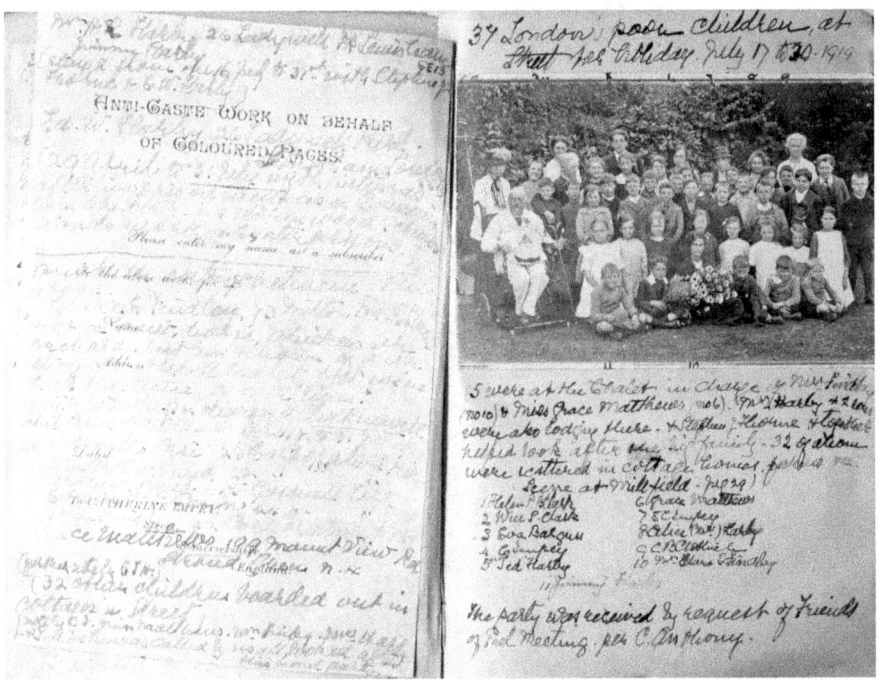

Figure 10.4 A page from Visitors at Askew showing a number of 'London's poor children' who visited Street for a holiday in 1919

racist taunts by street boys and the prejudices of his wife's family, but now he placed these in the context of the experiences of the black diaspora, identifying himself as an 'Anglo-African'. Coleridge-Taylor attended the Pan-African Conference as a delegate and arranged the musical programme. Five years later he collated *Twenty-four Negro Melodies*. The collection held great personal and political significance for Coleridge-Taylor and answered the call made by Dunbar in 1894 for black composers to rebuke and overcome the shame associated with 'Negro music'. Dvorak had argued that Nergro Melodies should be the basis of any serious and original school of composition in the United States, for these were America's folk-songs and all great musicians borrowed from the songs of the common people.[55] In claiming his African inheritance and presenting this collection to the public, Coleridge-Taylor hoped to do for black music what Dvorak had done for the understanding of the Bohemian and what Brahms had done for Hungarian folk-music.[56]

Political life in Street

Twelve pages of the visitors' book, all filled with black-inked tales and signatures, take the lives of Catherine and Ellen from 1898 through to 1900. Jane Metford and her servant and companion Maria West stayed for two weeks in March 1899, visiting Ivy Thorn Wood and attending Roger Clark's lecture on his recent visit to the South Sea Islands. In May, Alice and Henry Corder rode over. A downpour kept them prisoners overnight, 'but who cares for that whilst our cousins are so hospitable!' wrote Henry. Mary Tudor Pole had better luck with the weather when she cycled over to discuss vegetarianism in June 1899 before summer guests arrived for picnics and teas. During the first year of the new century the sisters prepared for their move to the smaller Old Tanyard House. Their Clothier grandparents, mother, aunts and uncle were born there and they adapted the space into a snug and picturesque home. In January 1901 Jane Metford sat in their new sitting room enjoying the morning sun as it came through the windows and lit up the flowers and pictures. The wood on the hearth blazed cheerily while outside the branches of the laurel trees swayed in the strong wind, their leaves glistening in the sunshine. Among the chorus of many birds she could pick out a woodpecker in the orchard of the farmhouse opposite. With the many changes of recent years, Jane Metford enjoyed being in a part of Street that had altered little and held bright and happy memories. Georgiana Simpson returned for almost a month in the summer of 1905. In the visitors' book she admitted to spending her first day in bed trying to adjust her body to the stillness of land after her voyage across the Atlantic. Back on her feet, she travelled to Bristol to attend a Peace Congress and Anti-Slavery Society meetings. As a tourist she visited Cheddar and Sidcot and attended many teas and enjoyable gatherings around Street before leaving on 10 July. She stayed again in 1913, arriving on 18 August for a 'spiritual uplift' and left on 2 September 'much richer for having come' (Figure 10.5).

In 1909 John Tengo Jabavu joined a delegation of 'native and coloured' men who travelled to England in order to lobby the British Government against the introduction of the 'colour bar' into the South African Constitution (Figure 7.1). They protested

Figure 10.5 Georgiana Simpson, who was one of the first three black American women to be awarded their PhDs at American universities in 1921. She stayed with the Impeys in 1897, 1905 and 1913

against the naked racism being openly inserted into the constitution and predicted that the proposal would inevitably sever white and coloured populations into opposite and hostile camps.[57] Despite help from high-profile colleagues, including W T Stead, their lobbying came to nothing. No doubt greatly despondent, Jabavu visited the Impeys on 25 October before he returned home. In August 1911 Jabavu visited Street once more, this time joined by his eldest son Davidson Jabavu and a friend from Natal. Davidson lived in Britain as a student, studying at the Colwyn Bay African Institute and also the University of London, where he received his BA.[58] For a while he acted as principal violinist for the Hampstead Brotherhood Orchestra.[59] Catherine encouraged him to visit the Tuskegee Institute to gain insights of the machinery of education in operation there and other education centres in the United States.[60] Davidson's decision to travel to the United States prompted Catherine to write to W E B Du Bois for the first time. They had not met before, but she asked Du Bois if perhaps he had heard of her in the days 'when I published the little monthly *Anti-Caste*'.[61] Du Bois acknowledged in his reply that he knew her well by reputation and was pleased to hear from her in person. Following on from her request he emphasized that he would be pleased to meet Davidson Jabavu if it could be arranged.[62] Catherine still played an important role in creating links in the networks between political activists and on Wednesday 8 October 1913, Davidson Jabavu recorded that he ' "did" New York. Interviewed Dr Du Bois, an intellectual giant.'[63]

Edith Allen travelled to Street from Drogheda in July 1914 to attend the opening of the Impeys' new Chalet. The Swiss-style boarding house built by Ellen and Catherine stood a mile and a half outside Street on the crest of Polden Hills amid miles of grassy downs and woodland. Within easy reach of the Mendip Hills, Somerset Levels and Glastonbury, it provided an ideal place for a holiday or respite and recuperation. Rooms could be taken with or without attendants or rented weekly by boarders, and men or women in adult education could apply for a third off the standard rate. The outbreak of war during Allen's visit shattered the tranquillity of the town, bringing consternation and a feeling of disorganization to the inhabitants of Street. By the end of August, when Connie and Hilda Clothier visited with Vera, a young German refugee, the town had regrouped. All of Street was deeply engrossed in bottle washing and jamming, preparing for the aid they anticipated would be badly needed over the winter. Friends continued to visit throughout the war, attending temperance and Quarterly Meetings and finding respite from the chaos of war in the Somerset town.

In the spring of 1919 a group of conscientious objectors posed for a portrait with Ellen and Catherine (Figure 10.6). They arrived as 'Prisoners on Leave' in March 1919 but left as free men in April. All the COs who visited the Impeys were Absolutists, conscientious objectors who refused to work for any government schemes connected to military action, and spent their service time in prison. William Nimmo had served more than two years in Winchester prison. Charles Phillips and his brother Albert

Figure 10.6 Party of conscientious objectors who visited Catherine and Ellen Impey in the spring of 1919

came from Canterbury prison. Walter John Abel had been in Wandsworth prison, as had Horace Herbert, Francis Victor Beecham, Edward William Harby and Stephen James Thorne.[64] Some of the men arrived very weak, but singing hymns and long evenings spent quietly talking about their experiences in prison with Catherine, Ellen and other sympathetic Friends in Street revived them.[65] Like Georgiana Simpson, Paul Laurence Dunbar and so many others, Walter Abel had his 'spirit set on fire by the energy and enthusiasm' of the Impey sisters. Abel was born and lived in Peckham, and worked as a manager in south London before the war. A Unitarian and a member of the Independent Labour Party and the Ethical Society, on hunger strike at Wormwood Scrubs he had been force-fed nine times and served more than two years in prison.[66] He felt poetry could better say what he wished to convey to the sisters and chose to leave four lines by Longfellow, repeating those Catherine had inscribed in her scrapbook as a teenager:

Trust no future, howe'er pleasant!
Let the dead Past bury its dead:
Act, – act in the living present!
Heart within, and God o'er head![67]

On 22 January 1921 Ellen wrote her last letter to the COs who had visited them. Addressing her 'Dear Comrades', she explained that she had been very ill since before Christmas and apologized for not replying to their enquiries and good wishes before. Three years after the war distressing events continued to happen across the world, but Ellen held onto her belief that these sad events represented God working out his purpose in his own and certain way, though at times she felt almost helpless. A simple and elegant card in Loving and Reverent Memory marks the passing of Ellen at the Old Tanyard House on 8 February 1921. A small obituary from *The Independent* sits below it, noting with regret the passing of a devout Quaker always keen to help individuals of other denominations and always interested in work for the betterment of other human beings. A more substantial obituary appeared in the *Central Somerset Gazette*. Here Ellen's commitment to teetotalism and racial equality, her life-long kindness to animals and her strong conviction in the principles of Liberalism complimented recollections of a woman of strong character and firm conscience. The paper sent its sympathy to Catherine in her bereavement and severance from her sister, with whom she had lived for so many years. As Georgiana Simpson later recalled, Ellen had been Catherine's staunchest support throughout her life and Ellen's death deeply affected her.

After inheriting her sister's estate of nearly £4000 Catherine began placing her affairs in order.[68] Her APS membership changed from The Misses Impey to simply Miss Impey. She placed the Chalet in the trust of the Middle Division of Somerset's Society of Friends. Its custodians were to continue the sisters' commitment to hospitality and the poor, providing three main functions for the community. First, offering facilities for holidays, rest or convalescence for anyone requiring them but particularly for people with limited means, with preference given to inhabitants of

Street and the immediate neighbourhood. Second, to provide food and refuge for members of the public and, third, to provide a guest house for recreational meetings, entertainments or educational purposes or for any other purpose which in the opinion of the trustees contributed to the social, moral and intellectual welfare and wellbeing of the community. Catherine included all the Chalet's furniture, tools, crockery and linen within the agreement. She hoped the committee would occasionally check the quantities and replace what may have been worn out or broken, but now it was their property to deal with as they saw fit. During the late 1920s families in Street enjoyed summer afternoons in the grounds with refreshments from the newly built tea-house. By 1931 the Chalet was no longer needed as a convalescence home and in April the trustees leased the Chalet at a nominal rent to Paul Dudley Sturge, Honorary Secretary of the Gloucestershire and Somerset branch of the Youth Hostels Association. Aside from a few years during the Second World War when it became a temporary home for evacuees, the Chalet remained and continues to be a YHA lodging.[69]

The final entry in the visitors' book is a note from Esther Winter that Miss Katie Impey died on 14 December 1923 and was buried four days later. At her funeral men and women from all classes mourned her passing and the *Central Somerset Gazette* attested that in Street no one was more highly honoured. Alongside their sorrow the *Gazette* reported a feeling 'which was remarkably manifest that though a rare worker had passed from sight, the influence she exerted on the life of the place is still and long will be living and powerful.'[70] Catherine's body was laid to rest in the Friend's Burial Ground in Street, where the simple gravestones are boarded by a high grey stone wall and in some parts sheltered by trees. Rows of graves are covered by grass and in the summer wild flowers decorate the soft carpet. Catherine's gravestone sits low to the ground next to Ellen's. Although the details of Ellen's memorial can still be clearly read, Catherine's gravestone has eroded away. Only fragments of the month she was born and the month she died can still be seen.

Two obituaries appeared in the *Anti-Slavery Reporter and Aborigines' Friend* for April 1924. First and with deep regret the Society recorded the death of Lady Scott, an active member of the Society's Committee who from her old-fashioned house in Cowley Street, Westminster, had provided gracious and informal hospitality to guests, including 'people of dark skin and colour' who frequently numbered among her guests. A far shorter entry noted that the society had recently learned of Catherine Impey's death. In the few lines they reminded readers that throughout her life Catherine was 'keenly interested in the wrongs of Native Races' and 'especially stirred by the conditions and treatment of Negroes in the United States' and for a time she edited a paper called *Anti-Caste* on the subject. The author remembered that 30 years earlier Catherine had often been in touch with the Anti-Slavery and Aborigines Protection Societies, but there was nothing on the hospitality she and Ellen had offered to guests who visited them in Street. The announcement records that a number of Catherine's papers and books had been given to the society by her relatives. It seems that this marks the origins of the papers now held among the Anti-Slavery Papers collection at the University of Oxford.[71]

Georgiana Simpson's memories of her old friend published in the *Journal of Negro History* were far warmer and personal. She described Catherine as one of the 'staunchest friends of humanity', a woman whose Quaker humanitarianism had produced a life devoted to work for human betterment.[72] Simpson recalled the importance of Catherine's trips to the United States in 1878 and 1886 in her understanding of the 'colour question' and her parallel struggles with the temperance orders. Simpson emphasized *Anti-Caste*'s final declaration for the Brotherhood of the entire Human Family, its broad network of contacts and its interaction with numerous organizations including the Negroes' Friend Society, the Indian National Congress Movement, the National Citizen's Rights Association, the Women's Loyal Union, the *Richmond Planet*, Maloga Mission, the British Foreign and Anti-Slavery Society, and the Aborigines Protection Society, as well as individuals including Harriet Colenso. Simpson remembered Catherine's kind hospitality and credited Catherine as the 'prime factor' in the movement that introduced Ida B Wells to the British public.[73] Catherine's support for black civil rights continued after her death. In September 1928, W E B Du Bois received a cheque for £10 from the executors of Catherine's estate.[74] They sent the money for use by 'the American Negro cause' and Du Bois promised to spend it as 'I think she would have liked'.[75]

The lives of black folk

Although black people might have once believed that 'the English treat our people badly everywhere except in the Islands of Great Britain', in the twentieth century the colour line Catherine believed to be rooted in the United States and the colonies became entrenched at home.[76] During the First World War a xenophobic atmosphere intensified, legitimating state and public harassment of black communities and their families in Britain.[77] 'Mixed race' couples found themselves facing increasing aggression in the British press and in their daily lives. Their attackers blamed both black men and white women for the violence and prejudice they faced. The year 1919 was a violent one across the world, with strikes, uprisings and riots occurring across the Empire, Europe and North America. In Britain race riots first erupted in Glasgow in January. By August, South Shields, Salford, Hull, London, Liverpool, Newport, Cardiff and Barry would also play host to a new geography of racial violence. During the riots black people including Africans, south Asians, Chinese, Caribbean and Arab men and women were attacked. Five people were killed, many were injured and over 200 arrested.[78]

Everyday forms of racism faced by black people on London streets between the wars are recorded in the surviving diaries of the Australian Aboriginal activist A M Fernando. He regularly faced the 'colour bar' and struggled to overcome its effects on his material and psychological well-being. He searched throughout London looking for rooms but even 'common lodgings' refused him because he was a black man. Unlike Ida B Wells' experience of London's public transport as an inclusive modern space, Fernando found himself abused on London trams and trains.[79] On one underground journey he had to listen to other passengers grumble that the presence of a black man in their carriage 'wouldn't be allowed in America'.[80] Working as a street trader, Fernando faced racist taunts on his arrival in East End markets and he observed that at times when he was refused space for a stall, even on the pavement, white traders were allowed to pitch their wares. When he was able to find a place in a market it was always temporary and often the stallholders would drive him away empty handed. One day, as Fernando walked through Bethnal Green Market, one of the stallholders greeted him with a 'good morning Darkie', along with the suggestion that he should wash his face. Fernando had been called far worse: 'coon', 'nigger', 'alien', 'dirty black dog', but on this occasion he retaliated.[81] Fernando hit a stallholder over the head and then to the astonishment of the surrounding crowd pulled out a gun. In the resulting court case, as a number of Australian newspapers reported, Fernando spoke forcefully about British racism from the dock of the Old Bailey in 1929:

> The black man, he asserted, was the only foreigner in this country who was not treated well. Holding up his coat to the view of the Court, he shouted: 'Look at my rags. I can't make ends meet. All you hear is "go away, black man, go away"'.[82]

Fernando had come to London as a British subject but saw himself treated only with contempt and injustice. His experience was not unique. Maria Davis wrote to the popular black American entertainer Florence Mills from her home at 12 Featherstone Buildings, London, on 12 September 1926. The night before, she had seen Mills on stage in a performance of the wildly successful show *Blackbirds*. As she sat in the audience Davis felt sure that 'never was there a heart prouder than mine'. Maria Davis greatly admired Mills as an artist. Her singing was 'like a nightingale', and her dancing was 'also divine', but the pride Maria Davis felt was the 'race pride' of seeing a woman of colour successfully performing on stage. As a black woman, or as Maria put it, 'a colour woman like yourself', she wrote to thank Mills and the entire company 'for being able to show the White People, who think we are nobody – because we are "colour" that we can stand side by side & beat them at their own game.' Before signing off, Maria evoked the evolving ideas of the African diaspora in praising Mills once more, this time as 'a Daughter of the Mother Land'.[83] The hardening of the colour line in Britain, felt so painfully by Fernando and Davis, may have prompted the executors of Catherine's estate to send another donation of £15 to Du Bois in 1930.[84]

Una Marson's poem *Nigger* published in the July 1933 issue of *The Keys*, the quarterly journal of the League of Coloured Peoples, gave public expression to the pain inflicted upon black people by the colour bar and racist taunts thrown at them from the streets.

> ....
> What made me keep my fingers
> From choking the words in their throats?
> What made my face grow hot,
> The blood boil in my veins
> And tears spring to my eyes?

What made me go to my room
And sob my heart away
Because white urchins
Called me 'Nigger'?[85]
...

Unlike *Anti-Caste*, *The Keys* reported on the racial prejudice now regularly faced by black people in Britain. In Cardiff, Liverpool and London men and women were meeting daily with racial discrimination in their search for work and homes. As *The Keys* observed, many of them had 'served the Empire in the last war but that is no avail now.... Hotels, restaurants and lodging houses refuse us with impunity.'[86] These

Figure 10.7 An early issue of *The Keys*, journal of the League of Coloured Peoples founded on Tottenham Court Road in London 1931. *The Keys*, vol 1, no 2, October 1933

changes had been noted earlier in the decade by black American visitors who no longer lauded Britain as a country where the colour line did not operate. A headline in the *Chicago Defender* reported on Robert Abbott's visit to England in 1930. Having arrived from Europe, Abbott found that in England 'hospitality, especially to dark people' was almost unknown. In London he had been refused entry to some 30 hotels, but though 'England, like America' appeared under the 'Yoke of Race Prejudice' the practices operated differently.[87] Abbott had seen 'Negroes married to white women' living in 'high class' neighbourhoods and 'not only was there no attempt to oust them or bomb them out of their homes as in America', but they were found to be on the best of terms with their white neighbours. In Cardiff he noted that there was no segregation in the Bute Town settlement nor in Liverpool, where white and black lived together in the same buildings and their children played in the same playgrounds and attended the same schools.[88] However, the racism presented in the British press he found on a par with even the worst papers in the American South and he heard stories from families whose 'mixed race' children had been mocked and tormented at their schools and from students who felt 'they met an enormous amount of racial prejudice' and of the difficult employment conditions facing the black working class.[89]

The League of Coloured People's focus on domestic concerns did not detract from their reporting on international oppression and their sense that the rise of fascism meant that the oppression of white communities must be included in that world view. The need for an inclusive activist community was laid out in the first issue of *The Keys*, published in July 1933.

> Little is known in England of the legal disabilities under which the African labours in South Africa. The tragic plight of the aboriginal in Australia is a closed book to many at present. The recent persecution of the Jews in Germany, and the apathy with which the news was received by the rest of the world was appalling.[90]

Although *Anti-Caste, Fraternity* and the *Bond of Brotherhood* may not have drawn such clear lines of solidarity between the politics of oppression in Europe and Empire, those who read them between 1888 and 1897 certainly knew about the plight of African and Indian labourers in South Africa and the terrible treatment of Indigenous people in Australia. But Catherine, Celestine Edwards and the networks they and their pioneering colleagues had created were now largely lost and disconnected from the new generation of activists.[91] White men who promoted the politics of racism had succeeded in establishing the doctrine that 'multi racial democracy was an impossibility.'[92] The absence of Catherine, Edwards, Williams and other earlier antiracist activists from British cultural memory reflects the difficulties in maintaining continuity in activist campaigns and how tough it was for individuals to continue their work in the face of financial inequality, ill health, personal disagreements, global wars and the crushing success of white supremacy. The hope expressed by the *Central Somerset Gazette* that Catherine Impey's legacy would live on proved sadly misplaced.

Figure 10.8 The Chalet built as a convalescence home by Catherine and Ellen Impey became a YHA hostel in 1931

Notes

1. Quoted by Schneer, *London 1900*, 215.
2. Fryer, *Staying Power*; Saunders, 'From Trinidad to Cape Town'.
3. Killingray, 'Significant black South Africans'. Killingray notes that Alice Kinloch returned to South African in February 1898.
4. Geiss, *Pan-African Movement*, 177.
5. Geiss, *Pan-African Movement*.
6. Williams to Washington, 29 June 1900, BTW Papers, vol 5, 570; Williams to Bourne quoted in Sherwood, *Origins of Pan-Africanism*, 68.
7. Walters, *My Life and Work*, 262. Published 17 years after the conference, Colenso and Saunders caution that Pan-African scholars have found Walters' recollections to be unreliable, Colenso and Saunders, New Light on the Pan-African Association: Part I.
8. Quoted in Sherwood, *Origins of Pan-Africanism*, 95–96.

9   Williams to Washington from Dublin, 17 July 1899, Booker T Washington Papers, vol 5, 158; Hamedoe, 'The first Pan-African conference of the world, 223–231; Gilroy, *Black Atlantic*.
10 The African Association, *Liverpool Mercury*, 27 April 1899.
11 *Fraternity*, November 1893, 14. For material on Southampton's multi-ethnic dock communities in the early twentieth century, see Kushner, 'Not that far? Remembering and forgetting cosmopolitan Southampton'.
12 Burton, *Heart of Empire*; Bressey, 'Looking for work'.
13 In 1897 he had spoken to a group of working men in Belfast at a meeting organized by the National Thrift Society. Telling the audience that the prosperity of the nation depended upon the prosperity of the working classes, he also implied the responsibility to care for this prosperity lay in their thriftiness, without which they would not be able to maintain comfort and happiness in their homes. *The Belfast News-Letter*, 12 August 1897.
14 Williams to Washington, 17 July 1899. Booker T Washington Papers, vol 5, 158.
15 Smith, *Photography on the Color Line*.
16 *Pan-African*, October 1901, 4.
17 Sherwood, *Origins of Pan-Africanism*.
18 Richings, *The Christian Recorder*, 4 May 1899.
19 *Pan-African*, October 1901, 1.
20 On reviews in the Trinidad *Mirror* see Sherwood, *Origins of Pan-Africanism*.
21 Catherine Impey presented the balance sheet at the Band of Hope annual meeting, *The Bristol Mercury and Daily Post*, 12 October 1898, 12. Obituary, *Central Somerset Gazette*, 21 December 1923.
22 *The Times*, 19 October 1903, 3.
23 Personal: Georgiana R. Simpson, *The Journal of Negro History*, 29:2, 1944, 245–247; http://www.lib.uchicago.edu/e/webexhibits/IntegratingTheLifeOfTheMind/GeorgianaSimpson.html, accessed 1 August 2013.
24 Visitors at Askew, original emphasis.
25 Smethurst, *African American Roots of Modernism*.
26 Turner, 'Paul Laurence Dunbar', 1.
27 Fryer, *Staying Power*.
28 Green, *Samuel Coleridge-Taylor*.
29 Richards, 'A Pan-African composer?'.
30 *Fraternity*, January 1894, 12.
31 *Fraternity*, January 1894, 13, original emphasis.
32 Downing to Washington, 2 September 1902, biographical note on Henry Francis Downing, Booker T Washington Papers, vol 6, 507.
33 Dunbar to Dunbar, 28 February 1897, in Martin and Hudson, *Paul Laurence Dunbar Reader*, 439.
34 Dunbar to Moore, 26 March 1897, in Martin and Hudson, *Paul Laurence Dunbar Reader*, 442.
35 Dunbar to Moore, 23 May 1897, in Martin and Hudson, *Paul Laurence Dunbar Reader*, 446.
36 Dunbar to Moore, 7 March 1897, in Martin and Hudson, *Paul Laurence Dunbar Reader*, 441.
37 Green, 'The foremost musician of his race'.
38 Diary of Helen Priestman Bright Clark, MIL 69, 1896–1898, Alfred Gillet Trust, Street, Somerset.

39 Visitors at Askew.
40 Dunbar to Nelson, 20 July 1897, in Martin and Hudson, *Paul Laurence Dunbar Reader*.
41 'fleeting' seems most likely, although the word is no longer clear. Visitors at Askew; Dunbar, *Lyrics of Love and Laughter*.
42 Published in *The Independent* on 16 September 1897, 'England as seen by a black man', Martin and Primeau, *In His Own Voice*, 176–180.
43 Dunbar to Dunbar, 28 February 1897, in Martin and Hudson, *Paul Laurence Dunbar Reader*, 439.
44 Dunbar, 'England as seen by a black man', in Martin and Primeau, *In His Own Voice*, 177.
45 Dunbar, 'England as seen by a black man', in Martin and Primeau, *In His Own Voice*.
46 Turner, 'The rejected symbol'.
47 Dunbar, 'England as seen by a black man', in Martin and Primeau, *In His Own Voice*, 179.
48 Dunbar, 'The Garrett', *Lyrics of the Hearthside*.
49 For example see *New York Age*, 14 July 1888, 1; 'The African In Europe', taken from the *New York Age* and reprinted in *Fraternity*, January 1894, 11.
50 On Green, see Gatewood, *Aristocrats of Color; Cleveland Gazette*, 24 March 1894, 1.
51 *Fraternity*, January 1894, 11.
52 For more on 'mixed' families in nineteenth-century London, see Bressey, 'Geographies of belonging'; Visram, *Asians in Britain* on earlier periods see Chater, *Untold Histories*.
53 *The Times*, 14 November 1900, 14.
54 Martin and Primeau, *In His Own Voice*, 178.
55 *Fraternity*, September 1893, 16.
56 Coleridge-Taylor, 'Preface' to *Twenty-four Negro Melodies*.
57 Dr A Abdurahman, draft letter to *The Times*, W P Schreiner Papers, University of Cape Town archives and manuscripts, BC 112.
58 Killingray, 'Significant black South Africans'. The notice that DDT Jabavu was the first South African Negro graduate of the University of London is on a flyer within his memoirs, Tuskegee DDT Jabavu, My Tuskegee Pilgrimage, 1913, part 2, University of South Africa, http://hdl.handle.net/10500/6452, accessed 24 June 2013.
59 Jabavu, My Tuskegee Pilgrimage, 1913, part 2, University of South Africa, http://hdl.handle.net/10500/6452, accessed 24 June 2013.
60 Jabavu, My Tuskegee Pilgrimage, 1913, part 1, University of South Africa, http://hdl.handle.net/10500/6452, accessed 24 June 2013.
61 Impey to Du Bois, 31 August 1913, W. E. B. Du Bois Papers (MS 312).
62 Du Bois to Impey, 19 September 1913, W. E. B. Du Bois Papers (MS 312).
63 Jabavu, My Tuskegee Pilgrimage, 1913, part 2, University of South Africa, http://hdl.handle.net/10500/6452, accessed 24 June 2013.
64 My thanks to Cyril Pearce, who is compiling a database of British COs, for this information.
65 Diary of Helen Priestman Bright Clark, Alfred Gillet Trust, MIL 69, 1918–1921.
66 My thanks to Cyril Pearce for this information.
67 The verse comes from Longfellow's poem A Psalm of Live (1838).
68 Ellen Clothier Impey, 1921, England & Wales, National Probate Calendar (Index of Wills and Administrations), 1861–1941.

69 Bundle of papers connected to deeds of the Chalet and other properties in Street. Somerset Record Office DD/SFR. m 90; Jack Dawe, 1959, 'Standing on a street corner', *Clarks Courier*, 13 November, 5.
70 *Central Somerset Gazette*, 21 December 1923.
71 *Anti-Slavery Reporter and Aborigines' Friend*, 14, 1, April 1924, 30.
72 Simpson, 'Notes', 104.
73 Simpson, 'Notes', 106.
74 Letter from Clothier to Du Bois, 20 September 1928, W. E. B. Du Bois Papers (MS 312).
75 Letter from Du Bois to Clothier, 3 October 1928, W. E. B. Du Bois Papers (MS 312).
76 Fortune to Washing, BTW Papers, vol 5, 154, 14 July 1899.
77 Tabili, *Global Migrants*.
78 Jenkinson, *Black 1919*.
79 Though Wells felt the internal design of London trains left much to be desired, with narrow compartments and passengers' knees rubbing against those of entire strangers, Wells reflected that 'primitive as are these railway carriages, I as a Negro can ride in them free from insult or discrimination on account of colour, and that's what I cannot do in many states of my own free (?) America.' Duster, *Crusade for Justice*, 172.
80 Quoted in Paisley, *The Lone Protestor*, 110.
81 Quoted in Paisley, *The Lone Protestor*, 109.
82 Quoted in Paisley, *The Lone Protestor*, 120.
83 Davis to Mills, 12 September 1926, Florence Mills Papers, Schomburg, HAJ.
84 Du Bois to Clothier 10 November 1930, W. E. B. Du Bois Papers (MS 312). This material comes from the AHRC-funded project Drawing Over the Colour Line (AH/I027371/1), based at The Equiano Centre, Department of Geography, UCL, with Caroline Bressey and Gemma Romain.
85 *The Keys*, July 1933, 8.
86 *The Keys*, July 1933, 1–2.
87 Robert S Abbott founded the *Chicago Defender* in 1905. On hotels in London etc., My Trip Abroad, IX, We Arrive in England, *Chicago Defender*, 4 January 1930, 1–2. My thanks to Robbie Aitken for passing on these references.
88 *Chicago Defender*, My Trip Abroad, X, 11 January 1903, 1–3.
89 My Trip Abroad, IX, We Arrive in England, *Chicago Defender*, 4 January 1930, 1–2; *Chicago Defender*, My Trip Abroad, X, 11 January 1903, 1–3.
90 *The Keys*, July 1933, 2.
91 For a reflection on telling stories of inter-generation memory see Alexander, 'Do grandmas have husbands?'.
92 Lake and Reynolds, *Drawing the Global Colour Line*, 6.

11

Hauntings

On a walk to the galleries used by Autograph ABP on Rivington Place, I pass through the newly chic streets of Shoreditch in East London. It is a bright, sunny and warm summer afternoon. I scold myself for pausing to look into shop windows and restaurants that I pass with a reminder of the images of death I am on my way to see. I received some warning of what I am about to encounter having sat in the audience for a panel discussion on the decision to hold the exhibition.[1] As I draw closer to Rivington Place my mood becomes more apprehensive and unsettled. I have come to see *Without Sanctuary: Lynching Photography in America*. This is the first time this collection of lynching photographs, postcards and memorabilia from the 1880s to the 1960s has been shown in Britain.[2] I am hoping I might see an original print of 'A Lynching Scene in Alabama' among the images displayed in the exhibition. I am uneasy as to why I am hopeful at the thought of seeing any lynching images at all; why I am briskly walking towards a room filled with the violent traces of racism, torture and murder when I could be outside in the sun or sitting in a cafe watching people pass along the street.[3]

When I arrive at the gallery I am tempted to browse the books on display in reception. I consider looking through the book that accompanies the exhibition. It is a large hardback volume bound in black cloth, which Shawn Michelle Smith has described as a 'kind of macabre coffee-table book'.[4] I know I am putting off going up to the gallery; stopping here is now the last chance to delay my own personal encounter with the images of misery and hate I have come to see. Walking down towards the gallery door at the end of the corridor I register the member of staff sitting outside the door. The distressing nature of the material inside the room has prompted the gallery to arrange for someone to sit outside the space ready to speak to visitors and help answer their questions. When I walk inside the gallery space I realize that I am alone. At first I am deeply unsettled and uncertain that I want to stay. I then think how exceptional it will be to encounter the images by myself. When first displayed in the United States in 2000, hundreds of people queued in the cold Manhattan weather to view *Witness: Photographs of Lynchings from the Collection of James Allen and Jon Littlefield*, at the small Roth Horowitz Gallery, an art space on the Upper East Side.[5] Authorized to hold 30 visitors at a time, the gallery had to issue tickets to manage the crowds and limited visitors to 200 a day.[6]

Because the images are mostly small photographic prints or postcards, I have to lean in very close to see them and unpack their detail. But that brings me far too near to faces of hatred and dead bodies. As I walk round the exhibition I repeat a rocking motion moving in close for as long as I can before an instinctive break – an internal cry which shouts 'enough!' – pushes my body back abruptly. From this more solid footing I meet the gaze of ghosts. They are nearly always white for the eyes of the black bodies rarely look into the camera. The images are all deeply upsetting to look at. I am surprised to see pictures of lynched white men and shocked by the image of a son and his mother, Laura Nelson, hanging from their necks from a bridge above a river in Okemah, Oklahoma, on 25 May 1911; Laura Nelson's dress seems dirty and is ripped, her struggles for her family so cruelly and violently disregarded. Along the bridge above them over 50 men, women and children lean against the railings for the photograph: a woman holding up her child in her arms, a man leaning down over the bridge for another look of the body of the young man with his trousers torn down around his ankles. At times I find I have stopped breathing. I inhale deeply to help rock my body back away from the picture before me. Seeing the verso of postcards and the writing on them brings home that these photographs of murder were personal objects, possessions expressing the excitement people felt when they took part in these events – that they were proud of their actions and wanted to keep a memento. One picture, of Thomas Shipp and Abram Smith killed on 7 August 1930 in Marion, Indiana, is framed behind glass and set in a rough and unprofessionally cut mount, with the personal pencilled inscription 'Bo pointn to his Niga', and with the more factual 'Klan 4th Joplin, Mo. 33' on the outer mount.[7] Pressed between the glass and the second larger mount is the trophy of a souvenir hunter. Not a lock of hair, but a mess of hair. To see the hair from the body of a dead man framed. To know that someone grabbed, carefully snipped, roughly cut off or bought the materiality of what was left from that body and kept it. I do not lean in.

As I reach the end of the exhibition a small group of people come in – three people, all adults, two men and a woman. They are quiet at first and I decide to stay and walk around the exhibition again to see how the atmosphere changes now the space is one that I am sharing, to see how the viewing of the images changes with other people in the room, to overhear what they say to each other. I wonder, because they are not alone, if they will vocalize some of the emotions I have encountered but have not shared except with the air that has absorbed my contracted gasps. I walk back to the first set of postcards and prepare to view them for a second time, but I realize that I cannot look at them again. I have had enough of being so confronted. I feel disgusted and nauseous. I am also, I realize, disappointed. 'A Lynching Scene in Alabama' is not here. I open the door and walk straight down the corridor. I do not stop to speak to the person sitting on the chair waiting to share my grief.

After *Witness* closed at the Roth Horowitz Gallery, it re-opened at the New York Historical Society as *Without Sanctuary: Lynching Photography in America*. The Society drew on its own collections to provide contextual materials which did not appear in the first version of the exhibition.[8] Reflecting on *Without Sanctuary*, Susan Sontag asked if the lynching images had retained their power because they were so rarely seen.[9] Clearly people were drawn to witness this resurrection of the American past: 50,000 people attended the exhibition during its first four months.[10] The images had been brought to the public through James Allen, a white American antique collector, who created his own archive of lynching postcards. Picture postcards had seemed trivial to him until he saw a brittle image of Leo Frank, a white Jewish man killed on 17 August 1915 in Marietta, Georgia. Looking at the card he was bewildered not only by the body joined to the oak tree, but by the 'canine-thin faces of the pack, lingering in the woods, circling after the kill'.[11] This encounter with Leo Frank and the lingering pack prompted a quest to seek out others whose death had been photographed and pictured on a postcard.

Without Sanctuary travelled from New York throughout the United States, attracting thousands of visitors to the Andy Warhol Museum in Pittsburgh in 2001, the Martin Luther King Jr National Historical Site in Atlanta in 2002, Jackson State University and Charles H Wright Museum, Detroit, in 2004 and then the Chicago Historical Society in 2005. The journey of the exhibition and the context of each space resulted in slightly different forms of the exhibition being displayed. In Atlanta, part of the exhibition focused on the campaigns against lynching led by the NAACP and Ida B Wells' pioneering work in the United States and Britain.[12] In each place, the exhibition became situated in local political understandings of the past and contemporary racial and cultural politics. In New York, images were displayed the year after Amadou Diallo, a 22-year-old Guinean immigrant and unarmed street vendor, had been killed by 41 shots fired by New York Policemen as he stood in the entrance of his apartment building in the Bronx.[13] The acquittal of the four white policemen accused of killing him in February 2000 coincided with the opening of *Witness* on the Upper West Side.[14] The visual record of the lynching photographs was directly connected to Diallo's murder and provided for some an illustration that black people continued to be lynched in the United States with impunity.[15]

In Atlanta, Duane Corpis and Ian Fletcher considered the historical images alongside the placing of nooses in some workplaces to intimidate black employees, the bombing of a gay bar and the then recent beating of two black men by skinheads in an 'alternative' neighbourhood.[16] The Atlanta exhibition also provided a space for families who had survived the trauma of lynching to meet. After the murder of Anthony Crawford in Abbeville, South Carolina, because he argued over the price of cotton with a white storekeeper in 1916, his land was seized and his family forced to leave.[17] His descendants from Chicago and South Carolina came together for a reunion in the grounds of the Atlanta exhibition, and other families came hoping to find information and possibly photographs of fathers and grandfathers ripped from them by racial violence.[18]

The development of the exhibition in the United States and in Britain placed the images of lynchings in the context that Catherine, Wells, Edwards and Mitchell sought to use them. Curators and viewers inverted their meanings so that the racial hatred and white supremacy celebrated within them is faced and challenged. The curators of the exhibition in London held *Without Sanctuary* in conjunction with a retrospective of photographic works by the Nigerian-born artist Rotimi Fani-Kayode, highlighting the 'complex notions of sexuality and cultural dislocation' present in his work.[19] The curators showed these two collections of work together in order to 'create a platform to discuss the spectacle of the black body on display' and to provide a space where difference, race and representation, as well as civil rights, intolerance and homophobia, could be discussed.[20] But over the two months *Without Sanctuary* remained at

Rivington Place, fewer than 4500 people visited the exhibitions.[21] A few young black men who shared their responses to *Without Sanctuary* with the gallery spoke of their visit as a 'transformative experience' and returned with friends to see the exhibition again.[22] While other visitors were 'overwhelmed and deeply touched' by the works on display, their responses also clearly reflected a sense that they struggled to understand and relate to the violence on display and the complexity of their experience.[23] They were little helped by the British press, who largely ignored the presence of the photographs in the city.[24] There were few attempts to situate the images within the context of global political intolerance as presented by the curators, nor to place the images in an historical context of racism or antiracist campaigners in Britain like the League of Coloured Peoples or Ida B Wells, Celestine Edwards or Catherine. Perhaps they were not seen as important to British history by contemporary observers. Yet the practice of lynching played an important role in galvanizing the Victorian antiracist community in Britain, and an understanding of international solidarity remained key to their discussions around the politics of race.

The second half of the twentieth century celebrated successes against racist political structures including the defeat of Nazism, the end of colonialism and apartheid. In Britain we tend to assume that we have progressed a great distance from the politics of our Victorian ancestors. In many aspects of social and political life this is true. Racial politics changed dramatically over the twentieth century, but the legacy of racism's spectacular successes before the end of the Second World War remains part of everyday life in Britain. How we deal with these realities without reversing the successes of the civil rights campaigns of the late twentieth century is a contentious issue. As Catherine illustrated to her readers month after month, the official ending of slavery did not end racial prejudice or the legal effects of social oppression it gave birth to. The process of eradicating racism may take many generations, although the ideologies of racism may never die because, as Primo Levi observed, 'nothing ever dies. Everything returns renewed'.[25] In a time when racism is supposed to have 'faded away', as Paul Gilroy observes, 'racial abuse, like racial inequality, remains'.[26] In the second decade of the twenty-first century, many of the questions that Catherine and Celestine Edwards had raised in *Anti-Caste* and *Fraternity* remain part of our multiplicity of discourse networks. Since 9/11 the 'whole question of the right relations between white and coloured races' has once again become one of worldwide importance.[27] In these days of globalization and widespread immigration, debates about a new 'clash of civilisations' and the simultaneous 'failure of multiculturalism' has dominated discussions on migration and integration on both the left and right of politics in the West.[28] The need for a greater understanding of Islam in Europe is reflected in many debates on immigration and social cohesion. Hajee Browne's hope that Europe would soon put aside its understanding of Islam as a 'religion of blood' seems hopelessly optimistic. Following the events of 9/11 and 7/7 Britain built discriminatory laws upon the legacies of state racism forged against black and Irish activists and non-activist members of their communities in earlier parts of the twentieth century and placed ideas of multiculturalism increasingly under attack.[29] The role of consumers in networks of consumption and exploitation continues to be questioned through the campaigns by NGOs and charities. The wars in Afghanistan and Iraq following 9/11 again raised questions about the opaque links between British military foreign interventions and capitalism.

Geographies of optimistic imaginings

Catherine and Celestine Edwards challenged and developed their readers' knowledge of oppression beyond that of many Victorian socialists, positivists and anti-imperial nationalists. The textual community created by their readers produced new networks of solidarity and political engagement. In response to requests as to how they might further the cause against lynching Ida B Wells replied, 'Tell the world the facts.'[30] Supporters were asked to purchase and distribute pamphlets and books so they might enter the general circulation of humanitarians, editors, teachers and preachers. Like Catherine, Wells believed that once the 'Christian world' knew the truth and extent of injustice in the United States, 'some means would be found to stop it'.[31] They shared this optimistic view with other nineteenth-century journalists such as W T Stead, who felt that the press played an active role in social change by placing evidence of wrongdoings in the public domain; it was then the government's responsibility to enact the changes required.[32] *Anti-Caste* did not realize the promising potential of the foundations created in 1893, primarily because of a personal dispute, but also because of the rigid principles Catherine maintained for herself and her subsequent refusal to remain part of the SRBM that maintained unity through the *Bond of Brotherhood*. Her determination to live according to the principles she preached is to be commended, but perhaps the anticaste movement also failed to develop because Catherine relied too heavily on ideas of internalized individual action. The knowledge *Anti-Caste* and *Fraternity* brought before people undoubtedly stirred the compassion of many readers, but as Susan Sontag observed, compassion is an unstable emotion; it is an emotion that needs to be translated into action or it will whither away.[33]

Reading played an important role in the making of political actors, particularly women. *Anti-Caste* formed part of a voluminous print culture that made up a discourse network for those building a radical political outlook, be they Quakers, vegetarians, feminists, socialists or civil rights workers augmenting *Anti-Caste* with material from their membership of other overlapping reading communities. News circulation, statistics, opinions, observations and testimony are essential components in the process of political transformations. They are not, on their own, the kind of action that forces political change. Catherine argued that it was neither money nor patronage, nor cheap condescension, that oppressed people needed, but an outpouring of brotherly love and a just and fair spirit of neighbourliness. But Frederick Douglass, whom she greatly admired, believed rather more forceful actions were required.[34] During an address to celebrate the anniversary of the emancipation of the enslaved in the West Indies, Douglass argued that those involved in continuing struggles against oppression had to be prepared for action that might involve more than words. His words on 'the philosophy of reform' reminded his audience that throughout history in 'the progress of human liberty' all concessions 'made to her august claims' had been born out of struggle.[35] Struggle formed an essential part of the politics of transformation:

> If there is no struggle there is no progress. Those who profess to favor freedom and yet deprecate agitation, are men who want crops without plowing up the ground, they want rain without thunder and lightning. They want the ocean without the awful roar of its many waters.

> This struggle may be a moral one, or it may be a physical one, and it may be both moral and physical, but it must be a struggle. Power concedes nothing without a demand. It never did and it never will. Find out just what any people will quietly submit to and you have found out the exact measure of injustice and wrong which will be imposed upon them, and these will continue till they are resisted with either words or blows, or with both.[36]

Although Douglass gave his speech in an era before the abolition of enslavement in the United States, twentieth-century struggles against oppression, by suffragettes, by anticolonial, anti-apartheid and civil rights activists, have shown that successful movements must contain people who are willing to be imprisoned for their struggle and accept they may die because of their willingness to challenge the structures of power within their society. Martin Luther King had been arrested at least 18 times before he was assassinated on the balcony of the Lorraine Motel in Memphis in April 1968, barely three months after his 39th birthday. He argued that being part of political struggle changes people.[37] As oral histories undertaken by History Workshop in the 1970s illustrated, what people remember from partaking in a political struggles is not formal resolutions of conferences or organizational structures, but the sense that being involved in a political organization gives a feeling of hope and meaning to their lives.[38] People are changed by and through the process of political struggle. How these personal moments are directed towards political ends or action is a key moment in the development of solidarities.[39]

Letters from readers of *Anti-Caste* and *Fraternity* suggest the periodicals contributed, though partially and in a myriad of ways, to some individuals feeling a sense of being part of a political organization that gave meaning, and in some cases hope, to their lives. Catherine and Edwards held Britain and other Western powers to account in their demand for equality for all and struggled through personal humiliation, financial hardship and illness to maintain their contribution to that struggle. But aside from the influence the movement held for individuals, the anticaste movement failed. Racial inequality clearly still exits in Britain, the United States, Australia and other regions reported in these two periodicals, and critical race studies continues to struggle with the possibilities of a 'post race' world and the utopian language that might be used to describe it. Nonetheless, the work of Catherine and the anticaste movement reminds us that antiracist work has a long tradition that can be located in the progressive politics of the late Victorians and it is a legacy that can be reclaimed. *Anti-Caste* created a 'discourse network' that sat alongside others that are better remembered perhaps because they had a more palatable and less confronting message and have been more easily included in the myth-making of British liberalism and radical thought.

The trajectory of a struggle is transformed by its imagination and the legacies of its memories. *Anti-Caste* and *Fraternity* were bold contributions to late nineteenth-century print culture. Their editors imagined other worlds were possible, believed these should be reality and saw their periodicals as practical interventions into the making of these utopian geographies. Establishing the intergenerational and integrated histories of antiracism since the late nineteenth century as a 'philosophy of reform' is an important part of antiracism's continuing revolutions. Catherine recognized that the

Figure 11.1 Catherine and Ellen Impey

forms of racism expressed during the era of enslavement were linked but different to those that took shape during Reconstruction in the United States and high imperialism in Britain. These were challenged by the ideologies of anticaste liberalism, and in turn anticaste activists were challenged by the politics of 'the colour line' which dominated politics for much of the twentieth century. As Catherine argued, resistance to struggles for equality changes, so those striving to challenge it must transform their methods and the sites of their battles. Drawing on an historical legacy of antiracism can inform the choices of current and future activists. The knowledge Catherine and Edwards gathered may still influence a community of readers who engage, reinterpret, blog, tweet, edit, skip and augment passages as they choose.

Notes

1. Panel discussion on *Without Sanctuary* hosted by Amnesty International, Human Rights Action Centre, London, on 28 June 2011.
2. This version of *Without Sanctuary* was curated by Autograph ABP and shown at Rivington Place, London, from 27 May to 30 July 2011. The exhibition was brought to London through the efforts of Mark Sealy, Autograph ABP's Director.
3. For discussions of responses to *Without Sanctuary* exhibitions in the United States, see Apel, *Imagery of Lynching* particularly Chapter 1, 'On Looking' and Sontag, *Regarding the Pain of Others*, especially 81–84.
4. Smith, *Photography on the Color Line*, 119.
5. Raiford, *Imprisoned in a Luminous Glare*.
6. Barnes, 'On Without Sanctuary'; Apel and Smith, *Lynching Photographs*.
7. For a detailed analysis of this image see Smith, 'The evidence of lynching photographs'.
8. Lee, 'Introduction'.
9. Sontag, *Regarding the Pain of Others*.
10. Lee, 'Introduction'.

11 Allen, 'Afterword', 204.
12 Corpis and Fletcher, 'Without Sanctuary'.
13 Fritsch, 'The Diallo Verdict: The overview', *New York Times*, 26 February 2000.
14 Vulliamy, 'Cold rage engulfs the Bronx, observer', 27 February 2000, www.guardian.co.uk/world/2000/feb/27/theobserver3, accessed 13 June 2013; Fritsch, 'The Diallo verdict: The overview, *New York Times*, 26 February 2000, www.nytimes.com/2000/02/26/nyregion/diallo-verdict-overview-4-officers-diallo-shooting-are-acquitted-all-charges.html?pagewanted=all&src=pm, accessed 13 June 2013.
15 Editorial, 'Police lynchings law of the land', *News & Letters*, www.newsandletters.org/Issues/2000/April/4.00_ed.htm, accessed 13 June 2013.
16 Corpis and Fletcher, 'Without Sanctuary', 282–285.
17 Atoning for segregation: Justice Delayed, *The Economist*, 16 June 2005, www.economist.com/node/4085834, accessed 13 June 2013.
18 Barnes, 'On Without Sanctuary', 86–91.
19 Rivington Place, Rotimi Fani-Kayode (1955–1989), Without Sanctuary: Lynching Photography in America, press release 2011.
20 Email correspondence with Renée Mussai, Autograph ABP, 22 January 2013. My thanks to Renée Mussai, Curator/Head of Archive at Autograph ABP, for discussing these issues with me and providing information on visitor numbers.
21 Email correspondence with Renée Mussai, Autograph ABP, 22 January 2013. Audience figures for the joint *Without Sanctuary* and Rotimi Fani-Kayode exhibitions at Rivington Place were 4368.
22 Email correspondence with Renée Mussai, Autograph ABP, 11 February and 13 June 2013.
23 Email correspondence with Renée Mussai, Autograph ABP, 13 June 2013.
24 Renée Mussai notes a feature by Candace Allen on Nightwaves, BBC Radio 3, 31 May 2011, as an exception, email correspondence with Renée Mussai, Autograph ABP, 22 January 2013.
25 Levi, Return to Auschwitz, 216.
26 Gilroy, 'My Britain is fuck all', 382.
27 An appeal concerning the treatment of Coloured Races; MSS. Brit. Emp. s.20 E5/8.
28 Kundnani, *The End of Tolerance*; Gilroy, 'My Britain is fuck all'.
29 See Sivanandan, 'Race, terror and civil society'; Dickson, 'The detention of suspected terrorists in Northern Ireland and Great Britain'.
30 Wells-Barnett, *On Lynching*, 151.
31 Wells-Barnett, *On Lynching*, 151.
32 Hampton, *Visions of the Press*.
33 Sontag, *Regarding the Pain of Others*.
34 *Anti-Caste*, August 1889, 2.
35 Two Speeches by Frederick Douglass; West India Emancipation...And the Dred Scott Decision, The Frederick Douglass Papers at the Library of Congress (Series: Speech, Article, and Book File A: Frederick Douglass, Dated), 21.
36 Two Speeches by Frederick Douglass; West India Emancipation...And the Dred Scott Decision, The Frederick Douglass Papers at the Library of Congress (Series: Speech, Article, and Book File A: Frederick Douglass, Dated), 22.
37 Honey, *Going Down Jericho Road*.
38 Mulgan and Worpole, *Saturday Night or Sunday Morning*.
39 Featherstone, *Solidarity*.

Bibliography

Archive material

Newspaper articles published before 1924 are cited in the notes and are not included in this list of references.

Periodicals, newspapers, journals

Anti-Caste. Library of the Society of Friends, London, available on microfilm at the British Library (March 1888–March/April 1893, and 1895).
Fraternity. (1893–1894 and 1896–1897). The British Library.
Fraternity. (1895). History, Philosophy, and Newspaper Library, University of Illinois.
Imvo. South African National Library, Cape Town.
Lux. The British Library.
New York Age, Cleveland Gazette, Richmond Planet, Schomburg Center for Research in Black Culture, New York Public Library.
Southern Letter. New York Public Library.
Village Albums. Alfred Gillet Trust, Street, Somerset.

Papers

Albion W. Tourgée Papers. Chautauqua County Historical Society, Westfield, NY.
Catherine Impey's Scrapbook and *Visitors at Askew*. Private family archive.
Davidson Don Tengo Jabavu. My Tuskegee Pilgrimage, 1913 (parts 1–3). University of South Africa.
Frederick Douglass Papers. Manuscript Division, Library of Congress, Washington DC.
Ida B Wells Papers. Special Collections Research Center, University of Chicago Library.
Papers of the Anti-Slavery Society (MSS. Brit. Emp. s). Including *Anti-Caste* May/June, 1893. The Bodleian Library of Commonwealth and African Studies, University of Oxford.
Papers of Dr W. E. A. Axon. The John Rylands Library, University of Manchester.
W. E. B. Du Bois Papers. Special Collections and University Archives, University of Massachusetts Amherst Libraries.

Unpublished PhD thesis

August, Anita. 'Rival Radical Feminists – Frances Willard and Ida B Wells: The Rhetorical Slugfest of Two Nineteenth-Century Queen Bees over Lynching,' University of Texas at El Paso, 2009.

Duffield, Ian. 'Duse Mohamed Ali and the Development of Pan-Africanism 1866–1945,' Edinburgh University, 1971.
McLisky, Claire. 'Settlers on a Mission: Faith, Power and Subjectivity in the Lives of Daniel and Janet Matthews,' University of Melbourne, 2008.
Mitcham, Roderick E. 'Geographies of Global Humanitarianism: The Anti-slavery Society and the Aborigines Protection Society, 1884–1933,' Royal Holloway, University of London, 2001.
Moses, Jennifer. 'Writing *The Age*: T. Thomas Fortune, the African American Press, and the unfolding of Jim Crow America, 1880–1930,' University of Delaware, 2011.
Silkey, Sarah Lynn. 'Evolving Morality in a Transatlantic Society: Ida B Wells, Anti-lynching Activism, and British Interest in American Race Relations, 1877–1914,' University of East Anglia, 2006.

Primary sources

Works published before 1924

Aked, Charles. 'The race problem in America.' *Contemporary Review* 65 (1894): 818–827.
Beatrice, Lindsay. *An Introduction to the Study of Zoology with 124 Illustrations and Diagrams*. London: Swan Sonnenschein, 1899.
Browne, Haji A. *Bonaparte in Egypt and the Egyptians of To-Day*. London: T. Fisher Unwin, 1907.
Coleridge-Taylor, Samuel. *24 Negro Melodies, Transcribed for the Piano by S. Coleridge-Taylor with a Preface by Booker T. Washington*. Boston: Merrymount, 1905.
Cooper, A. J. *A Voice from the South*. Ohio: Aldine Printing House, 1892.
Coppin, Fanny Jackson. *Reminiscences of School Life, and Hints on Teaching*. Philadelphia: AME Book Concern, 1913.
Du Bois, W. E. B. *The Souls of Black Folk*. New York: Dover, 1994. First published 1903 by A. C. McClurg.
Dunbar, Paul Laurence. *Lyrics of the Hearthside*. New York: Dodd, Mead, 1899.
——. *Lyrics of Love and Laughter*. New York: Dodd, Mead, 1903.
Edwards, Celestine. *From Slavery to a Bishopric or the Life of Bishop Walter Hawkins*. London: John Kensit, 1891.
Fortune, T. Thomas. 'Correspondence, Afro-American or negro?' *Outlook* 62, no. 6 (1899): 359.
——. 'On syndicating news.' *AME Church Review* 8 (1891): 231–242.
Hamedoe, S. 'The first Pan-African conference of the world.' *The Colored American Magazine* 4 (1900): 223–231.
Jabavu, D. D. T. *The Life of John Tengo Jabavu: A Great Bantus Patriot*. Lovedale, South Africa: Lovedale Institution Press, 1922.
Lumholtz, Carl. *Among Cannibals: Account of Four Years Travel in Australia, and of Camp Life with the Aborigines of Queensland*. London: J Murray, 1889.
Mayo, Isabella Fyvie. *Recollections, of What I Saw, What I Lived Through, and What I Learned During More than Fifty Years of Social and Literary Experience*. London: John Murray, 1910.
National Negro Business League. *Report of the Seventh Annual Convention*. Boston: Charles Alexander, 1906.

Penn, I. Garland. *The Afro-American Press and Its Editors*. Springfield, MA: Willey, 1891.
Post-Office. *Glasgow Directory for 1892–1893*, Printed by William Mackenzie for the Postmen of the Post Office, 1892.
Ray, Cordelia. *Poems*. New York: Grafton Press, 1910.
Robertson, Thomas William. *Caste: An Original Comedy in Three Acts*. Boston: Walter H. Baker, 1913.
Stowell, Charles. *A Healthy Body*. New York: Silver, Burdett, 1891.
Sumner, Charles. *The Question of Caste: Lecture*. Boston: Wright and Potter, 1869.
Walters, Alexander. *My Life and Work*. New York, Chicago, Toronto: Fleming H. Revell Company, 1917.

Secondary sources

Works published after 1924

Abbott, Lynn and Doug Seroff. *Out of Sight: The Rise of African American Popular Music, 1889–1895*. Jackson, MS: University Press of Mississippi, 2002.
Abd-Allah, Umanr F. *A Muslim in Victorian America: The Life of Alexander Russell Webb*. Oxford: Oxford University Press, 2006.
Alexander, Ann Field. *Race Man: The Rise and Fall of the "Fighting Editor," John Mitchell Jr*. Charlottesville, VA: University of Virginia Press, 2002.
Alexander, Sally. '"Do grandmas have husbands?": Generational memory and twentieth-century women's lives.' *The Oral History Review* 36, no. 2: 159–176, 2009.
Alexander, Shawn Leigh. *An Army of Lions: The Civil Rights Struggle before the NAACP*. Philadelphia, PA: University of Pennsylvania Press, 2012.
——. *T. Thomas Fortune, the Afro-American Agitator: A Collection of Writings, 1880–1928*. Gainesville, FL: University Press of Florida, 2008.
Allen, James. 'Afterword.' In *Without Sanctuary: Lynching Photographs in America*, edited by James Allen, Hilton Als, John Lewis and Leon F. Litwack, 203–205. Santa Fe, NM: Twin Palms Publishers, 2010.
Allen, Kerri and Alison Mackinnon. '"Allowed and expected to be educated and intelligent": The education of Quaker girls in nineteenth-century England.' *History of Education: Journal of the History of Education Society* 27, no. 4 (1998): 391–402.
Apel, Dora. 'Lynching photographs and the politics of public shaming.' In *Lynching Photographs*, edited by Shawn Michelle Smith and Dora Apel, 42–78. Berkeley: University of California Press, 2007.
——. *Imagery of Lynching: Black Men, White Women and the Mob*. New Brunswick, NJ: Rutgers University Press, 2004.
Arendt, Hannah. *The Origins of Totalitarianism*. New York: Schocken, 2004.
Attwood, Bain. *Rights for Aborigines*. Crow's Nest, NSW: Allen and Unwin, 2003.
Attwood, Bain and Andrew Markus. *Thinking Black: William Cooper and the Australian Aborigines' League*. Canberra: Aboriginal Studies Press, 2004.
Bailey, Julius H. *Race Patriotism: Protest and Print Culture in the AME Church*. Knoxville, TN: University of Tennessee Press, 2012.
Barnes, Natasha. 'On Without Sanctuary.' *Nka: Journal of Contemporary African Art* 20 (2006): 86–91.
Barthes, Roland. *Camera Lucida*. London: Vintage, 2000.

Berger, Martin A. *Seeing through Race: A Reinterpretation of Civil Rights Photography*. Berkeley: University of California Press, 2011.
Bernstein, Patricia. *The First Waco Horror: The Lynching of Jesse Washington and the Rise of the NAACP*. College Station, TX: Texas A & M University Press, 2005.
Berreman, Gerald D. 'Caste in India and the United States.' *American Journal of Sociology* 66, no. 2 (1960): 120–127.
Bondfield, Margret Grace. *A Life's Work*. London: Hutchinson & Co, 1949.
Booth, Michael R. 'Robertson, Thomas William (1829–1871).' *Oxford Dictionary of National Biography*. Oxford University Press, 2004.
Bowden, Henry Warner. 'Tanner, Benjamin Tucker.' In *African American Lives*, edited by Henry Louis Gates Jr. and Evelyn Brooks Higginbotham, 799. Oxford: Oxford University Press, 2004.
Brake, Laurel. '"Time's Turbulence": Mapping journalism networks.' *Victorian Periodicals Review* 44, no. 2 (2011): 115–127.
Brake, Laurel, Bill Bell, and David Finkelstein. 'Introduction.' In *Nineteenth-Century Media and the Constructions of Identities*, edited by Laurel Brake, Bill Bell, and David Finkelstein, 1–7. Hampshire: Palgrave, 2000.
Brake, Laurel and Marysa Demoor, eds. *Dictionary of Nineteenth Century Journalism in Great Britain and Ireland*. Gent: Academia Press, 2009.
Bressey, Caroline. 'Anti-racism and feminism in Britain.' *Women: A Cultural Review* 21, no. 3 (2010): 279–291.
———. 'Looking for work: The black presence in Britain, 1860–1920.' *Immigrants and Minorities* 28, no. 2/3 (2010): 164–182.
———. 'Reporting oppression: Mapping racial prejudice in Anti-Caste and Fraternity, 1888–1895.' *Journal of Historical Geography* 38, no. 4 (2012): 401–411.
———. 'Geographies of belonging: White women and black history.' *Women's History Review*, published online 24 April 2013. doi: 10.1080/09612025.2012.751767.
Brosseau, Marc. 'Geography's literature.' *Progress in Human Geography* 18, no. 3 (1994): 333–353.
Brown, Lucy. *Victorian News and Newspapers*. Oxford: Clarendon Press, 1985.
Burton, Antoinette. *Brown over Black: Race and the Politics of Postcolonial Citation*. Gurgaon: Three Essays Collective, 2012.
———. 'New narratives of imperial politics in the nineteenth century.' In *At Home with the Empire: Metropolitan Culture and the Imperial World*, edited by Catherine Hall and Sonya Rose, 212–229. Cambridge: Cambridge University Press, 2006.
———. 'Tongues untied: Lord Salisbury's "Black Man" and the boundaries of imperial democracy.' *Comparative Studies in Society and History* 42, no. 3 (2000): 632–661.
———. *At the Heart of Empire: Indians and the Colonial Encounter in Late-Victorian Britain*. Berkeley: University of California Press, 1998.
———. 'The white woman's burden: British feminists and the Indian woman, 1865-1915.' *Women's Studies International Forum* 13, no. 4 (1990): 295–308.
Bush, Julia. *Women against the Vote: Female Anti-Suffragism in Britain*. Oxford: Oxford University Press, 2007.
Carby, Hazel. 'White woman listen! Black feminism and the boundaries of sisterhood.' In *The Empire Strikes Back: Race and Racism in 70s Britain*, edited by Centre for Contemporary Cultural Studies, 212–235. London: Hutchinson, 1982.
Carey, Jane. 'The racial imperatives of sex: Birth control and eugenics in Britain, the United States and Australia in the interwar years.' *Women's History Review* 21, no. 5 (2012): 733–752.

Carrigan, William D. *The Making of a Lynching Culture: Violence and Vigilantism in Central Texas, 1836–1916*. Urbana, IL: University of Illinois Press, 2004.
Cato, Nancy. *Mister Maloga*. St. Lucia: University of Queensland Press, 1993.
Champness, E. I. *Frank Smith, M.P. Pioneer and Modern Mystic*. London: Whitefriars Press, 1943.
Chandra, Shefali. *The Sexual Life of English: Languages of Caste and Desire in Colonial India*. Durham and London: Duke University Press, 2012.
Chater, Kathleen. *Untold Histories: Black People in England and Wales during the Period of the British Slave Trade, c. 1660–1807*. Manchester: Manchester University Press, 2009.
Cimbala, Paul Alan and Randall Martin Miller, eds. *The Freedmen's Bureau and Reconstruction: Reconsiderations*. New York: Fordham University Press, 1999.
Claeys, Gregory. *Imperial Sceptics: British Critics of Empire, 1850–1920*. New York: Cambridge University Press, 2010.
Clements, Theresa. *From Old Maloga: The Memoirs of an Aboriginal Woman*. State Library of Victoria: Fraser & Morphet Pty. Ltd., http://www.slv.vic.gov.au/rareltpam/gid/slv-pam-aaa17900, accessed 20 March 2013.
Cohen, Lara Langer and Alexander Stein Jordan. 'Introduction: Early African American print culture.' In *Early African American Print Culture*, edited by Lara Langer Cohen and Alexander Stein Jordan, 1–16. Philadelphia, PA: University of Pennsylvania Press, 2012.
Colenso, Gwilym and Christopher Saunders. 'New light on the Pan-African association: Part I.' *African Research and Documentation* 107 (2008): 27–45.
——. 'New light on the Pan-African association: Part II.' *African Research and Documentation* 108 (2008): 89–109.
Corpis, Duane J. and Ian Christopher Fletcher. 'Without sanctuary.' *Radical History Review* 85, no. 1 (2003): 282–285.
Cowman, Krista. '"With a lofty moral purpose": Caroline Martyn, Enid Stacy, Margaret McMillan, Katharine St. John Conway and the cult of the good woman socialist.' In *Heroic Reputations and Exemplary Lives*, edited by Geoffrey Cubitt and Allen Warren, 212–224. Manchester: Manchester University Press, 2000.
Crawford, Elizabeth. *The Women's Suffrage Movement in Britain and Ireland: A Regional Survey*. Oxon and New York: Routledge, 2006.
Dabakis, Melissa. 'Martyrs and monuments of Chicago: The haymarket affair.' *Prospects* 19 (1994): 99–133.
Davis, Peter 'Backhouse family (per. c.1770–1945).' *Oxford Dictionary of National Biography*. Oxford University Press, 2004; online edn, May 2010.
Davis, Thomas J. *Plessy vs Ferguson*. Westport, CT: Greenwood Press, 2012.
Dearborn, Kerry. *Baptized Imagination: The Theology of George MacDonald*. Burlington, VT: Ashgate, 2006.
Decosta-Williams, Miriam, ed. *The Memphis Diary of Ida B Wells: An Intimate Portrait of the Activist as a Young Woman*. Boston: Beacon Press, 1995.
de Grout, Joanna. 'Metropolitan desires and colonial connections: Reflections on consumption and empire.' In *At Home with the Empire: Metropolitan Culture and the Imperial World*, edited by Catherine Hall and Sonya Rose, 166–190. Cambridge: Cambridge University Press, 2006.
Delap, Lucy. *The Feminist Avant-Garde: Transatlantic encounters of the early 20th Century*. Cambridge: Cambridge University Press, 2007.
Delap, Lucy and Maria DiCenzo, 'Transatlantic print culture: The Anglo-American feminist press and emerging "modernities".' In *Transatlantic Print Culture*

1880–1940, edited by Ann Ardis and Patrick Collier, 48–65. Basingstoke: Palgrave Macmillan, 2008.

Dennis, Brad. 'The debate on the early "Armenian Question", 1877–1896: Strengths, weaknesses, lacunae and ways forward.' *Middle East Critique* 20, no. 3 (2011): 271–289.

Dickson, Brice. 'The detention of suspected terrorists in Northern Ireland and Great Britain.' *University of Richmond Law Review* 43, no. 3 (2009), http://lawreview.richmond.edu/the-detention-of-suspected-terrorists-in-northern-ireland-and-great-britain/#_ftn46, accessed 14 June 2013.

Draper, Christopher and John Lawson-Reay. *Scandal at Congo House: William Hughes and the African Institute Colwn Bay*. Llanrwst, Wales: Gwasg Carreg Gwalch, 2012.

Dray, Philip. *At the Hands of Persons Unknown: The Lynching of Black America*. New York: Random House, 2002.

Dunbar, Paul Laurence. *The Paul Laurence Dunbar Reader: A Selection of the Best of Paul Laurence Dunbar's Poetry and Prose, Including Writings Never before Available in Book Form*. Edited by Jay Martin and Gossie Harold Hudson. New York: Dodd, Mead, 1975.

——. *In His Own Voice: The Dramatic and Other Uncollected Works of Paul Laurence Dunbar*. Edited by Herbert Woodward Martin and Ronald Primeau. Athens, OH: Ohio University Press, 2002.

Durbach, Errol. 'Remembering Tom Robertson (1829–1871).' *Educational Theatre Journal* 24, no. 3 (1972): 284–288.

Duster, Alfreda, ed. *Crusade for Justice: The Autobiography of Ida B. Wells*. Chicago: University of Chicago Press, 1972.

Elliott, Mark. *Justice Deferred: Albion Tourgée and the Fight for Civil Rights*. Westfield, NY: Chautauqua County Historical Society, 2008.

Elliott, Mark and John David Smith, eds. *Undaunted Radical: The Selected Writings and Speeches of Albion W. Tourgée*. Baton Rouge: Louisiana State University Press, 2010.

Fahey, David. 'Why some black lodges prospered and others failed: The good templars and the true reformers.' *Ethnic and Racial Studies* 36, no. 2 (2012): 337–352.

——. *Temperance and Racism: John Bull, Johnny Reb and the Good Templars*. Lexington, KY: University Press of Kentucky, 1996.

Fahey, David M., ed. *The Collected Writings of Jessie Forsyth, 1847–1937: The Good Templars and Temperance Reform on Three Continents*. Lewiston, NY: Edwin Mellen, 1988.

Featherstone, David. *Solidarity: Hidden Histories and Geographies of Internationalism*. London: Zed Books, 2012.

Flanagan, Maureen. *Seeing with Their Hearts: Chicago Women and the Vision of the Good City, 1871–1933*. Princeton and Oxford: Princeton University Press, 2002.

Foreman, P. Gabrielle. 'Reading/Photographs: Emma Dunham Kelley-Hawkins's *Four Girls at Cottage City*, Victoria Earle Matthews, and The Woman's Era.' *Legacy* 24, no. 2 (2007): 248–277.

Foner, Eric. *Reconstruction: America's Unfinished Revolution, 1863–1877*. New York: Perennial Classics, 2002.

Fraser, Hillary, Stephanie Green, and Judith Johnston. *Gender and the Victorian Periodical*. Cambridge: Cambridge University Press, 2003.

Fryer, Peter. *Staying Power: The History of Black People in Britain*. London: Pluto Press, 1986.

Fuller, C. J. 'Caste, race, and hierarchy in the American South.' *Journal of the Royal Anthropological Institute* 17, no. 3 (2011): 604–621.

Gandhi, Leela. *Affective Communities: Anticolonial thought, Fin-de-Siècle radicalism, and the politics of friendship*. Durham and London: Duke University Press, 2006.
Ganter, Regina. *Mixed Relations: Asian/Aboriginal Contact in North Australia*. Crawley: University of Western Australia Press, 2006.
Gatewood, Willard B. *Aristocrats of Color: The Black Elite, 1880–1920*. Bloomington: Indiana University Press, 1990.
Geiss, Imanuel. *The Pan-African Movement: A History of Pan-Africanism in America, Europe, and Africa*. New York: Africana, 1974.
Giddings, Paula J. *Ida: A Sword among Lions, Ida B Wells and the Campaign Against Lynching*. New York: Amistad, 2009.
Gilroy, Paul. *The Black Atlantic: Modernity and Double Consciousness*. Cambridge, MA: Harvard University Press, 1993.
———. 'My Britain is Fuck All': Zombie multiculturalism and the race politics of citizenship.' *Identities: Global Studies in Power and Culture* 19, no. 4 (2012): 380–397.
Gooding-Williams, Robert. *In the Shadow of Du Bois: Afro-Modern Political Thought in America*. Cambridge, MA: Harvard University Press, 2011.
Gray, F. Elizabeth. 'Introduction.' In *Women in Journalism at the Fin de Siècle: Making a Name for Herself*, edited by F. Elizabeth Gray, 1–20. Basingstoke, Hampshire: Palgrave Macmillan, 2012.
Green, Barbara. 'The feminist periodical press: Women, periodical studies, and modernity.' *Literature Compass* 6, no. 1 (2009): 191–205.
Green, Jeffrey. *Samuel Coleridge-Taylor, a Musical Life*. London: Pickering and Chatto, 2011.
———. 'Fuller, Joseph Jackson (1825–1908).' *Oxford Dictionary of National Biography*. Oxford University Press, 2004.
———. '"The foremost musician of his race": Samuel Coleridge-Taylor of England, 1875–1912.' *Black Music Research Journal* 10, no. 2 (1990): 233–252.
Gregory, James. *Of Victorians and Vegetarians: The Vegetarian Movement in Nineteenth-Century Britain*. London: I. B. Tauris, 2007.
Groves, Harry E. 'Separate but equal: The doctrine of Plessy v. Ferguson.' *Phylon* 12, no. 1 (1951): 66–72.
Gunning, Sandra. *Race, Rape and Lynching: The Red Record of American Literature, 1890–1912*. New York: Oxford University Press, 1996.
Hall, Catherine. *Macaulay and Son: Architects of Imperial Britain*. New Haven and London: Yale University Press, 2012.
———. *Civilising Subjects: Metropole and Colony in the English Imagination 1830–1867*. Chicago: University of Chicago Press, 2002.
Hampton, Mark. *Visions of the Press in Britain, 1850–1950*. Chicago: University of Illinois Press, 2004.
Hansen, Drew D. *The Dream: Martin Luther King, Jr., and the Speech that Inspired a Nation*. New York: Ecco, 2003.
Heartfield, James. *The Aborigines' Protection Society: Humanitarian Imperialism in Australia, New Zealand, Fiji, Canada, South Africa, and the Congo, 1837–1909*. London: Hurst, 2011.
Hein, David and Gardiner H. Shattuck Jr. *The Episcopalians*. New York: Church Publishing, 2004.
Hill Collins, Patricia. 'Introduction.' In *On Lynchings*, edited by Ida B Wells, 9–24. Amherst, NY: Humanity Books, 2002.
Hofmeyr, Isabel. *Gandhi's Printing Press: Experiments in Slow Reading*. Cambridge and London: Harvard University Press, 2013.

Hollingworth, Brian Charles. 'Axon, William Edward Armytage (1846–1913).' *Oxford Dictionary of National Biography*. Oxford University Press, 2004.
Holton, Sandra Stanley. 'Challenging masculinism: Personal history and microhistory in feminist studies of the women's suffrage movement.' *Women's History Review* 20, no. 5 (2011): 829–841.
———. *Quaker Women: Personal Life, Memory and Radicalism in the Lives of Women Friends, 1780–1930*. London: Routledge, 2007.
———. 'Kinship and friendship: Quaker women's networks and the women's movement.' *Women's History Review* 14, nos. 3 & 4 (2005): 365–384.
———. 'Segregation, racism and white women reformers: A transnational analysis, 1840–1912.' *Women's History Review* 10, no. 1 (2001): 5–26.
———. 'The suffragist and the "average woman."' *Women's History Review* 1, no. 1 (1992): 19–24.
Honey, Michael K. *Going Down Jericho Road: The Memphis Strike, Martin Luther King's Last Campaign*. New York: Norton, 2011.
Horton, Carol A. *Race and the Making of American Liberalism*. New York: Oxford University Press, 2005.
Howell, Philip. *Geographies of Regulation: Policing Prostitution in Nineteenth-Century Britain and the Empire*. Cambridge: Cambridge University Press, 2009.
Howe, Stephen, ed. *New Imperial Histories Reader*. London: Taylor & Francis, 2008.
Hunter, Kathryn. 'Rough riding: Aboriginal participation in rodeos and travelling shows to the 1950s.' *Aboriginal History* 32 (2008): 83–96.
Hyslop, Jonathan. 'The imperial working class makes itself.' *Journal of Historical Sociology* 12, no. 4 (1999): 398–420.
Impey, Ethel Jane. *About the Impeys*. Edited by Irene Clephane. Assisted by D. A. Impey. Worcester: Ebenezer Baylis, 1963.
Innes, Christopher, ed. *A Sourcebook on Naturalist Theatre*. London: Routledge, 2000.
Jackson, Kate. *George Newnes and the New Journalism in Britain, 1880–1910*. Burlington, VT: Ashgate, 2001.
Jauss Hans Robert. 'Literary history as a challenge to literary theory.' In *The History of Reading*, edited by Shafquat Towheed, Rosalind Crone, and Katie Halsey, 71-79. London and New York: Routledge, 2011.
Jenkinson, Jacqueline. *Black 1919: Riots, Racism and Resistance in Imperial Britain*. Liverpool: Liverpool University Press, 2009.
Jones-Wilson, Faustine, Charles A. Asbury, Margo Okazawa-Rey, D. Kamili Anderson, Sylvia M. Jacobs, and Michael Fultz, eds. *Encyclopaedia of African-American Education*. Westport, CT: Greenwood Press, 1996.
Kellogg, John. 'Negro urban clusters in the postbellum South.' *Geographical Review* 67, no. 3 (1977): 310–321.
Kercher, C. 'Ida B Wells and her allies against lynching: A transnational perspective.' *Comparative American Studies* 3, no. 2 (2005): 131–151.
Killingray, David. 'Significant black South Africans in Britain before 1912: Pan-African organisations and the emergence of South Africa's first black lawyers.' *South African Historical Journal* 64, no. 3 (2012): 393–417.
———. 'Rights, land and labour: Black British critics of South African labour policies before 1948.' *Journal of South African Studies* 35, no. 2 (2009): 375–398.
Kirakosiân, Arman Dzhonovich. *British Diplomacy and the Armenian Question: From the 1830s to 1914*. Princeton, NJ: The Gomidas Institute, 2003.

Kirk, Neville. *Comrades and Cousins: Globalization, Workers and Labour Movements in Britain, the USA and Australia from the 1880s to 1914*. London: Merlin, 2003.

Kittler, Friedrich A. *Discourse Networks 1800/1900*. Translated by Michael Metter, with Chris Cullens, Standford: Standford University Press.

Kneale, James. 'The place of drink: Temperance and the public, 1856–1914.' *Social & Cultural Geography* 2, no. 1 (2001): 43–59.

Korhoen, Kuisma. 'Textual communities: Nancy, Blanchot, Derrida.' *Culture Machine* 8 (2006), http://www.culturemachine.net/index.php/cm/article/view/35/43, accessed 1 August 2013.

Kundnani, Arun. *The End of Tolerance: Racism in 21st Century Britain*. London: Pluto Press, 2007.

Kushner, Tony. 'Not that far? Remembering and forgetting cosmopolitan Southampton in the 20th Century.' In *Southampton: Gateway to the British Empire*, edited by Miles Taylor, 185–207, London: I B Tauris, 2007.

Laity, Paul. 'Peckover, Priscilla Hannah (1833–1931).' *Oxford Dictionary of National Biography*. Oxford University Press, 2004.

Lake, Marilyn and Henry Reynolds. *Drawing the Global Colour Line: White Men's Countries and the International Challenge of Racial Equality*. Cambridge: Cambridge University Press, 2008.

Langa, Helen. 'Two antilynching art exhibitions: Politicized viewpoints, racial perspectives, gendered constraints.' *American Art* 13, no. 1 (1999): 10–39.

Lee, Anthony W. 'Introduction.' In *Lynching Photographs*, edited by Shawn Michelle Smith and Dora Apel, 1–9. Berkeley: University of California Press, 2007.

Lerner, Gerda. 'Early community work of black club women.' *The Journal of Negro History* 59, no. 2 (1974): 158–167.

Lester, Alan. *Imperial Networks: Creating identities in Nineteenth-Century South Africa and Britain*. London: Routledge, 2001.

Lester, Alan and David Lambert, eds. *Colonial Lives across the British Empire: Imperial Careering in the Long Nineteenth Century*. Cambridge: Cambridge University Press, 2006.

Levi, Primo. 'Return to Auschwitz.' In *The Voice of Memory: Primo Levi, Interviews, 1961–1987*, edited by Marco Belpoliti and Robert Gordon, translated by Robert Gordon. New York: The New Press, 2001.

Lewis, David Levering. *W E B Du Bois: Biography of a Race, 1868–1919*. New York: Henry Holt, 2003.

Lincoln, C. Eric and Lawrence H. Mamiya. *The Black Church in the African American Experience*. Durham, NC: Duke University Press, 2003.

Lodwick, Kathleen L. *Crusaders against Opium: Protestant Missionaries in China, 1874–1917*. Lexington, KY: University Press of Kentucky, 1996.

Lorimer, D. 'Reconstructing Victorian racial discourse: Images of race, the language of race relations and the context of black resistance.' In *Black Victorians/ Black Victoriana*, edited by G. Gretchen, 187–208. New Brunswick: Rutgers University Press, 2003.

Lynch, N. 'Defining Irish nationalist anti-imperialism: Thomas Davis and John Mitchel.' *Éire-Ireland* 42, nos. 1 & 2 (2007): 82–107.

Macknight, Campbell. 'The view from Marege: Australian knowledge of Makassar and the impact of the trepang industry across two centuries.' *Aboriginal History* 35 (2011): 121–143.

Mansfield, Bruce. 'The origins of "White Australia".' *Australian Quarterly* 26, no. 4 (1954): 61–68.

Martin, Sandy Dwayne. *For God and Race: The Religious and Political Leadership of AMEZ Bishop James Walker Wood*. Columbia: University of South Carolina, 1999.

Martin, Herbert Woodward and Robert Primeau, eds. *In His Own Voice: The Dramatic and Other Uncollected Works of Paul Laurence Dunbar*. Athens, OH: Ohio University Press, 2002.

Mathurin, Owen Charles. *Henry Sylvester Williams and the Origins of the Pan-African Movement, 1869–1911*. Westport, CT: Greenwood Press, 1976.

McDaniel, Donna and Vanessa Julye. *Fit for Freedom, Not for Friendship: Quakers, African Americans and the Myth of Racial Justice*. Philadelphia: Quaker Press, 2009.

McHenry, Elizabeth. '"An association of kindred spirits": Black readers and their reading rooms.' In *The History of Reading*, edited by Shafquat Towheed, Rosalind Crone, and Katie Halsey, 310–322. London and New York: Routledge, 2011.

McGarvie, Michael. *The Book of Street: A History from the Earliest Times to 1925*. Buckingham: Barracuda Books with C & J Clark, 1987.

———. *Guide to Historic Street: A History of Street as Shown in Its Buildings*. Street: C & C Clark, 1986.

McKay, C. H. 'A journal of her own: The rise and fall of Annie Besant's, our corner.' *Victorian Periodical Review* 42, no. 4 (2009): 324–358.

McLisky, Claire. 'The location of faith: Power, gender and spirituality in the 1883–84 Maloga Mission revival.' *History Australia* 7, no. 1 (2010): 8.1–8.20.

———. 'Colouring (in) virtue? Evangelicalism, work and whiteness on Maloga Mission.' In *Creating White Australia*, edited by Jane Care and Claire McLisky, 67–84. Sydney: Sydney University Press, 2009.

———. 'Professions of Christian love: Letters of courtship between missionaries-to-be Daniel Matthews and Janet Johnston.' In *Evangelists of Empire?: Missionaries in Colonial History*, edited by Amanda Barry, Joanna Cruickshank, Andrew Brown-May, and Patricia Grimshaw. Melbourne: University of Melbourne eScholarship Research Centre, 2008. http://www.msp.unimelb.edu.au/missions/index.php/missions, accessed 1 August 2013.

McMurry, Linda. *To Keep the Waters Troubled: The Life of Ida B. Wells*. New York: Oxford University Press, 2000.

Midgley, Clare. 'Bringing the empire home: Women activists in imperial Britain, 1790s–1930s.' In *At Home with the Empire: Metropolitan Culture and the Imperial World*, edited by Catherine Hall and Sonya Rose, 230–250. Cambridge: Cambridge University Press, 2006.

———. 'Estlin, Mary Anne (1820–1902).' *Oxford Dictionary of National Biography*. Oxford University Press, 2004.

———. *Women against Slavery: The British Campaigns, 1780–1870*. London and New York: Routledge, 1995.

Moore, Lindy. 'A notable personality': Isabella Fyvie Mayo in the public and private spheres of Aberdeen.' *Women's History Review* 22, no. 2 (2013): 239–252.

———. 'The reputation of Isabella Fyvie Mayo: Interpretations of a life.' *Women's History Review* 19, no. 1 (2010): 71–88.

Moropa, Koliswa. 'African voices in *Imvo Zabantsundu*: Literary pieces from the past.' *South African Journal of African Languages* 30, no. 2 (2010): 135–144.

Mulgan, Geoff and Ken Worpole. *Saturday Night or Sunday Morning: From Arts to Industry, New Forms of Cultural Policy*. London: Comedia, 1986.

Nair, Janaki. 'Uncovering the Zenana: Visions of Indian womanhood in Englishwomen's writings, 1813–1940.' *Journal of Women's History* 2, no. 1 (1990): 8–34.

Nelson, George E. 'James, Thomas Shadrach (1859–1946).' *Australian Dictionary of Biography*, National Centre of Biography, Australian National University, http://adb.anu.edu.au/biography/james-thomas-shadrach-10610/text18855, accessed 20 March 2013.

Nicholson, Bob. '"You kick the bucket; we do the rest!": Jokes and the culture of reprinting in the transatlantic press.' *Journal of Victorian Culture* 17, no. 3 (2012): 273–286.

Ogborn, Miles. *Indian Ink: Script and Print in the Making of the English East India Company*. Chicago: University of Chicago Press, 2007.

——. '*Geographia*'s pen: writing, geography and the arts of commerce, 1660–1760.' *Journal of Historical Geography* 30 (2004): 294–315.

O'Mally, K. 'Metropolitan resistance: Indo-Irish connections in the inter-war period.' In *South Asian Resistances in Britain, 1858–1947*, edited by R. Ahmed and S. Mukherjee, 125–139. London: Continuum, 2012.

Olsen, Otto H. *Carpetbagger's Crusade: The Life of Albion Wingegar Tourgée*. Baltimore: John Hopkins Press, 1965.

Owen, N. *The British Left in India: Metropolitan Anti-Imperialism, 1885–1947*. Oxford: Oxford University Press, 2007.

Paisley, Fiona. *The Lone Protestor: A M Fernando in Australia and Europe*. Canberra, ACT: Aborigines Studies Press, 2012.

Paterson, Lachy. 'Print culture and the collective Māori consciousness.' *Journal of New Zealand Literature* 28, part 2, Special Issue (2010): 105–129.

Perloff, Richard M. 'The press and lynchings of African Americans.' *Journal of Black Studies* 30, no. 3 (2000): 315–330.

Plaskitt, Emma. 'Mayo, Isabella (1843–1914).' *Oxford Dictionary of National Biography*. Oxford University Press, 2004.

Porter, Bernard. *Critics of Empire: British Radicals and the Imperial Challenge*, 2nd ed. London: I.B. Tauris, 2008. First published 1968 by Macmillan.

Powell, William Stevens. *Dictionary of North Carolina Biography*, vol. 2. Chapel Hill, NC: University of North Caroline Press, 1986.

Pratt, Mary Louise. *Imperial Eyes: Travel Writing and Transculturation*. London and New York: Routledge, 2009.

Punshon, John. *Portrait in Grey: A Short History of the Quakers*. London: Quaker Books, 2006.

Raiford, Leigh. *Imprisoned in a Luminous Glare: Photography and the African American Freedom Struggle*. Chapel Hill, NC: University of North Carolina Press, 2011.

Rao, Anupama. *The Caste Question: Dalits and the Politics of Modern India*. Berkeley, Los Angeles, London: University of California Press, 2009.

Rappaport, Helen. *Encyclopedia of Women Social Reformers*, vol. 1. Santa Barbara, CA: ABC-CLIO, 2001.

Regan-Lefebvre, J. *Cosmopolitan Nationalism in the Victorian Empire: Ireland, India and the Politics of Alfred Webb*. Basingstoke: Palgrave Macmillan, 2009.

Rendall, Jane. 'The condition of women's writing.' In *At Home with the Empire: Metropolitan Culture and the Imperial World*, edited by Catherine Hall and Sonya Rose, 101–121. Cambridge: Cambridge University Press, 2006.

Richards, Paul. 'A Pan-African composer? Coleridge-Taylor and Africa.' *Black Music Research Journal* 21, no. 2 (2001): 235–260.

Richmond, Lesley M. 'Wigham, Eliza (1820–1899).' *Oxford Dictionary of National Biography*. Oxford University Press, 2004.

Rief, Michelle. 'Thinking locally, acting globally: The international agenda of African American clubwomen, 1880–1940.' *The Journal of African American History* 89, no. 3 (2004): 203–222.

Ronnick, Michele Valerie, ed. *The Autobiography of William Sanders Scarborough: An American Journey from Slavery to Scholarship*. Detroit: Wayne State University Press, 2005.

Rose, Jonathan. *The Intellectual Life of the British Working Class*, 2nd ed. New Haven, CT: Yale University Press, 2010.

Ross, Andrew C. 'Stewart, James (1831–1905).' *Oxford Dictionary of National Biography*. Oxford University Press, 2004; online edn, May 2006.

Rowbotham, Sheila. *Dreamers of a New Day: Women Who Invented the 20th Century*. London: Verso, 2010.

Royster, Jacqueline. *Southern Horrors and Other Writings: The Anti-lynching Campaign of Ida B. Wells, 1892–1900*. Boston: Bedford, 1997.

Ryan, James. *Picturing Empire: Photography and the Visualization of the British Empire*. London: Reaktion Books, 1997.

Sadleir, Michael. 'Jacobs, William Wymark (1863–1943).' Rev. Sayoni Basu, *Oxford Dictionary of National Biography*. Oxford University Press, 2004; online edn, January 2011.

Samuel, Raphael. *Theatres of Memory Volume 1: Past and Present in Contemporary Culture*. London: Verso, 1999.

Saunders, Angharad. 'Literary geography reforging the connections.' *Progress in Human Geography* 34, no. 4 (2010): 436–452.

Saunders, Christopher. 'From Trinidad to Cape Town: The first black lawyer in the cape.' *Quarterly Bulletin, NLSA* 44, no. 4 (2001): 146–161.

———. 'Ngcongco, Javabu, and the South African war.' *PULA Journal of South African Studies* 11, no. 1 (1997): 63–69.

Schneer, Jonathan. *London 1900: The Imperial Metropolis*. New Haven, CT: Yale University Press, 1999.

Schoolman, Martha. 'Violent places: Three years in Europe and the question of William Wells Brown's cosmopolitanism.' *ESQ: A Journal of the American Renaissance* 58, no. 1 (2012): iv–35.

Senchyne, Jonathan. 'Bottles of ink and reams of paper: Clotel, racialization, and the material culture of print.' In *Early African American Print Culture*, edited by Lara Langer Cohen and Alexander Stein Jordan, 140–158. Philadelphia, PA: University of Pennsylvania Press, 2012.

Sherwood, Marika. *Origins of Pan-Africanism: Henry Sylvester Williams, Africa and the African Diaspora*. New York: Routledge, 2011.

Silkey, Sarah Lynn. 'Redirecting the tide of white imperialism: The impact of Ida B Wells's transatlantic antilynching campaign on British conceptions of American race relations.' In *Women Shaping the South*, edited by A. Boswell and J. McArthur, 97–119. Columbia, MO: University of Missouri Press, 2006.

Simpson, Georgiana R. 'Notes: Catherine Impey.' *The Journal of Negro History* 10 (1925): 104–106.

Sivanandan, A. 'Race, terror and civil society.' *Race and Class* 47, no. 3 (2006): 1–8.

Slate, Nico. *Colored Cosmopolitanism: The Shared Struggle for Freedom in the United States and India*. Harvard and London: Harvard University Press, 2012.

Smethurst, James Edward. *The African American Roots of Modernism: From Reconstruction to the Harlem Renaissance*. Chapel Hill, NC: University of North Carolina Press, 2011.

Smith, Shawn Michelle. 'The evidence of lynching photographs.' In *Lynching Photographs*, edited by Shawn Michelle Smith and Dora Apel, 10–42. Berkeley: University of California Press, 2007.
Smith, Shawn Michelle. *Photography on the Color Line: WEB Du Bois, Race and Visual Culture*. Durham, NC: Duke University Press, 2004.
Sontag, Susan. *Regarding the Pain of Others*. London: Penguin, 2004.
——. *On Photography*. London: Penguin, 1979.
SoRelle, James M. 'The "Waco Horror": The lynching of Jesse Washington.' *The Southwestern Historical Quarterly* 86, no. 4 (1983): 517–536.
Stewart, Robert. *Breaking the Fetters: The Memoirs of Bob Stewart*. London: Lawrence and Wishart, 1967.
Strieby, Secretary. 'Caste in America.' *American Missionary* 37, no. 12 (1883): 376.
Stunt, Timothy C. F. 'Newman, Francis William (1805–1897).' *Oxford Dictionary of National Biography*. Oxford University Press, 2004.
Sturge, Elizabeth. *Reminiscences of My Life and Some Account of the Children of William and Charlotte Sturge and of the Sturge Family of Bristol*. Bristol: Privately Printed, 1928.
Tabili, Laura. *Global Migrants, Local Culture: Natives and Newcomers in Provincial England, 1841–1939*. Basingstoke: Palgrave Macmillan, 2011.
——. *We ask for British Justice: Workers and Racial Difference in Late Imperial Britain*. Ithaca, NY and London: Cornell University Press, 1994.
Tate, Claudia. *Domestic Allegories of Political Desire: The Black Heroine's Text at the Turn of the Century*. New York: Oxford University Press, 1992.
Taylor, Ula. 'The historical evolution of black feminist theory and praxis.' *Journal of Black Studies* 29, no. 2 (1998): 234–253.
Taylor, Yuval. *I was Born a Slave: An Anthology of Classic Slave Narratives*, vol. 1. Chicago: Lawrence Hill Books, 1999.
Terborg-Penn, Rosalyn. *African American Women in the Struggle for the Vote, 1850–1920*. Bloomington and Indianapolis: Indiana University Press, 1998.
Thomas, Clarence. 'The virtue of defeat: Plessy v. Ferguson in retrospect.' *Journal of Supreme Court History* 22, no. 2 (1997): 15–24.
Thompson, Andrew S. 'The language of imperialism and the meanings of Empire.' In *New Imperial Studies Reader*, edited by Stephen Howe, 306–322. London: Taylor & Francis, 2008.
Thompson, Becky. 'Multicultural feminism: Recasting the chronology of second wave feminism.' *Feminist Studies* 28, no. 2 (2002): 337–360.
Tillman, Katherine Davis Chapman. *The Works of Katherine Davis Chapman Tillman*. Schomburg Library of Nineteenth-Century Black Women Writers. New York: Oxford University Press, 1991.
Towheed, Shafquat, Rosalind Crone, and Katie Halsey. 'Reading communities.' In *The History of Reading by Shafquat Towheed*, edited by Rosalind Crone and Katie Halsey, 273–274. London and New York: Routledge, 2011.
Tucker, David M. 'Miss Ida B. Wells and Memphis Lynching.' *Phylon* 32, no. 2 (1971): 112–122.
Turner, Arlin. *George W. Cable: A Biography*. Baton Rouge: Louisiana, Louisiana State University Press, 1966.
Turner, Darwin. 'Paul Laurence Dunbar: The rejected symbol.' *The Journal of Negro History* 52, no. 1 (1967): 1–13.

Tusan, Michelle. 'Humanitarian journalism: The career of Lady Isabella Somerset.' In *Women in Journalism at the Fin De Siècle: Making a Name for Herself*, edited by F. Elizabeth Gray, 91–109. Basingstoke: Plagrave Macmillan, 2012.

Tusan, Michelle Elizabeth. *Women Making News: Gender and Journalism in Modern Britain*. Urbana, IL: University of Illinois Press, 2005.

Van Toorn, Penny. 'Authors, scribes and owners: The sociology of nineteenth-century aboriginal writing on Coranderrk and Lake Condah reserves.' *Continuum: Journal of Media & Cultural Studies* 13, no. 3 (1999): 333–343.

Vargo, Gregory. '"Outworks of the citadel of corruption": The Chartist press reports the empire.' *Victorian Studies* 54, no. 2 (2012): 227–253.

Visram, Rozina. *Asians in Britain: 400 Years of History*. London: Pluto Press, 2002.

Vincent, David. 'Reading and writing.' In *The History of Reading*, edited by Shafquat Towheed, Rosalind Crone, and Katie Halsey, 161–170. London and New York: Routledge, 2011.

Wallinger, Hanna. '"Shrinking at no lofty theme": The race literature of Victoria Earle Matthews, Gertrude Mossell, and Katherine Tillman.' In *Loopholes and Retreats: African American Writers and the Nineteenth Century*, edited by John Cullen Gruesser and Hanna Wallinger, 189–203. Vienna: Lit Verlag, 2009.

Ware, Vron. *Beyond the Pale: White Women, Racism and History*. London: Verso, 1996.

Warner, W. Lloyd. 'American caste and class.' *American Journal of Sociology* 42, no. 2 (1936): 234–237.

Warren, Lynne. '"Women in conference": Reading the correspondence columns in Woman, 1890–1910.' In *Nineteenth-Century Media and the Construction of Identities*, edited by Laurel Brake, Bill Bell, and David Finkelstein, 122–134. London: Palgrave, 2000.

Weaver, Valeria W. 'The failure of civil rights 1875–1883 and its repercussions.' *The Journal of Negro History* 54, no. 4 (1969): 368–382.

Wellbery, David E. 'Foreword.' In *Kittler, Friedrich, Discourse Networks 1800/1900*, translated by Michael Metteer with Chris Cullens, vii–xxxiii. Stanford: Stanford University Press, 1990.

Wells-Barnett, Ida B. *On Lynchings*. Amherst, NY: Humanity Books, 2002.

Wood, Amy Louise. *Lynching and Spectacle: Witnessing Racial Violence in America, 1890–1940*. Chapel Hill, NC: University of North Carolina Press, 2009.

Woods, G. S. 'Clayden, Peter William (1827–1902).' Rev. H. C. G. Matthew, *Oxford Dictionary of National Biography*. Oxford University Press, 2004.

Yarwood, A. T. *Attitudes to Non-European Immigration*. Melbourne, VIC: Cassell Australia, 1968.

Zackodnik, Teresa. 'Ida B Wells and "American Atrocities" in Britain.' *Women's Studies International Forum* 28, no. 4 (2005): 259–273.

Zeleny, Rachael Baitch. '"Self-appointed executioner": The late nineteenth-century actress and George Paston's "A Writer of Books".' *Interdisciplinary Literary Studies* 14, no. 2 (2012): 133–149.

Index

Note: Locators with '*f*' denote figures; 'n' denotes notes

Abbott, Lynn 246
Abd-Allah, Umanr F. 150
Aberdeen 34, 78–80, 86–7, 90, 91, 183, 185, 186, 189, 190, 192, 197, 198, 215, 216
Aberdeen Evening Express 117
Aberdeen Weekly Journal 192
Aborigines' Friend 153–4
Aborigines Protection Board (Australia) 163–4
Aborigines Protection Society (APS) 21, 37, 51, 63, 65–6, 129, 132, 152–3, 171, 193, 211, 228, 231, 242, 228, 244
Activism, 11, 12, 67, 180, 193, 223, 227, 228.
activists
 middle-class 21, 31, 181, 229–30
 networks of 78–81, 134, 174, 183, 221
 working-class 181
advertisements 20, 84, 177
Afghanistan 256
African Association 222, 227–9
African diaspora 103, 194, 222, 227–9, 232, 237, 245
African Methodist Episcopal (AME) Church 37, 131
African Methodist Episcopal Zion Church 7, 62
African Romances 234
Afro-American journalists 96
 see also Thomas Fortune, H C Smith, John Mitchell Jr
Afro-American League 63, 80, 107, 130, 166, 211
Afro-American newspapers 96, 97, 99, 159
 see also *Cleveland Gazette*; *Free Speech*; *New York Age*; *Richmond Planet*
Afro-American Press Convention 96–7
agriculture 7, 42, 99, 162, 177, 178, 233

Aked, Charles 92, 189, 192, 193, 200
Alabama Plantation Missionary 132
alcohol 30–1, 45, 67
 see also temperance
Alexander, Shawn Leigh 97
Allen, James 253, 254
Allen, R. V. 185
AME Church Review 37, 132, 143, 182n. 28, 212
American Atrocities 89, 141
American Baptist 75–6
American Baptist Home Missionary Society 75
American churches 7, 35, 43, 54, 57, 206
American indigenous communities 55, 145
American Missionary 55
American Missionary Association 55
'American Negro' 107, 131, 133, 193, 198, 229, 232, 244
AMEZ see African Methodist Episcopal Zion Church
Among Cannibals 165
Anglo-Boer conflict 22, 157, 222
Anglo-Indian Temperance Association 211
Anti-Caste
 content of 66, 95–172, 178
 editorial voice 18, 51–2, 62, 68, 99, 100, 101, 103, 131, 138, 146, 152–3, 220
 editorship of 21–2, 62, 153, 177, 186
 established 21, 23, 31, 42–6, 87–90
 financial support 67
 first issue 46, 51, 167
 focus of 51–2, 173
 format 60*f*
 for free distribution 23, 134
 front page of 19, 122
 geographies of 20–5
 inaugural issue 25, 129

layout 61, 90
network expansion 68–70
newsprint networks 151, 211
political typographies 100
production of 14, 24, 59, 61, 62, 69, 90, 137, 174, 178, 181, 211
readership 24, 25, 63, 65, 66, 67, 102, 103, 131, 134, 138–9, 148, 167, 181, 211, 223
re-establishment of 215
relaunching 208–15, 221
scissors and paste technique of reporting in 20, 99
subscribers 21, 24, 38f, 46, 65–7, 70, 101, 134, 135f, 138–9, 143, 178, 179, 183, 186, 194, 198, 204, 205, 211, 216, 217, 231, 232
subscription forms 6, 45f
success of 52, 257–8
support for 23, 78–9, 132, 138
anti-caste liberalism 54–6, 222, 259
anti-imperialism 21, 22, 24, 227
antilynching 9, 18–19, 79, 101, 119, 122, 186, 189, 192, 195, 223, 255
Anti-Lynching Committee (England) 192, 194–5, 198, 213
antiracism 19, 22, 24, 51, 80, 100, 168, 175, 209, 222–3, 258–9
language of 13, 19, 166
anti-racist 19, 24, 54, 56, 58, 101, 180, 222, 258
activism 228
campaigners 256
international 7
periodicals 98
anti-Semitism 148n. 27, 166, 168, 247
antislavery movement 21, 28, 67, 70, 79–80, 88, 89
Anti-Slavery Reporter and Aborigines' Friend 243
Anti-Slavery Society 21, 27, 33, 37, 44, 46, 63, 66–7, 79, 91, 244
Apel, Dora 125, 126, 259
APS *see* Aborigines Protection Society
Arendt, Hannah 152
Armenia 67, 146, 165–6
Assam tea gardens 161, 168
Associated Press Association 98
see also news agencies

Australian Aboriginal peoples 21–2, 103, 160, 162–5, 166, 168
A M Fernando 244–345
Australian labour policies 151, 160
Australian press 160, 162, 164
Axon, William Edward Armytage 101, 162, 187, 221

Bahamas 132, 134, 166, 184
Bailey, Julius H. 48, 71
Balgarine, Florence 194–5, 198, 213, 215
Band of Hope 30
Baner ac Amseau Cymru 82
Barbados Tax-payer 133
Barnes, Natasha 138, 259, 260
Barthes, Roland 127
Beatrice, Lindsay 67
Belfast News-Letter 37
Berger, Martin A. 127
Bermuda 141
Bernstein, Patricia 126, 127
Berreman, Gerald D. 70
Besant, Annie 18, 98–100
Bible Society Rooms 88
Birmingham 80, 89, 137–8, 140, 143, 192, 197–8, 216
Birmingham Daily Post 192
Blackbirds 245
black newspaper editors *see* Edwards, Celestine; Thomas Fortune, H C Smith, John Mitchell Jr
Blair, Henry W. 204
Bondfield, Margret Grace 182
Bond of Brotherhood (The) 198, 199, 203, 205–9, 208f, 210f, 215–16, 221, 222, 247, 257
Booth, Michael R. 70
Boston Courant Philadelphia Sentinel 132
Boys, Be Chivalrous! 176
Brake, Laurel 20, 25, 26, 105, 118
Bressey, Caroline 15, 182, 248, 250, 251
Bricks without Straw 63
Bristol 6, 83, 85, 89, 95, 134, 137, 189, 212, 218, 235, 239
Bristol Mercury 64
Bristol Women's Suffrage Society 67
British colonialism 51, 66, 151–8, 218, 256
British Friend (The) 51, 52, 68, 137, 141

British Women's Temperance Association 214
Brosseau, Marc 105, 181
Brotherhood 18, 21, 32, 39, 56, 80, 88, 90, 98, 119, 142, 144, 147, 173, 206, 209
  also see Society for the Recognition of the Brotherhood of Man and *Bond of Brotherhood*
Brown, Lucy 104, 105
Brown, William Wells 33, 43, 47n. 36
Browne, Haji A. 142, 150, 194, 256
Browne, P. N. 194
Burton, Antoinette 22, 24, 26, 71, 72, 149, 182, 225, 248
Bush, Julia 182

Cable, George W. 39–41, 63, 130, 156, 211
Cape Times 147
capitalism 13, 152, 155, 158, 218, 256
  see also Rhodes, Cecil
capital punishment 231
Carby, Hazel 105
Carey, Jane 182
Carrigan, William D. 125
Caste (play) 53–4
caste 53, 54, 55, 56, 62, 63, 108, 111, 118, 130, 132, 206
  see also colour/color line
Caribbean 70, 73, 95, 99, 129, 134, 168, 184, 195, 199, 227, 238, 244
  also see West Indies
Cato, Nancy 171, 172
Central Anti-lynching Association 211
Central Somerset Gazette 242–3, 248
Champness, E. I. 225
Chandra, Shefali 125
Chartered African Companies *see* Rhodes, Cecil and South Africa Company
Chater, Kathleen 250
Chicago Defender 246
Chicago Historical Society 255
Chicago Record (The) 232
Christian (The) 164
Christian Evidence Society 83–4, 89, 91
Christianity 18, 38, 40, 41, 43, 82, 83, 85, 89, 103,165, 217
  religious institutions 63, 153
  religious language 18
Christian Recorder 37, 62, 131, 143

Christian Weekly 217
Christian World 192–3
Church of England Temperance Society 83, 228
Civic Church 141
civil rights 9, 11, 22, 25, 27, 39–40, 51, 63, 68, 73, 75, 77, 96, 124, 131, 168, 236, 255–8
Claeys, Gregory 26, 169, 225
Clarks 7, 12
class 28, 179, 236
  see also working class
Clements, Theresa 171
Cleveland Gazette 22, 123, 129–30, 133, 145, 204
Clifton Ladies Anti-Slavery Society committee 67
Clothier 5, 6, 29, 205, 239, 241
CMS Mission in Uganda 154
Cohen, Lara Langer 178, 182
Colenso, Gwilym 248
Colenso, Harriet 66, 89, 153, 155, 244
Coleridge-Taylor, Samuel 232, 233, 234, 236, 237, 249, 250
Colonialism 152–8, 256
colonial secretary 153, 163
Colored American 133, 228
'Color Line Justice' 111
colour/color line; colour bar 23, 27, 32, 34–42, 43, 56–7, 65, 74, 101, 107–12, 140, 206, 215, 222, 227–51, 259
  see also racial segregation
'colour caste' 18, 45, 52, 55–6, 107, 120, 167–8
'coloured people' 43, 62, 123, 138, 141, 155, 167
'coloured races' 19, 44–6, 56, 256
Colwyn Bay African Institute 239
Congregational Church 73, 235
Congregational Theological Institute 134
Contagious Diseases Acts, repeal 67
Contemporary Review 73, 130, 133, 192
Cooper, A. J. 232
Corpis, Duane J. 255, 260
Cornwall Times (The) 133
Cowling, F. B. (Rev) 73
Cowman, Krista 224
Crawford, Elizabeth 182

Creole Days 39
Critics of Empire 22
cross-cultural analysis 102
cross-cultural dialogue 142
Crusade for Justice see Wells, Ida B
Cuba 22, 218, 220

Dabakis, Melissa 104
Daily Chronicle 192
Daily News 133, 141, 192, 214
Daily Post 130
Darwinism 82–3
Davis, Peter 149
Davies, T. 64
Davis, Thomas 22
Davis, Thomas J. 71
Dearborn, Kerry 48
Declaration in Favour of Women's Suffrage 177
de Grout, Joanna 170
Delap, Lucy 180, 181, 182
Demerara Daily 133
Democratic politicians 204
Dennis, Brad 171
Despatch on Inland Emigration 161
DiCenzo, Maria 181
Dickson, Brice 260
Douglass, Frederick 11, 27, 29, 44, 51–2, 59, 63, 66–7, 79, 81, 108, 112, 139, 188–9, 203, 212, 205, 257
Draper, Christopher 94
Dream Lovers 234
Dress Reform Society 66
Du Bois, W. E. B. 9, 15, 59, 107, 113, 121, 122, 124, 166, 229, 239, 240, 244, 245, 250, 251
Duffield, Ian 201
Dunbar, Paul Laurence 7, 232–7, 241, 249, 250
Dundee Courier 64, 218
Durbach, Errol 70

Edinburgh 64, 79, 80, 81, 134, 143, 157, 177, 186, 216
Edinburgh Evening Gazette 88
Edinburgh Society for Women 67
editors
    black 76, 98, 195 see also Thomas Fortune, H C Smith, John Mitchell Jr

newspaper 66, 192, *see also* news and newspapers
Edwards, Celestine 73, 81–7f, 88 – 92, 102, 103, 134, 136, 137, 139, 140, 142, 143, 151,152, 153, 154, 157, 166, 174, 175, 178, 183, 184–5, 189–90, 195, 197–8, 214, 216, 220, 221, 256.
    see also *Lux* and *Fraternity*
Elliot, G. M. 67
Elliott, Mark 71, 93
Emancipation League 79–80, 87–8
English Woman's Journal 18, 100
Episcopal Church 84, 138–9
equality
    civil 207
    gender 31
    human 44, 222
    nominal 31
    political 22, 39
    racial 31–2, 44, 176, 220, 222, 242
    social 39
    universal 18, 20, 25
Ethical Society 242
exhibition 107, 145, 203, 206, 253–6
    see also *Without Sanctuary* (exhibition)
expansion
    capitalist 17, 153
    imperial 22–3, 152, 158

Fabian Society 222
Fahey, David M. 15, 47, 48, 49
Featherstone, David 24, 26, 245, 260
Feminism *see* women's movement
Ferdinands, George 79, 87, 91, 186, 196, 198
Finkelstein, David 105
Fireside Magazine 133
First World War 13, 241, 244
Flanagan, Maureen 180, 182
Flemming, J. L. 77
Foner, Eric 15
Fool's Errand by One of the Fools (A) 19
Ford, Isabella Ormston 18, 177, 187, 205
Foreign Anti-Slavery Society 46, 211
Foreign Missionary Society 68
Foreman, P. Gabrielle 224
Fortune, Thomas 43, 62, 63, 70, 76, 77, 79, 81, 96, 98, 101, 104, 105, 130, 133,

136, 149, 166, 168, 172, 178, 188, 190, 211
Forum (The) 133, 156
Fraser, Hillary 105, 174, 176, 181, 182
Fraternity
    arrival of 91
    control of 176, 184, 216
    editing 153, 198, 217
    editorship of 140, 184, 216, see also Edwards, Celestine
    employment opportunities 124
    financial difficulties 183, 184, 216
    first issue of 90–2
    free distribution of 137, 138
    lynchings in 123
    production 216, 218
    reading 133, 139–42, 148
    subscribers 184
    women writing in 142–4
    working-class readers 181
free-exchange agreements 137, 151
Free Russia 218
Free Speech 76, 96, 192
French Revolution 39, 41
Friend of China 159
'Friends of Justice and Humanity' 88–9
Friend (The) 52
From Slavery to a Bishopric 84
Fryer, Lucy 121–2
Fryer, Peter 47, 71, 93, 94
Fuller, C. J. 70

Gandhi, M. K. 62, 175
Ganter, Regina 171
Garnet-Barbza, Mary H. 68
Garrett, Edward 78
Garret (The) 236
Gatewood, Willard B. 250
Geiss, Imanuel 248
geographical imagination 129, 168
geographies
    of distribution 134–8
    imaginative 129, 168
    of journalism 97
    of oppression 129, 221
    of optimistic imaginings 257–9
    of writing 99–100
Giddings, Paula J. 92
Gilroy, Paul 248, 256, 260

Girl's Own Paper 176
Glasgow 79–80, 88, 110, 135, 218, 219, 244
Glasgow Herald 110, 117
Gold Coast Methodist Times (The) 133
Gooding-Williams, Robert 124
Gray, F. Elizabeth 104, 182
Green, Barbara 182
Green, Jeffrey 249
Green, Stephanie 174
Gregory, James 182
Groves, Harry E. 71
Gunning, Sandra 125
Gunthorpe, George 141

Hall, Catherine 47
Halsey, Katie 105
Hamedoe, S. 249
Hampstead Brotherhood Orchestra 239
Hampton, Mark 71, 101, 105, 181, 260
Hansen, Drew D. 71
Havas 98
    see also news agencies
Hayford, J E Casely 194
Headlight 76
Heartfield, James 25, 72, 169
Hein, David 149
Henry Fox Bourne 62, 153, 228, 231
Hiawatha's Wedding Feast 234
Hindostan 133
History Workshop 258
Hofmeyr, Isabel 105, 178, 182
Hollingworth, Brian Charles 150
Holton, Sandra Stanley 15, 21, 25, 26, 47, 72, 94, 182
Home Words 133
Honey, Michael K. 127, 260
Horton, Carol A. 25, 70, 225
House of Commons 21, 64, 66, 155, 218
Howe, Stephen 26
Howell, Philip 26
Hull Daily Mail 117
humanitarian
    campaigns 21
    group 51
    journalists 180
humanitarianism 21, 51, 163, 180, 243
human rights 39, 41–2, 45, 112, 180–1
Hunter, Kathryn 171
Hyslop, Jonathan 127

Illustrated Police News 117
'imagined communities' 23, 46, 52, 115, 131
Impey, Catherine 1, 2, 3, 4, 6, 9, 10, 11, 12, 13, 17, 18, 19, 21, 24, 25, 27, 29, 31, 34, 35, 36, 39, 41, 42, 43, 44, 51, 52, 62, 66, 79 – 80, 99, 108, 120, 129, 135, 162, 166, 167,168, 173, 175, 178, 179, 180, 187, 190, 205, 207, 209, 211, 212, 214, 221, 231, 243 see also *Anti-Caste*
   account of SRBM 198
   analysis of caste 55, 57, 165, 222
   anticaste network 18, 173
   disagreement with Mayo, Isabella 185-7, 189, 199
   domestic duties 29, 37, 68-9, 78, 214, 223
   editorship 25, 51, 62, 68, 99, 100, 101, 103, 109, 129, 131, 136, 145, 153, 168, 217
   Edwards, Celestine and 139, 168, 177
   faith, 7, 18, 41, 120, 165
   first editorial of *Anti-Caste* 52, 211
   geographical imagination 168
   ideals of social inclusion 181
   ideas of the self 42, 80, 162
   international links 19
   kinship networks 21, 29, 135, 221
   last contribution to *Bond of Brotherhood* 207
   letter to W E A Axon 221
   letter to W E B Du Bois 240
   meeting with Matthews, Daniel 164
   politics 9, 11, 12, 13, 17, 21, 25, 29, 173, 207, 231,
   portrait 2*f*, 14*f*, 28*f*, 241*f*, 259*f*
   racial prejudice 17, 19, 27, 39, 107, 120, 138, 206
   reputation 186, 189-90, 220
   scrapbook 11*f*, 12*f*, 28, 242
   temperance politics, 1, 30-1, 36, 39, 52
   vegetarianism 162
   visits the United States of America 27, 34-5, 37, 44, 77-8, 167, 244
   white supremacy, column on 204
Impey, Ellen 6, 7, 12, 13, 21, 29, 42, 66, 68, 69*f*, 79, 86, 91, 99, 177, 178, 187*f*, 205, 208, 212, 214-15, 220, 234-5, 239-43, 241*f*, 248*f*, 259*f*
Imvo Zabantsandu 64, 129, 132, 155-7, 211
Independent 192, 242
Independent Labour Party (ILP) 217, 218, 242
Independent Order of Good Templars (IOGT) 30-1
   Mission 43, 203
   movement 33
   Order 32
   Politics 31
India 129
Indian 145
Indian and Political General Agency (London) 23
Indian Magazine 133
Indian Messenger 161
Indian National Congress 211, 218, 222, 243
Indian Opinion 62
Industrial Missionary Association 67
Innes, Christophser 70
Inquirer 192
Institute for Colored Youth, Philadelphia 68
international networks 9, 97, 145-8
International Society for the Recognition of the Brotherhood of Man 218, see also SRBM
Inter-Ocean 10, 117, 133, 179, 190, 235
IOGT see Independent Order of Good Templars
Ireland 37, 63, 134, 160, 166, 168
Irish activism 22, 23, 38, 63, 256-7
Islam 13, 142, 256
Islamic missions in England 142
Isle of Wight Express 133

Jabavu, D. D. T. 169
Jabavu, Tengo (editor of *Imvo Zabantsandu*), 156*f* 133, 155, 157, 239, 240
Jackson Coppin, Fanny 7, 52, 62, 68, 78, 79, 108, 134
Jackson, Kate 71, 105
Japan 142
Jass, Hans Robert 105

Jenkinson, Jacqueline 182, 250
Johannesburg Sanitary Board 158
Johannesburg Star 133, 155
Johnston, Judith 105, 174, 181, 182
Jones, Marion 119
Jones, William 160
Jordan, Alexander Stein 178, 182
Journal of Negro History 243
Julye, Vanessa 15

Kercher, C. 15
Keys (The) 245, 247
Killingray, David 225, 248, 250
King, Martin Luther, Jr. 57, 124, 258
kinship networks 21, 29, 52, 65, 135f
Kirakosiân, Arman Dzhonovich 171
Kirk, Neville 172, 225
Kittler, Friedrich A. 20, 24, 26, 100, 104, 105
Klu Klux Klan 74, 146
Kneale, James 25, 47, 104
Knight, Broughton (Rev) 134
Korhoen, Kuisma 105
Kundnani, Arun 260
Kushner, Tony 248

Labour Chronicle 219
Labour Copartnership 219
Labour Leader 192–4, 218–20
Lady's Pictorial 179
Lagos Standard 218–19
Laity, Paul 49
Lake, Marilyn 23, 26, 70, 71, 77, 127, 225, 251
Lambert, David 26
Langa, Helen 126
Lawson-Reay, John 94
League of Coloured Peoples 247
League of Universal Brotherhood 203, 222
Lee, Anthony W. 259
Leeds Mercury 133
Leisure Hour 133
Lerner, Gerda 224
Lester, Alan 26
Levi, Primo 256, 260
Lewis, David Levering 15
Liberal Association of Bristol 189
liberalism 57, 258
liberty 41, 146, 159, 257

Life of Frederick Douglass 63
Lincoln, C. Eric 15, 132
Liverpool 32, 80, 83–6, 88–91, 131, 139, 142–3, 146, 189, 197, 198, 216, 222, 228, 232, 244, 246–7
Liverpool Daily Post 66, 131, 133, 146, 165, 192
Living Way (The) 75
Lodwick, Kathleen L. 170
London 1, 6, 7, 11, 13, 20, 23, 29, 32, 36–7, 39, 41–2, 53, 64, 66–8, 78, 82–6, 89, 95, 98, 107, 118, 132–5, 137–8, 141–2, 146, 155–6, 164, 173–4, 178, 180, 185–7, 189–92, 194–5, 198, 214, 218, 222, 227, 229, 231–6, 240, 242, 244–7, 253, 255
London Daily News 191
London Echo 192
London Missionary Society 153, 159
London Peace Society 204
Lord Salisbury (Prime Minister) 63, 64, 65, 147
Lorimer, D. 15
Lumholtz, Carl 165, 171
Lux 81–7
    advertising space 84
    agent locations 86f
    aims 153
    cost 84
    editorial 85, 154
    founding members 85
    readership 84
    women's column 143, 144, *see also Fraternity*
Lynch, N. 26
lynching photography 19, 107, 112–22, 253, 255
lynchings
    analysis of 110
    before British audiences 175
    in British press 109, 117, 218
    children present 113, 118, 119
    of C J Miller, 116, 117, 118, 119, 140
    of Edward Coy 109
    of Italians 125n. 15
    justification among whites 111, 115
    photographs 107, 115, 117, 118, 122, 255
    postcards 113, 254

rape, 18, 109, 110, 111, 112,121, 173, 196
  reporting on 109, 115, 146, 215
  Roosevelt's policy 222
  scene at Clanton 114f
  special issue on 80
  violence of 17, 108, 114, 206, 218
  Well's analysis 110–11, 175
  in white American press 117
  of Will Stanley 112
  of William Shorter 119
Lyrics of Love and Laughter 235
Lyrics of Lowly Life 232, 234

McDaniel, Donna 15
McGarvie, Michael 14, 15
McHenry, Elizabeth 104, 105
McKay, C. H. 104, 228
Macknight, Campbell 171
McLisky, Claire 26, 171
Malins, Joseph 5, 27, 31, 32, 33, 34, 36, 37, 42, 43, 208, 209
Maloga Mission 22, 163, 164, 169, 211, 244
Mamiya, Lawrence H. 15
Manchester 63, 67, 79, 80, 83–5, 88–9, 162, 187, 189, 197–8, 228
Manchester Courier 110
Manchester Evening News 110, 117
Manchester Guardian 63, 133
Mansfield, Bruce 170
Markus, Andrew 171
Martin, Herbert Woodward 250
Martin Luther King Jr National Historical Site 255
Martin, Sandy Dwayne 15
Mathurin, Owen Charles 26
Matthews, Daniel 162–4, 168, 169, 214
Mayo, Isabella Fyvie 78, 175, 177, 180, 183, 185, 191, 196–7, 204, 215, 217, 220
Memphis Commercial 77, 192
Memphis Daily Appeal 74
Metford, Isabella 5–6, 21, 38, 89, 205, 212
Metford, Jane 34, 36, 69, 239
Methodist Boys High School 66
Methodist churches 7
Methodist Times 192
metropolitan-focused networks 174

Midgley, Clare 21, 25, 72
migrants 168
Minneapolis Appeal 132
missionaries 138, 163
  see also Maloga Mission
Mitcham, Roderick E. 21, 25
Mitchell Jr, John 115, 116f, 117, 146–7, 211, 255
  editorial cartoons 146–7
Mitchel, John 22
'mixed race' communities 111, 175, 237, 244, 247
modernity 9–10, 59, 62, 146, 161, 166, 176, 244
  inclusive modern space 244
Monitor (The) 133
Moore, Lindy 149, 175, 181, 201
Moropa, Koliswa 169, 170
Moses, Jennifer 104
Mulgan, Geoff 260
multiculturalism 256

NAACP *see* National Association for the Advancement of Colored People
Naoroji, Dadabhai 23, 64, 89, 148, 175, 218
Narrative of William W. Brown 33
Nash, Elizabeth 134
Nashville Citizen 133
National American Woman Suffrage Association 179
National Association for the Advancement of Colored People 58, 119, 121, 225
National Citizens' Rights Association 80, 211, 243
National Congress Movement 132, 243
National Indian Association 63, 133
National Indian Congress 216
National Negro Business League 166
National Reform Union 3
National Society of Women's Suffrage 177
National Thrift Society 228
National Union of Working Women 177
Nation (The) 22
Native Races Association 222
NCRA *see* National Citizens' Rights Association
Negroes' Friend Society 243
Negro Mission Fund 43

Negro Welfare Association 228
Nelson, George E. 171
negro supremacy 207
New Journalism 101
new literary community 203–6
Newman, Francis William 67, 86, 205
News 20, 95, 96, 99, 101, 133, 196, 211,
    233 see also individual newspaper
    titles and editors
  British 20, 117, 133, 159, 176
  clippings 1, 39, 144, 168,
  international 97–8, 129, 146, 178, 221
  local 87, 133, 146, 155, 164, 219
  networks 130–4, 151
  scissors and paste, print cultures 20, 99
  syndication of 97, 98, 103
  news agencies 97–8, 133, 168
  white press 76, 97–8, 111, 157
  women's press 18, 173–4, 179–80
New York City 211
New York State 31, 42, 77–8
New York Age 22, 77, 96, 130, 133, 145,
    190, 218–19
New York Freeman 63
New York Times 109
Nicholson, Bob 25, 104, 134
Nimmo, William 241
Nineteenth Century 133

Ogborn, Miles 26, 100, 105
Old Waverly Temperance Hotel 79
Olsen, Otto H. 25, 26, 225
O'Malley, Kate 23
oppression
  international 247
  legalized 46
  political 151, 166
  racial 39, 46, 51, 52, 101, 129, 153,
      165, 168, 173, 199, see also racial
      segregation
  religious 151
  reporting 228
  social 22, 44, 46, 168, 256
Our Corner 98
Owen, N. 26

Paisley, Fiona 219, 251
Pall Mall Gazette 64–5, 117, 164
Pan-African Association 229, 231

Pan-African Conference 107, 227–8,
    231–2, 237
Pan-African politics 227–31
Paterson, Lachy 26
Peace Society 203, 217
periodicals 20, 23, 24, 62, 98, 100, 102,
    133, 140, 141, 174–7
Penn, I. Garland 104, 148, 150
penny pamphlets 84
Perloff, Richard M. 125, 126
personal responsibility 42, 161, 207
Philippines 22
Phillips, Charles 241
photography 10, 115, 253
  see also lynching photography
Phule, Jotirao 55
Pioneer Club 179
Plantation Missionary 132
Plaskitt, Emma 92
political prisoners 168, 207
political rights 9, 108
  see also civil rights
politics
  collaborative 22
  contemporary 143
  cultural 255
  imperial 178
  international 222
  local 42, 102
  party 96
  personal 25, 27, 67, 108
  progressive 22–3, 67, 70, 138, 258
  of transformation 257–8
politics of labour 158–62, 178, 215, 218, 222
  Australia 158–9, 160, 161
  capitalism 158
  exploitation of workers 160–1, 168
  exploitative trade relations 159, 161
  imperial expansion 158, see also
      working class
  and trade union movement 215
  trafficking of Pacific Islanders 158
Porter, Bernard 26
Powell, William Stevens 66, 72
Pratt, Mary Louise 98, 104
Priestman, Anna and Mary 89, 189
Primeau, Robert 249, 250
Prison Service Review 219
Punshon, John 46, 47

Quakers 21, 27, 28, 29, 52, 80, 257
    families 28–9
    women 27–33
    see also Society of Friends
Queen Victoria 213
Queensland 164–5, 168
    Kanaka contract system 159
    sugar plantations of 158–9
Question of Caste (The) 54

race
    constructions of 19, 51, 69
    language of 51, 100, 194, 222
    politics of 25, 27, 39, 63, 166, 199, 222, 256
    riots 181, 244
    typology of 165–9
racial hierarchy 17, 55–6, 69, 103, 174
racial prejudice 17–19, 23, 43–4, 55, 57, 58, 69–70, 76, 89, 102, 108, 114, 132, 145, 156, 177, 206, 207, 211, 215, 227, 237, 244–5
racial segregation 9, 18–19, 22, 27, 37, 52, 54–5, 59, 74, 107, 108, 123, 168, 204, 206, 208–9 *see also* colour/color line
racial stereotypes (cartoon) 194
racism *see* antiracism; civil rights; colour/color line; lynching; racial segregation
radicals 18, 22, 56, 70, 96, 173, 229
Raiford, Leigh 127, 259
Rao, Anupama 70, 125
Rappaport, Helen 149
Ray, Cordelia 143, 150
Readership *see Anti-Caste* and *Fraternity*
Red Record 110, 111, 114f, 118
Reform Act 1867 4, 64
Regan-Lefebvre, J. 26, 47
Rendall, Jane 104
Reuters 110
Review of Churches 192
Review of Reviews 133, 192
Reynolds, Henry 23, 26, 48, 70, 71, 127, 225, 251
Rhodes, Cecil 11, 92, 148, 151, 152, 154, 155, 158, 168, 219, 220
Richards, Paul 249
Richings, G. F. 198, 205, 206, 212, 223, 231

Richmond, Lesley M. 72
Richmond Planet 22, 108, 115, 117, 132–3, 145–6, 218–19, 244
Rief, Michelle 182
Right Worthy Grand Lodge of the World *see* RWGL of the World
Robertson, Thomas William 70
Robinson, Ellen 88
Ronnick, Michele Valerie 150
Rose, Jonathan 26
Rose, Sonya 26
Ross, Andrew C. 170
Rotherham Independent 110
Rowbotham, Sheila 18, 25, 181
Royal Astronomical Society 138
Royal Humane Society 123
Royal Scottish Geographical Society 157
RWGL of the World 32–3, 37, 39, 43–4
Ryan, James 125

Sadleir, Michael 149
Saffron Walden Girls' School 68
St Paul's Cathedral 36, 133
Samuel, Raphael 125
San Francisco Call 133
Sanjibani 161
Saratoga session 42–3
Sastri, Sivra N 68, 161
Saunders, Angharad 104
Saunders, Christopher 148, 170, 248
Schneer, Jonathan 26, 248
Schoolman, Martha 47
Scottish Leader 80, 121
Second World War 122, 243, 256
segregation 9, 23, 32, 56, 58, 59, 74, 107, 108, 207, 209
    see also colour/color line
selfishness 40, 219
    economic 19
    suppression of 41, 161
Senchyne, Jonathan 20, 25
sensationalist 101, 174
sexual assaults *see also* lynching, rape 18, 109–12, 121, 173, 196
sexuality 111, 175, 255
SFBM *see* Society for the Furtherance of the Brotherhood of Man
Shafts 177, 179
Shattuck, Gardiner H., Jr. 149

Sheffield Christian Evidence Society 85
Sheffield Evening Telegraph 117
Sheffield Independent 133
Sherwood, Marika 201, 248, 249
Silkey, Sarah Lynn 15, 124, 125, 181
Sierra Leone Missionary 62
Silent South 39, 63
Simpson, Georgiana R. 7, 177, 182, 232, 239, 240, 241, 242, 243
Sivanandan, A. 260
slavery
 abolition of 39, 44, 207
 in the United States 9, 35, 55–6, 68, 110, 159
 legacy of 10, 17, 35, 112, 115, 139, 207
 'Slaves of Navassa' 205
 statutory 207
 trans-Atlantic 67, 138, 140
Slavery (Gulamgiri) 55
Smethurst, James Edward 15, 249
Smith, Goldwin 54
Smith, John David. 93
Smith, Shawn Michelle 248, 259
social change 96, 173, 178, 257
social cohesion 256
social equality 30, 39
social oppression 22, 168
social reformers 42
social rights 39–40, 44, 52
socialism 98, 193, 218, 222
socialist pamphlets 102
Society (play) 53
Society for the Abolition of Capital Punishment 231
Society for the Furtherance of the Brotherhood of Man (SFBM) 87, 88, 89, 90
Society for the Recognition of the Brotherhood of Man (SRBM), 87, 90–1, 103, 137, 139–44, 173, 175–6, 178, 181, 183–6, 187*f*, 188–90, 194–9, 203–9, 215–16, 220, 222, 227, 257
 charter status of SRBM 102, 140
 temporary council 197–8, 205
 textual community 23, 222
Society of Friends 7, 11, 29, 31, 42, 88, 186, 191, 220, 242
 see also Quakers

solidarity 7, 102–3, 113, 115, 124, 220, 247, 256
Sontag, Susan 15, 125, 127, 254, 257, 259, 260
SoRelle, James M. 125, 126, 127
Souls of Black Folk (The) 59
South Africa (including southern Africa), 57, 95, 99, 124, 132, 141, 146, 151–7, 198, 213, 218, 220, 227–9, 247
South Africa Company 152, 153, 154
 see also Rhodes, Cecil
South Australian Register 162
Southern Christian Recorder 166
Southern Horrors 110, 121
Southern Letter 59
Southern Press Association 98
Spaces of reading 100–2
Stanford, Peter 143
Star (The) 192
Star of Zion 62
Stead, W. T. 141, 240, 257
Stewart, Bob 101
Stewart, Henry 76
Stewart, James 157
Stewart, Robert 105
Still, William 10, 77, 79
Stowe, Beecher 63
Stowell, Charles 149
Street, Somerset 1, 6–7, 12, 178–9, 194, 199, 212, 218, 220–1, 231–44, 253, 255
 political life in Street 239–44
 visitors to Street 231–8
Strieby, Michael E. 70
Stuart, John 133
Stunt, Timothy C. F. 72
Sturge, Elizabeth 28, 46, 47
Sumner, Charles 54, 55, 70
Sun (The) 192
Sunderland Daily Echo 83
surveillance 157
Sydney 73, 160
syndication of news 96, 98, 103

Tabili, Laura 225, 250
Tanner, Benjamin 7, 37–9, 43, 62
Taylor, Ula 182
Taylor, Yuval 47

tea plantations 160, 161, 168
telegrams 64, 109, 110, 148
temperance 1, 6, 20, 27, 29, 30, 31, 41, 38, 51, 52, 54, 56, 67, 78, 79, 81, 82, 83, 134, 139, 180, 219, 231
Temperance Watchword 51
Thomas, Clarence 25
Thomas Wingfold 36
Thompson, Andrew S. 225
Thompson, Becky 25, 173
Thorne, Stephen James 241
Three Years in Europe 33
Tillman, Katherine 143
Times (The) 151, 195, 233
Tourgée, Albion 11, 22, 52, 55, 58, 63, 77, 80, 113, 188
Towheed, Shafquat 105
Trade Union 90, 215, 217–18 *also see* workers and Independent Labour Party
trafficking 158
trans-Atlantic reprinting 20, 56, 117, 131, 140, 145
trans-Atlantic telegraph cable 97
transnational approach 24, 151
Tucker, David M. 92
Turnbull, W. W. 43
Turner, Arlin 48
Turner, Darwin 249
Tusan, Michelle Elizabeth 25, 100, 104, 105, 173, 174, 181, 182
Twenty-four Negro Melodies 237
Tyneside Geographical Institute 205

Uganda 153–4, 159, 192
Uncle Tom's Cabin 63
Underground Railroad (The) 10, 77
underground railway 33, 123
United States 6–7, 8, 9, 10, 17, 19, 22, 24, 31–2, 37, 38, 43, 54, 55, 56, 57, 63, 77, 97, 98, 101, 103, 107, 108, 111, 123, 124, 151, 155–6, 162, 195, 218, 205, 233, 236, 258
  Afro-Americans in 166
  black press 95–6, 205
  campaign against unification 43
  Catherine Impey visits 27, 34–5, 37, 77, 167, 244
  Catherine's report on mission 37

civil rights organization 63
Civil War 9, 39, 54–5, 131, 146, 191–2
citizenship rights 22
  lynching in 17, 18, 73, 107–24, 146, 192
  in British press 109, 117
  in white American press 117
  Reconstruction, 9–10, 44, 96, 108
  SRBM in 140
  suffragist campaigners 180
universal rights 181

Van Toorn, Penny 26
Vargo, Gregory 223
vegetarianism 30, 67, 88, 139, 162, 222, 239, 257
Vegetarian Messenger 138
Victoria, Queen 213
Village Album 12–13, 21, 27, 29, 31, 34–5, 39–40, 42, 100, 206
Vincent, David 105
violence 9, 10, 13, 17, 78, 108, 115, 120, 165, 244, 253, 255
  see also lynching; *Without Sanctuary* (exhibition)
Visram, Rozina 71, 250
Voice of the Negro 143
voting 3, 4, 9, 43, 57, 68, 108, 180
vulnerability 96

Wallinger, Hanna 150
Walters, Alexander 228, 248
Ware, Vron 9, 15, 21, 25, 47, 175, 176, 181, 182, 201, 224
Warner, W Lloyd 52, 70
Warren, Lynne 105, 149
Washington, Booker T. 59, 108, 166, 228
Washington DC 36, 57, 77–8, 138
Washington, Jesse 122
Watson, Robert Spence 89
Watts, Edward 154
WCTU *see* Women's Christian Temperance Union
Weaver, Valeria W. 92
Webb, Alfred 23, 89, 153, 154, 187f, 205
Wellbery, David E. 25
Wells, Ida B. 9–10, 25, 75f, 79, 125, 126, 213f, 260
  career success and reputation 74–6

Crusade for Justice 15, 92, 93, 94, 126, 170, 172, 182, 200, 201, 251
   entry in Askew's visitors' book 8f, 9, 13
   and Isabella Fyvie Mayo 78–81, 86–8, 91, 175, 176, 178
   on lynchings 18, 79, 110, 114f, 257
   1894 tour 73, 189–95
Western Mail were *117*
Western New York Anti-Slavery Society 33
West Indies 92, 138, 140–1, 155, 161–2, 211, 218, 228–9, 257
   also see Caribbean
Westminster Budget 192
Westminster Gazette 192
white communities 18, 52, 58, 103, 110–11, 196, 207, 247
white supremacy 9, 10, 17, 19, 22, 103, 112, 115, 119, 124, 129, 204, 207, 248, 255
white women 18, 109–11, 119, 140–1, 174, 179–80, 192, 196, 233, 244, 246
Whitsett, Virgie 144
Williams, Henry Sylvester 227, 230f, 233
Without Sanctuary (exhibition) 253–6
womanhood 111, 176, 196, 199
Woman's Signal (The) 179
women in adult education 241
women's advocacy 177–81
Women's Christian Temperance Union 62, 213
Women's Era Club 180, 192
Women's Herald 180
Women's Liberal Association of Bristol 189
Women's Loyal Union 211, 243

women's movement 18, 20, 70, 107, 139, 174, 177, 179, 180–1, 196, 173, 257
women's suffrage 18, 173–5, 177
Women's Temperance Convention 214
Women's Working Society 67
Woods, G. S. 200
Woollahra Congregational Church 73
Workers *see also* working class and trade union
   black 124, 131, 159, 168, 181, 194, 205, 229, 247
   Chinese Restriction Act 133, 160
   factory 161
   market traders 245
   pauperism 237
   postal 113
   protesting 96
   railway 90, 145
   white 124,
working class 3, 24, 30, 37, 56, 84, 101, 115, 135, 142, 159, 177, 181, 188, 194, 218, 219, 228, 229, 230, 236, 247, 257
World Travel 133
Worpole, Ken 260
Writers' Club 228

Yarwood, A. T. 170
Yeames, J. (Rev) 43
YMCA 63, 88, 90, 101
Yorkshire Evening Post 117
Youth Hostels Association 243

Zackodnik, Teresa 94
Zeleny, Rachael Baitch 70
Zulu Defence Committee 66, 155

www.ingramcontent.com/pod-product-compliance
Lightning Source LLC
Chambersburg PA
CBHW050135240426
43673CB00043B/1678